Religious Freedom in Islam

Religious Freedom in Islam

The Fate of a Universal
Human Right in the Muslim
World Today

DANIEL PHILPOTT

OXFORD
UNIVERSITY PRESS

OXFORD
UNIVERSITY PRESS

Oxford University Press is a department of the University of Oxford. It furthers
the University's objective of excellence in research, scholarship, and education
by publishing worldwide. Oxford is a registered trade mark of Oxford University
Press in the UK and certain other countries.

Published in the United States of America by Oxford University Press
198 Madison Avenue, New York, NY 10016, United States of America.

CIP data is on file at the Library of Congress
ISBN 978–0–19–090818–8

9 8 7 6 5 4 3 2 1

Printed by Sheridan Books, Inc., United States of America

In Memoriam: Alfred Stepan

In gratitude: Timothy Samuel Shah

Contents

List of Figures and Tables

Figures

Tables

Preface

IS ISLAM HOSPITABLE to religious freedom? Many will bristle at such a question. Religious freedom is a Western principle, some will say, and to pose it to Islam is to impose it on Islam. Others will object that to speak of an entire religious tradition recklessly flattens diversity and muffles dissonance. Still others will ask why I, a Westerner, and a Christian at that, deign to ask why a religion other than my own is free. Should not Western Christians first acknowledge the plank of religious repression in the eye of their own tradition before concerning themselves with the speck in another tradition's eye, to borrow a metaphor from Christianity's founder?

Yet I persist in inquiring into religious freedom in Islam because I believe the question holds high stakes for peace, stability, and justice in the world. I also believe that scholars have a responsibility to speak to the important controversies of their day. The controversy at hand is the intense public debate over Islam in the West. It has flared up every time the headlines have reported Muslims involved in violence, at least as far back as the attacks of September 11, 2001. ISIS. Orlando. Paris. San Bernardino. Benghazi. London. Madrid. "Islamoskeptics" hold that violence and repression are hardwired in Islam's texts and traditions and that the West must gird up for a struggle of decades. "Islamopluralists" counter that Islam, like all religions, is diverse and mostly peaceful but contains a fringe of violent extremists and counsel the West to engage in dialogue, avoid provocation, and own up to its historical role in the problems of the Muslim world.

This public debate is at times so heated that it resembles a culture war. As is true in all culture wars, the two sides fail not only to listen to each other but even to talk to each other, convinced that the other side's position is outside the walls of acceptability. By contrast, this book aims to dignify both sides—as well as that fragile commodity, civil democratic debate—by entering the argument. It does so for the reason that much is at stake in this debate—for the foreign policies of western states toward Muslim-majority states, for the treatment of Muslims within the West, for the treatment of religious minorities in the Muslim-majority world, for the religious vitality of Islam, for the reduction of terrorism and civil war, and for the success of constitutional democracy and peace. The book therefore addresses fellow westerners who are engaged in this lively dispute, a group that certainly includes Muslims living in the West, but also hopes to engage the arguments and perspectives of Muslims around the world and indeed of all who agree that this debate has great stakes.

Which side, then, is right? The book's criterion is religious freedom—a universal human right that demands respect for the full citizenship rights of people who differ in their answers to ultimate questions. I apply this criterion to the 47 (or so) countries where Muslims are in a majority and then look more broadly at the Islamic tradition.

I find that Islamoskeptics and Islamopluralists are both right and both wrong—an answer that might reduce the temperature of the debate and point the way toward constructive relations.

From a satellite view, the landscape of Muslim-majority states favors the Islamoskeptics. Of 47 Muslim-majority states, 36, more than three-quarters, have strong restrictions on religious freedom. Taken as a whole, the set of Muslim-majority states is far less religiously free than the global average or the set of Christian-majority countries.

To adopt this landscape view as our conclusion, though, is to overlook important contours that come into focus when we zoom in from a satellite view to a close-up view of the Muslim-majority world—namely the presence of religious freedom and the factors that account for its absence. Here, the Islamopluralists prove insightful. If there is a relative dearth of religious freedom in the Muslim world, Islamic doctrine is not necessarily the cause of it. We discover that some 42% of the Muslim-majority states that have low levels of religious freedom are governed not by a radical form of Islam but rather by an aggressive form of secularism imported from the West. We also discover that 11 Muslim-majority countries are religiously free—far more than outliers—and that they are free not despite Islam but because of their very interpretation of Islam.

True, 58% of the countries with low levels of religious freedom are "Islamist," meaning governed by a regime that deploys highly restrictive laws and policies to promote a strongly traditional form of Islam—which stands as evidence for the Islamoskeptic position—but even these have modern origins and are too simply deemed the real and true Islam. We discover, too, Muslim movements, parties, and intellectuals who espouse and advocate for religious freedom. When we turn our focus to the Islamic historical tradition, we also discover "seeds of freedom"—seven in particular—which carry potential for germinating into full religious freedom in the Muslim world. The long road of the Catholic Church toward freedom offers a model for how a religious tradition can undergo reform through its own historical commitments.

The result is a synthesis that is both honest and hopeful. As argued in the first chapter, what we learn from Islamoskeptics is honesty. Considered in the aggregate, the Muslim-majority world is comparatively religiously unfree. What we derive from Islamopluralists is hope. Both the reality and the potential for religious freedom can be found in the Muslim-majority world and in the broader Islamic tradition as well. The book, then, aims to present a picture of Islam that is fuller and more balanced than either side of today's public debate provides. The final chapter derives from this picture recommendations for action that can guide Western countries in their engagement with the Muslim world and contribute to an expansion of religious freedom around the globe.

Acknowledgments

THIS BOOK BEGAN in 2011 as a contribution to a body of research on religious freedom being fostered by the Religious Freedom Project at the Berkley Center for Religion, Peace, and World Affairs at Georgetown University. On a grant from the John Templeton Foundation, the Religious Freedom Project convened a group of scholars to investigate religious freedom and brought us together periodically to discuss ideas and drafts. In 2016, the Religious Freedom Project became the Religious Freedom Institute, a nongovernmental organization (NGO) in Washington, DC, and I continued to participate in its work. The numerous seminars, workshops, symposiums, and conversations convened in these settings were an ideal intellectual atmosphere: rigorous, collegial, good humored, and embodying a diversity of perspectives that is rare in today's academy.

I am indebted to the leaders whose creative vision and tenacity made all of this possible: Thomas Banchoff, who was founding director of the Berkley Center from 2006 to 2017 and is now Vice President for Global Engagement at Georgetown University; Thomas Farr, who was Director of the Religious Freedom Project from 2011 to 2016 and is now President of the Religious Freedom Institute; Timothy Samuel Shah, who was Associate Director of the Religious Freedom Project from 2011 to 2016 and is now Senior Director of the South and Southeast Asia Action Team at the Religious Freedom Institute; and Kent Hill, who joined the Religious Freedom Institute as Executive Director in 2017. I am grateful as well to the staff in these programs who worked faithfully and tirelessly to organize the many events: Jeremy Barker, Nicholas Fedyk, Abigail Galvan, Kyle Van der Meulen, A. J. Nolte, and Claudia Winkler. Not least, I thank the fellow scholars for their critique and encouragement: Ilan Alon, Anthony Gill, Brian Grim, William Inboden, Karrie Koesel, Timur Kuran, John Owen, David Novak, Ani Sarkissian, Rebecca Samuel Shah, Mona Siddiqui, Monica Duffy Toft, Roger Trigg, Bradford Wilcox, and Robert Woodberry.

I have benefited capitally from opportunities to present versions of the book's arguments. I thank the James Madison Program at Princeton University for its invitation to deliver the Charles E. Test, MD, Distinguished Lectures on April 27–29, 2016. I also presented portions of the book at the Annual Law and Religion Roundtable in Chicago, Bar Ilan University, Brigham Young University Law School, Georgetown University, Northwood University, the Notre Dame Islamic Studies Colloquium, a Religious Freedom Institute conference in Rome, Italy, the Transatlantic Academy in Washington, DC, the United States Institute of Peace in Washington, DC, and the University of Michigan. I am also grateful to several publishers of the book's ideas: *Acta Philosophica, America, The Journal of Law and Religion* (with Timothy Samuel Shah), *Lawfare, The New York Daily News, Public Discourse,* and *The Washington Post.*

I am indebted to numerous people who provided feedback on the manuscript. Those who commented on the entire manuscript include Jonathan Fox, Kent Hill, Habib Malik, Timothy Samuel Shah, and Nukhet Sandal. Conveying useful comments on portions of the text were Mustafa Akyol, Jeremy Barker, Paul Elhallal, Brian Grim, Robert Hefner, Jeremy Menchik, and Gabriel Reynolds. I am grateful to Timur Kuran, one of today's most important scholars of Islam, for reading the entire manuscript and taking the time to talk through a range of important issues with me. Three reviewers for Oxford University Press provided very helpful feedback.

Among the most profitable sources of feedback were two review sessions whose participants agreed to read the manuscript and spend several hours discussing it. The first of these took place at the University of Notre Dame on May 5, 2017, and was supported by generous grants from the Institute for the Study of the Liberal Arts and the Tocqueville Program for Inquiry Into Religion and Public Life at Notre Dame. Its participants included Sahar Aziz, Robert Dowd, C.S.C., Richard Garnett, Scott Hibbard, Mark Hoipkemeier, Farahnaz Ispahani, Ahmet Kuru, Anna Moreland, and Mun'im Sirry. I thank Tocqueville's Director Phillip Muñoz for his generous support, and Program Coordinator Jennifer Smith for a virtuoso job in organizing the event. The second workshop took place on May 26, 2017 and was organized by the Religious Freedom Research Program at Georgetown University's Berkley Center. Its participants included Matthew Anderson, Marjorie Balzer, Jacques Berlinerblau, Jennifer Bryson, Gabrielle Girgis, Kent Hill, David Hollenbach, S.J., John Langan, S.J., Paul Manuel, Paul Marshall, Jane McAuliffe, Ismail Royer, Angela Senander, Denis Sokolov, Sayyid Syeed, and Sufian Zhemukhov. I am grateful to Timothy Samuel Shah for conceiving and initiating this event and to Jeremy Barker for cheerfully organizing it.

On a topic on which there is so much fierce public debate, it is especially worth stressing that the views in the book are solely my own and should not be imputed to any of the many people who commented on the manuscript.

A number of research assistants provided critical help, including Faisal Baluch, Andrew Bramsen, Sean Braniff, Caleb Hamman, Mark Hoipkemier, Ji Eun Kim, Sarah Miller, Elizabeth Mullen, Paul Nauert, Anna Peterson, Josiah Ponnudurai, Nilay Saiya, Carolyn Sweeney, Afiya Webb, and Cynthia Weber. I thank Josiah Ponnudurai and Hailey Vrdolyak for fact-checking the manuscript; Hailey Vrdolyak and Melody Wood for copy-editing and proofreading; Belinda Thompson of Notre Dame's Marketing Communications office for composing the maps; and the Political Science Department and the Joan B. Kroc Institute at Notre Dame for providing institutional homes. At Oxford University Press, I am grateful to editors Theo Calderara and Drew Anderla for their invaluable support, to Victoria Danahy for her outstanding copyediting, and to Felshiya Manonmani for production editing.

It is all too easy to overlook the importance of those who enable a book's writing more than any other—one's family. My wife Diana and my children Angela, James, and Peter supported the project through their love, their patience, their infectious joy, and their consistent dinner table query, "Dad, how is your book going?"

I dedicate the book to two people. A close reading of the following pages will reveal numerous influences of the work of Alfred Stepan, who, until his death on September 26, 2017, was one of the world's leading comparative political scientists and theorists of democratization, a pioneer in the study of religion and politics, and a friend to the University of Notre Dame (at one time a member of Notre Dame's Board of Trustees), all of this following early stints in the US Marine Corps and as a journalist for *The Economist*. Al was a kind and generous mentor to young political scientists, including a cohort of us who study religion and politics. May he rest in peace.

A close reading of the preceding acknowledgments reveals several mentions of Timothy Samuel Shah, who has been a constant collaborator and conversation partner since we were graduate students together in the early 1990s and a brother who lays down his life for his friends.

Introduction

IN JUNE 2009, Barack Obama, early in his first term as President of the United States, delivered a most unusual speech in Cairo, Egypt. Instead of directing his words to the citizens of a country, a parliament, or an international organization, President Obama spoke to the members of a world religion. "I've come to Cairo to seek a new beginning between the United States and Muslims around the world," he announced. It was perhaps the first time in history that a US president had chosen an entire religion as his audience. A host of the speech was Al-Azhar, one of Islam's oldest and most prestigious universities, and a patron who could help Obama project his message to Muslims—all Muslims, everywhere.

Why did President Obama direct his speech to such an unusual set of hearers? The previous year, Obama had campaigned for president on a promise to end the United States' wars in Iraq and Afghanistan. One of his charges against these wars was that Muslims around the world perceived them as being waged against Islam. In fairness, Obama's predecessor, George W. Bush, had made great efforts to communicate that the United States was fighting terrorists and a rogue dictator and not Islam, which Bush had called a "religion of peace." Still, Obama saw a need for a realignment in the relationship between the United States and Muslims—all Muslims, everywhere. "We meet at a time of great tension between the United States and Muslims around the world," he began his speech, and he elicited applause when he declared, "America is not—and never will be—at war with Islam."

The president proposed that the United States and the Muslim world could reduce tensions together by addressing several issues ranging from violent extremism to women's rights to nuclear proliferation—to religious freedom. Obama's inclusion of this last principle—religious freedom—was, to close observers of US foreign policy, noteworthy and far from inevitable. Just over a decade earlier, in 1998, the US Congress had passed the International Religious Freedom Act, mandating that the US government promote religious freedom around the world. Although religious freedom was a signature feature of America's heritage, the bill's architects reasoned, overseas it had become one of the most widely violated human rights, and the United States had not responded adequately. George W. Bush's administration spoke warmly and consistently of the principle, though it sometimes subordinated it to the fight against terrorism.

It was unclear, though, whether President Obama would take up the cause, one that critics portrayed as asserting Western superiority over Islam and fomenting a clash of civilizations—exactly what Obama was proposing to leave behind. In his Cairo speech, though, he spoke of religious freedom warmly and forcefully, stressing that the principle is particularly dear to the United States: "[F]reedom in America is indivisible from the freedom to practice one's religion." The United States hosts 1,200 mosques, he pointed out, including one in every state. Religious freedom's relevance is not confined to America's borders, he went on to argue, praising Islam for its tradition of tolerance but also taking to task Muslims who are intolerant of religious minorities, Muslims who practice violence against other Muslims whom they deem heterodox, and certain Western countries who discriminate against their Muslim citizens. "Freedom of religion is central to the ability of peoples to live together," he added.

President Obama was right: Religious freedom is a universal principle, rooted in human dignity, that is critical to peace between Western countries and the Muslim world as well as within the Muslim world. This is the premise of this book, which asks: Is Islam hospitable to religious freedom? Such a question could be asked of any religion—or country, or civilization—but for three reasons, it is urgent to ask it of Islam.[1]

First, a fiery public debate over the character of Islam has been raging in the West at least as far back as the attacks of September 11, 2001, and its outcome matters a great deal for relations between Western countries and the Muslim world. I will argue that religious freedom is not only a good criterion for assessing this debate, but also, when applied, this principle may well simmer it and redirect it toward more constructive relations between the West and the Muslim world.

Second, religious freedom is a "force multiplier" that expands important goods that are now lacking in the Muslim world but whose increase could greatly benefit Muslim countries and their relations with the West. Among these goods are stable democracy, civil and human rights, economic development, the advancement of women, reconciliation among people of different faiths, and the reduction of terrorism, civil war, and international war.

Third, religious freedom is a matter of intrinsic justice. It is a human right that enjoys a prominent place in international conventions and safeguards the dignity of persons and communities. Justice is most at stake for religious minorities living amid Muslim majorities, Muslims who dissent from the orthodoxy of surrounding Muslim populations, Muslim minorities within non-Muslim-majority countries, and predominantly Muslim populations ruled by secular dictatorships, which Western governments sometimes support.

Let us look closer at these reasons for urgency.

A Public Debate

On the morning of Sunday, June 12, 2016, Americans woke to gruesome news. In the wee hours of that morning, a gunman had killed 49 people and wounded 3 others in a gay nightclub in Orlando, Florida. It was the deadliest shooting in US history. Soon it was revealed that the killer, named Omar Mateen, was a Muslim. During the shooting ordeal, he had declared his fealty to the Islamic State and his outrage over US interventions in Iraq and Syria.

What ensued in the media was a debate that has been taking place again and again in the United States and other Western countries in recent years.

"Is it any surprise that a Muslim did this?" asked one side. Political correctness and multiculturalism have blinded people to Islam's violent character despite the headlines before their eyes: attacks in Paris and San Bernardino, California, in the past couple of years and a long litany of terrorist incidents around the world in previous years.

Amplifying this criticism was the concurrent presidential campaign, one of the most rhetorically bombastic in US history. In a speech the next day, candidate Donald Trump used the occasion to repeat his charge that radical Islam was threatening the United States and to excoriate his opponent, Hillary Clinton, for being unwilling to use the words "radical Islam" in describing terrorism. Victor Davis Hanson, writing in the *City Journal*, echoed Trump's point: "The inability of Barack Obama and the latest incarnation of Hillary Clinton to utter 'radical Islam' or 'Islamic terrorism' in connection with Muslims' murderous killing sprees again is exposed as an utterly bankrupt, deadly and callous politically correct platitude."[2] The same mentality, these critics averred, had prevented law enforcement officers from investigating Mateen prior to the shootings. They did not want to be branded Islamophobic, tantamount to racism.

Islam was not the problem, shot back the other side, but rather Omar Mateen, a deranged and disturbed young man. Islam, like every religion, is peaceful and tolerant, though it also has its extremists. Islamist terrorism is a "twisted interpretation of one of the world's great religions," President Obama said shortly after the attacks, echoing themes from his 2009 Cairo speech. Candidate Hillary Clinton charged that anti-Islamic rhetoric and Trump's calls for draconian immigration and antiterrorist policies "[play] right into the terrorists' hands."[3] Obama responded angrily to calls for him to voice the term radical Islam: "What exactly would using this label accomplish and what will it change? Will it make ISIL less committed to try to kill Americans? Would it bring more allies for military strategy than . . . is served by this? The answer is none of the above. Calling a threat by a different name does not make it go away. This is a political distraction."[4]

Although this debate may seem to be one of right versus left, the reality is more complicated. Stoking controversy was not only the identity of Mateen but also that of his victims. Mateen's atrocity took place nearly a year after the US Supreme Court had accorded same-sex couples the right to marry and at a time when the issue continued to burn in courts, legislatures, and many other forums. Gay rights helped to scramble familiar ideological coalitions. Voices on both the right and the left cited Mateen's atrocious deed as evidence of Islam's homophobia, and voices on both sides volleyed back that the problem was not Islam but rather the hostility to gays that resided either in American culture or else simply in the heart of Omar Mateen. What remained salient, though, was the divide over the character of Islam: Voices lined up clearly as hostile or sympathetic.

This debate often resembles a culture war. It is carried out in public—on the Internet, cable news, radio talk shows, and newspaper opinion columns. It is polarized, with its two sides squaring off sharply with little common ground between them.[5] As in other theaters of the culture war, combatants fire flaming words as their weapons, aiming as much to ignite the zeal—and the votes and the media consumption—of their supporters as to explode their enemies. The dispute has flared up every time an act of terrorism committed by a Muslim hits the headlines. Al-Qaeda's attacks of September 11, 2001, launched the hottest phase of this public debate. Subsequent events have fanned it: the United States' wars in Afghanistan and Iraq; the murder of Dutch filmmaker Theo van Gogh in fall 2004; bombings in Madrid in 2004 and London in 2005; Danish cartoons mocking the Prophet Mohammed published in 2005; the Regensburg Address of Pope Benedict XVI in September 2006; the controversy of 2010 over the building of an Islamic Center near the site of the September 11 attacks in lower Manhattan; Fort Hood; Benghazi; The Boston

Marathon; Parliament Hill in Ottawa; the Islamic State; San Bernardino; Paris; Nice; Berlin.

Much as in the Cold War, this public debate has hawks and doves, which I herein call "Islamoskeptics" and "Islamopluralists," respectively.[6] Table I.1 summarizes their positions in four parallel tenets.

Islamoskeptics believe first that violence and intolerance are widespread in Islam. Referring to President George W. Bush, Christian leader Pat Robertson quipped, "I have taken issue with our esteemed president in regard to his stand in saying Islam is a peaceful religion. It's just not."[7] In this school, it is dangerously naive to view Islam's violent extremists as a small and aberrant faction. "[T]hat faction, militant Islam," writes Islamoskeptic journalist Andrew McCarthy, "is plainly far more robust and extensive than the scant lunatic fringe the U.S. delusionally comforts itself to limn; and its killings, far from condemnation, provoke tepid admiration if not outright adulation in a further, considerable cross-section of the Muslim world."[8]

Islam's proneness to violence, a second tenet of Islamoskepticism runs, is hardwired into Islam's founding texts and so is unlikely to change or to vary from place to place. Writer and former US government official Reuel Marc Gerecht takes to task westerners who "won't probe too deeply, and certainly not critically, into how the Quran and the prophet's traditions, as well as classical Islamic history, have given all believing Muslims certain common sentiments, passions, and reflexes."[9] One of the most prominent Islamoskeptics, Somali-born writer, Ayaan Hirsi Ali, holds that violent extremism is a "symptom of a much more profound ideological epidemic that has its root causes in Islamic

Table I.1. Islamoskeptics vs. Islamopluralists

Tenet → Ideology↓	Extent of violence and intolerance in the Muslim world	Source of violence in the Muslim world	Muslim attitude toward democracy	Recommendation for the West
Islamoskeptics	Widespread	Hardwired in Islamic doctrines	Inhospitable	Gird up for enduring conflict
Islamopluralists	Limited; the Muslim world is diverse	Local and contemporary circumstances	Open	Pursue dialogue, find common ground, own up to the West's past injustices

doctrine."[10] A common charge is that Islam's violent nature results from its stress on divine commands and its lack of a robust role for reason. Violence is rooted in Islamic theology, claims this school, and is not simply a product of poverty, corrupt regimes, or Western colonialism.

A third tenet follows: Islam is inhospitable to democracy. "Enthralled by diversity for its own sake, we have lost the capacity to comprehend a civilization whose idea of diversity is coercing diverse peoples into obedience to its evolution-resistant norms," writes McCarthy, citing global polls showing a high percentage of Muslims favoring a strict form of *sharia* law. In recent years, Islamoskeptics have criticized Western liberals for naively expecting democracy to arise from the Arab Uprisings of 2011—once but no longer called "the Arab Spring." "Islamism, if mentioned at all, was dismissed as irrelevant; experts in the studios and newsrooms at home were positive that this Arab Spring marked the success of secular and progressive values just like those they themselves had," comments British author David Pryce-Jones.[11]

The fourth tenet of Islamoskepticism is a prescription for action: The West must gird up for a long struggle to defend its liberties and civilization against the Islamic threat. Islam "cannot be placated. It must be fought and, sadly, it must be fought continuously and fiercely," wrote Martin Peretz, editor of *The New Republic*, not long after the attacks of September 11.[12] Dialogue and accommodation will do little to change Islam's hostility. If westerners engage in dialogue at all, it must be a tough dialogue, one that raises the hard issues of Islam's violence and illiberalism. Otherwise the outcome will be, as *National Review* editor James Burnham warned, "the suicide of the West."

At times, Islamoskeptics will acknowledge some diversity within Islam. Ali, for instance, proposes a catalogue of fundamentalist "Medina Muslims," more peaceful "Mecca Muslims," and reformist "modifying Muslims." Among Islamoskeptics, though, such acknowledgments are a stage whisper, in contrast to their declamations of Islam's true nature, which are loud and central. Even Ali stresses that all schools of Muslims must deal with the violence that dominates the tradition.[13]

Islamopluralists, by contrast, hold that Islam is diverse, not predominantly violent—their first tenet. The "majority of mainstream Muslims hate terrorism and violence as much as we do," argues Georgetown University scholar of Islam John Esposito.[14] Like all religions, Islam has its extremists, but they are in a small minority. Karen Armstrong, who also writes on Islam, cites a Gallup Poll showing that only 7% of Muslims thought that the September 11 attacks were justified.[15]

Where violence and intolerance do exist in Islam, a second Islamopluralist tenet holds, it feeds off local and historically particular circumstances. One month after the attacks of September 11, 2001, journalist Fareed Zakaria wrote a cover story for *Newsweek* entitled, "The Politics of Rage: Why Do They Hate Us?," in which he identified economic backwardness, illiteracy, the demographic "youth bulge," corrupt autocrats, and the failure of socialism, nationalism, and modernization as the conditions in the swamp from which the monster of religious violence grows.[16] Armstrong adds colonialism, secularism, and western states' support for autocrats.[17] One might add the Cold War, which often rendered Muslim-majority states pawns of the superpowers. For Islamopluralists, then, violence is not inherent in Islam's teachings.

Third, Islamopluralists are more optimistic about prospects for democracy in Islam. In the book *Islam and Democracy*, Esposito and fellow scholar of Islam John Voll point to Islamic concepts like *shura* [consultation], *ijma* [consensus], and *ijtihad* [independent interpretive judgment], as favoring democracy, as well as to several actual democracies in Muslim-majority countries.[18] Islamopluralists often also cite liberal democratic trends among Muslims in the 19th and 20th centuries, which, they point out, were later quelled by Western-backed authoritarian rulers.

Islamopluralists' recommendation to the West, their fourth tenet, is to end politics that oppress Muslims and create a violent backlash and to engage in a two-way dialogue that can increase the sphere of shared understanding. They counsel against "orientalism," the term that the famous Palestinian-born Western public intellectual Edward Said used to describe a Western colonialist mentality that rendered Muslims as backward and intolerant and that justified imperialism.[19] In fact, argue Islamopluralists, the orientalist mentality and the policies that it spawns only serve to inflame violent backlash; shrill Islamoskeptics create the very problem that they identify. In a true dialogue, the West would own up to its own history of contributing to the problems of Muslims. It would also draw upon and develop further the sphere of beliefs shared by the "Abrahamic" faiths—Judaism, Christianity, and Islam—a sphere whose size Islamopluralists find impressive.

As with the post-Orlando debate, the argument between these schools is not the same as that between right and left. The ranks of Islamoskeptics include political conservatives and Christian conservatives, to be sure, but also feminists, atheists, gay rights activists, and other voices from the political left. Likewise, the ranks of Islamopluralists include multiculturalists and left-wing university professors but also those conservatives who decry the war on terror as an overextended foreign policy and who find common cause with Islam on marriage, sexuality, and family.[20]

Are there more nuanced positions whose complexity eludes both camps? Of course there are.[21] Some of them appear in the pages that follow. Still, it is striking how much public commentary replicates these schools, not only on talk radio, the Internet, and cable news shows, but also in universities and high-brow publications like *The New Republic*, *National Review*, *The New York Review of Books*, and *The Weekly Standard*.

This public debate matters. When a partisan of one side gains power, changes in policy and in relations between the West and Islam ensue. Once Donald Trump had taken office in January 2017, he translated the loud Islamoskepticism of his campaign into action through an executive order that halted the admission of all refugees for 120 days, temporarily banned immigration from seven Muslim-majority countries, and indefinitely banned refugees from Syria, a predominantly Muslim country convulsed in civil war. Then, and throughout his first year in office, Trump voiced anti-Muslim rhetoric, even tweeting out anti-Muslim videos. Just after his election, the Federal Bureau of Investigation issued a report showing that hate crimes against American Muslims had surged over the previous year, one in which Trump's anti-Muslim rhetoric had been voluble.[22] The spirit of Obama's Cairo speech was dead, at least in the White House.

Which school is right about Islam? Is it possible to sort out the question? Religious freedom comes to our assistance. Religious freedom is the civil right of persons and religious communities to practice, express, change, renounce, and spread their religion. It is a strong criterion for whether a religious tradition and its members are violent and repressive or peaceful and inclusive. To accept religious freedom is to respect enduringly the full citizenship and human rights of people who embrace profoundly different answers to the most important questions about human life. The question at stake in the public debate, then, can be rephrased: Is Islam receptive to religious freedom?

Is religious freedom really the right criterion? It might seem that democracy is a better concept through which to take stock of the public debate.[23] One of this debate's pivotal issues, after all, is Islam's compatibility with democracy. Democracy alone, however, does not capture what is at issue. Recent global history reveals numerous countries that have adopted some practices of democracy, like contested elections and a peaceful transfer of power, yet continue to violate the religious rights of their populations, not least their religious minorities. Illiberal democracies, Zakaria calls them.[24] The Muslim-majority world contains several such illiberal democracies, including Pakistan, Malaysia, Indonesia, and Bangladesh. Religious freedom, by contrast, demands something more—respect for the rights of people whose religious faith differs from the dominant faith of a country.

What about tolerance—another word that flies about in public debate? Tolerance will not do, either. It is too tentative, implying a truce that stabilizes but is temporary. One of history's most famous instances of tolerance was the Edict of Nantes in 1598, in which French King Henri IV ended a generation of religious civil war by allowing Protestant Huguenots permission to worship in a predominantly Catholic France. Two generations later, in 1685, Henri's grandson King Louis XIV revoked Nantes, outlawing and expelling the Huguenots. Religious freedom is more lasting, a principle that is not meant to change. Religious freedom also has more content. Tolerance implies mere respect for one another's security, whereas religious freedom also entails respect for the whole range of manners in which individuals and communities express and practice their religion.

More than democracy or tolerance, religious freedom expresses what is in dispute in the West's public debate over Islam. At issue in religious freedom is whether the members of one religion respect members of other religions as well as dissenters within that religion or whether they seek to subdue, forcibly convert, or otherwise relegate the others to second-class citizenship. As a civil right, religious freedom demands not only that citizens practice this respect in their words and their deeds but also that they enshrine and enforce this respect through law. Religious freedom is the principle that is most blatantly and frequently negated by Islamist terrorist attacks, the enforcement of blasphemy codes, strict government control of mosques, and the many forms of discrimination found in Muslim-majority countries. For a religious tradition to be called peaceful and just, religious freedom is the standard that it ought to meet.

Religious Freedom Is a Weapon of Peace

The second reason why the question of religious freedom in Islam is urgent is that religious freedom can do much to alleviate the violence and repression that afflict Muslim-majority countries as well as relations between these countries and the West. Disproportionately to countries populated by other religions, Muslim-majority countries suffer from a dearth of democracy and economic development and a surfeit of terrorism, civil war, and social inequality. Consider only a few statistics. My own research found that in 2007, 91% of all religious terrorist groups in the world proclaimed a radical Islamic message.[25] Political scientist Monica Toft finds that today about three-quarters of the world's 20 civil wars that are fought over religious issues involve at least one Muslim combatant; that since the end of the Cold War, 71% of these wars have involved a Muslim-dominated government and predominantly Muslim rebels groups; and that Islamist rebels are implicated in all 14 instances of this kind of war that have broken out since 2000.[26] Sharpening these figures is the fact that only about 24% of the world's population is Muslim. Political scientist Ahmet Kuru reports that whereas half of the world's countries are electoral democracies, only a fifth of Muslim-majority countries are electoral democracies.[27]

As I shall be arguing in the chapters to come—and as Kuru and other political scientists argue—these problems are not necessarily due to the Islamic religion even if they are concentrated among Muslim populations.[28] Plausibly, however, these problems have much to do with a lack of religious freedom. Social scientists have adduced evidence that religious freedom is a "force multiplier" that elicits derivative benefits.[29] Sociologists Brian Grim and Roger Finke, for instance, have demonstrated a high correlation between religious freedom and other components of liberal democracy, like the separation of powers, rule of law, freedom of assembly, and freedom of speech, along with other goods like the empowerment women and low levels of armed conflict and poverty.[30] Although correlation is not causation, it is not difficult to imagine why religious freedom would beget other freedoms. For one thing, the practice of religion itself involves speech, assembly, and communication through the media, all of which demand accompanying civil and human rights.

In 2011, Pope Benedict XVI argued in his annual statement for the World Day of Peace that religious freedom is a "weapon of peace."[31] Political scientist Nilay Saiya adopts Benedict's phrase as the title of a new book in which he argues that religious repression is a cause of religious terrorism both within countries and across borders.[32] In a separate article, he shows that religious repression is behind civil wars and conflicts between states that are fueled by religion.[33] Conversely, he holds, religious freedom mitigates the same ills. Others have shown that religious freedom spurs economic growth.[34] If religious freedom begets these other benefits, then its increase also will improve relations between Western and Muslim-majority countries, which have grown tense over the past generation, as attested to by the Iranian hostage crisis, the Iran–Iraq war, violent conflict in Israel and Palestine, terrorism in Western cities, and wars in Afghanistan and Iraq. Much indeed is at stake for a religion that contains 1.6 billion members and whose inhabitants form a majority in about 47 of the world's states.

Religious Freedom Is Just

The third reason for the urgency of religious freedom in Islam is justice. Religious freedom is a universal human right, one that is not only a legal right, having made its way into the major international human rights conventions, but also a moral right, protecting the dignity of human beings in their search for and practice of religious truth.

I elaborate and defend this claim in Chapter 1. Here, it is worth noting the simple but essential insight that religious freedom presumes that religion is good for human beings, essential to their welfare. This ought to help allay the anxiety of certain Muslims around the world who fear that religious freedom is a Western export packaged with sexual license, pornography, the fracture of the family, and antipathy toward religion as a constraint to individual expression. Muslims living outside the West are not wrong in noticing such a hostile secularism in the West. In the previous decade a band of critics of religion known as the "New Atheists" sold hundreds of thousands of books arguing that religion is irrational, violent, intolerant, and inevitably repressive. Author Sam Harris, for instance, diagnosed the problem of Muslim terrorism as the problem of religious belief in general. Peace and respect for rights, the New Atheists hold, will come only when religion exits the stage of history.[35]

Were religious freedom hitched to such an alien secularism, the possibility of its realization in the Muslim world would be slight. Indeed there would be little point in asking about religious freedom in Islam or any other religion. In the New Atheists' view, there will be freedom only when there is no religion. Religious freedom, though, has little to do with this form of secularism. It presupposes that religion is a good and precious pursuit, bound up with human dignity and worthy of protection. Religious freedom does not ask anyone to renounce his or her claims about truth, God, transcendence, the origin of the world, the source of meaning, the character of morality and justice, salvation, and the degree of truth found in other faiths. Instead it protects these very pursuits. It even permits the spread of religion, albeit through persuasion, not pressure or manipulation. Tellingly, it is often religious people who advocate religious freedom and do so on the grounds of their faith.[36]

The right of religious freedom, though, protects not merely religion, but also freedom—the free practice of religion. Otherwise, it would amount only to the right of religion. As I argue in the next chapter, the good of religion is achieved indispensably though inward commitment and thus cannot and should not be imposed, coerced, or rendered a matter of discrimination. This is what is at issue in Muslim-majority countries today. There, minorities of other religious faiths—Jews, Christians, Baha'is—commonly suffer severe discrimination and harsh repression. The same goes for Muslims whose beliefs are considered heretical by other Muslims who control the state: Shias in Sunni states, Sunnis in Shia states, and Ahmadis in Sunni states. Not to be overlooked are Muslim majorities who are stifled and controlled by repressive secular dictatorships, often propped up by Western governments, as well as the discrimination that Muslims sometimes experience within Western countries. In all of these cases, the dignity of human beings, and hence justice, is denied. It is, finally, out of a hope that the sphere of justice will be widened that the present inquiry into religious freedom is launched.

Preview of the Argument

Is there religious freedom in Islam? I will consider this question from different angles. Roughly the first half of the book looks at those countries where Muslims are in a majority. Again, there are about 47 of these—give or take a few depending on how one handles judgment calls—and they are highlighted on the map in Figure I.1.

This is a fair test. If countries in which Muslims have the popular power to dominate others prove to be religiously free, then the case for religious freedom in Islam accrues strength.

My answer will be nuanced, thus offering a calming balance and constructive sobriety to today's public debate. From a satellite view, the landscape favors the Islamoskeptics. Of 47 Muslim-majority states, only 11, fewer than one-fourth, have high levels of religious freedom according to the standards of the Pew Research Center.[37] Sociologists Brian J. Grim and Roger Finke, in their book of 2011, *The Price of Freedom Denied*, report that 62% of Muslim-majority countries manifest a moderate to high degree of persecution, compared with 28% of Christian-majority countries and 60% of all other countries. They cite an even sharper comparison showing that 78% of Muslim-majority countries contain high levels of government restrictions on religion, in comparison with 43% of all other countries and 10% of Christian countries.[38] Similar results arise from an analysis of the Religion and State Dataset compiled by political scientist Jonathan Fox, who ranks levels of "official restrictions" on a scale of 0, meaning the least restrictive and the most free, to 5, the most restrictive, where all religions are illegal. During the period 1990–2008, Muslim-majority countries average 2.6, whereas the global average was 1.77 and the average for the Christian world was 1.36.[39] In Fox's recent book, *The Unfree Exercise of Religion*, in which he examines religious discrimination, he shows that Muslim-majority countries score over four times as high as Christian-majority countries on a religious discrimination score.[40] Again, the Muslim world is far less free.

Shall we conclude, then, that Islam is inhospitable to religious freedom? No. Such a judgment is too simple and obscures both the presence of religious freedom in the Muslim world and the reasons for its absence. Zooming

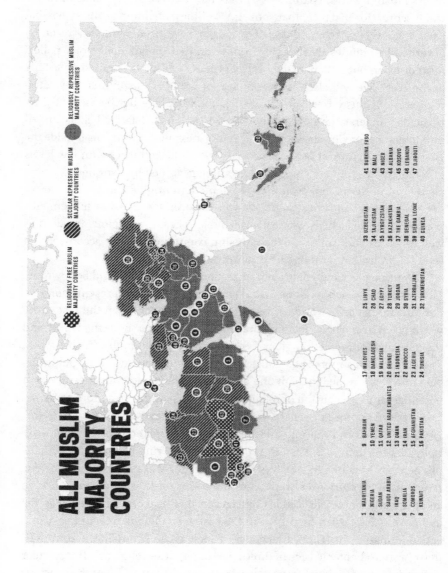

FIGURE 1.1. Global map

in from a satellite view to a close-up perspective that shows the history and circumstances of Muslim countries, the Islamopluralists' point about Islam's diversity takes on plausibility. If there is a relative dearth of religious freedom in the Muslim world, Islamic doctrine is not necessarily the cause of it. We will discover, for instance, that some 42% of the Muslim-majority states that have low levels of religious freedom are (or have been until very recently) governed by regimes that harshly impose on their populations not a radical form of Islam but rather an aggressive form of secularism inspired by sectors of the West. We will also discover that 11, or 23% of, Muslim-majority countries are religiously free not despite Islamic teachings but because of their particular understanding of Islamic teachings. Here, Islamic beliefs undergird tolerance for Christian and other minorities and for Muslims outside the Islamic mainstream. It is also true that 58% of the countries with low levels of religious freedom are "Islamist," meaning governed by a strongly conservative form of *sharia*, but even these have modern origins and are too simply deemed the real and true Islam. We will discover, too, Muslim movements, parties, and intellectuals who espouse and advocate for religious freedom as well as places and times in which Muslim communities have accorded high levels of protection for religious minorities.

Islamoskeptics and Islamopluralists, then, are both right and both wrong. Islamoskeptics teach us honesty. Taken as a whole, at the present moment, the Muslim-majority world is less free and more violent than the rest of the world taken as a whole. Islamopluralists teach us hope. Both the reality and the potential for greater religious freedom can be found in the Muslim world as well. Finding a more satisfying synthesis than either side of the public debate provides—rooted in a fair and even view of Islam, identifying sources of potential for the expansion of religious freedom, pointing to a more constructive Western approach to Islam—is the aim of the pages that follow.

Some critics will call into question the very foundations of this endeavor. Religious freedom is a Western principle and will ring strange and perhaps offensive to Muslims in much of the world, they will say. To pose religious freedom as a criterion of study is to impose it on those studied, much as colonists and imperialists did. Confronting this important challenge is the subject of Chapter 1, where I make the case for religious freedom as a universal human right. Then, I take a close look at Muslim-majority countries, devoting one chapter to each of three types of regime—religiously free, secular repressive, and religiously repressive—and one chapter to the Arab Uprisings of 2011, a spring that largely turned into winter, in good part because of the absence of religious freedom.

In the final three chapters, I aim to deliver on hope, first through a chapter that identifies "seeds of freedom" in the Islamic tradition that might sprout into a wider acceptance and practice of religious freedom in the Muslim world; then through a chapter that depicts a pathway through which this development might take place, a pathway eked out by the Catholic Church, which contained early seeds of a teaching of religious freedom, denied religious freedom in the political realm for many centuries, eventually came to espouse religious freedom definitively, and did so compatibly with its own enduring teachings. The final chapter offers practical recommendations for realizing religious freedom in Islam, ones that carry responsibilities for citizens in both the Muslim world and the West.

It is to the suspicion that religious freedom is little but a Western export that I now turn.

1

In Defense of Religious Freedom

ANY INQUIRY INTO religious freedom's place in Islam must confront not only today's public contretemps over Islam but also a growing public row over religious freedom.[1]

This latter controversy is of recent vintage and beset with amnesia. Until yesterday, the populations of developed democracies considered religious freedom to be one of the nonnegotiable principles that ground constitutional liberal democracy. Religious freedom was ensconced widely in Western Europe's constitutions by the early years after World War II, was extended into Eastern Europe's constitutions after the end of the Cold War, and enjoys foundational status in the norms and membership criteria of the European Union. It was just after World War II that religious freedom also was incorporated into global norms, appearing in Article 18 of the Universal Declaration of Human Rights in 1948, and in subsequent years that religious freedom was cemented in international law by the 1966 International Covenant on Civil and Political Rights, where the principle also appears in Article 18, and by the 1981 convention whose long-winded title should not occlude its remarkably thorough articulation of the principle: The Declaration on the Elimination of All Forms of Intolerance and Discrimination Based on Religion or Belief (hereafter the 1981 Declaration).

As President Obama pointed out in his Cairo speech, citizens of the United States in particular have taken pride in their country's history as a pioneer and upholder of religious freedom. Like the granite faces in Mt. Rushmore, religious freedom has been fixed in what it means to be American. Right and left, Americans have taken pride in being a home for religious people who have been persecuted or rejected elsewhere: Mennonites, Mormons, Muslims, Baptists, Jews, Huguenots, Catholics, Jehovah's Witnesses, Amish, Quakers, Seventh-Day Adventists, Scientologists, and even atheists. Americans regard the First Amendment to their Constitution as globally innovative and worthy of export and imitation. As recently as the 1990s, religious freedom's prestige among Americans was evidenced by two bills that the US Congress passed with overwhelming bipartisan majorities: the Religious Freedom Restoration Act of 1993 and the International Religious Freedom Act of 1998.

In recent years, though, even in the United States, religious freedom has come to appear less like a common heritage and more like one side of a culture war. Partisans of religious freedom vie against critics who view the principle as a mask for resisting progress, usually in matters of sexuality. A phalanx of intellectuals has taken up an argument against the principle *tout court*. Some ask what is so special about religious freedom that it merits a constitutional right of its own and call for it to be discontinued and folded into other freedoms like speech, assembly, and expression.[2] Others cast their skepticism globally, disputing religious freedom's universality, its place in the human rights conventions, and all efforts to export it overseas.[3]

Many of these critics inhabit universities and swim in their prevailing intellectual currents, among these a relentless invocation of plurality and difference, a strong suspicion toward claims of universality, a particular aversion to westerners' assertions of universality, and a revulsion to the imposition of Western values on non-Western peoples. Religious freedom fits perfectly into these proclivities and antipathies. Far from being a universally valid principle, their critique runs, religious freedom is the product—and the agenda—of one culture in one historical period: the modern West. And in the West it should stay—and be kept under strict surveillance.

Islam shows up frequently in these critics' arguments. Hailing from the left end of the political spectrum, fitting the description of Islamopluralists in the Introduction, they look upon religious freedom as a rhetorical tool through which the West asserts its moral superiority over Islam and cloaks its drive to dominate Muslims. Surprisingly and ironically, though, there is a resonance between their denial of religious freedom's universality and the arguments of certain Islamoskeptics who criticize Islam from the right. These latter voices regard religious freedom as a product of the West's Christian foundations and singular history, conditions they believe are unlikely to be replicated. True, they stress the uniqueness of religious freedom from a very different posture than that of the critics from the left. For them, religious freedom is to be celebrated as a unique and humane achievement of the West. Still, though for different reasons, both groups converge in doubting religious freedom's universality and counseling against its spread. Islamopluralist critics view religious freedom as one option among others, call for humble acceptance of this diversity, and warn against militant imposition. Islamoskeptic critics see religious freedom as a prized achievement, call for vigilance in guarding it, and warn against the militancy of those who reject it. Islamopluralists think that because religious freedom is Western and Christian, it should not be foisted on Muslims; Islamoskeptics think that because religious freedom is Western and Christian, Muslims are not capable of accepting it. Right or left, Islamoskeptic or Islamopluralist, the conclusion is the same: Religious freedom is not a universal principle that advocates ought to strive to ensure for everyone.

All of these critiques of religious freedom call into question the premise of this book's engagement with Islam, namely, that religious freedom is a universally valid human right derived from human dignity. The arguments must be engaged. Religious freedom will be unable to serve as a criterion in the public debate over Islam if it is, at the same time, a combatant. It cannot be a referee if it is but a member of one of the teams. Nor can we hope that religious freedom would increase in the Muslim world if it proves to be a principle that can be imposed on Muslims only from the outside.

In this chapter, I argue that religious freedom is a universal human right. Although a full defense of this right is more than I can offer here, I set forth some reasons why religious freedom is a principle to which every person and religious community makes a justifiable claim. The right to religious freedom is a natural right, one that is grounded in the dignity of every human being, a creature who asks the question of religious truth and lives out answers to it in the form of religious practices and beliefs. That is, the human right of religious freedom exists prior to its articulation in constitutions or international covenants. Indeed, it is because religious freedom is first and foremost a moral principle accessible to reason, lodged in the common morality of humankind, that we may hope and demand that constitutions and international conventions would clearly articulate it and that governments would vigorously defend it. We may also pose it as a criterion for world religions.

What Is at Stake

In 1996, an Egyptian appeals court declared null and void the marriage of Nasr Hamid Abu Zayd, a professor of Islam at Cairo University and a humanistic reformer of the Islamic faith, to his wife of 12 years, Ibtihal Younis, a professor of French literature at Cairo University. The reason? It is unlawful for a Muslim woman to be married to a non-Muslim man, and Professor Abu Zayd, the court judged, was no longer a Muslim man. Why? Because he was an apostate. Abu Zayd had not renounced his faith or converted away from Islam. "I'm sure that I'm a Muslim. My worst fear is that people in Europe may consider and treat me as a critic of Islam. I'm not," he once told an interviewer.[4] A judge had decided, however, that Abu Zayd's questioning of the historic Islamic poll tax on Christians and Jews and of the permissibility of owning slave girls were both contrary to Islamic scripture. Egypt's Court of Cassation upheld the verdict in 1996. Next, Egyptian Islamic Jihad—a later version of the organization that assassinated Egyptian President Anwar Sadat in 1981—called for Abu Zayd's death. Abu Zayd and his wife fled to Europe and lived and worked in the Netherlands until his death in 2010. During the same years, many other intellectuals and artists received similar verdicts in Egypt and elsewhere in the Muslim-majority world.

In 2009, Muslims were assailed for their religious beliefs in a very different part of the world—Murfreesboro, Tennessee, a city about 30 miles to the south of Nashville. The local Muslim population, which had expanded sharply over the previous decade, decided to build a new mosque and community center to accommodate its increased numbers. Some local residents opposed the project vociferously, and over the ensuing two years a public controversy ensued. Vandalism and arson besieged the mosque site. Opponents objected above all to Islam itself, which they associated with the terrorist attacks of September 11, 2001, and thought would bring similar violence to and destroy the way of life of middle Tennessee. Tennessee's Lieutenant Governor, Ron Ramsey, questioned whether Islam is "actually a religion, or is it a nationality, way of life, cult or whatever you want to call it" and judged Islam to be "a violent political philosophy more than [a] peace-loving religion."[5]

Other Tennesseans, though, defended the mosque, appealing to the principle of religious freedom. "Freedom of religion means freedom for all religions," declared Middle Tennesseans for Religious Freedom.[6] A pertinent historical observation on the controversy came from the newspaper *The Tennessean*, which noted that in 1929, the Ku Klux Klan had led opposition to the building of the Roman Catholic Church of St. Rose of Lima, arguing that Catholics would threaten their safety and way of life.[7] It finally took a federal court order to allow the mosque to be completed in 2012. The imam of the mosque, Ossama Bahloul, told his community, "[t]his is a day of forgiveness. We want to say that we have nothing bad in our heart against anyone."[8]

These cases, both involving Muslims, illustrate what is at stake in religious freedom. What Abu Zayd and his wife experienced under the gavel of the Egyptian courts and at the gunpoint of Egyptian Islamic Jihad, what Mufreesboro's Muslims experienced at the hands of their fellow citizens, what thousands of people around the world experience every year when they are sanctioned, threatened, or coerced on account of their religious beliefs, are violations of their universal human right of religious freedom. This, today's skeptics deny. They might well judge the treatment that Abu Zayd, the Muslims of Murfreesboro, and others have suffered to be unjust. They dispute, though, that religious freedom is a universally valid principle that is justifiably invoked by and on behalf of everyone on the planet. This is where I demur.

Religion: Something for Everyone

A right is a justifiable claim that a person makes upon other persons. When a right is a human right, it is all persons who justly make the claim, and it is all other persons upon whom they make it. Many rights involve a claim against the violation of some dimension of personhood: life, bodily integrity, political speech, property, control of one's labor, and so on. Religious freedom is a right of this sort. As a universal human right, it is a claim that every person justly makes upon every other person to refrain from violating something of great value. That something is religion.

This argument will grate against the Western academy, where scholars are widely skeptical that we can speak of a single entity called religion that has meaning and value for human beings as such. Many a conference among scholars of religion has died from exhaustion in attempting to scale the peak of defining religion. Some definitions of religion, the skeptics say, end up excluding cases of what most people regard as a religion—and often privileging Christianity. For instance, if religion is defined in terms of worshipping God, then Buddhism, which does not posit a God (at least in some versions), is excluded. Other definitions of religion end up being too wide, failing to rule out phenomena that most people do not regard as a religion. If religion is defined in terms of ardent, spiritual devotion, for instance, then nationalism, Marxism, and environmentalism might all be religions. "Some people dilute [religion] to the point of futility," observes the late scholar of religious studies, Martin Riesebrodt, "considering barbecues with guitar music, soccer games, shopping in supermarkets, or art exhibitions to be religious phenomena."[9] If the critics are right that religion cannot be defined, then it cannot be something that humanity shares in any meaningful sense.

This skepticism is deepened by doubts that religion will survive the modern world—the secularization thesis. Originating in the Enlightenment philosophical movement of 17th- and 18th-century Europe, the secularization thesis gained momentum in the 19th and 20th centuries in the thought of Friedrich Nietzsche, Charles Darwin, Karl Marx, Sigmund Freud, and Max Weber, and, by the 1950s and 1960s, reigned supreme in the Western university and among Western elites and Western-educated elites in Asia, Africa, and the Middle East. The thesis holds that religion is the product of premodern superstition and will eventually melt under the light and heat of science, democracy, free thought, economic and technological progress, education, and historical criticism of the sacred texts. Where religion does still exist, its irrationality makes it violent and divisive, as the New Atheists attest.[10] Today, the secularization thesis retains a tenacious grip on the Western academy. Scholars across many fields either voice it explicitly or assume its tenets in their analyses.

But not everyone. In recent years, many scholars have called the secularization thesis into question.[11] Among these, some make the case that religion is, after all, a universal, human phenomenon that is identifiable and knowable. They are hardly the first to make this case. Classical Western thinkers conceived of religion in this way, as did sages of Eastern religions. Here, I articulate briefly my own version of the case.

That there is something called religion that is of very great value to human beings is a matter of common sense. Do I mean that religion is obvious and that a person is blind not to see it? No, what I mean by common sense is subtler and does not call into question the faculties of those who disagree. To say that a concept or proposition is common sense is to say that a person can know it through ordinary experience without appealing to elaborate proofs, definitions, or theories. If we ask the average Joe or Jane on the street—or Vijay, Ahmed, or Nan—what religion is, he or she will neither deliver a sophisticated disquisition nor be baffled by the question but rather is likely to recount phenomena that he or she readily identifies with religion: acts of worship, prayer, and ritual; experience of God or gods; sacred texts; or accompanying virtues like compassion, mercy, and generosity. To him or her, these things manifest religion and no further explanation is required. There is no reason to doubt that Joe or Jane or Vijay knows what religion is. We trust that we are identifying a real phenomenon and that we can speak about it meaningfully even if we cannot define it precisely or thoroughly. There are many such concepts—difficult to define precisely yet readily understood and vital to our lives—that all of us employ regularly: the economy, the family, and the state are all examples. Religion is no different.[12]

What characterizes religion as ordinary people have experienced it? Let us begin with this observation: The human being is a creature who uniquely asks "the grand questions of life." Where do we come from? Where did the universe come from? What is the basis of our moral convictions? Why do we suffer? Is there help for us in our suffering? What happens to us after death?[13] Human beings have asked these ultimate questions across an astonishingly diverse array of cultures, geographic locales, and historical epochs. In an equally astonishing array of times and places, they have turned to religion for answers.

Religion offers answers to the grand questions of life through an affirmation of a superhuman, transcendent realm. Arguing along these lines is Riesebrodt, one scholar in the field of religious studies who was not convinced by the present-day academic consensus and whose important book of 2011, *The Promise of Salvation: A Theory of Religion*, argues that religion is a universal human experience spanning history and geography. The premise of any religion, says Riesebrodt, is that there exist superhuman powers that are critically important for the lives of human beings. These powers might take the form of a God or gods, or they might be more abstract. Religions, though, posit not merely that these powers exist or that they take a certain form, but also that they provide critical help in the lives of people. Riesebrodt's most central claim is that religion contains three forms of promise for the people who practice it: It wards off misfortune, helps people to cope with crises, and lays the foundation for salvation. It is through religious practices that human beings establish contact with these superhuman powers. At the core of these practices are worship and the liturgies—prayers, songs, chants, devotions, rituals—through which worship takes place. Contact with superhuman powers is not any old kind of connection but rather involves awe, homage, supplication, adoration, and repentance.[14]

Although Riesebrodt does not explicitly say that religion is an answer to the grand questions of life, he conceives religion as offering answers to problems much like those that these questions pose—the biggest problems that human beings face. Other features of religion, some of which Riesebrodt discusses, also merit mention. Most religions have a clerical profession or caste, a corps of people designated (or ordained) to help ordinary people who are not clerics establish relationships with superhuman powers. Virtually all religions involve a community, a body of people who practice the rituals together and build their lives around these rituals. Typical, too, is a moral code grounded in a transcendent realm. Genuinely religious practices can be found in Christianity, Judaism, Islam, Daoism, Jainism, Sikhism, Buddhism, Shintoism, Hinduism, the Baha'i faith, and other traditions, Riesebrodt finds.

A broad definition draws together what religion typically involves in peoples' lives. A religion can be thought of as *an interconnected set of beliefs and practices through which people answer the grand questions of life by seeking to live in harmony with a superhuman power that intervenes in the real circumstances of their lives. They do this most characteristically through worship. Religion typically involves related rituals, a community, a clerical profession, and a moral code grounded in a transcendent realm.*

It might be objected that not every religion embodies all of these features. Even if true, it does not undermine the case for religion as a universal human experience. All of the major religions embody most of these characteristics, although those that they include and omit will vary from religion to religion. Religions share what the philosopher Ludwig Wittgenstein called "family resemblances," meaning that they resemble one another but that there are not required, essential traits that make them members of the same family. On this view, we need draw no bright line between what is a religion and what is not. Rather, we can say that certain collections of beliefs and practices are stronger and weaker in their religious character, more and less a religion. The major world religions—those on Riesebrodt's list—would rank strong, whereas the luminous, transcendent sensation of the Guns and Roses concertgoer and the sensibility of the westerner who claims to be "spiritual but not religious," although not entirely lacking in religious qualities, would rank weak.[15]

Religion and Other Things

When we see religion as a practice through which humans orient themselves toward superhuman powers through worship, we can then answer the perennial question of academic conferences: Can religion be differentiated from other things that may sometimes look like religion but are not religion? In fact, it can. "Arnold treats his work like a religion!" exclaims Eleanor. Does Eleanor mean to say that there is no difference between the definition of work and the definition of religion? By no means. Rather she is drawing upon the definition of religion to make the point that Arnold's dedication to his work is so total that it resembles a religious person's devotion to God. She is able to tap religion for comparison only because religion carries a concrete, commonly understood meaning.

So it goes with nationalism, Marxism, and environmentalism. All of these, like Arnold's work habits, can be and sometimes are adhered to religiously, but none is essentially the same as religion. Take nationalism. A wide consensus of theorists agree that a nation is a group of people who live on a contiguous piece of land, share a common language, culture, and history, and aspire to political self-rule, usually, though not always, in the form of an independent state.[16] Nationalism is an ideology that involves a commitment to the nation and its political aspirations. It is not a religion. It involves no essential claims about the superhuman but is rather a collection of humans' shared notions about how they want to live together and about who belongs in what territory and under what government. It does not entail claims about the afterlife or how to deal with suffering.

Sometimes, of course, nationalism can seem an awful lot like a religion. Adolf Hitler and Joseph Stalin, for instance, demanded that the citizens of Germany and Russia give their total devotion and indeed their lives for Germany and Russia. They rendered the nation into an idol, an object of religious-like loyalty. Note the claim being made, though. It is much like Eleanor's claim about Arnold: His work has become so total that it is like a religion. Sometimes nationalism is so consuming that it is like a religion. This can only be said, though, if there is something called religion that is not itself nationalism and is something to which nationalism may be compared.

The nationalism of millions of other people who have not lived under Hitler and Stalin is even more clearly something other than religion. Theirs is a nationalism of patriotism or a "civic nationalism" whose commitment to the nation is real but relative, sincere but circumscribed. It is not uncommon for a commitment to the nation to be conditioned by religious faith. People in modern nation-states join the armed forces out of loyalty to their country but also attend a church, synagogue, mosque, or temple out of devotion to the divine, and they view these commitments as separate, though perhaps connected. I am the nation's good servant but God's first, a modern Thomas More might say.

Attesting further to the difference between nation and religion is the fact that some forms of nationalism combine with religion—Hindu nationalism in India, Buddhist nationalism in Sri Lanka—whereas others do not and are even decidedly secular, like that of the Jacobins who led the French Revolution or of many of the partisans who fought to unite Italy in the 1860s. The distinction between religious nationalism and secular nationalism would be intelligible only if there were something called religion that can combine with—or not combine with—nationalism in the first place.

The argument runs similarly for Marxism, environmentalism, and the like. Marxism is not a religion. Marx thought that only the material world was real and that God, gods, and all superhuman powers were illusory. Marxists, like nationalists and workaholics, can be "religious" in their devotion to their cause, but such a statement makes sense, again, only if there is something called religion to provide the adjective.

Not only is religion distinguishable from other phenomena that sometimes resemble it, but according to Riesebrodt, members of most religions have themselves understood religion to be distinguishable from other areas of life—economic, cultural, political, familial and recreational. Stroll down a street in Minneapolis, Bangkok, Jakarta, or Cairo. On the right you will see a marketplace where merchants are negotiating with customers. Then, on the left is a pub or a tearoom where people gather to eat and converse. Further down is a government office where clerks work at computers or typewriters conducting the business of the state. Next you come to a row of houses where family life takes place. Then you come to a structure whose architecture is designed to raise one's thoughts to a superhuman realm and where people inside are praying, chanting, singing, offering sacrifices, burning incense, or otherwise worshipping. Here, religion is practiced and is something different from the kinds of activities practiced in other plots alongside the road. It is a distinct sphere of life. It is not sealed off from the rest of life. Religious people will tell you that it governs what they do in the marketplace and in the home and in all that they do. If not sealed off, though, religion is meaningfully separated.

Buttresses

Although a full defense of this view of religion—mapping every side avenue, responding to every objection—cannot be performed here, several factors serve to buttress it.

First, "[r]eligion's promise . . . remains astonishingly constant in different historical periods and cultures," Riesebrodt writes.[17] It is constant because human beings are constant. "All humans belong to the same species," he elaborates, and manifest "universal characteristics . . . and thus are not arbitrarily or infinitely variable or unbridgeably different."[18] Merely one testament to this universality is the recent discovery of the Göbekli Tepe, an archaeological site in Turkey dating back to 9600 BCE that is believed be a structure for worship that predated and spurred the development of agriculture and the construction of settlements.[19] Religion, the site reveals, is at the origin of human experience.

Second, not only have ordinary people practiced religion widely across time and space, but philosophers and theologians have long thought something called religion exists. Riesebrodt's view that religion is human and universal may be fresh in today's academy but it is not new or exclusively modern. In the Western tradition, the ancient Roman philosopher Cicero discussed religion as a natural human virtue through which a person gives reverence to God. Early Christian thinkers like Augustine, Lactantius, and Tertullian wrote of religion as something practiced by a wide variety of people, not just Christians.[20] Medieval Christian philosopher Thomas Aquinas thought that religion is a virtue whereby one pays God the reverence due to God through worship. Importantly, Aquinas maintained that religion is a natural virtue, one embedded in human nature and apprehensible by human reason.[21] Long before the modern world ever came to be, then, philosophers thought that religion was a matter of worship and a universal human phenomenon.

Third, a related insight of Riesebrodt's is that most religions, both ancient and modern, have understood themselves to be one among several other religions. This implies, in turn, that they have viewed religion as a general category, different forms of which other humans practice. This is easily grasped in the case of Judaism, Christianity, and Islam, among which each historical successor has differentiated itself quite intentionally from its predecessor. It is also true, though, of ancient Buddhism, Jainism, Sikhism, Daoism, or Shintoism, Riesebrodt maintains.[22] They may not have explicitly articulated the concept of religion but they have thought of themselves much like religions who live in a world also inhabited by other religions. How religions have viewed and related to other religions has varied enormously. Over the course of history, religions have conquered, assimilated, massacred, and allied with other religions but also have undertaken interreligious dialogue in the friendliest spirit of cooperation, understanding, and loving-kindness. Whereas some contemporary critics of the concept of religion hold that it was colonialists, imperialists, missionaries, and generally Protestants of the 17th, 18th, and 19th centuries who introduced religion as a general concept to the world, in fact, the concept appears far earlier and more widely.[23]

Fourth, some cognitive scientists corroborate the naturalness of religion. "[B]ecause of the nature of human minds, religious expression in beliefs and practices is nearly inevitable in most populations and the majority of individuals within those populations," as one researcher, Justin Barrett, puts it.[24] Barrett shows that in the first five years of development, children typically come to believe that behind the visible world is an agent who is responsible for causing it. Children are even directed by their reason toward believing in a God who is invisible, omniscient, omnipotent, and immortal. None of these findings, of course, proves that there is a God or gods or still less settles the vexed question of whether the religious impulse evolved through natural selection. What they do suggest is that this impulse is ingrained in our humanity.[25]

Finally, religion has not gone away, and there is little evidence that it is going away, as the secularization thesis had predicted. Over the course of the twentieth century—the century that secularization theorists thought would bury religion once and for all—the portion of the world population adhering to Catholic and Protestant Christianity, Islam, and Hinduism jumped from 50% in 1900 to 64% in 2000. Sociologists Brian J. Grim and Roger Finke cite the findings of the World Values Survey that in the early 2000s, 79% of people surveyed in 50 countries across the globe reported belief in God, an increase from the late 1980s and early 1990s, when the number was 73%.[26]

Admittedly, global poll numbers are imprecise and conceal exceptionally un-believing regions like northwestern Europe as well as short-term dips in belief such as the recent rise of the "nones," or the religiously unaffiliated, in the United States.[27] The broad historical trajectory, though, reveals nothing like the wane in religion that the prophets of secularization predicted. It points far more strongly to the conclusion that religion is a universal human experience.

From Religion to Religious Freedom

Lurking in this description of religion is an important feature of religion: It is a good, that is, an end whose achievement brings fulfillment, flourishing, and fullness of being. In the thought of one recent school of philosophy that has come to be known as new natural law, religion is a "basic good," meaning that it is intrinsically valuable as opposed to being instrumental to something else.[28] People find in religion help and solace in their suffering, a pathway to happiness, and other answers to what are the most important and ultimate questions and problems that human beings face. The Witherspoon Institute's publication, *Religious Freedom: Why Now?*, puts it well: "It is self-evident that if truth about ultimate reality in fact exists, it is of paramount moral and practical importance. The knowledge of such truth would be singularly illuminating both of what is *real* and of how we should live our lives."[29]

To say that religion is fundamental to human flourishing is not in itself to say that religion actually corresponds to transcendent reality, that any religion is truer than the others, or that religions are all the same.[30] One need not be re-ligious to acknowledge religion's role in human life across time and place.[31] It is also not to deny that religious leaders and communities have inflicted great harm at times. It is only to say that the search for, embrace of, and practice of religious truth have been crucial to the flourishing of humans—not humans in this or that epoch or culture but human beings *simpliciter*.

Because religion is crucial to flourishing, it merits protection. It is to be protected not simply out of a commitment to protect whatever people want to believe out of conscience, with religion being one of innumerable pos-sible options, but rather because religion itself is part and parcel of human flourishing.

Why, though, must religion be free? If it is simply religion that merits protection, then governments might well protect their country's religion even through outlawing or legally restricting minority faiths, in direct violation of the human right to religious freedom. The reason why freedom is crit-ical is that religion is considered, investigated, pursued, and lived authenti-cally only when it is willed, reflected upon, and sincere. Inward assent plays a central role in all religions, which stress, *mutatis mutandis*, the heart, virtue, true worship, belief, faith, enlightenment, surrender to God, loving-kindness, and other qualities related to interior commitment. What religion would stress mere outward conformity to rules and regulations, absent any interior commitments? True, different religions render differently the role of rites, community, and conformity to religious and moral norms—what is usually meant by "external" behavior—but virtually all give a central place to internal commitment. If this commitment is to be genuine, it cannot be coerced. Were it coerced, or were it adopted out of fear of harm at the hands of others, for social approval, or to avoid shame, the commitment would not be a commitment. So, too, the search for and the ability to reject such commitments out of conscience is entailed in the very same freedom. The early Christian writer, Lactantius, made the argument vividly:

> [T]he butcher's trade and piety are two very different things . . . . If you want to defend religion by bloodshed, torture, and evil, then at once it will not be so defended: it will be polluted and outraged. There is nothing that is so much a matter of willingness as religion, and if someone making sacrifice is spiritually turned off, then it's gone, it's nothing.[32]

In a very different time and place, the first president of post-Suharto, democratic Indonesia, Abdurrahman Wahid, connected internal assent to religious freedom thus:

> The fact that the Qur'an refers to God as "the Truth" is highly significant. If human knowledge is to attain this level of Truth, religious freedom is vital. Indeed the search for Truth (i.e., the search for God)—whether employing the intellect, emotions, or various forms of spiritual practice—should be allowed a free and broad range. For without freedom, the individual soul cannot attain absolute Truth, which is, by Its very nature, unconditional Freedom itself.
>
> Intellectual and emotional efforts are mere preludes in the search for Truth. One's goal as a Muslim should be to completely surrender oneself [*islâm*] to the absolute Truth and Reality of God rather than to mere intellectual or emotional concepts regarding the ultimate Truth. Without freedom, humans can attain only a self-satisfied and illusory grasp of the truth, rather than genuine Truth itself [*haqq al-haqiqi*].[33]

Freedom is required for religion to be practiced as an authentic good.

If religion is of highest importance to humans and their flourishing and if the authentic practice of religion must be free, then it would be manifestly unjust to coerce, prevent, interfere, or unduly restrict it and manifestly just to protect it with the force of law. In brief, this is the argument for religious freedom.

Religious freedom, then, rightfully occupies its elevated perch in international law. Again, it is the 1981 Declaration that articulates the most full-bodied concept of the right, enumerating a remarkably wide range of dimensions of religious practice that merit protection. Every individual, this Declaration holds, has a right to manifest a religious faith in public or in private and in worship, observance, practice, and teaching. To protect the right of individuals to religious practice, though, also means protecting the communities in which this practice takes place. It means protecting group worship and assembly, the construction and maintenance of buildings where religious communities meet, the training of religious leaders, the appointment of religious leaders according to the standards of the community, the publication of literature, the running of charitable and humanitarian institutions, the manufacture and purchase of religious articles, the observance of holidays and days of rest, communication among members of the community, the religious education of children by the religious community, and the religious education of children by parents.

Other dimensions might be added to the 1981 Declaration's list. Religious freedom arguably entails the right to form religiously-based political parties. Meriting inclusion, too, is the right to share one's religion with others, to adopt a new religion, and to leave a religion. Muslim objections—to Muslims leaving their faith and to others converting Muslims to other faiths—prevented this dimension of religious practice from being included in the 1981 Declaration. It is indeed controversial, and a defense of it requires more elaboration than I can provide here.[34] The core of such a defense is that the free and interior practice of religion means little if it does not extend to the very adoption of a religion to which one is drawn as well as the relinquishment of a religion to which one does not consciously assent. Finally, religious freedom ought to include freedom from heavy discrimination. When religious minorities are denied access to positions in the public and private sectors, for instance, these minorities effectively suffer a strong restriction of their freedom.

In essence, religious freedom means that no person or community should have to pay a material penalty for the practice of his, her, or its religion. More formally, *religious freedom is the civic right of all persons and religious communities to express, practice, and spread their religion in all of its public and private dimensions and to be free from heavy discrimination on account of their religion.*[35] Not coincidentally, all of these dimensions of religious freedom are ones that modern authoritarian regimes have sought to suppress in brutal fashion. In Poland during the Cold War, the Communist regime tried to control and diminish the Catholic Church by opposing its right not only to worship but also to run schools, charity organizations, and camps for children, and to perform public religious rituals. The Church's successful defense of all of these dimensions of its religious freedom preserved for it an autonomous space from which it ultimately helped to bring down the regime. Once the Republic of Turkey was established in 1923, it sought to control Islam by restricting everything from seminary education to the content of Friday sermons to the religious education of children to the dress of Muslims. Curtailing all of these dimensions of religious freedom, the republic's founder, Kemal Atatürk, was convinced, was necessary to prevent Islam from putting a drag on Turkey's progress toward being a modern nation. Few understand the many dimensions of religious freedom better than dictators.

On the basis of this defense of religious freedom, let us consider some of the most assertive arguments of recent critics.

Not Impossible

Religion and religious freedom are not something for everyone but rather are different for everyone. These concepts have intractably diverse meanings. Therefore, an effort like my own to assess the state of religious freedom in Islam can only be cultural imperialism—an imposition of my meaning upon theirs. This is one of the central arguments of a school of scholars who have mounted a concerted and vociferous critique of religious freedom in recent years through a passel of books and articles. Let us call them "the new critics of religious freedom." The most succinct and accessible version of their arguments can be found in a 2012 forum sponsored by a blog, the *Immanent Frame*, which hosts sophisticated discussions of contemporary issues and intellectual developments regarding religion.[36]

One of the coeditors of the forum, legal scholar Winnifred Fallers Sullivan, presented a much longer and more elaborate version of her critique of religious freedom in her 2005 book, *The Impossibility of Religious Freedom*.[37] There, she tells the story of a court case, *Warner v. Boca Raton*, in which the plaintiffs appealed to religious freedom in defense of their right to place statues, crosses, plantings, and Stars of David on the graves of relatives, contrary to cemetery regulations requiring that all markers be level with the ground. As Sullivan explains, the case turned on the question, What is religion? Judges became theologians as they tried to determine whether the elegiac adornments were a valid exercise of religion that merits the protection of law. The problem, argues Sullivan, is that there simply is no good way to define religion—and thus to define what deserves freedom. America's contemporary lack of any shared consensus about what religion is, compounded by a gap between the official texts and teachings of religions and the "lived religion" of ordinary people, makes impossible the task of defining which religious words and deeds are covered by the right of religious freedom.

The impossibility of religious freedom, Sullivan argues in her *Immanent Frame* post, mortally wounds the cause of those who are making pleas for religious freedom in contemporary debates.[38] She and several other new critics argue that religious freedom differs so strongly in its meanings across time and place that there simply is no single thing to which everyone has a right.

In another post on the *Immanent Frame* forum, University of California Berkeley anthropologist Saba Mahmood observes that religious freedom is a bulwark of the West, where it is "widely regarded as a crowning achievement of secular-liberal democracies. . . . Conventional wisdom has it that religious freedom is a universally valid principle." From the standpoint of this principle, she argues, westerners believe themselves to be civilized and tolerant while the Muslim world is "afflicted with the ills of fundamentalism and illiberal governments."[39]

Like Sullivan, though, Mahmood thinks that westerners are wrong about religious freedom, guilty of expanding their own parochial values into universal principles. She echoes Sullivan in claiming that the "meaning and practice of religious liberty have shifted historically" and points to the Middle East as a site where religious freedom has found multiple and conflicting meanings over the course of history. Religious freedom "means very different things to different groups," she concludes.

Other contributors to the forum also assert the diversity of religious freedom's meanings. Elizabeth Shakman Hurd, a political scientist at Northwestern University, who coedited the religious freedom forum with Sullivan, echoes Mahmood in viewing religious freedom as the central plotline in a story told by westerners in which they are the "heroic saviors" who uphold international law, secular tolerance, democracy, human progress, and liberty while their enemies, particularly Muslims, are violent, premodern, primitive, and discriminatory. In Hurd's view, religious freedom is indeed a Western story, but it is only a Western story and is not the world's only or best narrative.[40]

Is religious freedom impossible, as the title of Sullivan's book suggests? It is not entirely clear what Sullivan means by impossibility. On one reading, she thinks that in our day and age there are so many different forms of religion—ranging from Pentecostal snake handlers to the spirituality of the Oprah

Winfrey show—that we just cannot say what religion is. The hapless judges in the Florida cemetery case found themselves forced to become theologians and define religion but their efforts were doomed: The task is impossible. If there is nothing that we can call religion, it follows that there is nothing that can be accorded a right of religious freedom. If this is Sullivan's reasoning, then my response is simply to point to my foregoing argument, which is that there is indeed something called religion, that it is universal and human, and that its free practice is worthy of protection.

At other times, though, Sullivan appears to mean something different by the impossibility of religious freedom, namely that it is impossible to find a criterion for balancing religious freedom against other freedoms and rights. In the Florida cemetery case, how do we balance the right of religious people to bury their dead according to their customs with the right of the cemetery owner to run his business as he pleases? There is no clear way to find such a balance, Sullivan holds. Such an argument weaves through many of the posts in the *Immanent Frame* forum. They insist relentlessly upon the extraordinary diversity and complexity of ways that religious freedom has been balanced with other freedoms and principles in the United States, let alone the rest of the world. They extend their argument by observing the astounding variety of relationships between religion and state across the globe.

The critics have a point. How religious freedom is to be balanced with other rights, obligations, and principles is the stuff of case law, which will always be contestable, complex, and evolving in any country whose laws endorse religious freedom. Consider some of the controversies over religion that courts have faced in the United States alone. May the Amish refrain from educating their children past the eighth grade? May citizens abstain from the Pledge of Allegiance on account of their religion? From military service? Is prayer permitted in public schools? At graduation events and football games? Can a religious club meet on school property? May native tribes employ otherwise illegal drugs in their rituals? May members of the military wear religious headgear? Are religious adoption agencies required to place children with gay couples if their religion forbids homosexual conduct? Are religious businesses, schools, universities, and charities required to provide services to which they object as a part of their employees' health plans? Or consider a version of these dilemmas that is common in the Muslim world: May sports teams require their players to fast for two or more days before a game during Ramadan?[41]

Other countries face similar controversies, though always tailored to their unique configuration of religion and state. England and several Scandinavian countries have established a Protestant church as their official church and exercise both support for and governance over this church in numerous ways. Countries like Poland give the Catholic Church a special status in their Constitution. Germany and other European countries impose a tax on their population for funding churches. France funds both public and Catholic schools. Numerous constitutions in Islamic-majority countries declare Islam as the official religion of the state; many stipulate that no law may be incompatible with Islam. In these and manifold other countries, religious freedom claims and controversies take place along the boundaries and fault lines that laws and institutions create.

The complexity and diversity of religious freedom cases cannot be denied. The imperative of balancing religious freedom with other principles arises in part from a commitment that any thoughtful defender of religious freedom affirms: Religious freedom is not absolute. Even the robust 1981 Declaration allows that religious freedom may be subject to limitations "as are prescribed by law and are necessary to protect public safety, order, health or morals or the fundamental rights and freedoms of others." Religious freedom can never serve as a justification for child sacrifice, for instance, or for mass suicide, as the people of Jonestown, Guyana, committed in 1978. The US Supreme Court ruled in 1878 that laws outlawing polygamy, practiced mainly by Mormons, were valid. Other cases will garner less of a clear consensus, both in the United States and elsewhere. May Muslim girls be prevented from wearing headscarves to school, as they are in France, or to universities, as they were until recently in Turkey? May women be required to wear headscarves in public, as they are in Iran? May prisoners in the United States drink communion wine despite prison regulations against alcohol? That religious freedom is not absolute means that dilemmas regarding its relationship with other rights and principles will proliferate.

To be sure, this book is not about finding principles through which religious freedom is properly balanced and bounded, but rather about to what degree religious freedom is present and can be expanded in Islam. The question, though, is whether complexity and diversity make religious freedom impossible, as Sullivan and other *Immanent Frame* authors contend. It is difficult to see how this is so. Their argument that diversity and complexity yield impossibility is guilty of the logical fallacy of non sequitur: It does not follow. From the fact that religious freedom is diverse in its application and subject to balancing against other principles, it does not follow that the concept has no core, universal meaning. From the fact that a concept has fuzzy boundaries it does not follow that the concept does not exist. It just means, well, that it has fuzzy boundaries. It would make little sense to speak of fuzzy boundaries were there not something that has boundaries in the first place.

To those who would say that the complexity and diversity of religious freedom makes religious freedom impossible—indefinable or so prone to eternal dispute that it is useless to promote or defend—a further question becomes this: What of Professor Abu Zayd? And what of the Muslims in Murfreesboro? What of the Muslims in the state of Gujurat, India, who were targeted and killed with the knowledge of a Hindu nationalist state government for being Muslims? Or of Helen Berhane, the gospel singer whom the Eritrean government held for over two years in a shipping container in the desert because she refused to renounce evangelism? Or Baha'is in Iran who are imprisoned and have their homes ransacked by the government for being Baha'is? Are these also endlessly indisputable dilemmas of religious freedom? If some cases are complex and call for religious freedom to be balanced and qualified, other cases are beyond complexity and are, on their face, egregious, straightforward, horrible violations of religious freedom. Although the complex cases fail to undermine the right of religious freedom, these cases bring great clarity to religious freedom—and all the more challenge the claim that religious freedom is impossible.

There is another sense in which the new critics are guilty of non sequitur. It does not follow from the fact that religious freedom is diverse that there is no universal principle of religious freedom. An assertion of diversity is a description of the world. A defense of the human right of religious freedom is a claim about moral obligations. One does not follow from the other. The fact that there are many understandings and applications of religious freedom does not rule out that some are more just than others.

Imagine that the issue is not religious freedom but rather torture, whose use against suspects of terrorism was the subject of heated public controversy in the West following the attacks of September 11, 2001. Religious freedom and the prohibition of torture admit of striking parallels. As with religious freedom, attitudes toward torture vary greatly across time and place. Think only of the medieval Inquisition; authoritarian regimes around the world over the past century ranging from Mubarak's Egypt to Hitler's Germany to Communist Vietnam; the views of present-day human rights activists; and the 41% of Americans who approved of torture in an August 2012 poll.[42] Another parallel: Just as religious freedom is not absolute, so too, some would justify torture in "hard cases" like the "ticking bomb scenario," in which thousands or even millions will die if officials cannot ascertain the whereabouts of an explosive from a captured terrorist. Like religious freedom, torture is subject to debates over its very meaning, as took place in the United States, where the difference between torture and practices like sleep deprivation or waterboarding was mightily disputed during the decade after the attacks of September 11, 2001. Like religious freedom, the right not to be tortured is espoused most strongly in the modern West and has become strengthened in international law. Six years after the 1981 Declaration on religious freedom came the 1987 Convention against Torture and Other Cruel, Inhuman or Degrading Treatment or Punishment.

Considering all of these ways in which torture, like religious freedom, admits of widely differing opinions, would any of the new critics then conclude that torture is not heinous and rightly subject to universal prohibition? Would any of them claim that the prohibition of torture is but a product of Western thought and history that is imposed on other cultures in neocolonialist fashion? It is difficult to see that they would. Academics swimming in the same cultural and intellectual waters that the new critics do were vociferous in their condemnations of the administration of President George W. Bush for its practice of torture and its rendition of terrorist suspects to countries that would torture them. In my own view, too, torture ought to be condemned whenever and wherever it takes place (unlike even religious freedom, which is not absolute). Wherever exactly one comes down on torture, though, the point is that the morality of torture is not determined by the world's plurality of views, the fact that there are hard cases, the Western provenance of the prohibition, and so forth. Moral convictions about torture are derived rather from what one believes that human dignity consists of and what sort of things cannot be done to a human being. When we make moral judgments, we are not simply describing the spread of opinion in a nation or the world but rather what we believe to be right or wrong about the matter.

As it is with torture, so it goes for religious freedom. If the fact of diversity does not stand in the way of a moral condemnation of torture, then why does it stand in the way of universally asserting the right of religious freedom? Why not extend the same moral concern to the Muslims in Gujarat and the Baha'is in Iran? A similar argument could be made with respect to slavery or, say, sexual trafficking. Both practices are subject to a diversity of interpretations in their meaning and their morality. Would the new critics then refrain from moral opposition to both? If the fact of diversity undermines universal moral judgment, then it must also do so for torture, sexual trafficking, the targeting of civilians in wartime, and a whole host of other violations of human rights. If diversity does not undermine universal moral judgment, then it does not do so for religious freedom.

A Modern Western Protestant Invention?

The new critics accompany their argument that religious freedom lacks universality with an explanation of exactly where religious freedom came from. It was a product of particular developments in Western history, especially the Protestant Reformation and the secularization that followed in its wake in the Enlightenment movement, they say.

The guru behind this claim, whom several of the new critics rely upon heavily, is Talal Asad, an anthropologist at the City University of New York. A first encounter with Asad's thought might suggest that he would be sympathetic to religious freedom. He is a strong critic of modern secularism, which considers religion dangerous, divisive, and baneful when it enters the political sphere and benign only if it remains in a strictly private realm. Such a marginalization of religion, Asad finds objectionable.

His view, though, does not translate into sympathy for religious freedom, which Asad believes to emerge from the same historical forces that gave the world secularism. Chief among these forces, indeed the incubator of secularism, was the Protestant Reformation, which revolutionized the West's way of looking upon religion. Whereas religion was once about rituals, practices, and embodied community, now it stressed an individual's belief and the sincerity of his faith, which amount to a "purely inner, private state of mind, a particular state of mind detached from everyday practices."[43] It was on this understanding of religion that European philosophers of the Enlightenment during the 17th and 18th centuries concluded that genuine faith cannot be coerced by the state or by any outside party—the idea of religious freedom.

Enlightenment philosophers also took a giant stride toward understanding politics in a more secular way. They followed Protestantism in widening the separation of religious and political authority and in establishing the state's authority over the church, but they also looked upon religion much more skeptically as a fissiparous force, an animal that needed to be leashed. It was these philosophers' view that religion ought to be private and that secularism was the *lingua franca* for public matters that ushered modern secularism onto the historical stage, Asad holds.

Asad takes modern secularism to task for proclaiming itself universally valid whereas in fact its views of religion and of the relationship between religious and political authority are but the notions of a particular time and place. "The *meanings* of religious practices and utterances are to be explained as products of historically distinct disciplines and forces," Asad writes.[44] Worse, the West has sought to export its parochialism through colonialism and imperialism. It is from this standpoint that Asad looks upon religious freedom—as a mile marker along the Protestant-secular pathway to the modern world. Asad concludes a recent essay by declaring that when the West foists the secularism of its own version of democracy on peoples who view religion differently, it violates the very spirit of democracy, which stresses listening and inclusivity.[45]

In a post on the *Immanent Frame* blog, Hurd adopts Asad's account of religious freedom's origins and deepens his dark judgment of rendering religious freedom a universal principle.[46] Such a rendering, she charges, privileges Protestant Christian forms of religion and leaves others out; subordinates religions in which inward belief is not central; "endows hierarchical authorities with the power to represent and pronounce on what is or is not religious belief deserving of special protection or sanction"; and "globalizes the secular state's power over the individual." The human right of religious freedom that appears in international law is a secularized Christian notion enforced by power. She closes her piece by calling religious freedom "mind control" and comparing it to the Inquisition of medieval Europe. Several other contributors reason similarly about the Western, Protestant, secular provenance of religious freedom and its resulting exclusivity.[47]

This argument of the new critics also contains some truth. It was a cluster of Protestant thinkers in the late 17th and early 18th centuries who injected the idea of religious freedom into debates about politics in the modern West.[48] Some of them, like John Locke, are considered major figures of the Enlightenment. They argued for toleration even as they applauded the state's establishment of authority over religion. Their advocacy of religious freedom favored individual, private belief, reflecting the ambition of Protestant reformers to scrape what they saw as the barnacles of ritual, hierarchy, and superstition from the hull of the Christian church and to disencumber the free commitment of the individual believer.

Yet, the new critics' historical claim that religious freedom is tightly bound to the rise of Protestant, privatized religion and the secular state—and is thus an exclusively Western idea that can only be imposed on the rest of the world—is riddled with difficulties, seven in particular.[49] The first is *Protestantism without religious freedom*. In the century-and-a-half after the Reformation, Protestant church leaders or theologians who advocated religious freedom were few and far between. Both Martin Luther and John Calvin, the most famous reformers, approved of the execution of heretics, whereas Protestant kings and princes persecuted Catholics and dissenting Protestants. Although, as just noted, some Protestants (mostly those on the receiving end of persecution) pressed for religious freedom in the subsequent period, other Protestants advocated its sharp curtailment well into the 19th century—Chancellor Otto von Bismarck in late 19th-century Germany and Anglicans in England well into the middle of the 19th century, for instance.[50]

A second difficulty is this: *the Enlightenment without religious freedom.* If some Enlightenment thinkers opened up space for religious freedom, others envisioned regimes that would brutally deny it. Even John Locke's *A Letter Concerning Toleration* of 1689, which argued for legalizing dissenting Protestant churches, rejected toleration for atheists, Catholics, and Muslims who professed loyalty to the Ottoman Mufti.[51] French philosopher Denis Diderot—whom one of the new critics, religious studies scholar Yvonne Sherwood, associates with the invention of religion as belief—is well known for his quip that "[m]en will never be free until the last king is strangled with the entrails of the last priest."[52] The French Revolution followed suit by emancipating Jewish and Protestant individuals while beheading resistant Catholic priests and requiring Catholics to take an oath swearing loyalty to the revolution and forswearing obedience to the pope. It is far too simple, then, to say that religious freedom was a component of a "secular state package" that was developed in the Reformation and the Enlightenment and was then imposed on the rest of the world.

A third difficulty: *the West without religious freedom.* The new critics' contention that religious freedom is a Western invention imagines a West far more monolithic than the one that actually has existed. Since the Enlightenment, Western states have ranged greatly in their respect for religious freedom. The US Constitution's First Amendment was a milestone in the development of religious freedom and opened America's gates to people of many faiths who were not tolerated elsewhere. On the other hand, the legacy of the French Revolution included harshly anticlerical regimes in France, Italy, Mexico, and many Latin American countries in the late 19th and early 20th centuries. For its part, the religion of the clerics, the Catholic Church, comprising the majority of West Europeans and Latin Americans, did not fully embrace religious freedom until 1965. Communist Soviet Union and Nazi Germany, both Western regimes, carried out history's greatest denials of religious freedom. Even considering Western Europe alone, religious freedom was more the exception than the norm until after World War II.[53]

A fourth difficulty: *religious freedom prior to Protestantism and the Enlightenment.* Jarring to the narrative of Asad and the new critics who follow him is the appearance of the precise concept of religious freedom centuries before Western modernity. Scholars such as Robert Wilken, Elizabeth DePalma Digeser, and Timothy Samuel Shah point to the concept in early Christian thinkers, whose espousal of religious freedom long predates the Protestant Reformation and its allegedly privatized vision of religion.[54] It is in the *Apology* of the Christian writer Tertullian, dated 197, that we arguably first find the phrase, "religious liberty" [*libertas religionis*], by which Tertullian meant exactly freedom from arbitrary religious coercion—an articulation that took place some 1,300 years before the European Reformation and some 1,500 years before the European Enlightenment. Important, too, was Lactantius, an adviser to the Emperor Constantine in the early 4th century who had been influenced by Tertullian and whose arguments for religious liberty are imprinted on the Edict of Milan, Constantine's declaration of religious liberty of 313.[55]

Religious freedom outside of Protestantism and the Enlightenment is a fifth difficulty. The new critics are hard-pressed to account not only for the dating of religious freedom but also for its appearance outside the tradition in which they place its origin. In India in the 3rd century BCE, the Buddhist Emperor Ashoka urged religious toleration by declaring that "a man must not . . . disparage [the sect] of another man without reason." In the 2nd century BCE, as described in the First and Second Books of Maccabees, Jews rebelled against King Antiochus, whose Hellenizing policies sought to coerce religious and cultural uniformity. In ancient Greek literature, Antigone, the heroine of Sophocles' play, defies the tyrannical decrees of King Creon—decrees that obstruct a central, binding obligation of piety and thus violate religious freedom. Nowhere in the text of any religious scripture is religious freedom expressed so forthrightly as it is in the Qur'an: "There is no compulsion in religion."[56] Finally, in the heart of that very church whose teachings and authority Protestants protested, the Second Vatican Council in 1965 issued a declaration, *Dignitatis Humanae*, stating that "all human beings ought to be immune from coercion" in religious matters. Religious freedom has never been consistently, much less irrevocably, intertwined with the Protestant religion.

A sixth difficulty is this: *religious freedom articulated far more widely than the Protestant notion of religion, as it is in the human rights conventions.* The conventions protect religious freedom not only as a matter of inward belief— the version of religion that the new critics find in Protestantism—but also as a matter of practice and in both individual and collective dimensions. Such is the case for the Universal Declaration of Human Rights of 1948, the International Covenant on Civil and Political Rights of 1966, and, most of all, the 1981 Declaration on the Elimination of All Forms of Intolerance and Discrimination Based on Religion or Belief. Today's religious freedom advocates strenuously resist the restriction of religion to beliefs or ideas.

A seventh and final difficulty: *the new critics' mischaracterization of Protestantism.* Each of the foregoing difficulties grants the new critics their depiction of Protestantism as inward belief and questioned whether there is a tight connection between Protestantism and religious freedom. But is this depiction accurate? Although "stripping the altars" was certainly a feature of the Reformation, most Protestant churches have retained ritual, hierarchy, strong community and a stress on "good works" seen as flowing from faith.[57] To be sure, these features vary among Protestant churches, which include at least six major international denominations and literally thousands of small and independent churches, whose styles differ from one another as much as they differ from the Catholic Church. A high Anglican church outdoes most Catholic Churches in its liturgical elaborateness, and Pentecostal churches have rituals of their own, albeit informal ones. Most Protestants, then, would find it strange to call their religion inward belief. And they demand freedom for far more than belief alone.

Religious freedom is not simply the upshot of an allegedly Protestant religion of private, inward belief or the product of modern Western history. Ironically, the new critics end up creating exactly the sort of binary that they decry—the West versus the Rest—even though binaries and essentialism are unforgivable sins for postmodern intellectuals. Their arguments contain too little and too much diversity. Too little, because the bifurcation of the world into the West and the Rest fails to allow that there are and have been both proponents and opponents of religious freedom in every religion and every part of the world—including the West—both prior to and during modern times. Too much, because religious freedom extends far more uniformly over time and place than they allow.

Part of what makes plausible the universality of the human right of religious freedom is its minimalism. Religious freedom does not prescribe the worldwide export of Thomas Jefferson's wall of separation between church and state, a Protestant way of doing things, or any one country's relationship between religion and state. Whether a state should proclaim a national religion (as do Pakistan, England, Israel, Cambodia, Denmark, and many others), whether the government should provide financial support for religious activities or fund religious schools, which, if any, religious holidays ought to be public holidays—these and many other questions are left unanswered by religious freedom.[58] Religious freedom does not proffer a blueprint for the edifice of religion–state relationships, but rather prescribes a floor, a set of prohibitions and obligations that everyone, everywhere ought to follow. For instance, no one should be killed, tortured, imprisoned, detained, robbed of their property, deprived of their houses of worship, and denied jobs, economic opportunities, and positions in public service on account of his or her religion. The truth that the new critics obscure is that the minimalist moral intuition of religious freedom as religious noncoercion, far from being parochial or peculiar to the modern West, enjoys a widespread resonance across history and across cultures.

A Weapon of the Powerful?

Behind the new critics' rejection of religious freedom's universality and their assertion of its modern, Western, Protestant provenance is their underlying conviction that what accounts for how religious freedom is defined in this or that place is the power and the interests of those doing the defining. Likewise, the historical evolution of religious freedom is a product of power struggles. The winners of these struggles will voice religious freedom when it suits them. One contributor to the *Immanent Frame* forum, writing a piece about Sri Lanka, states the view clearly and directly: "[R]eligious rights, as rhetoric, serve not as apolitical instruments, but as indicia of political alliances . . . . In this version of the story, religious rights, rather than conclude conflict and harmonize societies, signpost disagreement."[59]

Lurking behind this view is the ghost of 20th-century French philosopher Michel Foucault. Among the ideas for which Foucault was best known is his view of power. Power, he taught, is not straightforwardly coercive, as in: A makes B do something that B would not otherwise do. Rather, power is something far more subtle, pervasive, and indeed often unseen. It inheres in a society's notions of knowledge and its ways of speaking about truth—for instance, its norms of right and wrong or its standards of what can be known, as with scientific knowledge. Such power shapes people thoroughly. The moral standard of religious freedom, in a Foucauldian view, exerts power by defining some people as civilized, law abiding, tolerant, and democratic and others as violent, intolerant, and regressive.

Foucault has been a major influence on Asad's thinking. Mahmood cites Foucault as one of her key influences in her widely-acclaimed book of 2005, *The Politics of Piety*.[60] Her *Immanent Frame* post exudes Foucault, too. There, she writes that religious freedom has been a tool to promote Western Christian proselytizing among non-Christian peoples and to advance the power of western states over non-Western peoples. "[C]rucially, [religious freedom] is a technique of national and international governance whose proper exercise has always entailed realpolitik concerns."[61] Another contributor, scholar of religion Greg Johnson of the University of Colorado, Boulder, declares on the basis of what he learned from the "fantastic papers" in the forum that the promotion of religious freedom is "a form of social eugenics" and "social engineering." He resounds the sentiments of the other contributors in writing, "[t]he sought-after outcome of such agendas is to produce and reproduce a healthy social body—as defined by those who have the power to manipulate society at the level of policy."[62] Several of the *Immanent Frame* bloggers charge that the United States' promotion of religious freedom is an exercise of American domination; some add that it is a cause of the Christian right.

Circumstantial evidence for their claim exists. Over the course of the 20th century and into the 21st century, the United States has been both the world's greatest possessor of "hard power" (military, economic, etc.) and the leading champion of religious freedom. As legal scholar Anna Su documents, the United States promoted religious freedom in the Philippines during its occupation of these islands in the early 20th century; made religious freedom one of its major war aims in World War II; wrote religious freedom into the Constitution of Japan after World War II; ensured the principle's inclusion in the Universal Declaration of Human Rights in 1948; promoted the principle during the Cold War; and has incorporated religious freedom into its foreign policy over the past two decades including in its occupation of Iraq after 2003. The historical dominance of Protestant Christianity in the United States has much to do with its purveyance of religious freedom.[63]

But does it follow from the fact that religious freedom has been a cause of the world's most powerful state that religious freedom is but an instrument of this state's power? Again, we run into non sequitur. Clearly, religious freedom is a part of the purpose of the United States. It is far less clear how religious freedom promotes the power of the United States. A contemporary advocate of America's religious freedom policy might well wish that religious freedom were, in fact, so empowered. Since the US Congress established the Office of International Religious Freedom in the State Department, the office has played a marginal role in the making of American foreign policy. The ambassador-at-large for International Religious Freedom does not even serve directly under the secretary of state, as many other ambassadors do.

More broadly, despite religious freedom's incorporation into the architecture of US foreign policy, it has been trumped time and again by other foreign policy goals like fighting terrorism. Pakistan, for instance, has received little pressure from the United States to dismantle its blasphemy laws because it has been an ally (though a shaky one) in the war against terrorism. China, Saudi Arabia, Russia, and other major powers also face little trouble from the United States for their religious freedom policies despite their thorough denials of this human right.

That the United States would subordinate religious freedom to power is hardly new. During the Cold War, when the United States trumpeted religious freedom as one of the defining principles in its struggle against the Soviet

Union, it was perfectly willing to ally with arch-violators of religious freedom in order to gain advantage in that very struggle. For instance, the Central Intelligence Agency engineered the installation of the shah of Iran, who brutally repressed traditional Muslim clerics, in the early 1950s and remained steadfastly loyal to him right up until a coalition of conservative Muslims, socialists, and others overthrew him in 1979.[64]

Even when the United States militarily occupied Afghanistan and Iraq in the 2000s, exercising hard power in the most direct way possible, the United States did not deploy religious freedom as an instrument of this power. In Afghanistan, the United States consented to a new constitution that was unfriendly to religious freedom. In Iraq, the US government pushed harder for religious freedom in the Constitution but with mixed results, some of its provisions favoring religious freedom and others not. Even here, though, it is hardly clear that religious freedom was an instrument of power. In advocating for religious freedom, the American coalitional authorities risked political capital, in fact. They had to overcome the stances of powerful influential Iraqi political and religious leaders and thus risked instability.[65] Had they not pressed the issue of religious freedom, their already-difficult job of securing passage of a constitution would have been easier. In other cases—relatively rare—when the United States has incorporated religious freedom into the promotion of its core interests, it is its purpose, not its power, that has provided the impetus.

A variant of the religious freedom-as-power argument also stumbles upon the evidence: the claim that religious freedom is a tool not just of America but also of Christian America. To the weak extent that the United States promotes religious freedom in its foreign policy, it does so on behalf of all religions, not just Christians. Although an early version of the legislation that the US Congress passed as the International Religious Freedom Act (IRFA) focused more narrowly on Christians—and failed to pass in part for this very fact—the coalition of supporters behind the bill then expanded to a wide array of religious communities, who saw Congress pass the bill overwhelmingly in 1998. "[A]ssertions that the statute was mainly a product of the lobbying efforts of the Christian right are plain wrong," writes Su.[66] After IRFA passed and came to be implemented, both the State Department office and the US Commission on International Religious Freedom (USCIRF), an independent entity appointed by Congress, have been assiduous in addressing violations of religious freedom against a wide variety of religious people and communities, as they do in their annual reports.

A final problem with the power argument is that the human right of religious freedom is almost always invoked on behalf of the powerless—religious majorities suppressed by their regime, religious minorities, and alleged dissenters from their own religion's orthodoxy. On behalf of Muslims who experienced massacres in 2002 in the state of Gujarat, India, USCIRF successfully lobbied to have the United States deny a visa in 2005 to Gujarat's Chief Minister, Narendra Modi—a ban that was not lifted until Modi became prime minister of India in 2014. Religious freedom officials also have spoken on behalf of Ahmadis and Sufis in Pakistan; Christians in Vietnam; Yazidis and Chaldean Christians in Iraq; numerous other minorities; and, in some cases, religious majorities who are repressed by secular governments. What is true of all of these religious communities is that they lack power and there is little political incentive for anyone to take up their cause.

Religious freedom is not merely a product of power, modern Western thought, or Protestantism, nor a concept whose meanings are wildly diverse and unsettleable, but is rather a universal human right that demands the protection of every person's search for and embrace of religious truth. What was done to Professor Abu Zayd and the Muslims of Murfreesboro was universally wrong. If that is the case, then we may ask for Islam, as we may ask for any religion: To what degree does it allow religious freedom? This is the question to which we now turn.

2

Religiously Free States in the Muslim World

IS ISLAM HOSPITABLE to religious freedom? There is no better way to answer the central question of this book than by looking closely at the Muslim world. Is it religiously free? This chapter and the following two chapters undertake this investigation.

I focus on how governments treat the question of religious freedom in countries where Muslims are a majority. There are about 47 of these countries, and they are concentrated in the Middle East, North Africa, West Africa, and Southeast Asia (see the world map in Figure I.1 in the Introduction). Muslims are not confined to these countries and are scattered around the world, including in the West. India contains 172 million Muslims, one of the largest concentrations in the world, even though Muslims are only 14.2% of the population. Muslims also organize politically other than through governments—for instance, through parties and through transnational movements like the Muslim Brotherhood and Jamaat-e-Islami.

I focus on the governments of Muslim-majority states, though, because they serve as a strong test for religious freedom: How are dissenters and religious minorities treated in states where Muslims are the majority of the population and have the means of coercion at their disposal? If regimes in these states allow religious freedom, then the case for the Muslim world's openness to religious freedom is strengthened. Just as there are ways in which Muslims organize themselves other than the state, so, too, there are ways in which they—like people of any religious faith—can restrict religious freedom other than through the state. Nonstate actors—militant groups, mobs, and vigilante citizens—carry out acts of discrimination and violence, acts that the Pew Research Center terms "social hostilities." Although, in the chapters that follow, I will allude to both nonstate groups and nonstate violence, my central focus is on state governments.

Help for understanding governments' religious freedom policies comes from the Pew Research Center. Led by sociologists Brian J. Grim and Roger Finke, Pew's research team has scored 198 states and territories around the world on a Government Restrictions Index (GRI), the one that I will use most, as well as a Social Hostilities Index (SHI), measuring the violations that non-state actors commit. The GRI scores are a composite of 20 dimensions of religious freedom curtailments, whereas the SHI collates 13.[1] Each country is given a score on each index on a scale from 0 to 10, with 0 being the most religiously free and 10 being the highest level of restriction.

Pew's first report, *Global Restrictions on Religion*, appeared in 2009, and five subsequent reports have offered updated data, the most recent coming out in April 2017. Over the next three chapters, I rely mainly on the data for 2009, using them as the basis for my categorization of regime types. I chose 2009 as my benchmark for comparison because the data for that year depict the Muslim-majority world prior to the changes of the Arab Uprisings that began in 2011. I then devote Chapter 5 to looking at the changes that the Uprisings brought about (or, more commonly, failed to bring about). In this manner, the Arab Uprisings can be analyzed in isolation from the Muslim-majority world at large.[2]

Pew's indices offer a thorough and textured understanding of the extent of religious freedom in a country. The GRI aggregates a vast array of ways in which governments can curtail religious freedom. These curtailments can be directed against both Muslim citizens and non-Muslim religious minorities. The ones directed against Muslim citizens might include harsh laws against blasphemy or converting away from Islam; laws outlawing allegedly heterodox sects such as Shias (in Sunni-majority countries) or Ahmadiyyas (in Pakistan or Indonesia); and policies that restrict heavily the activities of mosques and the religious community more broadly. Restrictions against non-Muslim minorities might include curbs on practice and expression; policies that make it difficult to build new religious structures; and law or policies that forbid non-Muslims from holding certain political offices.

Table 2.1 shows the 20 criteria that make up the composite GRI.[3]

Again, these 20 criteria together comprise a score for an individual country on a scale from 0 to 10. Based on these scores, Pew divides the world's countries into four categories of restrictiveness: very high, high, moderate, and low. Figure 2.1 shows how Pew distributed countries into these categories in its initial report of 2009.

Table 2.1. The Criteria That Make up the GRI

Q.1   Does the constitution, or law that functions in the place of a constitution (basic law), specifically provide for "freedom of religion" or include language used in Article 18 of the United Nations Universal Declaration of Human Rights?

Q.2   Does the constitution or basic law include stipulations that appear to qualify or substantially contradict the concept of "religious freedom"?

Q.3   Taken together, how do the constitution/basic law and other national laws and policies affect religious freedom?

Q.4   Does any level of government interfere with worship or other religious practices?

Q.5   Is public preaching by religious groups limited by any level of government?

Q.6   Is proselytizing limited by any level of government?

Q.7   Is converting from one religion to another limited by any level of government?

Q.8   Is religious literature or broadcasting limited by any level of government?

Q.9   Are foreign missionaries allowed to operate?

Q.10   Is the wearing of religious symbols, such as head coverings for women and facial hair for men, regulated by law or by any level of government?

Q.11   Was there harassment or intimidation of religious groups by any level of government?

Q.12   Did the national government display hostility involving physical violence toward minority or nonapproved religious groups?

Q.13   Were there instances when the national government did not intervene in cases of discrimination or abuses against religious groups?

Q.14   Does the national government have an established organization to regulate or manage religious affairs?

Q.15   Did the national government denounce one or more religious groups by characterizing them as dangerous "cults" or "sects"?

Q.16   Does any level of government formally ban any religious group?

Q.17   Were there instances when the national government attempted to eliminate an entire religious group's presence in the country?

Q.18   Does any level of government ask religious groups to register for any reason, including to be eligible for benefits such as tax exemption?

Q.19   Did any level of government use force toward religious groups that resulted in individuals being killed, physically abused, imprisoned, detained or displaced from their homes, or having their personal or religious properties damaged or destroyed?

Q.20   Do some religious groups receive government support or favors, such as funding, official recognition or special access?

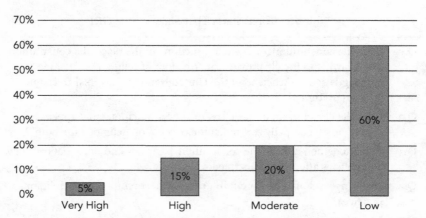

FIGURE 2.1. The range of restrictions on religious freedom (GRI) in the world's countries (Pew Research Center 2009 report)

At first, these numbers may not seem to paint a dire picture of religious freedom in the world. Only 5% of countries are in the very high range and 15% in the high range. Considering, however, that some of the world's most populous states fall into the two tiers of very high and high—China, India, Russia, Indonesia, and Turkey—the picture starts to look different. Pew's reports show that in 2014, 74% of the world's population lived in a regime where restrictions were very high or high—a number that had climbed to 79% in 2015.[4]

Pew's numbers are central to my argument about religious freedom but do not alone deliver it. One must look not only at the magnitude but also at the manner in which governments restrict religious freedom. By manner, I have in mind what we may call a regime's political theology, that is, a doctrine of political authority, justice, and the proper relationship between religion and state that is derived from more foundational theological and philosophical commitments. Political theology can be found in the statements and speeches of government leaders, in constitutional principles, and in the laws and norms that govern religion.[5] For instance, certain medieval Catholic political theologies held that the purpose of government authority was to inculcate virtue in its subjects, lead them to eternal salvation, and uphold the work of the Church, including through coercion, and that this authority was derived from a more basic doctrine of God's sovereignty over the world. A Marxist political theology holds that the state's purpose is to marginalize religion as much as possible, even to the point of elimination, given that religion is illusory and a promoter of economic oppression.

Turning to Islam, I categorize Muslim-majority countries according to a combination of Pew numbers and the political theology of regimes. I propose three categories of regimes as they are defined by their political theology. The first is "religiously free" states, which make up 11 out of 47 Muslim-majority states. These fit Pew's category of "low" restrictions on religious freedom on the GRI and are categorized by a political theology of religious freedom, meaning that they espouse, promote, and protect the freedom of people and communities to practice their religion.

The 36 Muslim-majority states that are not religiously free fit Pew's categories of moderate, high, or very high levels of restriction on the GRI. These states manifest different political theologies, though, and so can be divided into two categories. One of these—the second of my three categories—can be called "secular repressive" states. Numbering 15 in 2009, these states proffer a political theology of secularism, rooted in the West, holding that the public influence of Islam ought to be stifled so as to make way for nationalism, economic modernization, and modernity in general.

The other kind of Muslim-majority state that curtails religious freedom—my third category—I call a "religiously repressive" state. These states numbered 21 in 2009 and manifested a political theology of "Islamism" that envisions law and government policy as a vehicle for promoting a strongly conservative form of Islam in all spheres of life—family life, economy, culture, religious practice, education, dress, and many others.

Figure 2.2 shows the three categories of governance of religious freedom in Muslim-majority states.

These categories are at the heart of my argument about Islam and religious freedom. Recall from the Introduction that in the aggregate, the Muslim-majority world is far less religiously free than the rest of the world. Recall also that when we zoom in from this satellite view to a close-up view of the Muslim-majority world, the picture takes on complexity. These categories describe that more complex picture.

They show, first, that religiously free states do exist in the majority-Muslim world. They make up almost one-fourth (23%) of that world and so are more than outliers. Then, the religiously unfree portion of the majority-Muslim world must be understood in its complexity, too. About 32% of Muslim-majority states are secular repressive ones, fueled by an antireligious ideology borrowed from the West. The other 45% are religiously repressive, imposing traditional Islam. In this picture can be found grist for both sides of today's public debate. On the Islamoskeptics' side is the satellite view and the religiously repressive regimes. On the Islamopluralists' side is the complexity of

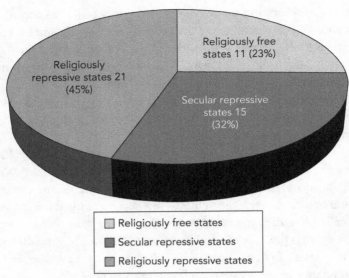

FIGURE 2.2. Categories of religious freedom in Muslim-majority states (as of 2009)

the close-up view and the presence of both religiously free and secular repressive regimes.

Let us look more closely at this picture by turning first to religiously free countries, the subject of the remainder of this chapter.

Religiously Free States in the Muslim-Majority World

Religiously free states are ones whose laws and government policies refrain from coercing or discriminating heavily against individuals and religious communities in their practice of religion. They adhere closely to international human rights conventions in matters of religion. They rate favorably on the 20 questions that make up the Pew Research Center's GRI.

Religiously free states are secular, but only in a certain sense of this fraught and protean word. In the West, where the word originated, secular regimes have taken both positive and negative forms, to borrow a distinction that Pope Benedict XVI made.[6] Positive secularism, Benedict explained, is a separation of authority of religion and state that is broadly friendly to religion. Religious communities must relinquish strong standing authority in political affairs but in turn are given broad freedom to express and practice their faith and to participate in democratic politics. Such reciprocal respect is what political scientist

Alfred Stepan called the "twin tolerations."[7] In negative secularism, by contrast, the state sharply constrains and controls religion, usually motivated by an ideology that considers religion baneful and destined to disappear from the world stage. Religiously free states are characterized by positive secularism.

Critically, religiously free states do not prohibit religious people or communities from building a religious society or from making religious arguments in the political realm. Nor must religiously free states replicate one particular configuration of religion and state. The Western democracies, almost all of which are religiously free today, range from the US model of wide separation of church and state, to England's established state church, to Germany's raising of taxes for the Catholic and the state Protestant church. Within the Muslim world, religiously free states are ones in which Muslim religious leaders promote the vigorous practice of Islam, the spread of Islam, and a robust Islamic culture while often enjoying direct state support for religious activities. Religious freedom means that religion is free, not that politics or society is free from religion.

Table 2.2 spells out typical features of religiously free Muslim-majority states.

As we shall see, not every religiously free Muslim-majority country exhibits all of these characteristics, but all of them possess enough of these characteristics to earn the rank of religiously free.

The 11 Muslim-majority states fitting this description appear in Table 2.3 and are shown in the map in Figure 2.3.

Note that between 2009 and 2015, the religious freedom scores of three of these countries, Lebanon, Kosovo, and Djibouti, worsened significantly. Lebanon and Kosovo moved down into Pew's "moderate" category, and Djibouti moved into Pew's "high" category. By 2015, then, only 8 of the 11 countries that were religiously free in 2009 were still religiously free.

The West Africa Seven

The most striking feature of the set of religiously free Muslim-majority countries is that seven of them are in West Africa. They are Senegal, Mali, Niger, Guinea, Burkina Faso, Sierra Leone, and The Gambia.[8] All of them remained religiously free between 2009 and 2015. They are the geographic heart of the religiously free Muslim world and together offer the strongest existing evidence for the possibility of religious freedom in the Muslim world. They are free not despite or apart from their Islamic character but rather because of their interpretation of Islam.

Table 2.2. What to Look for in a Religiously Free Muslim-Majority State

- The state's constitution carries robust provisions guaranteeing religious freedom for all citizens and religious communities
- The constitution is absent provisions imposing doctrinal tests on laws (i.e., conformity to Islam or to *sharia* or requiring approval by a council of scholars)
- Public schools don't force students to be instructed only in a religion other than their own, or don't teach religion at all; and religious private schools are permitted
- The state does not directly govern mosques, imams, or the education that religious communities provide
- If the government offers financial support for religious communities or activities, it does so equally for all religions
- If the state declares religious holidays, it does so for the holidays of minority religions as well as Islam
- Registration of religious groups either is not required or carries no onerous implications
- Personal status law and status law courts (governing families, marriage, inheritance, etc.) either do not exist; or, when they do exist, are only for Muslims and are not required to be used by non-Muslims; are optional; and/or are liberal in their interpretations of *sharia* law
- The government creates an interreligious council to encourage harmony and conflict resolution but does not use it to govern religious communities directly
- There are no laws prohibiting blasphemy or imposing restrictions on speech, including broadcasting
- There are no laws prohibiting conversion away from Islam
- There are no religious tests for office
- There are no laws governing dress
- The law affords women a high degree of equality in education and vocational opportunities

In most of these countries, Muslim majorities live side-by-side with Christian minorities. The Sufi form of Islamic spirituality is prevalent in the region, and some of these countries contain Shias and Ahmadis, whose beliefs diverge from those of mainstream Sunni Islam. Tiny communities of Hindus, Baha'is, Jews, and other religions live in these countries as well. All of these countries also contain citizens who practice traditional African religions that long preceded the arrival of Islam and Christianity. It is common for Muslims and Christians to combine their faith with elements of these religions, indeed so much so that it is difficult to determine how many of each religion inhabit each country. Table 2.4 shows each country's religious demography according

Table 2.3. Religiously Free Muslim-Majority Countries

Country	2009 GRI (mid-2006 to mid-2008)	2015 GRI (December 2013)
Kosovo	2.0	2.5
Lebanon	1.8	4.0
Djibouti	1.6	5.1
Niger	1.6	1.7
Albania	1.3	2.2
Guinea	1.3	2.1
Mali	0.9	1.8
The Gambia	0.8	1.8
Burkina Faso	0.7	1.3
Senegal	0.4	1.2
Sierra Leone	0.3	1.4

N.B: As explained in the text, the lower the number, the greater the freedom.

to US State Department estimates.[9] The numbers are uncertain, though, and estimates vary.

The kinds of Muslim beliefs, syncretistic practices, and non-Muslim minorities found in these countries are the kind that elicit repression elsewhere in the Muslim world—but for the most part, not here.

Religious freedom is articulated boldly in these countries' constitutions. They prescribe religious freedom explicitly and do not dilute it into a more generalized freedom of conscience or belief. They prescribe it robustly, too, according it to both individuals and communities and to both belief and practice. Absent are clauses declaring that the country is an Islamic state and the kinds of provisions that serve to restrict religious freedom in constitutions elsewhere in the Muslim-majority world, for instance, ones that say that no law shall contradict *sharia*, that *sharia* is the primary source of legislation, or that laws are subject to the approval of a council of religious leaders.

Some of the constitutions declare the government to be a secular one, but they mean secular in the positive sense, not in the antireligious sense. Senegal's Constitution, for instance, espouses *laïcité*, the French word for secular that is also found in France's Constitution, but means by it a regime that is much friendlier to religion than is France's regime. Senegal's first president, Léopold Senghor, a Catholic, described Senegal's *laïcité* in remarks in 1963 at the inauguration of the Great Mosque at Touba: "[l]aïcité, for us, is neither atheism nor anti-religious propaganda. I give as just one piece of

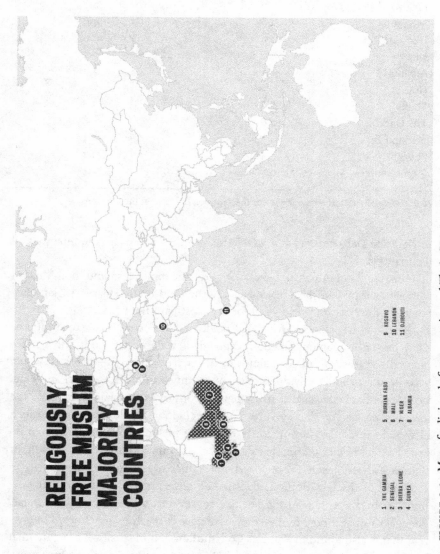

RELIGOUSLY FREE MUSLIM MAJORITY COUNTRIES

1 THE GAMBIA
2 SENEGAL
3 SIERRA LEONE
4 GUINEA

5 BURKINA FASO
6 MALI
7 NIGER
8 ALBANIA

9 KOSOVO
10 LEBANON
11 DJIBOUTI

FIGURE 2.3. Map of religiously free countries and Their GRI Score

Table 2.4. Religious Demography of West Africa

Country	Total population (millions)	Percentage Muslim	Percentage Christian	Percentage traditional religions	Notes
Burkina Faso	18.4	61	23	15	19% of population is Roman Catholic and 4% Protestant. Less than 1% is atheist or belongs to other religious groups.
The Gambia	1.9	90	9	1	Most of Muslim population is Sunni, but there are small numbers of Ahmadi and Ndigal Muslims. The Christian population is mostly Roman Catholic but includes various Protestant denominations. There is a small community of Hindus.
Guinea	11.5	85	8	7	Muslims are mostly Sunni. Christians include Catholics and various Protestant denominations. There are small numbers of Hindus, Buddhist, and adherents of traditional Chinese beliefs.
Guinea-Bissau	1.7	40	10	50	Numbers of Christians and Muslims are uncertain because of the high levels of syncretism. Most Muslims are Sunni. Christians include Catholics and various Protestant denominations.
Mali	16.5	95	<5	<5	Christians (2/3 Catholic, 1/3 Protestant) and traditional religions make up less than 5%.
Niger	17.5	>98	<2	<1	Muslims are 95% Sunni and 5% Shia. Christians are Catholic and Protestant. There are a few thousand Baha'i.
Senegal	13.6	94	5	1	Christians are Catholic and Protestant.
Sierra Leone	5.7	77	21	<2	There are small numbers of Baha'is, Hindus, Jews, and adherents of traditional religions.

evidence the articles of the Constitution that guarantee the autonomy of religious communities."[10]

Examples of the region's strong religious freedom clauses can be found in the Constitution of Sierra Leone, one of the two most religiously free countries in this religiously free region. Here are some passages from Article 24 of that constitution:

(1) Except with his own consent, no person shall be hindered in the enjoyment of his freedom of conscience and for the purpose of this section the said freedom includes freedom of thought and of religion, freedom to change his religion or belief, and freedom either alone or in community with others and both in public and in private to manifest and propagate his religion or belief in worship, teaching, practice and observance.

(2) Except with his own consent (or if he is a minor the consent of his parent or guardian) no person attending any place of education shall be required to receive religious instruction or to take part in or to attend any religious ceremony or observance if that instruction, ceremony or observance relates to a religion other than his own.

(3) No religious community or denomination shall be prevented from providing religious instruction for persons of that community or denomination in the course of any education provided by that community or denomination.

The Sierra Leone Constitution does not merely set forth standard religious freedom language but takes pains to protect dimensions of religious freedom that are widely denied elsewhere in the world.

Constitutional articles are far from sufficient for religious freedom. There are plenty of countries in the Muslim-majority world—and elsewhere—that articulate religious freedom perfectly well in their constitutions but who are perfectly repressive in their practice.[11] In several ways, the West African Muslim-majority states back up their constitutions with real religious freedom.

Any government that wants to shape the religious character of the populace will strive to control the vital turf of education. Schools are the most direct and potent means for influencing the minds and souls of citizens. Both secular repressive and religiously repressive governments, not just in Muslim-majority countries but also in many other countries, have reasoned that by getting into the minds of the youth, they can change the religious views of their people within a generation. In recent years, emotional battles in France and Turkey over whether girls may wear headscarves in schools and universities reveal how much people believe to be at stake in the religious character of education.

In a religiously free country, citizens have wide legal latitude to educate their children in their faith and are not forced to have their children educated in a faith not their own or in doctrines contrary to their faith. This is an ideal. Secular liberal democracies who score high on religious freedom approach religious education in a wide variety of ways and are replete with debates over religion's—or secularism's—place in education. Still, they approximate this ideal far more closely than religiously repressive states.[12]

Such is the case in Muslim West Africa. Here, in state-supported schools, religious education is either not mandated or else mandated flexibly so that students are either given a choice of which religion to learn or else required to learn about several religions. These states also permit religious private schools. It is common in West Africa for students of one religious faith to attend schools run by another religious faith. Here again, Sierra Leone is exemplary. Because enrollment in private religious schools is open to all, it is common for Muslim children to be educated in Christian schools and vice versa. Remarkably, the Ahmadiyya sect of Islam, which is persecuted in other Muslim countries like Pakistan and Indonesia, runs schools in Sierra Leone, indeed ones of high reputation that attract Christian and Muslim students alike.[13]

West African Muslim states are also generally free of the kinds of restrictions that unfree Muslim states impose. There are no "religious tests" requiring one to be a Muslim to hold a certain political office. Generally, these states lack laws that prohibit blasphemy, defamation, or conversion away from Islam, or that restrict broadcasting, newspapers, or other forms of public speech. In Fox's study of religious discrimination around the world, he finds such discrimination to be remarkably low in Muslim-majority states in this region.[14]

Another common source of religious restriction is requirements that religious communities register with the government, a tool through which governments inhibit certain communities from erecting buildings, conducting worship and rituals, educating their children, and any number of other activities. Although most West African Muslim-majority states have registration requirements—including Sierra Leone, Mali, The Gambia, Burkina Faso, Guinea, and Guinea-Bissau—these requirements almost always impose few restrictions on religious freedom. In Guinea, the government monitors religion more heavily through its Secretariat of Religious Affairs, but it does so mainly to restrict forms of Islam that are likely to be violent or otherwise to disrespect the religious freedom of others.[15]

In West African states, law is generally secular, meaning that it is not derived directly from the Qur'an or other Islamic sources. Among the ways in which more restrictive Islamic states apply religious law, one of the most common is what is known as personal status law, pertaining to marriage, divorce, inheritance, and the consequences of religious conversion for these matters. Often these states create special courts for this area of law that apply interpretations of family and of male and female roles that are strongly traditional and that disadvantage religious minorities. In West Africa, this kind of law and this kind of court are largely absent. Family matters, like all other matters, are governed by secular law that applies to everyone, Muslim and non-Muslim alike. Senegal offers Muslims the opportunity to choose to have family matters adjudicated under Islamic law but leaves it optional.[16] A stronger exception is The Gambia, whose *qadi* [judges] handle personal status cases for Muslims, while applying secular common law to non-Muslims.[17]

West African states sometimes provide direct support to religious communities but do so equally. The governments of Guinea and Senegal, for instance, subsidize the costs both for Muslims to participate in the *Hajj*, the pilgrimage to Mecca, and for Catholics to travel to pilgrimage sites.[18] Burkina Faso both subsidizes the travel costs for Muslim pilgrims and granted a large plot of land to the Catholic Church to build a new papal nunciature.[19] Likewise, the government of Niger foots the bill for the *Hajj* while it also financially supported Christian communities after Islamist militants burned 70 churches in a two-day assault in January 2015.[20] In Senegal, the government offers financial assistance to all religious groups to construct schools and buildings for worship—and even accorded the largest share of this funding to Christians, a small minority.[21] It is common across West Africa for governments to declare national holidays for both Muslim and Christian observances.

It is not only through light restrictions and impartial aid and recognition that West African Muslim-majority states promote religious freedom but also through active efforts to encourage harmony between religions. These societies are not without their religious tensions, exacerbated in the past decade or so by the rise of Islamist militancy, much of it supported from the outside. In response, government and religious leaders work together actively to prevent these tensions from disrupting their societies' religious harmony and enjoyment of religious freedom. Most of these states feature some form of interreligious council of religious leaders who work closely with the government to ensure peace and freedom. For the most part, this cooperation is voluntary and not mandated or forced.

Senegal does not have such a council but still features active coopera-tion between the government and religious leaders. Even though founding President Senghor was a Catholic—part of a tiny minority—he received the active support of Sufi brotherhoods, the country's most powerful re-ligious group, and reciprocated with respect and deference toward them.[22] Subsequent presidents, all Muslims, would maintain close ties with Muslim leaders while also supporting Christian churches. Commonly, Muslim and Christian political and religious leaders attend one another's ceremonies and pilgrimages.[23] These relationships, undergirding Senegal's impressive level of religious freedom, proved useful for quelling religious tensions, including riots between Sufi brotherhoods in 1980 and anonymous threats against Christian clergymen in 2004.[24]

In Mali, the government consults frequently with a "Committee of Wise Men," an informal group of religious leaders that includes Muslims, Catholics, and Protestants. The government has also formed umbrella groups among Muslim leaders—the Malian Association for the Unity and Progress of Islam in 1980 and the High Islamic Council in 2002—in order to unite the country's disparate Muslim groups and to build cooperation among them. As in Senegal, these ties undergird the government's commitment to religious freedom. Exemplifying this commitment was a 2003 incident in which main-stream Sunni Muslims attacked Wahhabists who were building a mosque. Despite the Wahhabists being a small, highly traditional and strict form of Islam, the government acted strongly on the Wahhabists' behalf, considering the matter a strong form of religious freedom violation. It sentenced 5 of the attackers to death and 84 others to prison terms of between three months' probation and 20 years.[25]

In Sierra Leone, an Inter-Religious Council of Sierra Leone, formed in 1997, not only has supported religious freedom but also has helped to bring peace to the country following a civil war that killed tens of thousands between 1991 and 2002. After the war, both Christian and Muslim leaders headed the country's Truth and Reconciliation Commission.[26] The government works loosely with the Council, as it does with the Council of Churches of Sierra Leone and the United Council of Imams.

The pattern is the same around the region. In Niger, interreligious dia-logue and cooperation as well as an advisory body of Muslim leaders, now called the Niger Islamic Council, have helped to alleviate tensions associ-ated with the rise of Salafist Islamists who wish to overturn the country's religiously free state and replace it with an Islamist one.[27] In The Gambia, an Interfaith Group for Dialogue and Peace meets regularly to discuss matters of religious freedom and religious harmony and consists of Muslims,

Christians, and even Baha'is, a religion that is ruthlessly persecuted in much of the Muslim world.[28] The government of Burkina Faso acted to promote religious freedom and cooperation in 2013 by passing a constitutional amendment that requires its senate to include representatives of Muslim, Catholic, and Protestant communities.[29] Guinea and Guinea-Bissau can boast of like-mannered forums for cooperation.

In recent years, Muslim West Africa's religious freedom regimes have faced sharp challenges, including violent attacks, from Islamist groups who, supported by resources and ideas from the outside, have gained strength throughout the region. Their political theology impels them to strive for the kind of regime that I have called religiously repressive. Islamists have been most formidable in Mali, where, in January 2012, they joined Tuareg rebels in liberating the northern Azawad region from the Malian government and then turned against the same rebels and installed a strict form of *sharia*. They were then overthrown by a coalition of the French military and African Union forces, who intervened on behalf of the Malian government in January 2013. Today, the government—and its religiously free institutions—remain intact.

Islamists have carried out violence elsewhere in the region as well. As previously mentioned, Islamist militants burned 70 Christian churches in Niger in January 2015, doing so in response to the president of Niger's attendance at an antiterrorism march in Paris following the Islamist attacks on offices of the French magazine *Charlie Hebdo* earlier that month. Like Mali, though, and indeed like all of the Muslim West African states, Niger has maintained its religiously free orientation.

Advocates of a stricter Islam have disputed the boundaries of religious freedom in other ways as well. Family law has been a particularly contentious stake in conflicts between Islamic and secular visions of society. The marabouts, or Sufi brotherhood leaders, of Senegal objected when President Senghor sought to pass a law to liberalize Senegal's Family Code in the early 1970s. Because the law discouraged polygamy, gave equal inheritance rights to women, and made it more difficult for husbands to divorce their wives, critics disparaged it as the *Code des femmes* [Women's Code]. Sufi religious leaders attacked the Family Code because it contradicted Islamic law, especially in the domains of marriage, divorce, and inheritance issues. Although proclaiming that they had no intention to intervene in the conduct of the affairs of the nation, they declared that it was their duty as religious guides to reject the legislation as violating the Qur'an and Sunna. The law passed but it remained unevenly enforced and thus allowed both sides to claim victory.[30]

Mali is another site of disputes over family law, the most recent taking place between 2009 and 2012. Here, too, the president, Amadou Toumani

Touré, sought to pass legislation that would liberalize family law. Because the law sought to remove language about a man being head of the family, placed husbands and wives on an equal legal footing in marriage, raised the age at which women could legally marry from 15 to 18, and declined to recognize the validity of religiously conducted marriage ceremonies if the parties did not also go through the secular governmental process, it stirred the ire of Islamic leaders, including the mainstream High Islamic Council. Finally, a law was passed that was largely consistent with the Islamic leaders' demands and contrary to the wishes of proponents of liberalization.[31]

Through these challenges from partisans of a stricter Islam, religiously free regimes in Muslim-majority West Africa have endured. To be sure, in facing Islamist threats, some countries have moved in a more restrictive direction. The government of The Gambia sometimes restricts groups that oppose rulings of the Supreme Islamic Council such as directives setting the date of the Islamic holiday, Eid. Although the Council is an independent group, such a partnership weakens religious freedom. The government also employs some religious officials and bans political parties organized on a religious basis. [32] Guinea monitors religious groups through its Secretariat of Religious Affairs and forbids religious groups from owning radio or television stations.[33] The government of Niger monitors religious expression and has established the Niger Islamic Council, consisting of Muslim clerics, through which it issues prayer licenses.[34]

These practices are inconsistent with yet do not strongly compromise West Africa's high levels of religious freedom. Most of them are in fact aimed at monitoring and restricting Islamist groups who would disturb religious freedom and interreligious harmony, including through violence. When President Yahya Jammeh of The Gambia dismissed the imam of the State House Mosque, he did so because the imam had denounced Ahmadiyya Muslims as "not part of the Islamic faith" and asserted that they should be expelled from the country.[35] None of these governments has strayed from its broad commitment to maintaining a religiously free polity.

Why Is Muslim West Africa Religiously Free?

What explains this zone of religious freedom in the Muslim world? One potential answer is demographics: Religious freedom in these countries results in some way from the distribution of Muslims among the population. But what exactly does a demographic explanation consist of? One account might hold that when Muslims amount to an overwhelming majority, say in the 90th-percentile range, of the population, they can afford to be religiously free because the tiny Christian minority poses little threat. Another explanation might be the opposite: When Muslims hold a slim majority or a plurality, they favor freedom as a kind of truce with Christians, whose large numbers pose a reciprocal threat.[36] In the first of these explanations, Muslim majorities favor freedom because they can afford to; in the other, they favor freedom because they have to.

Neither explanation fits the evidence in West Africa. Among these religiously free countries, one finds vast Muslim majorities, as in Senegal (94%) and Niger (98%), smaller majorities, as in Burkina Faso (61%) and Sierra Leone (77%), as well as pluralities in countries that are not strictly Muslim majority yet also stand as evidence for religious freedom in the Muslim world, including the Ivory Coast (39%) and Guinea-Bissau (40%) (see Table 2.4). The demographics of all of these countries differ, yet all are religiously free.

A comparison within these states also counts against both explanations. Within the category "religiously free," these states vary in their degree of religious freedom, yet this variation does not correspond to the share of Muslims in the population. At both the high and low ends of religious freedom we find both overwhelming Muslim majorities and slimmer Muslim majorities and pluralities. A comparison with states outside the region does not help a demographic explanation, either. We will see later in this chapter and in future chapters that we find all three categories of Muslim states—religiously repressive, secular repressive, and religiously free ones—among states with overwhelming Muslim majorities and slimmer Muslim majorities.

If demographics are not the answer, perhaps religiosity explains freedom in Muslim West Africa. The secularization theory holds that religion's absolute claims make it intolerant of others and thus an enemy of freedom.[37] If the secularists are correct, then we should expect Muslim West Africa to be freer because its Muslims are less religious.

The reality is starkly different. Sub-Saharan Africa, which includes West Africa, is arguably the most religious part of the world. A Pew Research Center report shows that all of the West African countries report high rates of religiosity according to global standards. Whereas in the United States, which is probably the most religious of the industrialized democracies, 70% of adults say that they are absolutely certain of God's existence, more than 80% say the same in West Africa countries. Whereas 57% of adults in the United States say that religion is very important in their lives, more than 75% of the populations in West African countries say the same.[38] A separate Pew report on the world's Muslims shows that Muslims in West Africa are the most devout of any in the world with the possible exception of those in Southeast Asia. The percentage of Muslims in West Africa who say that "religion is very important in their lives" ranges from 98% in Senegal down to 86% in Niger, compared with the Middle East–North Africa, which ranges from 89% in Morocco down to 56% in Lebanon.[39] Muslim West Africa is both highly free and highly religious.

More pointedly, Muslim West Africa is highly free not despite its religion but rather because of its religion, and further still, because of the kind of religion that is found in the hearts, minds, and habits of the people. Across the region is a culture of interreligious harmony that is unusual in the world. Christians and Muslims celebrate one another's holidays; marry one another and create interreligious extended families; sometimes attend one another's prayers; and even display tolerance for conversion to the other's faith. Political scientist Alfred Stepan reports that in the city of Popenguine, Senegal, Christians and Sufis joined in constructing the mosque and church of each community.[40] The Pew Research Center reports that in those West African countries covered here, Muslims "express overall positive views of Christians" at very high rates—92% in Senegal, 86% in Mali, and 72% in Guinea-Bissau.[41] Undeniably there are tensions, even violent tensions, between these faiths, ones that have increased in recent years, but the culture of harmony is strong enough to absorb, mitigate, and survive these tensions. This culture extends also to Muslims who dissent from Sunni orthodoxy—Shias, Ahmadiyyas, and Sufis—as well as to tiny non-Christian minorities, including Baha'is, Sikhs, Hindus, and Buddhists.

Responsible in good part for these habits of harmony is Sufism, the kind of Islam that predominates in West Africa. Sufism is a form of Islamic spirituality that stresses the mystical dimension of religion. Practitioners are members of orders with hierarchies and rituals of worship. Sufism has a strong presence among Muslims outside of the Arab Middle East, for instance, in West Africa and Southeast Asia. Today, one-fifth of Muslims identify with Sufism.[42]

Sufism should not be thought of as a modernist rejection of traditional Islam. Sufis are found among both Sunnis and Shias and take the Qur'an and Sunna as authoritative. Yet, Sufis find themselves sharply at odds with and often violently attacked by proponents of puritanical strains of Islam, including Wahhabism and Salafism. In the eyes of these Muslims, Sufism's openness to art, poetry, music, and culture, as well as its popular religiosity, including the veneration of saints and sheikhs, is unacceptably syncretic. In Muslim-majority religiously repressive regimes—the subject of Chapter 4— Sufis are frequently persecuted, as they have been in certain secular repressive regimes like Turkey.

Sufis are not inherently pacifist. In certain times and places, they have been fierce warriors, leading conquests in Central and South Asia and in southeastern Europe, and heading up resistance movements to European colonial governments in Africa and Asia and to countries like Russia that have sought to expand into Muslim areas.[43] Yet, Sufis are also known for their tolerance. Where they have conquered, they have taken on local practices and traditions. Their teachers stress the presence of God within every human being, respect for other religious traditions, and the free character of faith, all of which favor a political theology of religious freedom.

Stepan discovered these qualities in his interviews with Senegalese religious leaders and scholars. Senegalese Sufis' tolerance for other faiths is theologically grounded. They see every person as a religious being searching for God; cite Qur'anic verses stressing freedom and tolerance such as "there is no compulsion in religion"; and even affirm a right of "religious exit" and refrain from deploying the concept of an "apostate." They stress equality between men and women.[44] As scholar Sheldon Gellar describes, Sufis and Senegal hold that "in His wisdom God had given individuals freedom of belief," thereby allowing for a "great diversity of religious beliefs."[45] The Mouride Brotherhood, a large order in Senegal and The Gambia, is known for its strong religious devotion and its fanatical loyalty to its leaders, who in turn call their followers to avow religious freedom and respect for other faiths. Extremists of tolerance, Senegal's Sufis have strongly shaped civil society.[46]

It is also common in West Africa for Muslims, and in some places, Christians, to mix their rituals and beliefs with those of traditional African religions. In Sierra Leone, for instance, Christians and Muslims often practice traditional ceremonies, share a belief that all religious traditions share a comparable view of God, and see traditional indigenous beliefs as a common denominator.[47] Across the region, syncretism exists and encourages harmony. Still, it would be a simplistic mistake to attribute religious freedom in Muslim-majority West African countries to syncretism alone. This would ignore the remarkable devoutness with which West Africa's Muslims practice their Islamic faith. "[T]he Islam embraced by Muslim Africans comprised of the Five Pillars of the faith is no different from what Muslims elsewhere embraced," writes historian Lamin Sanneh.[48]

How, in turn, did West Africa's culture of harmony come about? In many centuries of history there lie two broad answers to this question: the way in which Islam came to West Africa and Muslims' relationships to European colonial authorities.

Islam came to West Africa gradually through traders and teachers between 1100 and 1600 CE—in contrast to Islam's swift expansion through the Middle East and North Africa through military conquest, beginning with the Prophet Muhammad. In West Africa, Muslims had to rely on the patronage of local rulers, who practiced traditional religions.[49] Even when some of these rulers converted to Islam, as did some of the kings of the great inland Songhai Empire of the 1400s and 1500s, they allowed their subjects to practice either the traditional religions or Islam—an early version of religious freedom.[50] The Sufi character of Islam, the tolerant nature of the traditional religions, and Muslims' syncretic adoptions from these religions contributed to tolerance as well. To boot, up until the 19th and 20th centuries, Muslims were minorities in the region. It was only in this latter period that Muslims sharply expanded to their present numbers.[51] Over the course of all of these centuries, West African Muslims nurtured a tradition of nonviolent expansion.[52]

Reformist *jihadi* movements, some of them violent, arose to challenge the predominant Sufi Islam between the 16th and 19th centuries. They hoped to purify Muslims, rid them of their syncretism, and establish regimes much like what this book calls religiously repressive. The most famous of these *jihadis*, Uthman dan Fodio of present-day Nigeria, said, "[t]he government of a country is the government of its king without question. If the king is a Muslim, his land is Muslim, if he is an unbeliever, his land is a land of unbelievers." These *jihadis*, though, were defeated, opposed by a combination of local populations of Muslims, a large proportion of local Muslim leaders, allies of local Muslims who practiced indigenous faiths, and, later, European colonial powers, whose defeat of the *jihadis* was welcomed by the local populations.[53]

The second major historical explanation for today's religious freedom in Muslim West Africa is the alliances forged between European colonial powers and West African Muslim leaders.

From the 15th century to the late 19th century, European involvement in West Africa consisted mainly of merchants—including slave traders up to the abolition of the slave trade in the 19th century—and missionaries, sometimes supported by military forces, coming from Britain, France, and Portugal. It was only in small coastal settlements that these European powers exercised governance. Then, between 1881 and 1914, there took place the Scramble for Africa, in which European powers established colonial territorial governance on 90% of the continent, having previously controlled 10%.[54] During this period were formed the colonies that became independent West African states between the late 1950s and early 1970s.

To exercise influence, then governance, in West Africa, European empires established "indirect control," meaning alliances with local rulers. Critical were ties with Muslim leaders, whose loyalty European powers elicited by granting them freedom to carry out their religious activities. The task was made easier by the tolerant culture of the region's Muslims, who were willing to live and mingle with Christians and adherents of traditional African religions. In virtually every one of today's seven Muslim-majority West African states, these kinds of alliances were formed and served to establish the roots of a positive secularism, a healthy separation of state and religion whereby the state respected the authority and sometimes promoted the welfare of religion.[55]

Stepan vividly tells the story of how alliances furthering religious freedom arose in Senegal. There was nothing especially enlightened about how it happened. France's military forces largely decimated the traditional African kings in the second half of the 19th century but were then challenged by Muslim, mostly Sufi, leaders. Both realized that neither could win and so accommodated each other.[56]

Essential for the accommodation was France's respect for Islam. As Stepan recounts, during the 19th and early 20th centuries, the French government financed pilgrimages to Mecca, established a Muslim tribunal, granted money for the construction of mosques, promoted training in Arabic in Islamic schools, and sent officials to major Sufi ceremonies.[57] In response, Muslims were willing to reciprocate with respect for French authority. Stepan quotes a letter written by Amadu Bamba, the founder of the Mouride Sufi order, who wrote, "I have decided to give . . . some advice to my Muslim brothers in order that they not be drawn into wars . . . . The French government, thanks to God, has not opposed the profession of faith but on the contrary has been friendly toward Muslims and encouraged them to practice [their religion]."[58] Thus forged was Senegal's *laïcité*, a positive secularism that contrasted with the negative secularism of France's own Third Republic.

French colonial authorities supported the religious freedom of Christians, too, in West Africa. They did not work hand in glove with Christians in their evangelization efforts, though, and often even discouraged missionaries' attempts to convert Muslims in the interior. The Christian church itself became a more progressively indigenous one from the late 18th century to the early 20th century, the period when Christianity grew most rapidly. The translation of the Bible into African languages and the adaptation of worship to African customs were decisive in this success. Prominent Christian leaders of this period, like Edward Blyden and Samuel Ajayi Crowther, were Africans who respected Muslims, cultivated friendships with them, and cooperated with them in efforts of social improvement. Muslims reciprocated this respect; many sent their children to Christian schools, and there was even intermarriage and the mingling of families. Finally, Christians generally enjoyed good relations with leaders and practitioners of traditional African religions, often adapting their customs into the Christian faith and benefiting from their tradition of tolerance. All in all, the Christian churches of West Africa contributed to the patterns of respect that persisted into the religious freedom of today.[59]

Islands of Freedom

Outside West Africa, a handful of religiously free Muslim-majority countries are scattered around Africa, the Middle East, and southern Europe. Their regimes, too, promote religious freedom through their constitutions, their schools, their laws, and their active commitment to interreligious harmony. Here too, though, religious freedom has also been challenged in recent years.

The first of these is Lebanon, a Muslim-majority state whose religious diversity is the most complex in the Middle East, perhaps in the world. To manage this diversity, Lebanon has developed a sophisticated and delicate set of institutions at the core of which is religious freedom. Its religious freedom is not pure or perfect but is impressive given the real and potential tensions between its religious communities, and it does much to mitigate these tensions. Heiner Bielefeldt, the United Nations Special Rapporteur on Freedom of Religion or Belief sums up:

> People generally practise their religion freely, and there is no religious persecution in the country. Moreover, Lebanon has successfully kept society united across religious boundaries, and built resilience in the face of religious extremism. These are major accomplishments and cannot be taken for granted.[60]

The Lebanese state recognizes 18 religious communities, 13 of them Christian, 4 of them Muslim, and the other Jewish. Three groups are most populous: Maronite Christians, Sunni Muslims, and Shia Muslims. What proportion of the population do the communities make up? A census has not been taken since 1932, but a research firm, Statistics Lebanon, estimates the population at 28% Sunni Muslim, 21% Shia Muslim, 35.5% Christian (the majority being Maronites), 5.3% Druze, and small numbers of Jews, Baha'is, Ismailis, Alawites, Buddhists, Hindus, and Mormons. Lebanon hosts the largest percentage of Christians in the Middle East. This country of 5.9 million people also hosts some 1.4 million refugees from Syria and Iraq (at the time of this writing) as well as a Palestinian refugee population of between 250,000 and 350,000, who arrived between 1948 and 1971.[61]

For centuries of rule under the Ottoman Empire, religious communities were governed by the Millet System, which, under Sunni Muslim governance, allowed each community to govern itself in matters of family status law. After World War I, upon the collapse of the Ottoman Empire, the French took control of Lebanon as a mandate and created a constitution that was completely secular in the sense that it took no account of citizens' religious affiliations.

The French came to realize, though, that legal accommodations had to be made for religion.[62]

In 1943, Lebanon became effectively independent and instituted an updated Millet System premised on the equality of religious communities. An informal but enduring "National Pact" provided that religious courts would be created for each (recognized) religious community and that authority would be apportioned in the government such that a Maronite Christian would be president, a Sunni Muslim would be prime minister, a Shia Muslim would be Speaker of the House, and cabinet posts and parliamentary seats would be spread out among the religious communities.

From 1975 to 1989, Lebanon experienced a major civil war that took the lives of more than 150,000 people.[63] It is disputed whether religious differences contributed to the war but undisputed that in the war, atrocities took place between religions and sects. Heightening tensions is the high probability that since the 1930s, the share of the Muslim population has increased while that of the Christian population has decreased, though the numbers are uncertain because of the absence of an updated census. There is good reason for this absence. A new census is likely to inflame tensions between religious communities—a sure sign of the delicacy of Lebanon's religious balance.

After the war, the *Taif* Agreement adjusted the "confessional system" of the pact so as to strengthen the (Sunni) prime minister, weaken the (Maronite) president, mandate equal representation in parliament for both Christians and Muslims and, most consequentially, add a provision to the Constitution declaring it a "basic national goal" to abolish the place of religious allocations in the government. As of today, though, the confessional provisions remain strong.

In this constitutional order, religious freedom is strong, though in certain respects curtailed to meet the demands of balancing confessions. Lebanon's constitution promotes positive secularism. It does not declare the state to be an Islamic one, or, for that matter, a Christian one, but is based rather on citizenship, "public liberties," and equality before the law. The preamble calls for freedom of opinion and belief, and Article Nine stipulates the free exercise of religion, freedom of conscience, and respect for all religious creeds. It also speaks of "rendering homage to the Most High," a phrase that flies in the face of any strict negative secularism. Lebanese law renders it permissible to convert away from one's religion, including from Islam, a liberty that is rare outside the zone of freedom depicted in this chapter.

The Constitution also provides for education that does not interfere with the "dignity of any of the religions or creeds." Private religious schools are not only allowed but also educate 70% of the students. Often private schools mix religions, whereas public schools tend to be of a single confession.[64]

Lebanon poses religious registration requirements that are capacious yet also restrict religious freedom to an extent. For a religious group to be recognized—which 18 are—it must submit a statement of principles to the government, avowing its commitment to Lebanon's constitutional norms. Upon gaining recognition, very important benefits are triggered—an exemption from taxes, eligibility of affiliated members to run for office, and permission to run religious courts that adjudicate matters of family law. By contrast, religious groups that are not recognized are distinctively disadvantaged. They enjoy no tax exemption; in a country that has no civil marriage, their members cannot get married through their religion; and their members cannot run for office. Often, in order to marry or run for office, members of an unregistered group must register through a recognized group, thus having to represent themselves according to a faith to which they do not belong. Unregistered groups include Baha'is, Hindus, and some Protestant churches.[65]

Lebanon also governs religion in certain religiously unfree manners. The government vets and pays senior clerics in the Sunni, Shia, and Druze communities and appoints and pays judges in Muslim religious courts. In doing so, the government is not discriminating in favor of Muslims and Druze but rather is restricting their independence and gaining influence over religious doctrine. By contrast, the regime leaves Christian groups to operate freely, as they wish to do, and thus to evade this form of control.[66]

Behind this broad but spotted religious freedom regime is a population with a strong shared identity of citizenship and a culture of conviviality among people of different faiths. Mixed marriages between Christians and Muslims are common. Religious mixing takes place in schools, especially private ones, professional workplaces, and residential neighborhoods, though some areas are homogeneous. Christians and Muslims have begun to celebrate March 25 as a joint, interreligious holiday. Civil society efforts to build interreligious harmony and to carry out interreligious dialogue are common, some of them bringing together religious leaders at the highest level.[67]

Countering this civility has been the violence of recent decades carried out by Islamist militant groups. Hezbollah, the largest of these, was founded as a Shia party and militia in 1982 in order to fight Israel's occupation of Lebanon. It was strongly supported by Iran, whose religiously repressive regime it sought to spread, and has launched terrorist attacks in Lebanon and upon embassies and airlines elsewhere in the world. It continues to declare itself an enemy of Israel, which it does not recognize as a legitimate state. In the 1990s it refashioned itself as primarily a political party and runs a wide variety of social services, including hospitals, but it maintains a highly fortified armed wing.

Since 2011, Lebanon has been drawn into the violence of neighboring Syria. From Syria, Sunni Islamist militias like the Islamic State and al-Nusra have exported their attacks on Shia in Lebanon; into Syria, Hezbollah exports its attacks on Sunnis; between Syria and Lebanon, violence has erupted along many cleavages. Because of this violence, Lebanon's SHI has been high, moving from an already high 5.1 in 2007 to a very high 7.9 in 2012 and down to a still very high 6.1 in 2013. It is no wonder that a Pew Research Center poll of 2011 and 2012 showed two-thirds of all Muslims, including approximately half of Shia and 80% of Sunnis, agreeing that sectarian tensions were a "very big or moderately big problem."[68]

In June 2015, Makassed, a Sunni Muslim philanthropic organization closely associated with Dar el-Fatwa, the highest Sunni authority in Lebanon, issued a statement, "The Beirut Declaration on Religious Freedom," strongly affirming religious freedom and the desire of Muslims to live alongside Christians, placing these commitments on Qur'anic foundations.[69] The statement was a sign that there are prominent Lebanese Muslims who hold a political theology of religious freedom and who treasure Lebanon's interreligious harmony. Whether their commitments or those of Hezbollah and the Islamic State carry the day in Lebanon is yet to be seen.

Other religiously free Muslim-majority states can be found in Albania and Kosovo, both in southeastern Europe. In Albania, Muslims are a solid majority, though the percentages of religions are a disputed and sensitive issue.[70] The Constitution's provisions for religious freedom are quite robust, proclaiming that there is no official religion and guaranteeing the free expression of religion to individuals and communities, in public and private life. The Constitution opens with these words:

> We, the people of Albania, proud and aware of our history, with responsibility for the future, and with faith in God and/or other universal values, with determination to build a social and democratic state based on the rule of law, and to guarantee the fundamental human rights and freedoms, with a spirit of religious coexistence and tolerance . . .

From the outset, Albania's Constitution places religion and "religious coexistence and tolerance" at the heart of the country's purpose. The country's State Committee on Cults applies a registry requirement but one that places little restriction on religious freedom.[71] Religious instruction is forbidden in the public schools, and religious schools must comply with requirements for the presence of secular content in their curriculum. Several religious holidays, both Christian and Muslim, are considered national holidays. An Interreligious Council of all major faiths issues public statements in support of religious freedom, and its leaders often attend one another's ceremonies.

What accounts for Albania's religious freedom? Some would point to the low level of religiosity among the population. The opening paragraph of Albania's Constitution seems to evince an ambivalence about religion, or at least a desire to accommodate irreligion, when it says, "faith in God and/or other universal values." Whatever their affiliation, Albanians do not practice their religion vigorously. Among countries in Europe, already the world's most unreligious continent, Albania's population ranks in the bottom one-third in religiosity according to a Gallup Poll of 2008–2009, which reports a low 39% answering "yes" to "does religion occupy an important place in your life?"[72]

Recall, though, the argument of this chapter that irreligiosity does not automatically yield religious freedom: high levels of religious freedom can exist in highly religious populations—as in West Africa—while religious freedom can be brutally repressed in the name of atheism. Again, we must look not merely at the level and intensity, but also at the character and content, of religion. Islam in Albania is known for being liberal. Only 12% of Muslims in Albania favor making *sharia* the law of their country, a number that is close to the low end of the world's Muslim-majority states, reports the Pew Research Center.[73] "Islam-lite" is how one journalist, quoting an Albanian, describes the country's faith, noting that "in the centre of the capital, Tirana, not a headscarf is to be seen, let alone a burqa."[74] Influential in Albania are Sufism, particularly the pacifist, *bektashi*, version, and followers of the Turkish religious leader Fethullah Gülen, who has articulated a politics of democracy and religious freedom. More broadly, Albanians subordinate their religious identities to their identities as Albanians and Europeans.

Albania's history is one of religious repression—the imposition of religion through conquest and of atheism through Communist dictatorship. Albania became Christian under the Byzantine Empire and remained so until it was occupied in 1506 by the Ottoman Turks, under whom much of the population became Muslim. In the 19th century, a nationalist movement arose, declaring that "the religion of Albania is Albanianism" and led the country to independence in 1912.[75] In 1944, Albania fell under the Communist dictatorship of Enver Hoxha, who sought to eradicate religion. In the first few years of his regime, he outlawed religion, nationalized religious properties, and had priests and *ulema* arrested, tortured, and executed. He especially persecuted the Catholic Church, which opposed his regime and demanded religious freedom, but he also suppressed Islam and Orthodoxy. A second wave of persecution, the Albanian cultural revolution, came in 1967–1968, in which Hoxha destroyed hundreds of mosques, numerous churches, and Islamic libraries; imposed prison sentences for preaching; and paved the way for the 1976 Constitution to declare that "the state recognizes no religion." Communism lasted until December 1990, when independent political parties were created and religious freedom was restored. In 1992, the communists were defeated in an election.[76]

Communism was devastating to religious belief in Albania, just as it was in countries like East Germany and Czechoslovakia. After Communism, though, Albanians supported religious freedom. In part, this support stemmed from a desire to meet the membership standards of the European Union. It also arose from a desire to put in the past a history of repression, one carried out both by religion and against religion. Although the cases of West Africa showed that a history absent conquest favors religious freedom, that of Kosovo and Albania shows that a country can learn from its history and chart a new course.

Kosovo, Albania's neighbor to the northeast, may not seem at first like a likely candidate for religious freedom. In 1998–1999, Kosovo's ethnic Albanians, who make up an overwhelming majority of Kosovo's population are predominantly Muslim, fought a violent war against Serbia for independence. Chief among the victims of the conflict were ethnic Serbians within Kosovo, who are mostly Orthodox Christians. Some 10,000 people died and one million were displaced (even while Muslim ethnic Albanians also suffered from Serbian President Slobodan Milosevic's violence against them). In recent history, Kosovo is known far more for ethnic cleansing than it is for religious freedom. The country's 2011 census reports a population of 95.6% Muslim, 2.2% Roman Catholic, 1.4% Serbian Orthodox, and less than 1% other, but as in Albania, the numbers are controversial in part because remaining Serbian Orthodox residents in the north boycotted the census.[77] After the war, when Serb forces left Kosovo, Serbs fled the region in numbers estimated to vary from 65,000 to 200,000.[78]

Yet, Kosovo's laws and institutions rank among the freest in the Muslim world. Its constitution contains strong religious freedom provisions; religious education is not required in the public schools, although religious schools are allowed; the country has created an ombudsperson for monitoring religious freedom and discrimination; and the government has created Interfaith Kosovo, which promotes religious harmony and religious freedom through civil society and educational initiatives.

As can be expected from a region that experienced mass violence so recently, Kosovo continues to experience regular incidents of hostility between

Albanian Muslims and Serbs as well as people of other faiths. Its score on Pew's SHI is in the high range, a 5.3.[79] Sometimes the hostilities involve the government. In 2014, for instance, the government threatened to tear down the unfinished Serbian Orthodox Church of Christ the Savior, which officials scorned as "Milošević's Monument" (referring to the former Serbian dictator).[80]

Still, for the most part, Kosovo's government promotes religious freedom despite these tensions. It perceives religious freedom as a vehicle of peace in the aftermath of violence between ethnic groups whose identities are shaped by their religion. Like Albania, Kosovo is at the crossroads of centuries of civilizational conquests. After World War II, Kosovo, with its vast majority of Albanian Muslims, was incorporated into the Yugoslavian Federation as an autonomous region of Serbia. As Yugoslavia disintegrated between 1990 and 1992, Kosovo attempted to secede from the rump federation, controlled by Serbia, but did not succeed. A pacifist leader, Ibrahim Rugova, carried out an independence campaign but was then supplanted by the Kosovo Liberation Army, who took up arms against Serbia. In 1999, NATO's military intervention drove Serbia out of Kosovo, but not before Serbian president Slobodan Milošević could conduct an ethnic cleansing campaign against Kosovo Albanians. In 2008, Kosovo declared independence and was recognized immediately by numerous surrounding powers with the notable exception of Russia. The newly independent state, desiring stability, places a premium on interreligious harmony. Religious freedom is also favored by Kosovo's kind of Islam, which follows the Hanafi school of jurisprudence, the most lenient of the schools, and hosts a strong streak of Sufism. Finally, Kosovo wishes to join the European Union and is thus incentivized to respect religious freedom.

Meriting mention is finally Djibouti. A tiny country on the Horn of Africa with a population of fewer than a million people, Djibouti is 94% Muslim with the remaining 6%, almost all of them foreigners and expatriates, scattered among diverse Christian communities and tiny populations of Hindus, Jews, and Baha'is. Pew's 2009 rankings show Djibouti to be a religiously free country. At that time, the constitution, laws, and government practice respected religious freedom, even allowing conversion away from Islam. A few restrictions existed such as a requirement that religions register with the government and that the president and other government employees take Islamic religious oaths, but none of these restrictions seriously constrained religious freedom.[81]

By 2015, the story was quite different. The GRI score had increased from 1.6 to a high range score of 5.1, and the government had strongly increased its authority over Islam. The Ministry of Islamic Affairs had seized authority over mosques, taking ownership of them and making imams government employees, and over private Islamic schools and the practice of Islam more generally. It surveilled imams' sermons and detained the imams when it deemed their message unacceptable. It banned women from wearing veils in government or commercial offices.[82]

What changed? The government had undertaken efforts to stamp out Islamic extremism, which it linked to terrorism. Djibouti's exposed geographical location made the country a dangerous post. Here, as elsewhere, the rise of Islamic violent extremist groups constitutes the greatest threat to the religious freedom of Muslim-majority countries. Whereas the other countries in the Islamic zone of freedom have remained free in the face of this threat, Djibouti has not.

What Does the Muslim Zone of Religious Freedom Teach Us?

There is a zone of freedom in the Muslim world. This zone is only a part of the Muslim world. Islamoskeptics in today's public debate will stress "a part," stressing that these countries are a minority of Muslim-majority countries. These countries may be free and may be Muslim, they will say, but they are not free because of Islam. Islamoskeptics will point out that the West Africa cluster is outside of the Islamic heartland—the Arab Middle East—and hosts a heterodox form of Islam. Albania is atheist, Kosovo is war torn, Lebanon is anomalously diverse, and Djibouti is no longer free. In the entire zone, religious freedom is threatened by rising Islamist extremism. The purer the Islam, the less likely religious freedom is, Islamoskeptics will say.

Islamopluralists will retort that one-fourth of Muslim-majority states are more than outliers. It is a distortion, they will say, to claim that Arab Islam is purer. Non-Arabs make up some 80% of the world's Muslim population and are not in any obvious sense less Islamic. Sufi Muslims, prevalent in West Africa and strong in Albania and Kosovo, are committed to the traditional teachings of Islam—usually Sunni, sometimes Shia—and, in West Africa, are highly devout. True, West African Islam is known for being syncretic, incorporating elements of traditional African religions, but even were the syncretic elements removed, the Islam of this region would remain a "pacifist" faith, committed to conversion solely through persuasion, as historian Lamin Sanneh argues compellingly in his book, *Beyond Jihad*.[83] True, Islamic extremism is on the rise in these countries, but religious freedom has generally been resilient.

In all of these countries, religious freedom is enabled by the type of Islam—more precisely, the political theology—of the inhabitants. Stressing the free character of religious commitment and the religious nature of every person, Sufi Islam is configured to favor religiously free regimes. These countries show that political theology is shaped not purely by doctrine but also by the lessons of history. Albanian Muslims have learned from centuries of conquest and, even more so, from the experience of Communist dictatorships, that freedom in religious matters is to be prized. West African Muslims look back favorably upon a history of religious respect that dates back seven or more centuries. Muslims in Lebanon derive their views of religious freedom from centuries of the Ottoman Millet System that evolved into equality of support for religion.

For all of these reasons, the religiously free zone covered in this chapter favors the Islamopluralists. The Islamoskeptics' best argument is the small number of religiously free Muslim countries. The remainder of the Muslim-majority world, they will argue, bears out Islam's propensity toward violence and intolerance. Whether this is true will be discovered in the next two chapters.

Partisans in today's public debate in the West would profit from one other conclusion that emerges from Islam's zone of religious freedom: Its religious freedom is not mainly an import from the West. Recall that Islamoskeptics believe religious freedom to be a Western invention and doubt that Islam is receptive to it. The new critics of religious freedom believe religious freedom to be a Western invention and protest against asking Muslims to accept it. Islamopluralists believe that Islam has its own resources for generating religious freedom.

Here again, the Islamopluralists are closer to the mark. Religious freedom in West Africa is derived from the type of Islam and of relations between Muslims and non-Muslims that were in place long before European colonists arrived. The contribution of colonialism to religious freedom was due far more to the pragmatics of colonial rule than it was to European ideology. Albania and Kosovo practice religious freedom in part because of their populations' Western orientation and their desire to join the European Union and thus conform to its human rights standards but are influenced also by their history of religious conflict and, in the case of Albania, by their reaction against Communism, itself a Western ideology. Lebanon's religious freedom is influenced in part by the contribution of the French to revising the *Millet* System in the direction of religious equality but is due also to the prior presence of a *Millet* System that was there to be revised and, more generally, to how Muslims have confronted religious diversity.

The next chapter will take this conclusion further, arguing that in a sizable portion of the Muslim-majority world the negation of religious freedom is due to Western ideology, not to a form of Islam.

3

Secular Repressive States in the Muslim World

THE LAST CHAPTER showed that there is religious freedom in the Muslim-majority world and that Islam is the source of it. Repression is not hardwired into Islam. The present chapter extends this insight by showing that even though there is much repression in the Muslim-majority world, Islam is not necessarily the source of it. A major pattern of repression is of a secular kind. Secular repression does not come from Islam but rather from the West. It also comes from a particular period in time, underlining that religious repression in the Muslim world is historically contingent.

The secular repressive model emanates from a Western strand of thinking, vivified in the French Revolution, which holds that the state must manage, control, and contain religion in order to make way for modern civilization. Kemal Atatürk, who founded the modern Republic of Turkey, aspired to build a modern nation—economically developed, scientifically advanced, marked by equality, unified by nationalism—in just this fashion. Many other Muslim-majority countries imitated him, making his republic the standard-bearer of secular repression in the Muslim world.

What Is A Secular Repressive State?

Let us no longer define—and divide—ourselves according to ethnic, tribal, and ancient religious loyalties! Our people may keep their customs and rituals but these will not serve as the basis of our nation or state. No, we are a modern nation that is headed for greatness! We will pave our roads, build bridges, and provide everyone with electricity, running water, and sanitation. Everyone—yes, everyone, boy or girl, regardless of caste or class—will receive an education that will teach math, science, civic virtue, and all that is needed for professional success and will shape them into secular individuals. We will advance in economics, science, technology, and military might and will not be hindered by traditional hierarchies and roles. European states have shown us the path to the future but they will no longer be our masters or colonizers.

To achieve this progress, we must keep religion in check. Our citizens may practice religion if it gives meaning to their lives and makes them more virtuous people, but religion will not define our public life—our politics, our economics, our education, or the symbols that represent these realms such as our flag, the architecture of our public buildings, and our leader's dress. Why must we keep religion in check? Because religion is irrational, super-stitious, and the source of hierarchies that impede equality, and it directs people's pursuits away from this world and their loyalties away from the state. Perhaps religion can become more serviceable to the public weal, but it must be reformed and modernized, and this will require oversight and governance from the state.

This is the narrative of secular nationalism, a story that certain people in certain times and places have told about their common life. Secular nation-alism is rooted in the European experience of the rise of the modern state and nation and became the governing ideal in many Muslim-majority states in the middle 20th century—and still is in many of these states today.

The standard-bearer of the pattern in the Muslim world is the Republic of Turkey, founded by Atatürk in 1923. After World War II, several Arab states adopted the model, the most influential of these being Egypt, others including Libya, Morocco, Jordan, Syria, and Algeria. Iran embodied the pat-tern under the shahs of the Pahlavi dynasty up until the shah's overthrow in 1979, as did Iraq under Saddam Hussein up until his ouster in 2003. Indonesia was a secular repressive state under the dictatorship of Suharto from 1967 to 1998. So, too, are the former Soviet republics of Central Asia, including Uzbekistan, Turkmenistan, Tajikistan, Kyrgyzstan, Kazakhstan, and Azerbaijan. Table 3.1 lists the 15 secular repressive Muslim-majority countries in 2009. They make up 32% of all Muslim-majority countries and 42% of those with low levels of religious freedom. These countries are then identified on the map in Figure 3.1.

Endemic to secular nationalism is the repression of religion. Secular re-pressive regimes are secular in the negative sense, to draw from the distinction of Pope Benedict XVI highlighted in the last chapter. The prototype of modern negative secularism is the French Revolution of 1789, which, motivated by a harsh skepticism toward religion, aspired to control the Catholic Church and ultimately to nullify its social influence. By 1815, the Revolution had failed

Table 3.1. Secular Repressive Muslim-Majority
States and Their GRI Score (according to 2009
Pew Report)

- Uzbekistan (8.0)
- Egypt (7.6)
- Turkey (6.4)
- Algeria (6.2)
- Turkmenistan (6.0)
- Libya (5.6)
- Tajikistan (5.5)
- Jordan (5.3)
- Morocco (5.3)
- Syria (5.2)
- Tunisia (5.1)
- Azerbaijan (5.1)
- Kazakhstan (5.0)
- Chad (3.9)
- Kyrgyzstan (3.7)

and the alliance of monarchy and established Church returned. In 1870, the Third Republic again instituted a regime on the principles of the Revolution, igniting a "war of two Frances" that pitted republican advocates of secularism against monarchists and their ally, the Church hierarchy.[1] By and large, the republicans won. They closed religious orders and expelled over 30,000 priests. Their biggest victories, though, were in education, which Pope Leo XIII called "the battlefield where it will be decided if the society will remain Christian or not." The republicans engineered a massive transfer of students from Catholic schools to public schools, where secularism would be taught to the next generation. Whereas in the 1876–1877 academic year, France hosted 51,657 secular schools (including public and private) and 19,890 religious schools, in 1906–1907 the numbers had reached 78,444 secular schools and 1,851 religious schools.[2] Consolidating the republican victory was the 1905 Law of Separation of Church and State, which laid the foundation for the French state's approach to religion to this day. The law disestablished the Catholic Church; banned state funding of religion, on which the Church depended greatly at the time; made Church buildings the property of the state, to be used by the Church at the state's pleasure; and required religious groups to register with the state. The law was not all bad for the Church. Disestablishment,

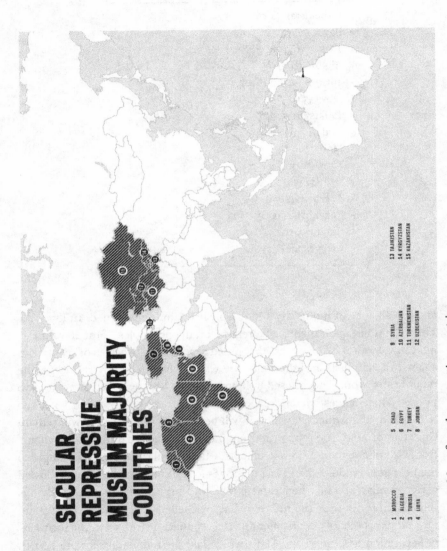

SECULAR REPRESSIVE MUSLIM MAJORITY COUNTRIES

1 MOROCCO
2 ALGERIA
3 TUNISIA
4 LIBYA

5 CHAD
6 EGYPT
7 TURKEY
8 JORDAN

9 SYRIA
10 AZERBAIJAN
11 TURKMENISTAN
12 UZBEKISTAN

13 TAJIKISTAN
14 KYRGYZSTAN
15 KAZAKHSTAN

FIGURE 3.1. Map of secular repressive countries

defunding, and the law's return to the Church of its right to choose its bishops enhanced the Church's independence in the long run. All in all, though, the Third Republic, which lasted until 1940, crippled the Church's social influence and awarded the state the upper hand.

After World War II, a rapprochement took place between the Catholic Church, which finally shed its hopes for a restoration of the French monarchy, and France's new constitutional republic, which guaranteed religious freedom on terms more favorable to the Church and provided state funding for religious education. Today, the negative secularism of the French Revolution is felt most acutely by France's Muslim minority, representing some 5%–10% of the population, who are subject to laws that restrict their religious practice, the most renowned of which prohibits girls from wearing headscarves in public schools.

Today, France shares with the other modern liberal democracies of the world a level of religious freedom that is high by global standards. Within this cluster, though, it stands on the restrictive end of the spectrum, the legacy of its history of negative secularism.[3] From a historical perspective, France's association with negative secularism is even stronger. The French Revolution and its legacy have served as the symbol and inspiration for negative secularism around the world, not least within the Muslim world.

The American Revolution represents the other major legacy of the West for the governance of religion—the positive secularism defined by Benedict XVI. Although the American colonies had been a checkerboard of religious freedom and religious repression, the First Amendment to the US Constitution, passed in 1791, mandated religious freedom at the national level and prohibited the establishment of a national church. The result was a noninterference pact by which religious communities enjoyed wide freedom to govern themselves and to practice their faith in exchange for renouncing special constitutional prerogatives. Among the religious communities that this arrangement has benefited have been American Muslims, who are allowed broad latitude to practice their faith and have been assimilated into society far more successfully than in Western Europe.

The secular repressive pattern in Islam follows the French Revolution, not the American Revolution, and is a rival to the Iranian Revolution in its low levels of religious freedom. In fact, secular repression within the Muslim-majority world well exceeds contemporary France in governing and restricting religion.[4] Most practitioners of the secular repressive pattern have been authoritarian rulers: Shah Reza Pahlavi of Iran, Saddam Hussein of Iraq, Egypt's Gamal Abdel Nasser, Syria's Assads. It is often through brutal force, including torture, that they restrict religion—and necessarily so because their populations are far more religious than they are. They will not proclaim their goal to be the eradication of religion in the brazen and ruthless manner that Communist regimes have done in the Soviet Union, China, and North Korea, though they may well expect religion to disappear. They may advertise their devoutness in their public appearances: lemonade in the open, whiskey behind closed doors. Most assuredly, though, they seek to contain and control religion uncompromisingly.

Typically, Islamic secular repressive rulers will "establish" a moderate version of Islam by supporting it, commending it, and closely controlling the governance of mosques, seminaries, universities, and schools; the content of curricula; the public expression of religion; the architecture of buildings; and even the dress of their citizens.[5] They will simultaneously suppress more traditional and radical forms of Islam, preventing clerics from holding positions of power and, if necessary, jailing them, torturing, or killing them. Secular leaders will present these religious figures as enemies of the state and use them to make the case for authoritarian rule: "It's me or the Muslim Brotherhood," Egypt's Hosni Mubarak would say to his critics. What results, then, is a unique form of Muslim governance that is neither wholly irreligious, nor purely Western, nor entirely un-Islamic, but rather a synthesis that is designed to subordinate religion in order to build a modern nation-state.

Table 3.2 sets forth features of secular repressive regimes.

Secular dictators also like to boast that they protect non-Muslim religious minorities from the depredations of the Muslim population. Sometimes they

Table 3.2. What to Look for in a Secular Repressive Muslim-Majority Regime

- Regime explicitly proclaims the secular nationalist narrative.
- The constitution stipulates that the regime is a secular one.
- A state ministry governs mosques, schools for training clerics, and other religious institutions so as to enforce a moderate version of Islam.
- The regime governs expressions of religion in publications, broadcasting, and dress so as to promote moderate Islam and prohibit conservative/traditional Islam.
- The regime suppresses clerics, intellectuals, parties, and movements who espouse a form of Islam other than a moderate one.
- The regime either prohibits the teaching of religion in schools or requires that a moderate version of Islam be taught; or it may outlaw religious schools.
- The state promotes the teaching of a moderate version of Islam at universities.
- Courts use secular law in their decisions and not *sharia*; personal status law courts are either absent or liberal in their interpretations.

do. As we will see, though, this protection is often unreliable, inconsistent from regime to regime, and sometimes accompanied by the same control that is imposed upon Muslims.

The pattern that I have been describing is what the great sociologist Max Weber called an "ideal type," a general description that captures the essence of something but admits of variation in particular cases. One regime fits the secular repressive pattern so well and was so influential on later regimes that it ranks as the flagship of the type: the Republic of Turkey.

The Turkish Standard

In the global perspective, the Republic of Turkey ranks low in religious freedom. This is clearly borne out by the Government Involvement in Religion (GIR) index created by political scientist Jonathan Fox, which captures restrictions, discrimination, and regulation of religion performed by the state. A high GIR index means low religious freedom. Figure 3.2, compiled with Fox's data, compares Turkey with the global average over the period 1990–2002. It shows starkly that Turkey lacks religious freedom.

The year 2002 is important, for it was then that the Justice and Development Party, known by its Turkish initials, AKP, won a sweeping electoral victory that gave it control of the parliament and the prime ministership. The AKP's goal was to make the Turkish political system more religiously free and friendly

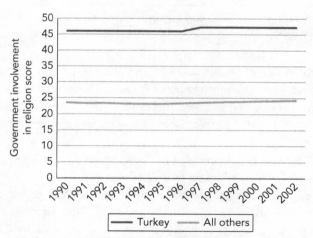

FIGURE 3.2. Turkish government involvement in religion, 1990–2002

Source: Religion and State Dataset, available www.rasdataset.org; chart compiled by Nilay Saiya

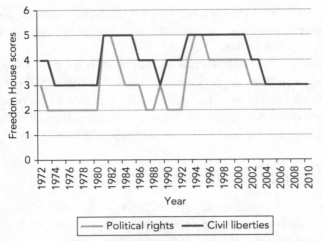

FIGURE 3.3. Political and civil liberties in Turkey, 1972–2010

Source: Freedom House, available at www.freedomhouse.org; compiled by Nilay Saiya

Table 3.3. Religious Freedom in Turkey, 1981–2009

Years Free	Years with moderate religious restrictions	Years with severe religious restrictions
1981	1982, 1983, 1986, 1987, 1993, 1994, 1995, 1996, 1999, 1998, 1999, 2000, 2002, 2003, 2006	1984, 1985, 1988, 1989, 1990, 1991, 1992, 1997, 2001, 2004, 2005, 2007, 2008, 2009

Source: Cingranelli and Richards Human Rights Dataset, available from ciri.org, compiled by Nilay Saiya.

to the participation of Muslims. On balance, progress toward these goals has been modest. The well-known index of Freedom House on political rights and civil liberties shows that in 2010, Turkey was little freer than it was in 1972, as Figure 3.3 illustrates. On Freedom House's scale, 0 is most free and 7 is least free.

This judgment is corroborated by the Cingranelli and Richards Human Rights Dataset, which affords a tracing of religious freedom in Turkey from 1981 to 2009. After coming to power in 2002, the AKP presided over two years of "moderate" restrictions—2003 and 2006—and five years of "severe" restrictions—2004, 2005, 2007, 2008, and 2009, as shown by Table 3.3.

The judgment is buttressed by the Pew Research Center, whose report of 2009 ranked Turkey 14th worst in the world in its GRI.

On a related measure, discrimination against religious minorities, the conclusion is the same: Turkey's average is far worse than the global average. Turkey's dearth of religious freedom is due to its treatment of Muslims who dissent from the orthodoxy of the majority Sunnis, including Alevis and Sufis, and of non-Muslims like Greek Orthodox Christians, Armenian Christians, and Jews. Figure 3.4 illustrates the problem, again using Fox's dataset.

How did Turkey become so religiously unfree? A momentous day was March 3, 1924, during the first year of the republic, when the Turkish National Assembly made two decisions: to abolish the Caliphate and to establish the Diyanet, or Directorate of Religious Affairs.[6] To abolish the Caliphate, whose assertion of religious leadership over all of Islam had been claimed by Ottoman sultans since the 14th century, was to assert a sharp break from Turkey's religious past. To establish the Diyanet was to assert strong control over Turkey's religious future. Both goals were essential to the secular repressive governance of religion that Atatürk established.

It was not inevitable that secular repression won out. The Ottoman Empire could boast of a record of harmony among its religiously plural population that, on balance, was impressive by the standards of its period in global history. In the middle of the 19th century, the empire made strides toward religious freedom for individuals through a succession of reforms that also included the establishment of a parliament and the first general popular election in Islamic history.[7] There emerged a number of liberal Muslim intellectuals and

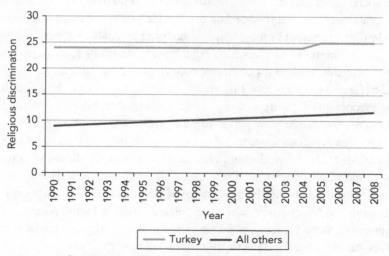

FIGURE 3.4. Religious minority discrimination, 1990–2008

Source: Religion and State Dataset, available www.rasdataset.org; compiled by Nilay Saiya

leaders, many of them known as "Young Ottomans," who thought that religious freedom was not only compatible with Islam but also could be rooted in Islam.

This Islam of religious freedom, however, faced two rival visions that correspond with the two Islamic patterns of repression described in this book. One was Islamism, which resurged in the sultanate of Abdülhamid II, who, after coming to power in 1876, quickly turned back the clock on democracy and religious freedom while pursuing other modernizing reforms up to the end of his reign in 1909. The other was secular repression, represented by a faction called the "Young Turks," whose vision is described well by scholar Erik-Jan Zürcher: "Anti-clericalism, scientism, biological materialism, authoritarianism, intellectual elitism, distrust of the masses, social Darwinism and nationalism . . . soaked up in the France of the *fin de siècle* was then transmitted by Young Turk thinkers and publicists to the Kemalist activists."[8] Kemalist refers to followers of Mustafa Kemal, later known as Kemal Atatürk, who was among the Young Turks.[9] As the Ottoman Empire hastily collapsed in the aftermath of World War I, Atatürk led the Turkish National Movement in the Turkish War of Independence, resulting in the founding of the Republic of Turkey with him as the first president in 1923.

Atatürk was not merely one in a succession of heads of state during an unstable time. Rather, he placed an imprint upon Turkey that endures to this day. He shared in the ambition of the Jacobins of the French Revolution and of so many programs that attained their full force in the 20th century to refashion the social fabric and the human soul. It was a secularizing vision. Positively, his goals were a nation modeled on the West in pursuit of economic modernization, advancement in science and industry, and equality between the sexes. The six principles of Kemalism, as articulated by Atatürk's party in 1935, were republicanism, statism (in economic policy), populism, laicism, nationalism, and reformism. To achieve this vision, religion would have to be confined and privatized, first within the walls of the mosque and the household, then within the souls of humans, ever shrinking, ultimately disappearing.[10]

Between Atatürk's founding of the republic in 1923 and his death in 1938, he unfolded this vision through reform after reform. By means of constitutional and public law, he sought to establish secularism as Turkey's national philosophy and to bring the governance of Islam under the regime's control. Although the Constitution of 1924 stipulated Islam to be the religion of the state as well as the principle of religious freedom, in 1928 the establishment of Islam was removed from the Constitution, and in 1937 secularism was added. Turkey's present Constitution, passed in 1982, contains a preamble stating "that sacred religious feelings shall absolutely not be involved in state affairs and politics as required by the principle of secularism" and declares sweepingly in Article 24 that "[n]o one can be allowed to exploit or abuse religion or religious feelings, or things held sacred by religion, in any manner whatsoever, for even partially basing the fundamental, social, economic, political, and legal order of the state on religious tenets . . . ."[11] The Kemalists eliminated the long-standing Ottoman coexistence of secular and religious law, abolished Islamic law, outlawed traditional religious courts, and adopted the Swiss Civil Code.[12] To oversee religion directly, they established the Diyanet, a large bureaucracy that today employees 106,000 civil servants and that hires and fires the country's imams, oversees religious facilities, controls religious education, and regulates religious dress, worship, observance, the publication of religious texts, and even the Friday mosque sermons, which are composed by Diyanet officials.

Key to the Kemalist program was education, which, as Pope Leo XIII perceived, is a regime's most potent tool for changing the hearts and minds of its citizenry. Turkey's Constitution grants the government oversight of religious and ethical instruction in the schools. In 1924, the Turkish parliament closed 479 *medreses*, or Islamic schools, and erected a nationwide school system that was secular and governed by a ministry of education. During the same period the government expunged religious instruction from the school curricula, outlawed private religious schools, founded "Imam Hatip" schools that were religious but government controlled, and then closed these same schools in 1930.[13] In 1933, it imposed reforms on the universities that removed professors who dissented from Kemalism, including two-thirds of the faculty at the University of Istanbul.[14] Political scientist Ahmet Kuru comments, "[t]he golden age for assertive secularists was the period from 1933 to 1949, when there was not a single legal school or university teaching Islam."[15]

Atatürk's ambition to give Turkey a moral and spiritual makeover did not cease with schools and mosques but reached far into the culture. He replaced the Arabic script with the Latin alphabet, adopted a Western calendar, and outlawed traditional clothing, polygyny, the Arabic call to prayer, and certain traditional titles.[16] He even sought to shape Turks' minds by controlling what was just outside of their minds—their hats. It was the top hat, a westernized form of headgear that replaced the traditional Ottoman fez, that Turkish men were required to wear. All of this was supposed to confine if not eradicate the "forces of superstition," as Atatürk called them, that stood in the way of progress.[17]

Kemalism curtailed the religious freedom not only of Turkey's vast majority of Sunni Muslims but also that of non-Muslim minorities and Muslim sects, Alevis and Sufis. The century prior to the founding of the Republic of Turkey had seen the breakup of the Ottoman Empire, a horrific history for minorities of every stripe that included wars of national independence among Christian populations that wrought the ethnic cleansing of Muslims and Jews; several episodes of large-scale massacres of Christians at the hands of the Ottomans; and the death of an estimated five million Muslims between 1821 and 1922. During the period of the republic, episodes of violence and continual discrimination against Jews and Christians have reduced the non-Muslim population from 2.78% in 1927 to fewer than 1% today.[18]

Although neither the Young Turks nor the Kemalist regime have been directly responsible for all of this violence, the regime's sharply discriminatory policies toward non-Muslims and Muslim sects have contributed to the repression of minorities. The 1923 Lausanne Treaty defined citizenship according to Islam and gave official recognition to some minorities while denying it to others. In the case of recognized minorities—which today include Armenian Orthodox Christians, Greek Orthodox Christians, and Jews—the state, acting in the spirit of Kemalist religious management, created a General Directorate for Foundations that governs their charitable foundations; regulates their religious practice; has at times expropriated their property and grossly overtaxed them; and has kept the seminary of the Greek Orthodox Church in Istanbul closed for more than four decades now, thus preventing the training of clergy and contributing to the decimation of this religious minority in Turkey. Alevis, a syncretic offshoot of Islam who amount to about 15% of the total population, have suffered sharp restrictions, including obligatory education into Sunni Islam, curtailments on the construction of meeting places, and lack of representation at the state level.[19] Sufis, practitioners of an Islamic mysticism, continue to exist underground after they saw their orders dissolved and their practices banned in 1925.[20] Christians experienced repressive violence continually during the first 12 years of the republic, pogroms directed against the Greek Orthodox Church in 1955, incidents of violence in 1963 and 1974, and several assassinations in the past decade-and-a-half.[21]

This control of religion Atatürk asserted through authoritarian means. Economist Jean-Philippe Plateau describes it well:

> The government, the bureaucracy, and the army were turned into a single body with Mustafa Kemal as its indisputable head. Interestingly, the only legitimate political opposition was short-lived. Allowed to form in 1930, the Free Republican Party (FRP) was abruptly terminated because it revealed the widespread discontent in the country and the unpopularity of the RPP [Kemalist party]. The enormous support for the rival FRP showed that the RPP's project of

social and cultural modernization had not been accepted by the mass of the population.[22]

Indeed, although the Republic of Turkey has always had a parliament, an institution that the Young Turks reestablished in 1908, it has likewise truncated democracy over most of its history. A singly party, the Kemalist Cumhuriyet Halk Partisi (CHP; in English, the Republican People's Party), ruled for 26 years beginning in 1924. Secularism has been enforced through a coalition of the president, the military, the Diyanet, the university, and allied sectors of the media and the political class. The courts have seen themselves as the civilian guardians of secularism and espouse the ideology forcefully. As Kuru wrote in 2009, "[f]or the court, secularism is beyond a political regime; it is 'Turkey's philosophy of life.' The court takes secularism as a comprehensive official doctrine, an overarching principle prior to all rights and freedoms, and a social engineering project to secularize society."[23] In the early years of the republic, Atatürk's regime created special tribunals to eliminate Islamist and Kurdish opponents and passed a Law on the Maintenance of Order that sanctioned the arrest of almost 7,500 people and the execution of 660.[24] Over subsequent decades, the regime arrested and imprisoned thousands of Islamic activists, took control of newspapers, and closed down the union of journalists.

Did Atatürk succeed? Assuredly, he created a secular republic that persists to this day. His aspiration to remake the souls of Turks and the social fabric of Turkey, however, has not succeeded. Religion has remained strong among the population, especially in the rural areas, and has walked hand in hand with the demand for democracy. Majority rule has always resulted in a challenge to Kemalism's enforced secularism. To this day, the CHP has never won the majority in parliament through a democratic election, whereas, in the past three decades or so, center-right parties, far friendlier to Islam, have won about 70% of the vote in national legislative elections.[25] So, too, the Kemalist sectors, especially the military and the courts, have consistently intervened to resist the gains of Islamic parties, staging coups every decade: 1960, 1971, 1980, and then the "soft coup" of February 28, 1997. The history of Turkey after Atatürk's death can be seen as a tug-of-war oscillating from democratic openings and Islamic gains back to Kemalist clampdowns.

Supporters of Atatürk's secularist program will argue that harsh measures were necessary for economic modernization. One of secularism's most prominent defenders, mid-20th-century sociologist Niyazi Berkes, whose writings Turkey's Constitutional Court endorsed in defining secularism in 1997, has made the case that Islam had upheld the medieval social order of the Ottoman

Empire and that "without the breakdown of the traditional structure and attitudes, modern economic and technical aid may produce little change conducive to economic growth." Berkes also rejected the separation of religion and state, which, he argued, only leaves intact religion's social influence.[26]

Is Berkes right? True, as political scientist Timur Kuran argues compellingly in his influential book of 2011, *The Long Divergence*, Islamic laws and institutions that arose in the Middle Ages served to stunt economic development in the Middle East over the course of the same centuries in which the West shot forward. Kuran is careful to argue, though, that Islam is not irrevocably destined by its texts or its foundational teachings to be antigrowth and that its economic norms are capable of change.[27] In fact, little in the history of the late Ottoman Empire or the early days of the Republic of Turkey serves to justify Kemalism's secular repression, which, apart from its inherent injustice, suffered from three major conceptual flaws.

First, it falsely portrayed Turkish Muslims as monolithic, ignoring the wide support for economic modernization among many of them, including the class of religious authorities, in the 19th and early 20th centuries, well before Atatürk took power. Second, much relaxation of religious strictures on economic exchange did in fact take place in the 19th century, as Kuran points out.[28] While, at the time that Atatürk took power, clerics still wielded economic influence through *waqfs*, or pious foundations, this influence had been greatly reduced over the course of the previous century. Third, Atatürk's aims were far more ambitious than whisking away remaining religious barriers to economic advancement. Rather, he sought to refashion minds, hearts, and even hats. Ironically, over the subsequent history of the Republic of Turkey, it has been religiously friendly center-right parties who have advocated not only greater democracy and religious freedom but also free-market economics, whereas the Kemalist party has promoted sclerotic, statist economic policies.

After World War II, under pressure wrought by widespread economic discontent and a newly established alliance with the United States, the Kemalist party agreed to allow multiparty elections, which took place in 1950 and were won by the Democratic Party (DP) and its leader, Adnan Menderes. For the first time in the history of the Republic of Turkey, a democratically elected party held power.[29] He steered Turkey toward free-market economic policies and away from socialist ones, aligned with the West and joined NATO, and effected modest relaxations on the governance of religion, for instance, opening 19 Imam Hatip schools, permitting Sufi brotherhoods, and allowing religious broadcasting on the public radio. Then, however, after Menderes won three national elections, Kemalist military officers staged a coup in 1960, shutting down the DP, purging the army and the university, and sending Menderes to the gallows. When, in the second half of the 1960s, a newly constituted Islamic party known as the Justice Party won elections and pursued policies similar to those of Menderes, it was again overthrown by Kemalist officers in 1971.

The 1970s brought the global resurgence of Islam to Turkey. Two strands emerged. One was an Islamist political movement, led by Necmettin Erbakan, who advocated turning Turkey away from the West and toward other Muslim countries, a statist economics, and a political–religious program inspired by radical Islamist intellectuals Sayyid Qutb and Abu Ala Al-Mawdudi and the Muslim Brotherhood of Egypt. The other was a more liberal Islam, inspired by the early 20th-century intellectual Said Nursi, that favored science, democracy, freedom, nonviolence, and cooperation with other faiths. Although Nursi was persecuted by the Kemalist regime, his followers numbered in the millions and, in the latter half of the 20th century, developed into a global movement under the preacher and imam Fethullah Gülen.[30]

In 1980, in what was becoming a decennial tradition, still another Kemalist coup took place and was followed yet again with the election of a reconstituted Islamic party, this one led by Turgut Özal, who served as prime minister for a decade and revived the policies of free markets, an orientation toward the West, and greater religious freedom. In the 1990s, the pattern repeated when Erbakan became prime minster and, though he backed away from his erstwhile Islamism and took a moderate line, was overthrown in a "soft coup" led by the judiciary in February 1997.

Still another Islamic party, the AKP, rose from the ashes and came to power in the 2002 national elections. Its leader, Recep Tayyip Erdoğan, became prime minister. This time, though, the Islamic party managed to stay in power for a considerable spell, winning pluralities in 2007, 2011, June 2015, and November 2015. Over its first nine years in power, the AKP governed in the tradition of Menderes and Özal and gained a reputation as an Islamic version of a European Christian Democratic party. It had won office upon the promise of pursuing membership in the European Union (EU), including meeting the EU's criteria for human rights and democratic governance. It favored the free market and led Turkey into an economic boom. And it sought to pry open the Kemalist regime's grip on the religion of the Turkish population.

Skeptics of the AKP, especially Kemalists, warned that the party is an Islamist wolf in a liberal democratic sheepskin, plotting to seize power in order to remake Turkey in the image of Saudi Arabia or Iran. They pointed to Islamist declamations by Erdoğan when he was mayor of Istanbul and styled himself the "Imam of Istanbul," and by prominent AKP leader Abdullah Gül, who announced the "end of the republican period" in 1996.[31] The AKP moderated its rhetoric, they claim, only to steer clear of the Kemalist military and courts.

What is the reality? Since 2011, Erdoğan's rule has become increasingly authoritarian. Still, we should not dismiss the commitment to liberal democracy among many AKP members or the party's track record in promoting freedom, especially up to 2011. Many in the party regard democracy as a legitimate vehicle for a social conservative agenda that supports the religion of the people and the traditional family. The party is indebted to the Nur and Naksibendi movements founded on the thought of Nursi, stressing democracy and religious freedom alongside piety and tradition. It finds a constituency in the fruit of another generational trend, the rise of an Islamic business community that combines devoutness with a commitment to political and economic modernity.[32] And it reflects a period in which Islamism remains a marginal view, as indicated by a 2006 survey that reports only 9% of Turks supporting an Islamic state based on *sharia* law.[33]

Political scientist Hakan Yavuz observed in 2009 that in the years after AKP came to power, it passed more political–legal reforms than were passed in the three previous decades, among these the abolition of the death penalty, the expansion of freedom of expression, increased cultural rights for Kurds, curtailment of military powers, and increased civilian control of the security forces.[34] In the realm of religion, Erdoğan articulated a positive secularism that avoids both religious dominance of the state and secular repression of religion. As he explained in a speech,

> Secularism, as the key guarantee of societal peace and democracy, is a concept with two dimensions. Secularism's first dimension is that the state should not be structured according to religious laws. This requires a standardized, unitary and undivided legal order. Secularism's second dimension is that the state should be neutral and keep an equal distance from all religious beliefs and should be the guarantor of individuals' freedoms.[35]

The AKP sponsored laws granting increased rights to religious minority groups; allowing religious minorities to open new places of worship; overturning restrictions forbidding religious associations; allowing minorities to reclaim previously seized land; removing restrictions on Imam Hatip schools, whose numbers had sharply increased over the previous twenty years; and relaxing restrictions on the teaching of Quranic courses.

The AKP also sought greater freedom in the most contentious of issues— Turkey's ban on women wearing headscarves in schools, university campuses, and many public buildings. With 69% of women wearing headscarves in 2007 and 78% of the population opposing the ban, the issue symbolizes the desire of the broad population to practice its faith freely.[36] In February 2008, a coalition in the Turkish parliament, led by the AKP, passed an amendment to the Turkish Constitution mandating equal access for women to public services and higher education—not a direct lifting of the ban but a principle that could be interpreted in favor of such a lifting.

The Kemalists fought back. That same year, the Constitutional Court nullified the amendment and, with a heavy hand, fined the AKP government for violating secularism.[37] In 1989, the court had ruled similarly, defending its decision with reasoning that could not be purer in its adherence to Atatürk's vision:

> The dress code is not just an issue of physical appearance. Secularism is a transformation of mentality. It is a must for a modern healthy society. An individual is a unity composed of his/her inner and outer lives, sentiments and thoughts, and body and spirit. The dress code is a means to reflect personal character. Regardless of whether it is religious or not, anti-modern dresses that contradict the Laws of Revolution cannot be seen as appropriate. Religious dresses, in particular, constitute a deeper incongruity since they contradict the principle of secularism.[38]

Here, Kemalism's aspiration to refashion the soul and the social fabric is on full display. In 2004, The Kemalist president of Turkey, Ahmet Necdet Sezer, also vetoed the AKP's bill lifting restrictions on the Imam Hatip schools. By and large, despite the AKP's efforts, much of the regime of secular repression has remained in place.

Again, since around 2011, Erdoğan's government—with him as prime minister from 2003 to 2014 and president from 2014 to the present—has become increasingly authoritarian, cracking down on popular protests, curtailing judicial independence, restricting the press and social media, committing electoral fraud, overseeing a rise in corruption, and accruing the power to oust and even imprison legislators. In suppressing a coup attempt in July 2016, Erdoğan arrested one-third of his generals and admirals, detained some 10,000 officers and soldiers, imprisoned about 50,000 people affiliated with the movement of Gülen, his chief rival, and had some 70,000 professionals—professors, journalists, businesspeople—and 150,000 public employees fired or suspended from their jobs.[39] Erdoğan has not resisted the trappings of a sultan, building himself a presidential palace of 1,150 rooms, costing $615 million and built with stone pillars and sheet glass.[40]

It is not clear, though, how Islamist Erdoğan's authoritarianism is. Some observers believe that he intends a traditional *sharia* state, others that he is more a thug than a puritan. Since 2011, he has issued calls for Turkish children to become a "pious generation," vastly increased funding for Imam Hatip schools, introduced Islamist textbooks in these schools, made religious education compulsory in primary schools (with exceptions only for Christians and Jews), required new schools to include prayer rooms, successively lifted rules banning women from wearing headscarves in state institutions (including schools, universities, the police, and the military), sponsored the building of mosques, and cracked down on Alevis. To be sure, these policies move Turkey in an Islamic direction, but do they transform the regime from a secular repressive to a religiously repressive one? Funding religious schools is little different from what many Western democracies do, and Imam Hatip schools contain only 10% of Turkish students.[41] The lifting of restrictions on headscarves is in fact a liberalizing move. Other policies are hardly new to Erdoğan, for instance, the repression of Alevis, which dates back at least to the 16th-century Ottoman Empire, and of Kurds, which took place throughout the Kemalist era. Still other measures are admittedly Islamist, for instance, the issuance of religious textbooks. Added up, though, these measures do not place Turkey in a different category of religious governance; it is not yet in the religiously repressive column. And Turkey most certainly is not religiously free. Whatever the truth about Erdoğan's Islamist intentions, his repressive rule greatly weakens the AKP's promise of transforming the Kemalist secular repressive republic into a democracy with religious freedom. This dream is now dead. Turkey has not gained accession to the EU and does not meet its criteria for democratic governance and human rights. In part, this is because it remains among the worst violators of religious freedom on the planet.

Egypt

Although Turkey is the oldest and strongest secular repressive state, Egypt's version of the pattern also stands tall in historical significance. Its designer was President Gamal Abdel Nasser, who took power in a coup with his fellow military officers in 1952, consolidated his power as head of state by 1954, and, like Atatürk, sought to reshape Egypt as a secular society until he died of a heart attack in 1970. Nasser led efforts to forge unity in the Arab world and was one of the most prominent figures of the "Bandung Generation," a group of heads of state in the Middle East, Africa, and South Asia who led their newly independent countries out of colonial servitude and sought to build them on the basis of nationalism, economic development, socialism, military power, nonalignment with superpowers, and a decided secularism.

Similar to Atatürk, Nasser did not want to erase the Sunni Islamic religion of Egypt's vast majority. He displayed his devoutness, making a pilgrimage [*hajj*] to Mecca in 1954. Rather, as political scientist Scott Hibbard put it, he sought to "tame Islam and employ it in the service of the state."[42] To take control of religion, he closed religious courts, seized religiously held land, and expanded the ambit of the Ministry of Religious Endowments to govern mosques as well as the influential Al-Azhar mosque and university complex. Paralleling Atatürk, Nasser promoted a liberal and modern version of Islam through controlling religious programming on the state-run television, religious content in the newspaper, religious education in the schools, mosque preaching, and funding for the university. Still, today, the government, largely through its Ministry of Religious Affairs, oversees mosques, supervises clerics, appoints and pays imams, closely monitors sermons, controls the training of imams, and restricts students from wearing the *hijab* [headscarf] in school.

True to the secular repressive pattern, Nasser also repressed traditional and conservative Islam and its call for integrating religion into public life, not privatizing it. Although Nasser allied with the Muslim Brotherhood, the popular Islamic revivalist group, in staging his coup of 1952, he then turned against the Brotherhood and its rival vision for society. After a member of the Brotherhood's armed wing tried to assassinate him in 1954, he used the occasion to break the influence of the organization by arresting more than 30,000 of its members and executing six of its leaders.[43] He placed a ban on the Brotherhood's participation in politics, one that would remain in place until 2011.[44]

Nasser was authoritarian. The previous period, 1922–1952, had been an experiment in liberalism, not without flaws, but nevertheless witnessing advances in political contestation, interfaith coexistence, and the influence of liberal Muslim intellectuals. Nasser ended the experiment, terminating political parties, closing newspapers, imprisoning dissenters, silencing opponents, bribing judges, and sharply restricting freedom of speech and public discourse, especially in the areas of religion and politics. His base of power resided in the military and universities and among supporters of his socialist policies. In 1967, he declared emergency rule, giving the executive extensive power to curb rights, including detaining people indefinitely without charge, a condition that lasted until 2012. In the decades following Nasser, the Egyptian government continued to violate human rights on a grand scale, even becoming an entrepôt of torture, a place where countries around the world would send their terrorist suspects to be interrogated.[45] On religious freedom, Egypt ranked in the worst 5% of all countries on government restrictions and just above the worst 5% on social hostilities according to the Pew Research Center's Report of 2009.[46]

As in Turkey, secular repression in Egypt could only be authoritarian because the population remained far more religious than the governing elites did. And, as in Turkey, repression failed to make the society secular. Beginning around 1970, Egypt experienced the global Islamic resurgence, a revival in religious devotion as well as in religious demands for social and political influence. In Egypt more than in Turkey, though, the state responded by enacting laws and policies that met Muslim demands—so much so that one may plausibly argue that Egypt ceased to be secular repressive and had become religiously repressive.

I contend, however, that Egypt continued to fit the secular repressive pattern up until the Arab Uprisings of 2011, though law and government admittedly took on a heavy admixture of Islamism. The state's governance of religion, its encouragement of moderate Islam, its crackdown on radical Islam, and its own professions to uphold secularism and to be a barrier to fundamentalism all persisted.[47] Most important, the governing regime never allowed Islamists to gain any real power. In a repeated pattern, it would relax its grip so as to allow Islamic groups to compete in politics but then squeeze its grip tight again as they gained in political strength. Without a doubt, the state enacted traditional Islamic laws and policies, but it did so in order to co-opt powerful Islamic popular forces. Over time, this co-optation accumulated so much that Egypt's strict governance of religion blended Islamist and secularist elements. The state, though, remained secularist in its overall standpoint.

The Islamic revival of the 1970s took place in part because of the failure of Nasser's economic policies, which left university graduates without opportunities; in part because Muslims felt excluded from the secularist state; in part because of Egypt's humiliating loss to Israel in the Six Day War of 1967; but also, as political scientist Carrie Rosefsky Wickham has stressed, because of Muslims' positive desire to create a religious society.[48]

The Muslim Brotherhood was the largest force for religious resurgence. Founded in 1928 by revivalist Hassan al-Banna, the Brotherhood dedicated itself to rekindling devotion to Islam among the population and in all walks of life. From the beginning, the Brotherhood has contained both moderates, who have favored the transformation of civil society and peaceful political engagement, as well as radicals who have advocated a violent overthrow of the regime. The Brotherhood's violent "Secret Apparatus" faction had been associated with several assassinations, including that of Egypt's prime minister in 1948, and with an attempt on Nasser's life in 1954, even while al-Banna's successor, Hassan Ismail al-Hudaybi, insisted upon nonviolence. In 1949, al-Banna himself was assassinated. [49] In the 1970s, the Brotherhood expanded rapidly, becoming the largest civil society organization in Egypt, its ranks swelling to more than 2 million by the 2000s, and its growth taking place particularly among university students and associations of engineers, doctors, and other professions. [50] Its quest was to encourage Egypt's Muslims to live a devout life and Egypt's culture, economy, and politics to be genuinely Islamic.

Nasser's successor, Anwar Sadat, determined to adopt free-market policies, forged an alliance with this burgeoning Islam against the left. He relaxed restrictions on the Muslim Brotherhood (though he kept it illegal), released thousands of its members and leaders from prison, supported Islamic laws and policies, and steered Al-Azhar University on a more conservative course. A new Constitution in 1971 established *sharia* as "*a* principal source of legislation," a change that was amended in 1980 to read "*the* principal (or primary) source of legislation."[51] For its part, the Brotherhood renounced violence and pledged good citizenship so long as it could advocate its version of Islam openly.

By the end of the 1970s, though, tensions returned between Sadat and revivalist Muslims. The most conservative faction of the Brotherhood, along with radical groups outside the Brotherhood, became vociferous critics of Sadat, especially after he made peace with Israel at Camp David in 1978. Sadat cracked down again. He denounced Islamic groups, banned the national student union, shut down the Brotherhood's newspaper, nationalized many private mosques, and expanded the Ministry of Religious Endowments' control over mosques. His quip, "those who wish to practice Islam can go to the mosques, and those who wish to engage in politics may do so through legal institutions," was vintage secular repression: Religion is private, politics is public.[52]

After members of the Egyptian Islamic Jihad assassinated Sadat in 1981, President Hosni Mubarak followed Sadat's previous course of relaxing constraints on the Brotherhood and promoting Islam in return for the Brotherhood's fealty to the political system. It was then that the Brotherhood took a turn toward active participation in politics, adopting elections, the separation of powers, and alliances with other political parties as its mode of pursuing an Islamic society.[53] Although the Brotherhood was not allowed to compete as a party, it fielded candidates through other parties and achieved increasing electoral success. By the early 1990s, Islamists had also infiltrated the leadership of mosques, the judiciary, Al-Azhar, and several government institutions. Court cases dealing with apostasy and artistic and intellectual freedom were increasingly decided in Islamist fashion.

Repeating the cycle, Mubarak cracked down again in the 1990s. He openly fought radical violent groups in a period of heavy violence between 1992 and 1997. He also suppressed more moderate groups, though, including the Muslim Brotherhood, whose leadership adhered to its renunciation of violence and its commitment to participation in the political system. Mubarak took control of the Brotherhood's leadership, undermining its control of professional organizations, arresting hundreds of its leaders and activists, and further nationalizing mosques. In 2005 and 2010, Muslim Brotherhood candidates stood for parliament as independents, but the Egyptian government sharply curtailed their victories through rampant electoral fraud. Even so, Brotherhood candidates won 88 out of 454 seats in the 2005 election.[54]

Political scientist Mohammed Hafez explains that what motivated Mubarak to suppress Islam so widely and disproportionately was the electoral gains of the Brotherhood, its expanding influence in civil society, and its open criticisms of the Mubarak regime for this regime's lack of freedom and democracy and for its practice of torture.[55] Like any secular repressive autocrat, Mubarak sought to keep conservative Islam in close check, partly through cooptation, partly through coercion.

Although secular repression was most centrally concerned with Sunni Islam, it contained strong repercussions for religious minorities. Egyptian law recognizes three religions—Islam, Christianity, and Judaism—and the Religious Affairs Department of the Ministry of the Interior has the final say on which religious groups are granted official recognition and which are not recognized and thus rendered a threat to the state. Egyptian administrative courts have issued rulings that non-Muslims must practice their faith in a way that does not "disrupt the harmony of society."[56]

Since the beginning of the republic and indeed well before it, Coptic Orthodox Christians have suffered mistreatment. Dating back to Jesus' Apostle Mark, the Copts constitute 10%-20% of the population and the largest Christian community in the Middle East. Most directly, Copts suffer violence at the hands of Islamic militant groups and sometimes mobs as well as discrimination at the hands of the surrounding Muslim population. The Muslim Brotherhood holds that Copts are *dhimmis*—citizens with minority status—and ought to be treated as such.[57] Islamist groups or individuals frequently assault Muslims who convert to Christianity and Muslim men who marry women who have converted to Christianity. Such violence and discrimination have increased since the Islamic resurgence of the 1970s.

Copts have also seen their freedom curtailed by the state, which, true to the secular repressive pattern, has sharply regulated their church. Most severely, Copts are restricted in building new churches, which require a permit from the government, a form of regulation dating back to the Ottoman Empire. As scholar of Coptic Christianity Samuel Tadros explains, the rationale for such regulations is the maintenance of order and the avoidance of provoking Muslims. The regulations, however, incentivize Muslims to instigate fury against the real or prospective building of a church and then to offer this anger as proof that building a church is unwise. The state has consistently turned a blind eye toward attacks on churches as well.[58]

After the Coptic Church protested state inaction against its mistreatment by Muslims in the late 1970s, President Sadat sought to remove Pope Shenouda from his position, had him confined to a monastery, launched a propaganda campaign against him, and arrested tens of priests and bishops. The Church refused to acquiesce to Shenouda's removal, but the episode revealed the state's proclivity for stricture. In 1985, President Mubarak restored Shenouda as pope in return for which Shenouda remained loyal to Mubarak until Mubarak's overthrow in February 2011.[59]

Religious communities who are not recognized—Shia Muslims, Baha'is, Mormons, and Jehovah's Witnesses—have it even worse. Until 2008, they could not obtain identification cards or birth certificates. Baha'is are not only denied recognition, but are also banned from constructing buildings for worship and conducting their religious activities. Jews, although they are recognized, suffer from strong anti-Semitism in the surrounding population and even in the state-controlled press. Over the course of Egypt's modern history, they have fled the country to escape pogroms, other violence, and the seizure of their property, often with the complicity of the government, dwindling from more than 100,000 people in the 1950s to about 12 in 2014.[60]

Arabian Secularism

Beyond Egypt, the secular repressive pattern—and the thinking that undergirded it—captured the imagination of leaders across the Arab world in the decades after World War II. The ideology was expressed vividly, for instance, in the Ba'ath Party, which was founded in 1947 with the aim of uniting Arab peoples, spread out over many borders created arbitrarily by colonial masters, into a single nation-state that would throw off colonial slavery and build a modern society. The Arabic word Ba'ath means "renaissance" or "resurrection," which was translated by the party's leaders into freedom from imperial rule, nationalism, equality, socialism, and other ideals borrowed from Europe. Like the vision of Atatürk and Nasser, Ba'athism was secular. Islam was an expression of "Arab genius," as the party's most prominent founder, Michel Aflaq, himself a Christian, put it, a co-optive rhetorical move implying that Arabic language and culture were not to be understood as expressions of "Islamic genius."[61] Arab nationalism came first, in the Ba'athist vision, and this meant that Islam could be an animator of souls but not of public life. With Ba'athists in charge, the state would police this boundary and serve as the primary prophet and revolutionary vanguard of the society's ideals. Until the people were suitably enlightened, the vanguard would have to remain in control.

Not surprisingly, Ba'athist states were dictatorships. Although Ba'athism originally envisioned a unified Arab state, Ba'athist parties took power only in Syria and Iraq, where they installed an authoritarian secularism upheld by detention and torture.

Syria came under Ba'athist rule in a coup that overthrew the government of the French mandate in 1963. In 1970, Ba'athist Hafez al-Assad took over the government and ruled until his death in 2000, when he was succeeded by his son, Bashar al-Assad, who remains president at the time of this writing. Members of the Alawite offshoot of Shia Islam, a sect constituting 16% of the population in a country comprising 74% Sunni Muslims, the Assads have given protection and professional privileges to Alawites as well as to the Christian population, which made up 10% of the population as of 2011. The Syrian Constitution contains some provisions that promote religious freedom as well as some that promote Islamism, the latter specifying that the president must be a Muslim and that Islamic jurisprudence is a principal source of legislation. It provides religious courts that rule on personal status law (marriage, divorce, custody, inheritance).

By and large, though, Syria is a repressive secular state. President Bashar Assad explicitly declared Syria secular as recently as 2013. The Islamist clauses were added to the Constitution in 1973 only after Sunni militants demonstrated violently. Over the decades, the Assads have repressed conservative and radical Islam and promoted a moderate Islam through controlling schools, religious education, the building and governance of mosques, and the content of sermons; conducting religious broadcasts on state-run radio and television; prohibiting women from wearing face-covering *niqab* in universities; outlawing the Muslim Brotherhood; and detaining Islamists in prison. Syria ranks among the biggest practitioners of torture in the world. Between 1979 and 1982, the regime fought a guerilla war against Muslim groups led by the Muslim Brotherhood, a rival to the secular Ba'ath Party since its earliest days in the 1940s, which ended finally when the Syrian Army quelled an uprising in the city of Hama by means of a massacre that killed between 10,000 and 40,000 people (estimates vary widely).

In Iraq, the Ba'ath Party came to power in 1968 through a military coup led by Saddam Hussein, who gradually took over governance until he formally became president in 1979. He and his party sought to bring electricity, industry, and other facets of modernization to Iraq through an authoritarian state and its secret police, the *Mukhabarat*. Saddam favored Sunni Muslims, who today make up 32%–37% of the population, over and against the Shia population, now a majority of 65%. He had a mixed record of protecting Christians, who numbered 1.5 million, or 6.5%, of the population, when he was overthrown in 2003. Between 1974 and 1989, he repressed them in an effort to assimilate them to the Arabic Iraqi nation. He also shielded, them, though, from Islamist threats.[62]

Whatever favor Saddam may have showed for this or that religious community, however, was overshadowed by the dominant theme of his rule: his close governance of religion in furtherance of a Ba'athist vision of secular nationalism. A Ministry of Endowments and Religious Affairs regulated and kept close track of mosques and clerics and gave permission for building and repairing places of worship and for publishing all religious literature. In the case of Shia Muslims, close governance is a vast understatement. Shia unrest toward Ba'athist secular rule had been growing over the course of the 1970s and accelerated after the Iranian Revolution of 1979. The regime's response was vastly, indiscriminately ruthless. Saddam and his security forces murdered, summarily executed, and arbitrarily arrested Shia leaders and followers; destroyed and desecrated mosques and holy sites; prevented Shia from performing religious rites, including Holy Day pilgrimages; controlled sermons; and deported tens of thousands of Shias to Iran in the late 1970s and early 1980s.[63] In 1991, Saddam suppressed Shia and Kurdish uprisings through operations that killed tens of thousands of civilians.

In 1993, responding to Islamic revival, Saddam launched a Return to Faith Campaign in order to encourage devotion to Islam among the population and to bolster loyalty to his regime among Sunni Muslims. The campaign's measures ranged among building and repairing mosques, publishing religious literature, opening up religious academic institutions, introducing religious curriculum in schools, creating a religious radio station, outlawing prostitution, requiring amputation for thieves, and introducing dimensions of *sharia* into the judicial system. This campaign was controlled by the government and supported only Sunni, not Shia, Islam. As in Egypt, it was a co-optative strategy that did not change the basic parameters of secular repressive governance.[64]

Tales of Arabian secularism also can be told about countries on Africa's northern coast during this same period: Algeria, Tunisia, Morocco, and Libya. After Algeria's National Liberation Front (FLN) won independence from France in 1962, it established a government whose approach to religion drew from the *laïcité* that France had established in Algeria a century earlier and that fit the mold of secular repression: nationalist, socialist, authoritarian, secularist, ruled by one party, and upheld by a secularist military. President Houari Boumédiène, who ruled from 1965 to 1978, promoted this vision most influentially. As in other Islamic secular repressive states, Algeria's Constitution declares Islam to be the state religion and promotes certain norms of *sharia* law, but this can be understood as the co-optative strategy of a regime that seeks to promote moderate Islam and contain conservative and radical Islam. As was true elsewhere in the Muslim world, Islamist revivalist movements, both moderate and militant, arose and grew in Algeria during the 1970s.[65]

In the late 1980s, the accumulated failures of socialism and an economic crisis precipitated unrest, leading President Chadli Bendjedid to allow multiparty elections in 1992. When the Islamic Salvation Front (FIS), the largest of the revival groups, was poised to defeat the long-governing FLN, the military intervened to cancel the election. It banned the FIS, the ranks of radical militant groups grew, and a civil war that took 150,000 lives ensued. Although, prior to the election, the FIS had declared goals of establishing an Islamic state and expanding *sharia*, it had not favored revolutionary violence. Only in the face of the government's subjugation did it become radicalized and less willing to compromise.[66]

Tunisia's Habib Bourguiba, who ruled as president for three decades after Tunisia gained its independence from France in 1956, epitomized his generation of leaders, aiming to cripple traditional Islam and to develop a modern secular nation.[67] He established a government in the same mold as Egypt's Nasser, Syria's Assad, and Algeria's Boumédiène. He secularized Zaytuna University, curtailed religious education in the schools, nationalized Islamic endowments, closed virtually all Quranic schools, outlawed polygamy, liberalized marriage and divorce, campaigned against the veil and the *hijab*, and enforced it all through 31 years of rule entirely lacking in a free election, which he knew he would certainly lose.[68] Zine El Abidine Ben Ali overthrew Bourguiba in 1987 and continued similar policies, persecuting Islamic movements, especially the popular Ennahda Movement, particularly brutally in the early 1990s. Tunisia was one locale where the secular government protected tiny communities of Christians and Jews and even permitted Baha'is.

Morocco belongs in the secular repressive category, too, though not as neatly so. Since independence in 1956, hereditary monarchs have governed the country: Mohammed V (1957–1961); Hassan II (1961–1999); and Mohammed VI (1999–present). All have been authoritarian. Hassan II was particularly repressive, whereas Mohammed VI has taken some steps toward democracy. Religion in Morocco, though, is less harshly restricted than it is in other secular repressive countries. Its Pew GRI score of 2009 was 5.3, which ranks "high" through not "very high."[69] The state refrains from regulating clothing. Voluntary conversion away from Islam is legal. *Sharia* courts are not highly concerned with punishing apostasy. The government protects the country's small Christian and Jewish communities so that they can conduct worship.

Still, Morocco merits a secular repressive designation because the state strongly regulates Islam in order to promote moderate Islam and to contain conservative Islam. It has a Ministry of Endowments of Islamic Affairs that governs and monitors mosques and generally regulates the practice of Islam in the ways that other secular repressive states do. The king appoints the members of the *ulema*, the body of authoritative scholars. The Supreme Ulema Council issues all *fatwas*. Religious parties are outlawed. The regime blocks the spread of literature that does not follow the official Maliki school of jurisprudence. Like other secular repressive governments, Morocco's has passed some Islamist laws, for instance ones censoring views critical of Islam and preventing the proselytism of Muslims. By and large, though, the state has hemmed in conservative Islam, especially following terrorist attacks in Casablanca in 2003. The Supreme Ulema Council itself took a historic step toward moderation in February 2017 when it issued a *fatwa* declaring that leaving Islam no longer merits the death penalty, a reversal of the Council's previous ruling of 2012.[70]

Libya did not seem to be a secular repressive society when Colonel Muammar Qaddafi proclaimed a cultural revolution in April 1973, four years after he had led the overthrow of Libya's hereditary monarch, King Idris. *Sharia* would replace all existing laws and Islamic thought would be promoted, he announced. Soon thereafter, though, he proclaimed himself a Muslim jurist and scholar, the authoritative interpreter of the Qur'an for the entire nation. Those who dissented from his interpretation would face the terror of his security forces. That interpretation was secular repressive. The revolution that he promised was a nationalist, modernizing one. He persecuted the Muslim Brotherhood, dissolving it in 1973, imprisoning and publicly executing its leaders, and ultimately exiling it.[71] He controlled mosques, made sure that they followed a moderate interpretation of Islam, and banned groups at odds with this interpretation. He allowed Christian churches—including the

Coptic Orthodox Church, with 60,000 members—to operate openly, though he limited every city to one church building of each denomination, creating a shortage of space for Libya's Christians.[72]

Jordan did not fit the secular repressive pattern for 30 years after it gained independence in 1946. A constitutional monarchy, Jordan was ruled by King Hussein from 1953 to 1999 and subsequently by his son, Abdullah. Until around 1980, Hussein exercised a light hand toward religious groups, allowing them considerable autonomy. In the late 1950s and 1960s, the regime allied with the Muslim Brotherhood, which was conservative but also pragmatic, and opposed nationalist groups—a coalition that hardly fits the secular repressive pattern. After the Iranian Revolution of 1979 created a popular movement of political Islam, the regime began to fear global *jihad* and created policies and institutions of the secular repressive kind. It took control of mosques, imams, holy shrines, sermons, religious instruction in schools, and public political commentary and required religious groups to apply for recognition. To promote moderate Islam, it created a research center for Islamic thought, established a Council of Fatwas to control religious directives, and sponsored conferences and other public projects promoting moderate Islam. Like other secular repressive states, it pursues some limited Islamist policies, including declaring Islam as the state religion, requiring that the king be Muslim, prohibiting conversion away from Islam in personal status courts, prohibiting slander of the Prophet, and banning Baha'is. [73] While Jordan is predominantly secular repressive, though, it does not repress severely, for here, Islamic groups, including the Islamic Action Front, the political wing of the Muslim Brotherhood, are comparatively moderate and willing to participate in the political system.[74]

The Secularist Stans

In February 1989, Muslim demonstrators gathered in Tashkent, Uzbekistan, to demand the resignation of the mufti of Central Asia, Shamsuddin ibn Babakhan, whom they accused of egregious misbehavior and the infraction of Islamic moral laws. Their protests succeeded. The Uzbek prime minister received an audience of 25 representatives of the demonstrators, after which the mufti resigned and a congress of Central Asian Muslims elected their own mufti.[75]

The incident reveals much about religion and state in the six Central Asian republics that the Soviet Empire had incorporated many decades earlier and that had received their political independence when the Soviet Union dissolved in 1991: Uzbekistan, Turkmenistan, Tajikistan, Kazakhstan,

Kyrgyzstan, and Azerbaijan. The mufti had been a part of the "official Islam" that the Soviet Communist government had created to contain and manage the rise of Islam that began in the region in the 1960s and grew through the 1970s and 1980s. The Soviets had deployed the mufti in Uzbekistan, the region's dominant state, most likely to control religion in the entire region. It was classic secular repression. Central Asian Muslims, however, demanded greater autonomy. In this case, the Uzbekistan government, still under Soviet authority at this point, appeased the Muslims' demands, doubtless fearing greater disorder.

Secular repression was not finished, though. It would become the uniform pattern of governance among the Central Asian republics following independence. These authoritarian states, often ruled by officials of the former Soviet communist government who shared its ideology of secularism, would closely manage and regulate the religion of their overwhelmingly Muslim populations. They would promote a moderate version of Islam, trading upon the prevalence of the Hanafi school of jurisprudence (Sunni Islam's most liberal) among the region's population.[76] They would repress traditional Islam, not merely *jihadi* terrorists, but also movements that participate peacefully in the political system in order to promote Islamic laws and governance. As with secular repression elsewhere, these elites ruled populations who were far more religious than they were, people whose voice the Tashkent demonstrators channeled in 1989.

The Soviet Union had incorporated the territories of all the Central Asian republics into its empire by the mid-1920s, less than a decade after the Bolshevik Revolution of October 1917. The government in Moscow sought to dominate the republics by drawing their borders inconsistently with ethnic and national lines, thus creating minorities and fomenting strife, and by encouraging Russians, the Soviet Empire's dominant nationality, to settle there. Faithful to Karl Marx in judging religion to be the "opiate of the masses," the Soviet government sought to destroy Islam, just as it sought to destroy the Orthodox Church, other Christian churches, and Jewry. The greatest repression took place under Joseph Stalin in the 1930s. In Tajikistan, a majority of mosques were destroyed and manifold religious leaders ousted, and in Azerbaijan, a thoroughgoing campaign of secularization reduced the number of mosques from 1,400 in 1928 to 17 five years later.[77] Similar repression took place in the other republics.

Islam proved resilient. It "survived in Central Asia despite 150 years of Russian and Soviet efforts to eliminate it," writes Shireen T. Hunter, an expert on the region.[78] Going underground, Islam was practiced in clandestine mosques and homes and persisted there even while, in the 1960s, the

Soviet government created "official Islam," opening mosques and madrassas under its supervision and training leaders. Earlier, the Soviet government had created "spiritual boards" to govern Islam. Meanwhile, violent militant groups also appeared, some coming from outside the region, some rising up indigenously. They were encouraged by the Iranian Revolution of 1979, by the Soviet–Afghan war of the 1980s, which Hunter calls "the midwife to militant and extremist Islam," and by the Soviets' own repressive policies, which stifled the educational and leadership structures of mainstream Islam, co-opted moderate Muslim leaders, and thus created a vacuum of legitimate authority that conservative, uneducated mullahs moved to fill.[79]

When the Soviet Union dissolved, though, it was not Muslims but rather secular repressive officials, many of them elites from the Soviet era, who seized power. They created regimes with laws, policies, and institutions much like the secular repressive ones in the Arab world: a government ministry to oversee religion; registration requirements for religions; governance of mosques and imams; the forbidding or close monitoring of the teaching of religion in schools; the restriction of religious publications; and the banning of religious parties (with the exception of Tajikistan, which decided to allow them in 1999).[80] All of these regimes justify these policies with secular ideology but also by appealing to the need to suppress Islamic terrorism and to prevent a repressive Islamic state. The region's religious minorities—Christians, Jews, sometimes others, typically totaling less than 5% of the population—are allowed to practice their faith but are heavily restricted, harassed, and strictly forbidden from proselytizing.

Among the republics, there are variations in specifics and severity. In 2014, the US State Department labeled Uzbekistan and Turkmenistan "Countries of Particular Concern," thus including them among the nine worst countries in the world for their levels of religious freedom. Azerbaijan, Kazakhstan, and Tajikistan (as well as Uzbekistan and Turkmenistan) all fall into the "very high" tier of Pew's GRI of 2014. Tajikistan has adopted harshly restrictive policies in recent years, which it justifies as necessary to fight terrorists. For instance, it has passed a law that prohibits young people (under 18) from attending religious activities, even setting up cameras at mosques to assess whether they are present; arrested imams for teaching religion to young people; restricted where Muslims can pray; closed hundreds of unregistered mosques and subjected groups operating without registration to fines, jail, and deportation; and forbidden women from wearing the *hijab* and men under 50 from wearing beards in public schools.[81]

The Central Asian republics imposed such repression at a time when their Muslim populations clamored to break free from privatized confinement and assert their public voice. Even in the penultimate years of the Soviet Union, the region's Muslims began praying openly in unofficial mosques, which greatly outnumbered official ones, opening Qur'anic schools, and publishing *samizdat* (i.e., banned by the state) religious literature.

Illustrative was Radbek Nisanbai, the holder of a position known as the Qazi in the city of Almaty, Kazakhstan, who, prior to the dissolution of the Soviet Union, defiantly had himself elected grand mufti of Kazakhstan independently of the official Soviet Muslim Religious Board based in Tashkent. Nisanbai opened Kazakhstan's first madrasa in 1991, printed a monthly Islamic newspaper, and published his own translation of the Qur'an into Kazakh.[82]

During these same years, Muslim organizations and parties were born. Although Islam competed with other causes like nationalism, tribalism, and environmentalism, Islam was a unifying force and rallying cry among diverse oppositional forces.[83] At first, the largest of these was the Islamic Renaissance Party (IRP) of Tajikistan, which aspired to bridge nation and ethnicity and unite the entire region through Islam. Initially, the party enjoyed popular strength in Tajikistan and also had a strong presence in Uzbekistan and Turkmenistan, but it was subsequently banned and today conducts political activity only in Tajikistan.[84] At a defining conference in 1990, the IRP called for establishing *sharia* courts and the teaching of Islam in public schools but did not call for an official Islamic state or endorse militant strategies. IRP's Islamism was a moderate one, striving to increase the presence of Islam in society while participating in politics peacefully and democratically. It claimed an impressive 20,000 members in December 1991, when Tajikistan's independence from the Soviet Union was recognized.[85]

Radical Islamic groups have also arisen in the region, proclaiming Islamic states with strong *sharia* law as their mission, some of them adopting violence, including terrorism. They have increased since 1998, are often sustained by sources in Afghanistan, Saudi Arabia, and Pakistan, and win followers at home by advocating a return to Islamic faith and opposing corruption, economic stagnation, and authoritarianism. There is the Islamic Party of Azerbaijan, a Shia group that was alleged to have close ties with Iran, formed during the period of transition to independence under the Soviet Union in December 1991, was given legal registration in 1992, but was then banned in 1996.[86] More successful among Islamist groups was Hizb ut-Tahrir (HT), a secretive international Sunni movement that envisions a transnational Caliphate and allegedly supports terrorist activity across the region. Among Islamist groups, HT has grown steadily across Central Asia from 1992 to 2007, according to political scientist Kathleen Collins, a scholar of Central Asia. In 2007, Collins judged it to be the largest Islamist opposition group in the region, estimating it to comprise 10,000–20,000 members in Uzbekistan, 3,000–10,000 in Tajikistan, 3,000–5,000 in Kyrgyzstan, and a few hundred in Kazakhstan.[87] Notable also is the Islamic Movement of Uzbekistan, which formed in 1998 with the goal of overthrowing Uzbeki President Islam Karimov but more recently has allied itself closely with international terrorist networks, declaring in 2015 that it was a part of ISIS. Although militant groups like these are unlikely to overthrow any regime, they contribute to internal discord, foment tensions among the republics, and give regimes pretexts for continued dictatorial rule.

Militant groups have multiplied in their ranks in good part in response to secularist authoritarian repression. In Uzbekistan, where President Karimov cracked down on religion shortly after independence and has jailed more than 6,000 political prisoners, "[e]very wave of repression has further radicalized the Islamic movements and creates a more receptive atmosphere for radical ideas," according to Hunter.[88] No region illustrates how repression begets radicalization as vividly and bloodily as Tajikistan. There, the neo-Communist government that emerged after independence did not wish to share power with anyone and banned all opposition parties and organizations in 1993, whether they were Islamic, nationalist, or democratic. The repression was so severe that it produced hundreds of thousands of refugees.[89] In response, the Islamic forces, led by the IRP, forged a coalition with secular organizations and waged war against the government—a conflict that lasted five years and took between 50,000 and 100,000 lives. The IRP's turn to violence was a dramatic change in its mission and identity and accompanied its embrace of more radical Islamist goals. A peace agreement in 1997 required the government to incorporate opposition parties in power structures, but in practical terms their participation has remained limited. After a 1999 referendum permitted religiously based parties to form, the IRP became one of the main opposition parties in the republic. After signing the peace agreement, it had reaffirmed its commitment to nonviolence, democratic participation, and a state that would not be explicitly Islamic—something much like a European Christian Democratic party. The party, however, failed to regain its political support, hampered by its ideological wavering, its internal divisions over what kind of Islamism to advocate, and its failure to establish networks of broad national support among the population.[90] It has never won more than about 10% of the vote in a national election, and in 2015, it was weakened further when the government banned it and designated it a terrorist organization. Although the Tajikistan government relaxed its secularist repression somewhat after the end of the country's civil war, it continues to harass and thereby contain its religious opposition.

Secular Repression and Religious Freedom in the Muslim World

Secular repression has widely meant detention without trial, torture, lengthy prison terms, and even death for its opponents. Imagine a candid (if unlikely) conversation in which a secular repressive dictator was asked to justify these abuses of human rights. His response might well begin with Mubarak's quip: "It's me or the Muslim Brotherhood." He would be saying, in the terms of this book, that the alternative to secular repression is inevitably religious repression: Iran, Saudi Arabia. Were I to throw open the country to full democracy, he might continue, this would spell the end of democracy. The Islamists would take over and would prevent future competition for power, just as the Nazi Party shut down democracy after coming to power with one-third of the popular vote in Germany in 1933. One man, one vote, one time.

The so-called moderates who profess to want to participate in the political system? It's only a tactic, he says. Once they are powerful enough, they will install an Islamist dictatorship. This would spell the end of protection for Christian minorities. The modernization of the country? That would end, too. Electricity and running water for rural villages? Forget about it. The building of the nation, scientific progress, opportunities for women? That will disappear. For women, it will be back to the *hijab*, and for all of us it will be back to superstition and feudalism.

One day we can have democracy and freedom for all, he might continue. We already have a parliament and constitutional provisions for religious freedom. Until agitators for Islamism can be quelled, though, free institutions will have to be constrained. Nattering westerners do well to remember that their own liberal democracies took centuries to develop.

Implicit in the dictator's argument, and in secularist ideology in general, is a skeptical view of Islam. Remember that Islamoskeptics claim that Islam is hardwired for violence and harsh intolerance and indisposed to liberal democracy. In the West, Islamoskeptics can be found among conservatives, secular liberals, and certain feminists. To this group can be joined the secularists who have held power in the Muslim-majority world over the past century. Islam must be privatized or perhaps refashioned, they hold, because its public influence is inimical to equality and social progress. It is because of the Islamic threat that more ample freedom is not possible yet, the secularist claims.

Is our dictator's skepticism supported by the experience of secular repressive regimes that we have explored in this chapter? No, his analysis is rife with problems.

The root problem with this view is its dichotomy of Western freedom versus Islamic unfreedom. Islamoskeptics commonly believe that the West is uniquely suited to religious freedom because of its Christian roots, its Reformation, its Enlightenment, or all of the above. Recall that, in an unholy alliance, the new critics of religious freedom share this dichotomy, for they, too, see religious freedom as the result of the Western liberal trajectory. They differ with Islamoskeptics in rejecting the superiority of Western religious freedom, call for more understanding and tolerance of Islam's differences, and warn against efforts to impose religious freedom on Islam or to see Islam as the enemy of it. Still, their analysis rests upon the dichotomy.

The dichotomy, however, is false, and the history of secular repression in the Muslim-majority world proves why. The Western experience cannot be equated with religious freedom, for it contains at least two paradigms of relationship between the state and religion: the French Revolution, which brusquely suppresses religious freedom, and the American Revolution, which favors it.

It was the French Revolution, not the American Revolution, that inspired Atatürk and the secular repressive rulers who followed in his wake. These rulers and their regimes did not discover Islam to be a threat. Rather, they proffered a vision by which Islam could only be a threat. Following Enlightenment philosophers, they thought that they had on their side pure reason, that their conclusions were ones at which any rational person would arrive were he or she unshackled from superstition, hierarchy, and ignorance. The march of reason through history required a vanguard to lead it, and they would be this vanguard. It was out of this reasoning that they governed mosques, seized religious property, required that secularism be taught in the schools, had their government ministers write Friday sermons, and jailed their opponents.[91]

What these rulers did not allow was that their version of rationality was only one version of rationality and that religious people, on the very basis of their convictions, might also support modern economies and institutions.[92] Ironically, Muslim religious parties have been some of the strongest advocates of greater democracy and religious freedom in the history of the secular repressive republics. It is unsurprising that they supported popular rule because the populations of these republics remained far more religious than their rulers, or that they wished to dismantle the apparatus of the secular repressive state because religious people like to conduct their own religious affairs. In Turkey, it was the Muslim parties who rose up to contest elections and were tamped down decennially when they became too successful. In Algeria, Egypt, and Tajikistan, too, Islamic parties demanded participation in electoral politics and were then repressed, eliciting violent unrest and civil war.

It cannot be denied that all of these republics also contained Islamists, including violent ones, who would impose religious repression were they to take power. The point is rather to challenge the dichotomy of Western and free versus Islamic and unfree. In these republics, religious repression was imposed not by Islam but rather by an ideology incubated in the civilization that is allegedly tolerant, whereas often, religious freedom was demanded by spokespeople for the civilization that is alleged to be inhospitable to freedom. The dichotomy cannot be sustained.

The Western provenance of most secular repressive republics is made somewhat more complex by the fact that most of them had been colonies of Western powers or else territories of the Soviet Empire. Espousing nationalism and anti-imperialism, they demanded freedom from imperial rule. Still, they sought to be modern like their erstwhile master. They wished to become modern on their own. Although Turkey, the standard-bearer of the pattern, had not been a colony, its predecessor, the Ottoman Empire, had experienced the cultural, political, and sometimes military interference of the Western great powers, while Atatürk voiced nationalism and anticolonialism as central themes.

Now we may offer a critique of our secular dictator's rationale for repression. First, this repression cannot be justified simply as a response to an Islamist threat. Again, the threat of Islamist violence is often real, not simply a product of secular repression, and is justifiably contained through force. The secular dictator's repression, though, is motivated by something beyond security, namely a mission to create a secular society, a mission that, given the religiosity of the surrounding population, must of necessity be illiberal and authoritarian. Our dictator is not merely defending the security of citizens; he is defending an ideology.

Second, secular repressive regimes do not simply repress radical or militant groups, contrary to their rhetoric. They also repress groups of more moderate Muslims who profess a commitment to political participation and engagement. These regimes suppress these groups when they show promise of electoral victory or else of staying in power long enough to begin to dismantle the apparatus of secular repression. Secular dictators disbelieve, or at least profess to doubt, the finding that sociologists Charles Kurzman and Ijlal Naqvi have demonstrated and will be explained in the next chapter, namely that when Islamist parties compete in elections they do not fare well.

Third, these regimes feed the problem they are trying to suppress. It is worth repeating again that secular repressive regimes are not the only cause of Islamist militancy. Their wide repression, however, has contributed to fierce backlash by convincing Islamists that only through the gun can they influence politics. Egypt under Sadat and Mubarak; Algeria under the FLN in the late 1980s and early 1990s; Tajikistan under neo-Communist rule; Turkey under its Kemalist military in the second half of the 20th century: In all of these cases, repressive, exclusionary tactics of regimes have contributed to the rise of violent Islamist groups. Our dictator says that democracy and freedom are not possible until these groups are tamped down, but he does not acknowledge that his tamping down leads them to rise up.

Fourth, secular repressive regimes have been weakened by their economic failures and their proneness to corruption. The socialist, state-led economic policies of Turkey, Egypt, and other newly independent Arab states stalled within a couple of decades of being adopted. Economic growth slowed and bureaucracies became calcified and stultified. As a result, these regimes suffered in their legitimacy and gave rise to demands for new policies, new parties, and the opportunity to compete politically—demands to which religious parties, among others, could appeal. When regimes failed to meet these demands, some of their political opponents turned to violence.

Finally, one rationale for secular repression turns out to be mixed in its merits: its protection for minorities. True, the Assads can be credited for protecting Alawites and Christians in Syria; Sadat and Mubarak for protecting Copts in Egypt; Qaddafi for protecting Christians in Libya; and Saddam Hussein for guarding Chaldean Christians in Iraq. There is no question that these and other minorities—Jews, Baha'is, Shias within Sunni populations, and others—suffer discrimination, harassment, and violence from surrounding populations. Can secularist ideology take credit for protecting these minorities against the zealous majority? Perhaps in part; a commitment to guarding minorities may well complement a commitment to preventing Muslim religious dominance. These regimes also derive a strong tactical advantage from protecting minorities, namely precious political loyalty in a milieu where their secularism leaves them outnumbered.

This same tactical dimension, though, means that protection for minorities will often be compromised. The allegedly more protective secular regimes will often look the other way when minorities are mistreated and even subject to vigilante violence at the hands of fellow countrymen—as when a Muslim converts to Christianity, for instance. There are some minorities for whom these same regimes provide little protection at all. Baha'is, for instance, can expect little but persecution at the hands of virtually any secular repressive regime (and even more so, any religiously repressive regime) in the Muslim-majority world.

Secular repressive regimes sometimes extend to minorities the same repressive controls that they place on Muslims: Witness Sadat's treatment of Pope

Shenouda, for instance. Other secularist regimes have quite poor records of treating minorities all around. Consider only Turkey's record of harsh control and discrimination against Sufis, Alevis, and Christians. Under almost every secular repressive regime in the Muslim world, Jewish populations, which in many of these countries numbered in the tens of thousands prior to secular rule, have dwindled to a small fraction of this number. True, the same can be said for their fate in many religiously repressive Muslim-majority countries. Still, this modern exodus detracts from the claim of secularist dictators that, despite their repression, they succeed in protecting minorities. Finally, secular regimes' protection of non-Muslim minorities sometimes has the perverse effect of rendering these minorities objects of attack at the hands of the regime's opponents, who regard them as allies of the regime.

These criticisms are naive, our interlocutor, the autocrat, will reply. It is all well and good to summon freedom when you don't have *jihadis* outside your door ready to take over. The autocrat's problem, though, is not just the *jihadi* threat but also his own quest for a New Society that is cold to his people's longings for the transcendent. There is an alternative to both secular and religious repression, which is religious freedom. It is an alternative that almost one-fourth of Muslim-majority countries have achieved and that major Muslim movements in countries like Tunisia and Indonesia advocate actively. The secular autocrat has not pursued this alternative robustly.

4

Religiously Repressive States in the Muslim World

ALTHOUGH THE LAST two chapters have argued that Islam is not hardwired for violence, even a casual consumer of contemporary news in the West is likely to ask these questions: What about Orlando, the episode recalled in the Introduction? Or Paris? Or the Islamic State? Or the attacks of September 11, 2001? A more informed observer might add this: What about the many Muslims around the world who have been victims of Muslim terrorism? These phenomena did not appear motivated by rationales of religious freedom or secular repression.

And: What about Asia Bibi?

Asia Bibi is a Catholic woman from a small village in Pakistan where, like many of Pakistan's Christians, she worked in a menial job, namely as a farmhand. Hers was the only family of Christians in a village of Muslims who frequently exhorted her to convert to Islam.

One day in June 2009, when Bibi was harvesting berries with other farmhands, she slaked her thirst using a metal cup lying next to a well. A neighbor, one whose family had been feuding with Bibi's over property, spotted her and inveighed against her for drinking from the same cup as Muslims, who consider Christians to be unclean. According to Bibi, in the heated argument that followed, the neighbor insulted her Christian faith, to which she responded, "I believe in my religion and in Jesus Christ, who died on the cross for the sins of mankind. What did your Prophet Muhammed ever do to save mankind?"[1] Her fellow villagers reported to a cleric that she had insulted Muhammad—that is, committed blasphemy.

In Pakistan, blasphemy is not merely an insult or an offense; it is a crime. Enforcing it are not only the police and the courts but also enraged fellow citizens. Hearing of Bibi's words, a mob visited her home and beat her and members of her family before the police came and protected her. Subsequently she was arrested and began her ordeal in Pakistan's court system. She was placed in solitary confinement in a Lahore prison after originally being sentenced to death by hanging by a Punjabi judge in November 2010.

Two prominent government ministers who advocated on her behalf, Salmon Taseer, the Muslim governor of Punjab, and Shahbaz Bhatti, minister of Minorities Affairs, were assassinated by Islamist militants. International human rights groups, Pope Benedict XVI, and 540,000 signers of a petition came to Bibi's defense. Many Pakistanis were less sympathetic toward her. A crowd in Rawalpindi demonstrated by chanting "hang her, hang her." On July 22, 2015, the Supreme Court of Pakistan suspended her death penalty sentence for the duration of the appeals process. Finally, in October 2018, the Supreme Court of Pakistan acquitted Bibi and released her from prison.

Pakistan is the first country to declare itself an Islamic state. The worldwide resurgence of Islam in the 1970s and 1980s brought to Pakistan the laws and the beliefs that later resulted in Bibi's arrest, legal fate, and treatment at the hands of her fellow citizens. As was true elsewhere, Islamist laws arose from popular pressure, then encouraged the further spread of Islamist beliefs among the population, and were often enforced by vigilante citizens who found the legal system insufficiently zealous.

Pakistan manifests the third pattern of governance of religion explored in this book: religious repression. The world's religiously repressive Muslim-majority regimes are listed in Table 4.1 and are represented on the map in Figure 4.1.

Religious repression is the pattern to which Islamoskeptics point to make their case. Where did this pattern come from? What are its underlying ideas? And how ought it to shape our judgments of Islam?

Islamism Straight Up: The Thought of Sayyid Qutb

It is hard to find a more forceful, pure, and influential articulation of Islamist thinking than in the writings of Egyptian intellectual Sayyid Qutb. Born in 1906, Qutb was a profound and prolific writer, having penned novels, poems, art criticism, and commentary on the Qur'an in addition to books on social justice and politics. Qutb spent 1948 to 1950 in the United States, where he was repulsed by everything from materialism to bad haircuts to sexual licentiousness, which he claimed to have observed even in churches, and was fortified in his commitment to Islam. Back in Egypt during the 1950s and early 1960s, he became the most prominent member of the Muslim Brotherhood,

Table 4.1. Religiously Repressive Muslim-Majority States and Their GRI Score (according to 2009 Pew Report)

- Saudi Arabia (8.4)
- Iran (8.3)
- Maldives (7.2)
- Malaysia (6.8)
- Brunei (6.7)
- Indonesia (6.6)
- Mauritania (6.5)
- Pakistan (6.5)
- Sudan (5.6)
- Afghanistan (5.3)
- Kuwait (5.0)
- Yemen (4.9)
- Iraq (4.8)
- Somalia (4.5)
- Oman (4.5)
- Bangladesh (4.4)
- United Arab Emirates (4.1)
- Bahrain (4.0)
- Qatar (3.9)
- Comoros (3.9)
- Nigeria (3.6)

the popular Islamic revivalist organization founded in Egypt. In 1952, he and the Muslim Brotherhood cooperated with Gamal Abdel Nasser and his Free Officers Movement in overthrowing Egypt's pro-Western government. After serving as a close adviser to Nasser, Qutb became disillusioned when he realized that Nasser intended to establish a secular nationalist regime, not an Islamist one. Qutb then broke with Nasser and joined in a plot to assassinate him in 1954. The Egyptian government foiled the plot, imprisoned Qutb, and eventually executed him in 1966. In prison Qutb wrote two enduring works: a 30-volume commentary on the Qur'an called *In the Shade of the Quran*, and a political tract, *Milestones*, published in 1964. After Qutb died—and in no small part because he died as a martyr—his writings inspired a generation of militant *jihadis*, not least Osama bin Laden and fellow ringleaders of Al-Qaeda.

Milestones stands as the most memorable statement of Islamism ever written. Parallels to Marxism come to mind. Like Karl Marx's *Communist*

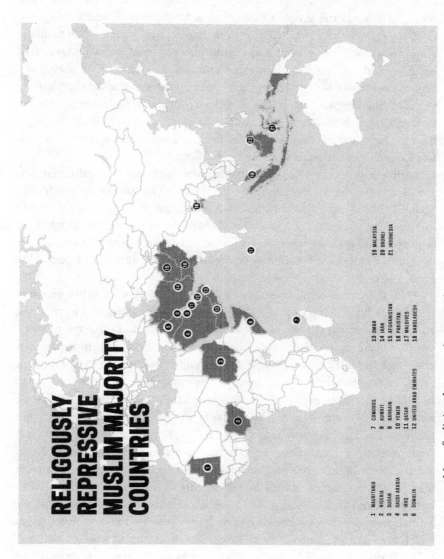

RELIGIOUSLY REPRESSIVE MUSLIM MAJORITY COUNTRIES

1 MAURITANIA	7 COMOROS	13 OMAN
2 NIGERIA	8 KUWAIT	14 IRAN
3 SUDAN	9 BAHRAIN	15 AFGHANISTAN
4 SAUDI ARABIA	10 YEMEN	16 PAKISTAN
5 IRAQ	11 QATAR	17 MALDIVES
6 SOMALIA	12 UNITED ARAB EMIRATES	18 BANGLADESH
		19 MALAYSIA
		20 BRUNEI
		21 INDONESIA

FIGURE 4.1. Map of religiously repressive countries

Manifesto, Milestones offers a diagnosis of global crisis, a revolutionary solution, and a strategy for achieving it. Qutb believes that he stands at a
turning point in history—a "crucial and bewildering juncture," he calls it.[2]
He diagnoses the world's illness as *jahiliyyah*, the darkness or barbarism that
prevailed prior to the Prophet Mohammad. *Jahiliyyah* is a rebellion against
God's sovereignty on earth, a state of servitude to human rather than to divine
authority.[3] Western European and Communist societies are *jahili*, Qutb tells
us, as are India, Japan, the Philippines, and Africa as well as "[a]ll Jewish and
Christian societies today." Then, Qutb jarringly avers that all of the "existing
so-called Muslim" societies are *jahili* as well.[4] Although their people may believe in God, they have substituted for God other systems of authority. Even
though Qutb does not mention Nasser by name, one can imagine that Nasser
was lodged in his mind as he sat in his cell writing.

Qutb's solution is revival. The Muslim community has been extinct for several centuries, and it is time to revive it.[5] Evoking Vladimir Lenin and Joseph
Stalin, Qutb calls for vanguard leadership to ignite in one country what will
eventually become a global revolution. What does a renunciation of *jahilliyah*
require? More than anything else, an acknowledgment of *tawhid*, or the oneness of God. All of society should be submitted to God, and every aspect of life
should be under God's sovereignty, Qutb exhorts.[6]

How will *tawhid* come to replace *jahilliyah*? Qutb's answer to this question
reveals much about his view of religious freedom. It is primarily by preaching
and persuasion that Islam will capture hearts and minds, he asserts, pointing
out that the Prophet Muhammad did not impose belief.[7] Qutb insists several times in *Milestones* that people should enjoy the freedom to choose their
religious beliefs, which cannot be forced or compelled, and that the Qur'an
mandates this freedom.[8] Perhaps it is surprising to hear this view from a
writer who is known for inspiring militants who have fought for anything but
religious freedom. Elsewhere in Qutb's writings, though, he articulates religious freedom even more strongly, indeed in terms strongly reminiscent of
the argument in this book. In his classic, *In the Shade of the Quran*, he makes
it clear that religion manifests the very nature of the person, who embraces
faith out of knowledge, reason, mind, and conscience. From this fact flows the
human right of religious freedom: "Freedom of belief is the first human right
which gives the attribute of 'insan' (humanity) to the human being. Whoever
robs a human being of freedom of belief in fact robs him of humanity," he
writes.[9] None other than history's most famous Islamist, then, unambigu-
ously endorses religious freedom and grounds it in the nature and dignity of
the human person.

Do we cast aspersions, then, when we associate Qutb with the aggressive promotion of Islam at the expense of other faiths? No, his reputation is deserved. For even while insisting that religion cannot and should not be coerced, Qutb calls for *jihad* against institutions and social structures—economic, cultural, political—that he believes stand in the way of people making a free choice for Islam, namely the structures of *jahili* societies. Qutb argues that Muslims are commanded to initiate coercive, military force against societies whose subservience to human authority amounts to an obstacle to its members' adoption of Islam. Islam, after all, is not merely a belief but a way of life that pertains to every realm. Thus, all beliefs, concepts, and political, social, economic, racial, and class structures that impede humans' freedom to accept the sovereignty of God must be fought both with preaching as well as with what Qutb calls "the movement"—a euphemism for coercion.[10] Qutb ridicules the notion that Islam prescribes only defensive responses to *jahili* societies. Muslims are commanded to fight. They are commanded to remove the chains that constrict other people from seeing and freely embracing the truth of Islam. What we have here is a doctrine of offensive warfare.

It is this doctrine—that laws, institutions, and social structures not oriented toward God in accordance with Islam are rightly subject to attack—that threatens religious freedom. Qutb never advocates explicitly the coercive restriction of worship or religious practice among Christians, Jews, Hindus, or other non-Muslims. He construes what is an obstacle to Islam so widely, however, that it is not hard to imagine how an interpreter of his could come to see another religion's worship and practice as a barrier to the free embrace of Islam—especially an interpreter disposed toward militancy. It is not hard to imagine, that is, how a reader of Qutb might end up attacking Ahmadis in Pakistan, burning churches in Indonesia, or torturing Baha'is in Iran.

What Islamists Believe

Qutb is the most famous Islamist but not the first or the only prominent Islamist. Widely regarded as pioneers of Islamism are Egypt's Hassan Al-Banna, who founded the Muslim Brotherhood in 1928, and Abu Ala Al-Mawdudi, a Pakistani who founded Jamaat-e-Islami (JI). Al-Banna and Mawdudi in turn drew from previous currents of thought like the Wahhabi and Salafi movements. To this day, both the Muslim Brotherhood and JI remain mass transnational movements that carry on their founders' vision of Islamic revival in all spheres of life, including the political. It was Qutb who took a turn toward a far more militant approach to revival, openly advocating violent *jihad.* The 1970s saw an explosion of Islamist parties and movements—a portion of which are terrorist groups—fueled by a popular revival of belief and practice throughout the Muslim world. Sharing in revival, too, have been the minority Shia Muslims. In 1971, Ayatollah Seyyed Ruholla Khomeini, writing from exile from Iran in the Iraqi city Najaf, made the case for an innovation in Shia tradition that would allow *ulema* to govern—his theory of guardianship of the jurist, or *velayat-e faqih.*

Foundational to Al-Banna's and Mawdudi's analysis and to all subsequent Islamist thought, as we saw in Qutb, is the diagnosis of *jahilliyah.* Islam had lost the glory that it had enjoyed centuries earlier when it had flourished as a civilization, Islamists have argued, largely because of secularism, a program for society that rejects the sovereignty of God. Behind secularism, in turn, was the West, whose ideas infected Islam both by being actively embraced by Muslims and through Islam's subordination to colonial rule, which, by the early 20th century, dominated Islam from West Africa to the Middle East to Indonesia. Nothing symbolized Islam's decline more saliently than the abolition of the Caliphate by the Republic of Turkey in 1924. From the time of the Prophet Muhammad's death, caliphs had claimed—though rarely with universal recognition—to rule over the *umma,* or entire community of Muslims. The last Ottoman caliph yielded to the founding of a secular, sovereign state modeled on the West.

The solution to *jahiliyyah,* Islamists believe, is a return to the first community of believers, who interpreted *tawhid,* the oneness of God, as well as the sovereignty of God to mean that Islamic law ought to pervade all of life. Islamists want to see secular orders replaced by ones in which religion is not separated from the legal and political spheres. Such conditions will enable Muslims to live good Muslim lives.[11]

Islamists are critical of the sovereign state, which they believe supplants the sovereignty of God and serves to divide the *umma.* Mawdudi, for instance, opposed statehood for Pakistan as a homeland for Muslims at the time of Pakistan's founding in the 1940s. Yet, although skeptical of the sovereign state, Islamists, like Qutb, propose to use the modern state in the short term as a vehicle to spread Islamic revolution. After the sovereign state of Pakistan became a reality, Mawdudi participated in Pakistani politics for three decades, though he always remained a reluctant nationalist and supporter of the state.[12] Within the state, the form of government is not greatly important to Islamists so long as it suffuses the society with Islamic teaching. There is no strong consensus among Islamists in favor of reviving the caliph.[13] With the exception of Khomeini, Islamists do not favor religious leaders holding political positions, though they look to them for guidance in politics.

Islamism is a political program. This is what makes it an "ism"—that is, an ideology—much like liberalism, Marxism, and Keynesianism. Islamism advocates using law, policy, and state power to promote a strict and strongly conservative form of the tenets of Islam in all spheres of life—family life, economy, culture, religious practice, education, dress, and many others. This political program takes place in a surrounding world that is hostile to it. Operating hand in hand with secularism is the legacy of colonial oppression; it is the rich and powerful states that most defile Islam. What is called for in response is a world revolution in which oppressive economic and political structures fall while Islam rises. Offensive war and violence are each a *modus operandi*. The state is a temporary vehicle for this revolution but will crumble one day before the united world *umma*. Resonant, again, are the dreams of Marx and Lenin.[14]

Not everyone who advocates adherence to strict Islamic teachings in the social realm is an Islamist. Scholar of Islam Olivier Roy distinguishes between Islamists and fundamentalists, who also advocate making the world thoroughly Islamic, but do not pursue an assertive political program. What sort of person becomes an Islamist? It is not the *ulema*, or religious authorities, who become Islamist, Roy points out; rather, the *ulema* scorn Islamists for their revolutionary agenda and heretical interpretations while being scorned by Islamists in turn. Although Islamists' beards and robes may manifest medievalism, they are products of the modern world. They are urban. They use cell phones and computers. Most are university educated, often in the sciences and engineering. Frequently, though, they were denied opportunity in the face of failing economies and corrupt regimes. So, their resentment was kindled.[15]

Islamism and Religious Freedom

The promotion of Islam by the state that Islamists envision results in the direct denial of religious freedom. Like Qutb, Islamists do not argue that the state can or ought to force people to believe. The vigorous enforcement of religious speech and behavior through law and policy in a quest for a thoroughly Islamized environment, though, frequently involves the restriction of faiths other than Islam as well as dissenters within Islam. Often, the restriction is harsh.

What are some of the Islamist state's tools for restriction? A clause in the constitution that declares Islam the official religion of the state or that no law shall contradict Islam often paves the way for a whole range of more specific restrictions. Notorious, too, are codes against blasphemy and apostasy.

Consider the law under which Asia Bibi was prosecuted, Section 295-C of the Pakistani legal code, "Defiling the Name of Muhammad," which mandates the death penalty for actions that Pakistan's Federal Shari'a Court has defined thus:

> Reviling or insulting the Prophet in writing or speech; speaking profanely or contemptuously about him or his family; attacking the Prophet's dignity and honor in an abusive manner; vilifying him or making an ugly face when his name is mentioned; showing enmity or hatred towards him, his family, his companions, and the Muslims; accusing, or slandering the Prophet and his family, including spreading evil reports about him or his family; defaming the Prophet; refusing the Prophet's jurisdiction or judgment in any manner; rejecting the Sunnah; showing disrespect, contempt for or rejection of the rights of Allah and His Prophet or rebelling against Allah and his Prophet.[16]

In many Islamist settings, terms like blasphemy and apostasy are invoked without precision, an ambiguity that enables exploitation. Harsh also are laws that declare an entire sect of Islam to be apostate, as do laws against the Ahmadiyya sect in Pakistan and Indonesia or against the Baha'is in Iran. Such laws are often enforced through sharp repression; in Iran, Baha'is are subject to imprisonment and torture at the hands of the Iranian government. Even when dissenting sects or religious minorities are allowed to operate, Islamist governments can make it difficult for them to build houses of worship, express their faith through the media, and practice their faith in a host of other ways. Islamist states exercise a strong hand in governing universities, schools, seminaries, and houses of worship, and they regulate spheres of life ranging from dress to marriage to observance of the faith. Table 4.2 summarizes ways in which religiously repressive regimes curtail religious freedom.

All of these restrictions constrain religious freedom not only directly but also through "multiplier effects." One of these is fear. If Islamist laws and policies prevent some citizens from speaking and practicing contrary to the regime directly through force, they deter many other citizens through the fear that they will suffer the same treatment. Restrictions on religious freedom imposed through law and policy also give a green light to militant groups to act as vigilantes and enforce Islamism on their own. To use Pew categories, government restrictions encourage social hostilities. To be sure, militant groups often act extralegally and through terrorist violence, but

Table 4.2. What to Look for in a Religiously Repressive Muslim-Majority Regime

- The constitution declares the state an Islamic state; may contain a clause saying that *sharia* is "a" or "the" source of legislation; and may contain a clause saying that no law may contradict *sharia*.
- Laws that prohibit and penalize apostasy and/or blasphemy.
- Laws that forbid conversion away from Islam; and/or proselytism.
- A state ministry governs mosques, schools for training clerics, and other religious institutions so as to prohibit a moderate version of Islam and to promote a conservative or traditional version of Islam.
- The regime governs expressions of religion in publications, broadcasting, and dress so as to promote conservative or traditional Islam and to hinder liberal Islam or secular views.
- The regime governs education so as promote a traditional or conservative version of Islam; may force non-Muslims to be educated in it; and/or may prohibit education in other religions.
- The regime outlaws or heavily restricts versions of Islam deemed heterodox.
- The regime outlaws, heavily restricts, or denies equality and religious freedom to non-Muslim religions.
- Personal status law is conservative and is adjudicated either through special courts or through general courts that apply it.

they do so with the implicit encouragement of the government and often with confidence in impunity. Just as government policy and law empowers Islamist groups outside the government, Islamist groups reciprocally pressure and empower governments to promote their agenda. When politicians see Islamism growing popular among the people, they fear losing support or even suffering violence should they refuse to take up the Islamists' agenda, but they also see the opportunity to bolster their power and perpetuate their rule so that they may pursue endeavors like economic modernization. Scholar of Islam Vali Nasr shows how, for instance, politicians in both Pakistan and Malaysia gained in power by allying with Islamists and promoting their cause.[17]

Religiously Repressive States

Let us see how Islamism is manifested in countries with Muslim-majority populations—the religiously repressive states.

Iran

The Supreme Leader of the Islamic Revolution: Thus runs the title of Iran's most powerful leader. The title expresses succinctly how Ayatollah Khomeini viewed the regime that he established when he overthrew Iran's monarch, Shah Pahlavi, in 1979. Espousing the revival of Islam in all spheres of life, flouting the imperialism of the Great Satan, the United States, and emitting a clear cry of revolution, Khomeini embodied the tenets of Islamism. Note what the title makes him the leader of: not the *Iranian* revolution but rather the *Islamic* revolution, one beckoning Muslims everywhere. Indeed, Islamists around the world were buoyed by this signal success. The Iranian Revolution did for Islamism what the Soviet Revolution of 1917 did for Communism—convince potential fellow travelers around the world that the revolution was on the march.

The Iranian Revolution did not succeed in unifying Islam. This was due in part to the demographics of the Shia sect, which is 90% of Iran's population but only 15% or so of the global Muslim population. Soon after its revolution, Iran became enemies with Saudi Arabia, which contains a Shia minority in the east, and with Iraq, whose dictator Saddam Hussein brutally repressed his country's Shia majority and with whom Iran fought a war that took over a million lives in the 1980s. Dictators in Muslim states around the world, fearing the fate of the shah, staved off revolution by preemptively establishing ties with clerics and adopting an Islamist agenda. Still, the Iranian Revolution was a landmark in the rise of Islamist politics.

The same revolution became a prototype for the Islamist suppression of religious freedom. Iran's government institutions were designed to promote Islamic law in every realm of life. The constitution declares that all laws and regulations must conform to Islam. A brand of Shia Islam known as Ja'afari [Twelver] is the official state religion. Heading the regime is the Supreme Leader of the Islamic Revolution—today, Ayatollah Ali Khamenei—who is chosen by a group of 86 Islamic scholars known as the Assembly of Experts and is empowered to defend the Islamic character of the state. He may veto the president's decisions and commands the army. An unelected Council of Guardians reviews—and may veto—all acts of the *Majlis* (parliament) and candidates for elected office according to the criteria of Islamic law. Absent from the Constitution are rights of Muslim citizens to adopt, change, or leave behind their religious beliefs. Two government ministries—the Ministry of Culture and Islamic Guidance [*Ershad*] and the Ministry of Intelligence and Security—keep a close eye on religious activity throughout the land.

Hitting nonconformists to Iran's official faith hardest are laws against apostasy and blasphemy. Anyone who commits blasphemy and any Muslim who commits apostasy is liable to execution. Although the regime has executed only a few people explicitly for apostasy, it has put many on trial for closely related crimes that include "friendship with enemies of God," "hostility towards friends of God," "corruption on earth," "fighting against God," "obstructing the way of God and the way towards happiness for all the disinherited people in the world," "spreading lies," "insulting the Prophet," "acting against the national security," "insulting Islam," "calling into question the Islamic foundations of the Republic," and, worst of all, *mohareb*, which is "making war against God and His Prophet." Many suspects of these crimes have been tried in Iran's revolutionary courts, which lack juries, where trials may last only a few minutes and lack appeal procedures, and where, according to Paul Marshall and Nina Shea, "judges are believed to know the 'right path' (*serate mostaqim*) and have accepted every means—including beating, lashing, solitary confinement, amputation, rape, sexual abuse, burning, starvation, and strangulation—to force defendants to follow it."[18]

The Constitution recognizes Christians, Jews, and Zoroastrians, all tiny minorities, as "people of the book," yet the government strongly restricts proselytizing, regularly arrests Christians and Zoroastrians for practicing religion, and closely monitors their activities, especially their schools. The government especially vilifies Jews. Recent President Mahmoud Ahmadinejad denied the Holocaust and called publicly for the destruction of Israel, and Ayatollah Khamenei called "Zionists" a "cancerous tumor." The Baha'is have it worst, suffering persecution just for being Baha'is, which Iran's Shia leaders consider a heretical sect of Islam. They suffer manifold forms of discrimination, including being barred from all leadership positions in the government, denied higher education, required to enroll their children in Muslim schools, and prevented from inheriting property. Since 1979, the government has executed some 200 Baha'is because of their religious beliefs and removed more than 10,000 from positions in universities and government. The government considers Baha'i blood to be *mobah*, which means that Baha'is may be killed with impunity.[19]

How did such repression of religion come about? If Iran's revolutionary regime is a prototype of the Islamist pattern of repression, its origins lie in a regime that fits almost perfectly the secular repressive pattern. Since the 16th century, Iran's Shia clergy had consented to a "Safavid contract" by which they accepted the rule of a monarch so long as the monarch agreed in turn to defend Shia as the religion of the realm. The shahs of the 20th-century Pahlavi dynasty abandoned this contract and imposed secularism instead. When the first of the Pahlavi rulers, Reza Khan, became shah through a coup in 1925, he followed in the footsteps of his neighbor Atatürk in setting Iran on a path to modernization and secularization. He built railroads, banned the veiling of women, established a modern national educational system, and marginalized the *ulema*. His son, Mohammed Reza Pahlavi, succeeded him in 1941, was restored to power through a coup backed by the US Central Intelligence Agency in 1953, and would retain close ties with the United States during the Cold War. He carried out his father's enterprise of making Iran modern and marginalizing Islam, quelling questioners through his secret police, the Savak.[20]

It was in this milieu of enforced secularism that Ayatollah Khomeini began to denounce the Shah, earning himself what would prove to be a 15-year exile in 1964. When he developed his teaching of *velayat-e faqih* in 1971, he had concluded that if Iran was to have an Islamic government, it would have to be one ruled by the *ulema*. By the end of that same decade, Khomeini had seized power through a coalition with Shia socialists, student radicals, and other secular forces, whom he then outmaneuvered and summarily sidelined. To this day, Iran remains a religious dictatorship. Popular opposition to it is strong, evidenced by the millions who took to the streets following the allegedly fraudulent elections of 2009, but how strong is unclear: All parties are outlawed except for conservative religious supporters of the Constitution. As for religious freedom, even after the election of a new president on a platform of moderation in June 2013, conditions continue to deteriorate, especially for Baha'is and Christians.[21]

Saudi Arabia

1979, the year of the Iranian Revolution, was also a tumultuous one for Iran's neighbor across the Persian Gulf, the Kingdom of Saudi Arabia. Fired by events in Iran, the Shias of eastern Saudi Arabia, 10%-15% of the country's population, mounted several uprisings against the Sunni monarchy. In an entirely uncoordinated event, an armed messianic sect seized control of the Grand Mosque of Mecca, one of Islam's holiest sites.[22] Both challenges, though suppressed, put a scare in the government of the land where stand Islam's two holiest sites, Mecca and Medina. The monarchy responded through a rigorous regimen of Islamism, building itself into a rival of Iran for its promotion of strict Islam at home and abroad.

Islamism was nothing new in Saudi Arabia, dating back to an 18th-century alliance between two founders—that of the Al Saud family dynasty and that of Wahhabism, one of the strictest sects of Islam. The alliance was renewed in 1932, when the modern Saudi state was founded and took on a third set of partners, the US government and US oil companies, after oil was discovered in 1938. The alliance meant that the Saudi government would promote, enforce, and export a puritanical form of Islam, that the *ulema* would hold strong authority, and that the arrangement would be upheld by vast wealth derived from the export of oil.

Although religious strictures were relaxed somewhat in the 1960s and early 1970s, the demand for more Islamist governance increased in the 1970s. Wahhabis flush with oil money began a campaign to spread their form of Islam around the world, a campaign that continues to this day and has expended tens of billions of dollars. In the 1980s, the monarchy fortified religious norms, shutting down cinemas and music shops, banning photos of women, sharpening gender segregation, and increasing religious instruction in the schools. In 1992, the monarchy introduced the Basic Law, which declared the Qur'an and Sunna to be the country's Constitution. Governance functions are concentrated in the king, whose decrees constitute the country's legislation. No parties or national elections are allowed. Judges follow the Hanbali school of jurisprudence, distinguished by its literalist interpretation of Islam, and make decisions largely according to their judgment of the Qur'an's meaning and without reference to precedent or any codification of *sharia*. Frequently, judges' interpretations of the Qur'an mean death for defendants. A total of 345 public beheadings took place between 2007 and 2010, and the number reached 157 in 2015.[23] Saudi Arabia invests extensive temporal authority in the *ulema*, who exercise a strong influence on Saudi Arabia's educational and judicial systems, a monopoly in religion and social morality, and the power to approve every successor to the throne and all decrees. Like Iran, Saudi Arabia exports *jihad*, supporting movements in Afghanistan, Bosnia, and elsewhere.

As in Iran, Saudi Islamism leaves little religious freedom for Saudis—or for the large population of foreign workers, whose numbers are estimated to be anywhere from 5 to 12 million out of a total population of 28 million in Saudi Arabia and who include Muslims from various schools, Christians, Jews, Hindus, Buddhists, and Sikhs. Like Iran, Saudi Arabia also has a formidable religious police force, the Committee for the Promotion of Virtue and the Prevention of Vice, whose 3500–4000 members patrol the streets enforcing sex segregation, religious observance, dress codes, and other norms. The government allows religion to be practiced in public only when it conforms to the official interpretation of Islam, closely supervises the operation of mosques, and prohibits the construction of nonofficial mosques, churches, synagogues, and other non-Muslim places of worship. Those whose beliefs do not conform to the official Islam of the regime are required to practice their faith in private and risk being detained, harassed, discriminated against in numerous ways, and deported. Shias suffer particularly severe discrimination. Nobody enjoys freedom to change or leave his or her religion. Apostasy and blasphemy carry the death penalty. Although no executions for these crimes have been reported since 1992, arrests and long prison sentences for them are common. Reinforcing religious repression are mosque speakers who pray for the death of Christians and Jews, including at mosques in Mecca and Medina, and school textbooks that sanction the killing of "polytheists," a term that includes Shias, Sufis, Christians, Jews, Hindus, and Buddhists.[24]

When this book went to press, Saudi Arabia had come under the authority of Crown Prince Mohammed bin Salman, who has moved to relax some of Saudi Arabia's strict religious laws, including its ban on women driving. These reforms, though, are a far cry from a wholesale revision of Saudi Arabia's religiously repressive governance, and they indeed exercise and reinforce the regime's control over religious policies. Authoritarianism continues unabated even while it liberalizes, at least somewhat.

Sudan

Like Iran and Saudi Arabia, Sudan promotes Islam assertively through law and policy. Sudan's Interim National Constitution declares Islam to be a source of law. Blasphemy and apostasy carry strong penalties, and conversion from Islam warrants death. Other laws enforce Islamic norms in matters ranging from dress to civil procedure to education, where religion classes that teach Islam are mandatory, even in Christian private schools. Like other Islamist states, Sudan has created a large bureaucracy that regulates religious practice, known as the Ministry of Guidance and Social Endowments, as well as a body of 40 religious scholars who advise the president.

Sudan's chief minority—the 3% of its population that is Christian—enjoys greater religious freedom than do minorities in Iran and Saudi Arabia, although this is admittedly not a high standard. Christians are free to worship and hold positions in government, and they benefit from the Sudan Interreligious Council, which promotes interreligious dialogue and addresses issues regarding religious freedom. Still, restrictions are strong and discrimination is common.

Islamism in Sudan began to gain momentum in the 1960s under the leadership of Hasan al-Turabi, a young intellectual who belonged to an offshoot of the Muslim Brotherhood. Increasingly popular among Sudan's middle class and supported by Saudi money, Islamists infiltrated the army, other government offices, and the financial system during the 1970s. By 1982, Islamist influence was strong enough to induce the Sudanese government to institute Islamic law. Thieves' hands would be cut off, adulterers stoned, alcohol banned, and alleged apostates hanged, as was religious leader Mahmoud Mohammed Taha in 1985. In 1989, Turabi's group, the National Islamic Front, seized power in a coup that installed Omar al-Bashir as president with Turabi as the power behind the throne. The new government consolidated power through purges, executions, and the widespread torture of military and government officials and expanded Islamist laws.[25]

The Bashir regime also intensified the government's war with the south of the country, which it had begun in 1982 as an attempt to unify Sudan through imposing Arab Islam on a population whose religions are animist, Christian, and minority Muslim and whose culture is Arab. The war took over two million lives and lasted until 2005, when a peace accord was signed that allowed the southern Sudanese to vote on independence, which they overwhelmingly chose in 2011.

Nigeria

In Nigeria, Africa's most populous country, Islamism also suppresses religious freedom, though in a different pattern. The country's Constitution contains a strong guarantee of religious freedom and explicitly prohibits either the federal government or a state government from adopting an official religion. However, the Constitution also provides for *sharia* courts, ones at the state level as well as a Federal Court of Appeal, to hear cases regarding Islamic law on civil matters like marriage, divorce, inheritance, and other matters. *Sharia* courts now exist in 12 out of 36 states.

Sharia courts are nothing new in Nigeria, dating back to before the country's independence in 1960. The trouble is that since 1999, when Nigeria returned to democracy and the rule of civilians, the states with *sharia* courts have been expanding the sphere of *sharia* law in ways that are constitutionally dubious and that violate religious freedom. They have established penal codes and punishments based on *sharia*, including amputation, flogging, and being stoned to death. Although no stoning sentences have been carried out, amputations and floggings have taken place. The same states regulate religion more and more. Several have created religious affairs bureaus to govern religious practice. They have decreed new regulations on dress, speech, and behavior, many of these falling disproportionately on women and the poor and some of them falling on non-Muslims. For instance, Kano state ruled in 2003 that all schoolgirls, Muslim and non-Muslim alike, must wear headscarves.

Five states have formed police units called Hisbah to enforce *sharia* law. In 2012, Hisbah in Kano arrested 20 people who did not observe the fast during the holy season of Ramadan.[26]

Worse than the direct constriction of religious freedom, though, are the massive violent riots between Christians and Muslims that the expansion of *sharia* law has touched off. Nigeria's population is 46% Christian and 52% Muslim, a balance whose delicacy is exacerbated by the desire of people of both faiths to make their religion public. The Pew Research Center on Religion and Public Life reported in 2010 that 70% of Christians in Nigeria favor "making the Bible the official law of the land," whereas 71% of Muslims favor "making Sharia the official law of the land."[27] Behind this balance is a history of tensions between Christians and Muslims that dates back to missionary efforts by both religions in the 19th century, to a strategy of indirect rule by the British colonial government that divided religious regions against one another, and to episodes of conflict between the faiths that have recurred since the 1960s.[28] History and demographics thus render the relationship between religions in Nigeria as a teetering, swaying structure that the expansion of *sharia* law strikes like a blast of wind. A 2004 report claims that violence between Muslims and Christians had taken some 10,000 lives since 1999.[29]

Although, to be sure, ethnic, economic, and regional tensions overlay the violence, the religious causes are undeniable. To cite just one example, in 2002, Isioma Daniel, a journalist for the paper *This Day*, commented on a controversy surrounding Nigeria's hosting of the Miss World competition by writing, "What would Mohammed think? In all honesty, he would probably have chosen a wife from one of them." Riots resulted, killing more than 200 people. Although Daniel publicly apologized for her statement, Muslim authorities put out a fatwa that called on Muslims to kill her. Nigeria's federal government declared the *fatwa* invalid, but Daniel nevertheless fled the country out of fear for her life.[30]

Nigeria stands as a strong example of a country where Islamist governance provokes violence between citizens. Often it is vigilante Islamist groups who carry out this violence, sometimes claiming to act on a green light from the government, sometimes claiming to act where governments fail. Today the most formidable purveyor of *sharia* is Boko Haram, a terrorist group whose name means "Western education is a sin" and who is responsible for legion armed attacks on government buildings, Christian churches, schools, and villages. Against Boko Haram and other armed Islamists, Nigeria's government enforces the law only weakly. The violence continues unabated.

Islamist Democracies

Four other countries—Pakistan, Bangladesh, Malaysia, and Indonesia—illustrate that harsh Islamist suppression of religious freedom can take place even under regimes with contested elections. Electoral democracy does not necessarily spell religious freedom.

Some important studies in recent years have shown that democracy—here, meaning competitive elections—can succeed in the Muslim-majority world. Thus challenged are secularists who claim that religious belief can only be an obstacle to democracy, as well as Islamoskeptics, who hold that Islamic teachings stand in the way of democracy. Although some Islamoskeptics have predicted that elections in Islamic countries will result in the victory of extreme parties who will prevent further elections, these predictions have proven overly alarmist. Political scientist Vali Nasr, for instance, traces what he terms "The Rise of 'Muslim Democracy'" in five countries—the four that we will look at shortly as well as Turkey—between the early 1990s and 2005. In each of these countries, he finds political parties who have significant Islamic identities but who do not promote religious governance in the aggressive manner that Islamist parties and factions do. Most of all, they are willing to play the democratic game, compete for votes, and, crucially, stand down if they lose elections. Nasr compares these parties to Christian Democratic parties in Latin America and Europe, whose platforms have been shaped by religion (albeit in yesteryear more than today) and who abide by the rules of electoral democracy. When these moderate Islamic parties have competed in elections with Islamist parties, they have generally prevailed. In each of these countries, multiple open electoral competitions have taken place during the period of Nasr's study.[31] Democracy in Islam exists almost entirely outside the Arab world—an observation that Nasr makes and that political scientists Alfred Stepan and Graeme Robertson confirm in their own careful study.[32] Still, looking at the Muslim-majority world as a whole, electoral democracy is significantly present.

The compatibility of Islam and electoral democracy is further confirmed by two sociologists, Charles Kurzman and Ijlal Naqvi, who studied democratic elections that took place over 40 years, between 1968 and 2008, in countries whose populations are at least 30% Muslim. Islamic parties participate in electoral democracy, they find, noting that the share of elections in which Islamic parties were involved increased from 28% in the 1960s to 35% in the first decade of the 21st century. Further, they find, the more democratic a Muslim country is, the more likely it is to have parties that are Islamic in their identity. Among the most democratic Muslim countries, 48% of elections have involved Islamic parties; whereas in less democratic countries, Islamic parties have been involved in only 28% of elections. Electoral democracy attracts, rather than repels, Islam. Still another finding is directly relevant to the present chapter. When Kurzman and Naqvi narrow their analysis to Islamist parties—those who advocate the aggressive promotion of *sharia* by the state—they discover that these parties have fared poorly; that more moderate Islamic parties fare far better; and that in stronger and more competitive democratic systems, the electoral success of Islamist parties is even lower.[33]

If Islam is compatible with electoral democracy, however, the suppression of religious freedom is compatible with electoral democracy, too.[34] In some Muslim countries, competitive elections coexist with laws and policies that closely manage the religion of the entire population and treat harshly religious minorities and dissenting Muslim sects. How does such a combination of practices arise? Electoral democracy can actually encourage the suppression of religious freedom, although it is hardly necessary for this suppression. Indeed, it can be said that electoral democracy encourages the Islamist denial of religious freedom without contradicting Kurzman and Naqvi's findings that Islamist parties fared poorly electorally. Here's why: In democratic systems, parties compete for voters and often shift their platforms to increase their electoral share. When traditional Islam surges among a population, as it did throughout the Muslim world in the 1970s, parties have an incentive to adopt policies that appeal to it. These parties need not be Islamist themselves. In fact, in the cases that follow, we see that large parties that broadly define themselves in more secular terms adopt Islamist measures in order to co-opt Islamist parties and prevent them from increasing their electoral share. They succeed in this parrying move even while remaining broad-based parties that are more moderate than the Islamist parties.

The suppression of religious freedom in Islamist democracies is particularly forceful when its proponents succeed in entrenching the repressive laws and policies in their country's constitution or bureaucratic apparatus, where these laws and policies are immune from easy democratic remedy.

Pakistan

Although Pakistan has oscillated over the course of its history between military rule and democratically elected governments, restrictive Islamism has grown steadily and is heedless of the presence or absence of popular rule. At Pakistan's founding in 1947, neither its Islamism nor even its independence was inevitable. Its destiny to become both a separate sovereign state and a homeland for the Muslims emerged through the erratic events of Britain's departure from its India colony.[35] After Pakistan had become independent, founding father Mohammed Ali Jinnah urged religious freedom, proclaiming in a speech:

> You are free to go to your temples, you are free to go to your mosques or to any other place of worship in this State of Pakistan . . . . You may belong to any religion or caste or creed—that has nothing to do with the business of the State . . . . We are starting with this fundamental principle that we are all citizens and equal citizens of one State.[36]

Pakistan did not take this course, though. The 1956 Constitution declared the country to be the Islamic Republic of Pakistan and contained a crucial clause prohibiting any law from being passed that is contrary to the Qur'an and the Hadith. Islamist laws and institutions continued to expand gradually until they ballooned under the military rule of President Zia ul-Haq, a general who seized power in 1978 in a coup against Prime Minister Zulfikar Ali Bhutto, whom Zia had executed.

Following the guidance of Pakistan's most powerful religious party, Jamaat-e-Islami, Zia instituted Islamist reforms that persist to this day. His most sweeping move was to change the Constitution to create a *Majlis-e-Shoora*, or an Advisory Council, that consists of religious scholars and that assesses all potential laws for their compatibility with Islam. Zia also created Federal Sharia Courts whose judges were *ulema*; mandated harsh Qur'anic penal codes; passed strict blasphemy laws; outlawed the Ahmadi sect, whom Sunnis consider heretical; and established a school curriculum that portrays Pakistan as an outworking of Islamic destiny and inculcates revulsion for Hindus and Sikhs.[37] Zia did not belong to an Islamist party, but he followed closely the agenda of JI, the most powerful of these parties, appointing many of its members to high places, including his cabinet. It was also during the 1980s that Pakistan's Inter-Services Intelligence (ISI) grew in importance because of its strategic role in Pakistan's alliance with the United States in support of the *mujahideen* opposition to the Soviet Union's occupation of Afghanistan. Since that time, the ISI has been a stronghold of Islamists, affecting Pakistan's domestic and foreign policies alike.

Pakistan is a democracy according to its Constitution and has held elections over the course of its history, though it has also experienced military coups and periods of emergency rule. It held national elections in 2008 and 2013, and its current government is democratically elected. Yet, Pakistan ranks among the most religiously unfree countries in the world. In December 2011, its GRI score on the Pew Research Center index was in the "very high" category and the 13th highest in the world. That same year, it became the first country ever to score a 10 out of 10 on the Social Hostilities Index.[38] The mobs who chased down Asia Bibi and the militants who assassinated the Governor of the Punjab and the Federal Minister for Minorities Affairs illustrate the reason for this ranking as well as the ways in which religiously repressive regimes elicit religious hostility among their citizens.

Bangladesh

Bangladesh, formerly a territory of Pakistan known as East Pakistan, can also be categorized as an Islamist democracy, though democracy here is as equally uncertain as it is in Pakistan, whereas Islamism is milder in law and policy but equally as harsh when promoted by groups outside the government.

Divided from Pakistan by land, language, and ethnicity and having suffered strong discrimination since Pakistan's founding in 1947, the Bengali people fought Pakistan in a colossal war of secession that culminated in independence in 1971. The then-dominant Awami League, which prioritized Bengali freedom over Islam, founded Bangladesh as a secular state, crafting a Constitution that banned religious parties and other associations. Islamists, including members of JI, opposed independence, believing union with Pakistan to be far more propitious for Islamic governance.

At the outset, then, Bangladesh was not an Islamist state. Neither was it a democracy, having become authoritarian quickly after independence. Paralleling Pakistan's history, Islamism arrived in the late 1970s and early 1980s under the military authoritarian rule of a leader whose popular name was the same as Pakistan's contemporary head of state: General Zia (formally Ziaur Rahman). To legitimize his rule, Zia turned to Islamism, appealing to a rising Islamic sentiment among the population and seeking to accommodate the growing power of the JI, a party that has never come close to winning power but has consistently played the role of kingmaker. Zia founded the Bangladesh Nationalist Party (BNP), which has favored Islamic governance and has ruled in coalition with the JI. He amended the Constitution so as to remove secularism and to legalize Islamic parties and associations and promoted Islam in rhetoric and in policy. After Zia was assassinated in 1981, one of his successors, General Hussain Muhammad Ershad, declared Bangladesh an Islamic Republic.

Islamism expanded in law and policy. Traditional village arbitration practices known as *salish* evolved in a religious direction, becoming an instrument for clerics to enforce a strong form of *sharia* law, particularly against women. Local clerics enforced *sharia* by issuing *fatwas*, or religious edicts.[39]

Laws regulating speech and the press on behalf of religion have emerged. Islamism, though, has never been as harsh in Bangladesh as it has been in Pakistan. The Supreme Court has guarded the secularism of the Constitution, banning *fatwas* in 2001, for instance, and the legislature has never passed blasphemy and apostasy codes like those of Pakistan.[40]

Bangladesh's most zealous Islamists are groups outside the government. As is true elsewhere, they derive encouragement from their government's laws and policies but also surpass the ambition of these laws and policies, often through vigilante violence. It is these groups who most threaten religious freedom. They impose their own punishments, for instance, against allegedly adulterous women. They attack dissenting Muslims like the Ahmadis and religious minorities like Hindus. In one outbreak of organized violence in 2005, Islamist militants detonated 450 bombs across the country within a single hour.[41] Because of this militancy, Bangladesh ranks above 95% of the world's states in the Pew Research Center Social Hostilities Index.[42]

Democracy came in 1991, when national elections were held, and has more or less persisted through today, though it was punctuated by emergency rule in 2007–2008 and was weakened by patronage and corruption. Far from muffling Islamism, democracy empowers it. Islamism waxes when the BNP is in power in coalition with the JI and wanes when the Awami League is in power. During the rule of the BNP–JI coalition between 2001 and 2006, according to one analyst, "[p]olitical violence, acts of Islamist terror, and extrajudicial killings reached all-time highs, with the perpetrators often receiving protection from the BNP-JI government."[43] Subsequently, the Awami League was reelected, capitalizing on the voters' desire for a return to normalcy. In 2010, the Supreme Court nullified Zia's amendment to the Constitution, thus reinstating secularism and reintroducing the ban on religious parties and associations. In fact, though, Islamist parties continue to participate in Bangladeshi politics, though under a somewhat more secularized cover.

Malaysia

Is it permissible for non-Muslims to use the word Allah to refer to God? Allah, of course, connotes the God of Islam around the world. If, however, the word Allah is also simply the word for God in Arabic and in other languages to which the word has migrated like Malay, then why should not, say, Christians or Jews who speak these languages use Allah when they utter God in the context of their own faith? That this question is the source of great controversy and even violence in Malaysia says much about the state of religious freedom in this country, which stands as another example of an Islamist electoral democracy.

Malaysians are justifiably proud of their history since gaining independence in 1957. The country has grown economically at consistently high rates, it is a model of healthcare provision, it educates its citizens at impressive levels, and it has mostly remained peaceful. These achievements were made possible by forging national unity among the majority Malays, about 60% of the population; ethnic Chinese, about one-quarter of the population; and ethnic Indians, about 7% of the population. Accommodating religion has been critical to this unity. Muslims make up 61.3% of the population, Buddhists about 20%, Christians 9%, Hindus about 6%, and traditional Chinese religions about 1%.[44]

Malaysia's Constitution guarantees religious freedom. It accords all citizens the right to practice their faith freely. It prohibits forcing citizens to undergo education in religions outside their own, gives parents the right to decide the religion of their children, and forbids legislatures from passing emergency laws that override religious freedom. Certain strands of the Constitution, however, point to a more repressive reality. Article 3 makes Islam the state's official religion. Article 11 gives state and federal governments the power to "control or restrict the propagation of any religious doctrine or belief among persons professing the religion of Islam."

In summary, the Constitution allows non-Muslims to practice their faith as long as they do not interfere with Islam, which has pride of place in Malaysia. What it means to interfere with Islam, though, has been interpreted broadly—and thus restrictively of non-Muslims—over the past 30 years on the part of the federal and state governments and sometimes the courts, all of which are controlled by the majority, predominantly Muslim, Malay ethnic group.[45]

Indeed, religious freedom in Malaysia has descended to troubling levels. The Pew Forum reports that by December 2015, the country showed a GRI score of 8.0—the sixth worst in the world—and a "high" Social Hostilities Score of 5.4.[46] Why the rating? For many reasons. Malaysia maintains a dual court system, requiring that its Muslims pursue religious and family issues in *sharia* courts that apply strongly traditional standards. The government heavily restricts Islam. It governs mosques, influencing the content of sermons, conveying political messages, and preventing certain imams from speaking, and it severely prohibits 56 "deviant sects," including Shias, whose members are subject to detention and "rehabilitation," as well as Ahmadis and Baha'is. It often refuses non-Muslims permits to construct houses of worship and destroys unauthorized ones. Government officials have harassed and detained numerous Muslim intellectuals for challenging Islamist doctrines and interpretations. In the past year, the home minister broke up a Christian revival meeting and the police reacted passively to several abductions and disappearances of Christian pastors. The purveyors of these actions are influenced in part by outsiders: Saudi Salafists and voices of the Egyptian Muslim Brotherhood.[47]

Muslims are free to proselytize but not to convert to other faiths, whereas members of other religions are free to convert to Islam but not to proselytize among Muslims. Most of Malaysia's states have passed laws against proselytization since the mid-1980s. Leaving the Islamic faith requires a certificate from a Syariah Court [Malay for Sharia Court], which these courts are loathe to grant. When a woman named Azalina Jailani converted from Islam to Christianity in 1998, taking the name Lina Joy, and sought to have her identity card changed accordingly, the civil courts refused to hear her case, thus consigning her to *sharia* courts, where she would be treated as an apostate.[48] *Sharia* courts also assert the right to overrule families' wishes regarding the religious character of burial rites.[49] Malaysia's highest court made a stride in the direction of religious freedom, though, in January 2018, when it ruled that children may not be forced to convert to Islam by one parent against the will of the other parent.[50]

The two states of East Malaysia, Sabah and Sarawak, which joined with Malaya to form the Malaysian Federation in 1963, have seen intensive efforts on the part of the state to convert Christians to Islam. Sarawak is the only Malaysian state with a Christian majority, and Sabah has a large Christian minority. Both states were accorded religious freedom at the time that they joined. In recent decades, however, the Malaysian government has directed large amounts of funding to Islamic institutions, including *sharia* courts, in these states, and has encouraged the illegal immigration there of hundreds of thousands of people from the Philippines and Indonesia so as to dilute the Christian population. Christian children are actively encouraged to convert to Islam in schools as well.

Then there is the issue of language. It was in 1991 that the government banned non-Muslims from using several words that are essential to Islam, including Allah, despite these words having become a part of Malay, the national language. Malaysian Christians had used the word Allah for several hundred years. When a Catholic newspaper took the issue to court in 2008–2009, it received a favorable ruling from the high court of Kuala Lumpur, which declared the prohibition on the newspaper's use of the word Allah unconstitutional. Violence ensued, as extremist Islamists perpetrated arson and vandalism on 12 churches, 2 Muslim prayer halls, 1 mosque, and 1 Sikh temple.[51]

Then, momentum shifted in the legal battle. Appeals resulted in Malaysia's highest court upholding the ban in June 2014, a blow for religious freedom.[52]

Like Bangladesh and Pakistan, Malaysia did not chart an Islamist course when it became independent (as Malaya) in 1957. True, under British colonialism, Islam helped to motivate the struggle for independence. The first prime minister under independence, Tunku Abdul Rahman, however, defined the state as a secular one. "[T]his country is not an Islamic state as it is generally understood," he declared, adding, "[w]e merely provide that Islam shall be the official religion of the state." What he had in mind for Islam was largely ceremonial.[53]

Reflecting the global trend, an Islamic revival took place among the population in the 1970s and 1980s and created a demand for Islamism in politics and society. The Malaysian Islamic Party (PAS), which formed in 1951, responded by strengthening its already Islamist platform. In turn, the United Malays National Organization (UMNO), the erstwhile secular nationalist dominant party, parried with a tactic that it came to employ repeatedly, namely co-opting PAS by taking on an Islamist agenda of its own. In 1981, UMNO's Mahatir Mohamad became prime minister and began to lead the country toward the Islamism of today. Politically, UMNO succeeded, keeping PAS at bay as a small electoral minority, but its strategy has compromised Malaysia's religious freedom. Shortly after the attacks of September 11, 2001, when Mohamad was still prime minister, he declared that Malaysia was "an Islamic state." Although his words were similar to those of his predecessor, Rahman, he had in mind something far more than ceremonial.[54]

Like Pakistan and Bangladesh, Malaysia's status as an electoral democracy must be qualified. Although Malaysia regularly hosts contested elections, for most of its history, it has been a one-party democracy, governed by a coalition dominated by UMNO. UMNO represents the Malay majority, an ethnic group that not only consists almost entirely of Muslims but is also defined by the Constitution as being Muslim as well as being the country's official indigenous people. Minority Chinese and Indian populations, who arrived under British colonial rule, are generally more prosperous than native Malays and have sometimes come into violent conflict with Malays but have accepted a tacit grand bargain by which they are granted full citizenship in return for allowing the Malays to govern.[55] UMNO has secured its dominance by blocking opposition parties from having equal access to the media and restricting their campaigning activities.[56] From this position, UMNO has been a potent promoter of Islamist politics. However, in May 2018, for the first time in Malaysia's history, UMNO was defeated in a general election. What the change means for democracy and religious freedom in Malaysia is yet to be seen.

In fairness, Malaysia also hosts organizations, coalitions, and voices that oppose the Islamist trend and advocate for interreligious harmony.[57] They represent Malaysia's promise of religious and ethnic unity. In recent decades, though, Islamism and the truncation of religious freedom have proven to be far more formidable vectors.

Indonesia

The memorable role of Muslim mass organizations in bringing down the 31-year dictatorship of Indonesia's Suharto in 1998 and in establishing electoral democracy thereafter might well engender befuddlement over the placement of Indonesia in the religiously repressive category. Indonesia has indeed become the world's largest electoral democracy in a Muslim-majority population, one that has staged four genuinely contested and largely peaceful national elections. This achievement owes much to the Nahdlatul Ulama (NU), an Islamic movement that includes 30–50 million people, and Muhammadiyah, another that contains 29 million members, both of whom were critical to the mass protests that deposed Suharto and are critical to sustaining democracy and a tradition of religious tolerance. Over the course of Indonesia's elections, voters, even pious Muslim ones, have offered only weak support for Islamic parties.[58]

Deepening the puzzle, a healthy tradition of religious pluralism is grounded in Indonesia's Constitution, which, established in 1945, sets forth a national philosophy of *Pancasila* that proclaims "belief in one God," and recognizes six religions: Islam, Catholicism, Protestantism, Buddhism, Hinduism, and, as of 2006, Confucianism. In a country where Muslims make up 87% of the population—and are the world's largest concentration of Muslims at that—such a provision protects minorities, especially the 7% Protestants, the 3% Catholics, the 1.5% Hindus, and a smaller number of Buddhists and Confucians.[59] What is more, the Constitution guarantees religious freedom for every citizen. During the constitutional debates of 1945, Islamists demanded that certain words be appended to "belief in one supreme God," namely, "with the obligation to live according to Islamic law for Muslims," which became known as the Jakarta Charter. They did not succeed in this quest, though, even after continuing to pursue it in subsequent years, including after the fall of Suharto. In the past generation, one of the strongest Muslim articulators of religious freedom has been Indonesia's first democratically elected president, the late Abdurrahman Wahid, who held office from 1999 to 2001 and who strongly defended religious freedom as a universal human right with a foundation in both Islamic theology and human nature. All of this evinces what anthropologist Robert Hefner calls "civil Islam."[60]

Why call Indonesia religiously repressive, then? Recall that this book's designations refer to a regime's governance of religion and, in the case of regimes that curtail religious freedom, the rationale for this curtailment. The designation does not describe the country or the government as a whole. With respect to religion, Indonesia has veered decidedly unfree.

In the last months of 2016, another Muslim protest coursed through the streets of Jakarta, this one not in support of electoral democracy but rather in opposition to Jakarta's first Christian and Chinese governor, whose references to the Qur'an were alleged to have violated Indonesia's anti-blasphemy laws. Around 200,000 conservative Muslims took to the streets to demand his removal. These protests point to a broader conclusion that a closer look at laws and policies at both the national and local levels reveals—namely, that despite Indonesia's Constitution, national philosophy of *Pancasila*, and broad achievement of interreligious peace, religious freedom has suffered sharp curtailments because of the pressure of Islamists during the period since the fall of Suharto. The Pew Research Center makes a similar judgment, ranking Indonesia as the world's fifth highest violator of religious freedom as of the end of 2014.[61]

At the beginning of Suharto's rule, Indonesia's governance of religion resembled the secular repressive pattern. Suharto banned religion from party platforms, subdued Islamist movements, and built structures to manage Islam.[62] By the 1990s, though, he had come to ally with and empower Islamist groups in order to co-opt Indonesia's Islamic resurgence and to weaken opponents situated in the army and the population. When Suharto fell in 1998, Islamists were poised for power.[63]

Today, "Indonesia's pluralism is in peril," reports analyst Benedict Rogers.[64] How is religious freedom restricted in Indonesia? Much of the curtailment takes place through the government's apparatus for governing religions. Shortly after the Constitution was passed in 1945, a Ministry of Religious Affairs was established to empower and regulate all of the official religions. The ministry is dominated by Muslims and favors Islam with attention but also regulates Islam, judging and discouraging deviancy, for instance.[65]

In 1975, the government created the powerful Indonesian Council of Ulema (MUI), which is semiofficial in that it issues *fatwas* that carry no direct political authority but that are taken quite seriously by public officials and sometimes even enforced by the attorney general and other ministries.[66] In 2005 President Susilo Bambank Yudhoyono addressed the MUI, promised its members "a central role in matters regarding the Islamic faith," and pledged to "open our hearts and minds to receiving the thoughts, recommendations, and fatwas from the MUI at any time." Days later, the MUI issued *fatwas* calling for the banning of the Ahmadiyya, a sect that mainstream Sunnis consider heretical, and denouncing "pluralism, secularism, and liberalism."[67]

Among the many ways that the Indonesian government restricts religious freedom is its harsh discrimination against sects who are not among the country's officially recognized religions, for instance, through denying their members their critical government identification card.[68] At times, the government has banned Baha'is and Jehovah's Witnesses. It also places heavy requirements on building houses of worship that have burdened Christians especially.[69] In 2006, the government added even more stringency to requirements that it had established in a 1969 decree.[70]

Proselytism, blasphemy, heresy, conversion, and alleged expressions of hatred are all restricted and often prosecuted, almost always in cases where Islamic law is alleged to be violated. The government's virtual ban on proselytism dates back to tensions between Muslims and Christian missionaries during the colonial period and typically prohibits Muslim conversions to Christianity.[71] A blasphemy law passed in 1965 has been enforced more strongly in recent years and was upheld in 2010 by Indonesia's Constitutional Court even though a broad coalition of organizations demanded its repeal.[72]

Among the communities whose religious freedom is violated most is the Ahmadiyya, the same community that is under attack in Pakistan and elsewhere, whose members number 500,000 in Indonesia. In the wake of the MUI's *fatwa* of 2005, violent attacks on the community began. In 2008, the government issued a joint ministerial decree that ordered the community to refrain from religious activity unless it renounced its claim to be Islamic.[73] Numerous provincial and local authorities followed with their own anti-Ahmadiyya regulations, which sparked still more maltreatment of Ahmadiyyas at the hands of fellow citizens. Sufis, Shias, Buddhists, Baha'is, and atheists all suffer discrimination, restriction, and harassment as well.[74]

During President Yudhoyono's tenure from 2004 to 2014, he made his office the source of religious restriction through his remarks, decrees, support for regulations, and failure to enforce laws against religious violence and illegal discrimination. Andrea Harsono of Human Rights Watch has remarked that Yudhoyono is "the president who laid down the most sectarian regulatory infrastructure in Indonesia." As of 2011, there were in place at least 147 "discriminative laws and public policies in regards to religion."[75]

Along with having a president who has constricted religious freedom, Indonesia has seen the rise of Islamist political parties, the most prominent being the Prosperous Justice Party (PKS), founded in 1998 on the inspiration of Egypt's Muslim Brotherhood. It has become the country's fourth largest party and has averaged about 7% of the vote in national elections in 2004, 2009, and 2014, and its members hold ministerial positions in the cabinet.

Some of the strongest governmental restrictions on religious freedom in Indonesia can be found at the local level. Although estimates vary, one report in 2013 identified 169 *sharia* regulations spread across 51 out of 497 districts. The regulations variously regulate consumption, prescribe reading the Qur'an, require a religious tax [*zakat*], ban Ahmadis, restrict churches, regulate Islamic dress, and impose harsh punishments for crimes like stealing and adultery.[76]

The largest and most violent attacks on religious freedom in Indonesia, though, come from groups outside the government. The Pew Research Center ranks Indonesia as thirteenth in the world in its level of social hostilities and places it on the cusp of the "very high" tier.[77] The Setara Institute, a human rights nongovernmental organization in Jakarta, has tracked incidents involving the harsh violation of religious freedom or belief and shows that they increased from 200 in 2009, to 216 in 2010, to 244 in 2011, and to 264 in 2012.[78] Salafi and Wahhabi movements have been growing, supported by Saudi Arabia, Yemen, and other countries. The Islamic Defenders Front, founded in 1998 shortly after Suharto's fall, commits widespread violence and harassment in the name of enforcing morality and doctrinal purity, and contributes words of hate and intolerance to Indonesia's political discourse. Islamist gangs and paramilitaries were involved in clashes with Christians that took some 8,000 lives in Maluku between 1999 and 2002 and caused around 1,000 deaths in Sulawesi around the same period. Shortly after Suharto's departure from power in May 1998, radical Islamist paramilitaries sprang up all over Indonesia.[79] Even among journalists, a harsh Islamism is gaining favor. A 2011 report based on research conducted by the Pantau Foundation shows that 63% of journalists approved of a series of conservative *fatwas* issued by the MUI and that 64% supported banning the Ahmadiyya.[80]

As is often true with religious hostilities, the distinction is not sharp between those committed by social actors and those by the government. Hefner makes the case that following Suharto's fall, Indonesia's state institutions became weak, porous, and easily penetrated by Islamist militant groups, who both pressured and formed alliances with state officials.[81] As a result, certain officials and agencies have chosen not to prevent or punish violence and sometimes even to support armed Islamist militant outfits—"[a] subcontracted, supplementary form of state power," as political scientist John T. Sidel puts it.[82] The government was indeed involved in creating the Islamic Defenders

Front, seeking a way to co-opt and contain Islamist passions, and has continued to support it. The Front, however, has not been pliable.[83]

Reinforcing religious freedom's troubled condition have been trends in public opinion. "It is people on the putatively 'moderate' centre of Indonesia's political spectrum, rather than those on the radical fringes, who ultimately determine the government's stance on religious tolerance," writes political scientist Greg Fealy. Fealy reports a number of figures that show that Indonesians on the whole are low on tolerance and getting lower. He cites the Denny JA Foundation as showing that 47% of Indonesians disapprove of having Ahmadis as neighbors and that 42% said the same of Shias. These numbers have risen since 2005, when the numbers were 39% toward Ahmadis and 27% toward Shias. Some 52% of Indonesians objected to non-Muslims performing religious ceremonies near their homes, and 64% were against having non-Muslim houses of worship built near their homes. In Western nations, in comparison, Fealy points out, levels of negative attitudes toward religious differences range from 2% to 25%, depending on the question.[84]

It is worth repeating that to categorize Indonesia as religiously repressive is not to ignore the country's many people and organizations that work assiduously to promote religious freedom, peaceful pluralism, and interfaith harmony. The 2008 decree on Ahmadiyya, for instance, was opposed by heads of NU, including Wahid, and of Muhammadiyah. Voices such as these would never be heard in Saudi Arabia or Iran. Still, these voices speak as loudly as they do because there is a problem to be confronted: the assertive promotion of Islam through governmental restrictions, social hostilities, and a combination of the two that violate the religious freedom of others.

Afghanistan and Iraq

A survey of the Islamist pattern cannot ignore two other Islamist countries that have been prominent in the global headlines because of US military intervention there—Afghanistan and Iraq. In both cases, US government officials debated to what extent the United States ought to promote religious freedom. Both countries remain Islamist.

When the United States invaded Afghanistan shortly after the attacks of September 11, 2001, it overthrew an Islamist regime renowned for its cruelty—the Taliban. Although religious repression abated somewhat under the Taliban's successor regime, it remains severe. The Taliban itself hardly disappeared from action, staying around to kill and kidnap members of the country's tiny Christian minority, foreign Christians whom they suspected of proselytizing, Muslim converts to Christianity, and Muslims who openly dissent from Islamist orthodoxy. Afghanistan's Constitution, though developed in consultation with the US government, contains numerous articles that enable a severe Islamism, designating Afghanistan as an "Islamic Republic," asserting Islam as the "state religion," requiring that no law be "contrary to Islam," forbidding political parties that contradict Islam, and even ensuring "the elimination of traditions contrary to the principles of the sacred religion of Islam." The president, the courts, the legislature, the police, and local governments have interpreted the law to mean the prosecution and harsh punishment of blasphemy, apostasy, and conversion, including through execution.[85]

Since the United States overthrew Saddam Hussein in 2003, religious freedom has likewise been precarious in Iraq. A good portion of the violations have taken place in the context of Iraq's ensuing civil war, which, among other cleavages, arrayed the majority Shia community (60%–65%) against the minority Sunni community (32%–37%). This should not obscure, though, the deliberate targeting of religious minorities, especially Christians, Mandaeans, Yazidis, and Baha'is, by armed Islamist groups. The country's population of Christians has plummeted (using conservative estimates) from an estimated 1.5 million in 2003 to fewer than 450,000 in 2013, most of them driven into neighboring Jordan and Syria. The government is not much help, doing little to enforce the religious freedom that the 2005 Constitution declares. Another article in the Constitution, unfortunately, prohibits any law that "contradicts the established provisions of Islam" and guarantees "the Islamic identity of the majority of the Iraqi people." As we have seen elsewhere among Islamist states, such provisions typically provide license for courts, legislators, executive officials, police, and vigilante groups to curtail the religious freedom of minorities and dissenters. Under Shia rule, the government has done little to include Sunnis and Kurds in the ranks of power, leaving them underrepresented in the civil service and important positions of leadership. During the civil war, Shias massacred Sunnis. Such treatment created the conditions on which the rebel Islamic State of Iraq and Syria capitalized in capturing a large portion of the country in 2014.

Smaller Islamist States

The preceding states are major Islamist states because of their size, their geopolitical significance, the international attention that their Islamism garners, and their roles as exemplars for other Islamist states. Eleven other states make the list of Islamist states but are minor ones because they lack these characteristics and are all fairly small. They share the elements of an Islamist state, though with variations and to different degrees. That is, their constitutions declare them to be Islamic republics and usually contain provisions declaring that Islam is the state religion, that Islam or *sharia* is the source of law, or that all laws must be compatible with Islam or *sharia*. They usually contain a government bureaucracy that regulates Islam in schools, mosques, charities, pilgrimages, doctrine, and much else. They typically outlaw Baha'is, where they exist, as well as other religions and sects that they deem heretical. In some of these states (though not others) other religions are allowed to practice and even accorded a constitutional right to religious freedom, but this practice is often truncated and balanced by other laws that privilege Islam. For instance, Buddhists or Christians might be allowed to worship, but this worship, like their religious speech and practice more generally, must take place in private. Proselytism is typically forbidden, as is Muslim conversion away from Islam, which is sometimes rendered a capital offense. Commonly, Muslim men may marry non-Muslim women, though they must usually be Christians or Jews, whereas Muslim women may not marry non-Muslim men. Utterers of blasphemy or, if it is not called blasphemy, public speech against Islam or Muslim leaders, will find themselves prosecuted and potentially severely punished in most of these countries. When these states include sizable populations of non-Muslims or of multiple schools of Islam, they typically have special courts that rule on family and religious matters when Muslims are involved. Nine of these countries score "very high" or "high" on Pew's GRI for 2013; the other two nevertheless fit the Islamist pattern.[86]

Six are Gulf States, surrounding Saudi Arabia and forming the coastline of the Arabian Peninsula: Kuwait, Yemen, Bahrain, Qatar, the United Arab Emirates, and Oman. One of the most prominent features of these countries' religious landscape is their large populations of foreigners who are not citizens and who migrated to the Gulf in order to work in the oil and related industries. Coming largely from elsewhere in the Arab world and from South and Southeast Asia, they are a diverse lot consisting of Muslims (of different schools), Christians, Hindus, Buddhists, and people of other religions. In Qatar and the United Arab Emirates, citizens are in fact only a small percentage of the population—12% and 11%, respectively. In countries like Oman, the portion of citizens is more substantial at 67%, but its share of foreign workers is still high.[87]

How the Gulf States treat these foreign populations is critical to their religious freedom profile. Qatar wishes to communicate to the world its religious tolerance. Although it is not even remotely democratic—a dictatorship among dictatorships—it aspires to be an entrepôt for international commerce, both in goods and in ideas like interreligious understanding. For over a decade, the Doha International Center for Interfaith Dialogue (DICID), a quasi-governmental entity, has hosted an annual conference on interreligious dialogue, a recent one bringing in 300 participants from more than 70 countries.

But is there religious freedom outside the conference facility? Qatar boasts that its law recognizes Christians and Jews—"people of the book"—and allows them to worship freely. This, though, takes place in a strongly Islamist atmosphere. Even people of the book must keep their worship private; religious ideas contrary to those of Islam (Sunni or Shia) have no place in public forums like the media. Proselytism is strictly outlawed, as is conversion away from Islam, which is a capital offense (though never enforced since the country's independence in 1971). The government exercises heavy censorship of the media. It does not legally recognize—meaning that it does not authorize worship facilities for—religions other than Judaism and Christianity, despite the fact that Hindus are 30% of the population of non-citizens and Buddhists are 7%. The government strongly regulates Islam as well as other faiths and manifests most of the other typical features of Islamist states. Qatar, then, is an Islamist cosmopolis that practices tolerance at best, and a highly circumscribed version at that. True to the Islamist pattern, it falls far short of international standards for religious freedom.[88]

The other three cases of minor states are ones that do not contain large populations of noncitizens and fit the Islamist description quite well. The Maldives, an archipelago in the Indian Ocean, prohibits the practice of anything but Sunni Islam and ranked fifth worst among Islamic countries in Pew's GRI of 2009. Brunei, a tiny state in the southeastern Pacific, and three African states—Mauritania, Somalia, and Comoros—all make the list of Islamist states as well.

Islamism in the Debate Over Islam

What do Islamist states teach us about religious freedom in Islam? Islamist states would seem to make the strongest case for the Islamoskeptics' view. Are they not exactly what these skeptics have in mind? There can be no question that Islamist thought is inimical to religious freedom and that Islamist states are arch-violators of religious freedom. It is in these states that we find a strong restriction of religion among the entire population, brutal violence against minorities of other faiths and Muslim dissenters, and a consequent atmosphere of fear. Nor cannot it be denied that Islamist doctrines and theology motivate this violence and fear.

Islamoskeptics are justly suspicious of certain commonly voiced arguments that explain away Islamism—as the result of poverty and under-development, for instance. Several of the most repressive Islamist states are among the richest states in the world. Qatar tops the International Monetary Fund's list of states ranked by per capita gross domestic product, and Bahrain, Saudi Arabia, the United Arab Emirates, Oman, and Brunei rank in the top 34 of 187 states. Even Iran, one of the standard-bearers of Islamism, is in the top half, standing at 78 or 187. It will be replied that although the wealth is formidable in these states, it is concentrated in a few hands, a situation of gross inequality that creates the conditions for religious extremism. The trouble here, though, is that several studies of the economic basis of Islamist movements show no strong connection between economic deprivation and either Islamist militancy or Islamist movements.[89]

If these Islamoskeptic judgments capture undeniable dimensions of Islamism, however, a close-up view of the Muslim landscape again reveals more complexity. Side by side with the dynamics that Islamoskeptics rightly identify are dynamics of the kind that Islamopluralists like to stress. One is history. An Islamoskeptic tenet is that a tendency toward violence and intolerance is hardwired in Islam's founding texts and events. This once-and-for-all view of things, however, misses a key feature of Islamist states: They are products of modernity. As we have seen, Islamism arose in the modern world, criticized the modern world, and adopted features of the modern world in order to advance a program of overcoming the modern world. Islamism offers an interpretation of history that is intelligible in only a certain moment in history: Islam had greatly declined from the glory that it had enjoyed in previous centuries because of both internal decay and domination at the hands of European colonial powers who imposed on them a rigid Western secularism. Historian Nikki R. Keddie shows that virtually every militant Islamist movement in the modern era, with the admittedly important exception of Wahhabism, arose as a reaction to Western colonialism.[90] Fittingly, Hassan al-Banna founded the Muslim Brotherhood only four years after the Turkish parliament dissolved the last Caliphate in 1924. Now, the West's own decay yields an opportunity to recover that glory. Such a recovery involves adopting the modern world's quintessential political form: the sovereign state.[91] Islamists view the state as a vehicle for the global Islamic revolution even as they believe that the state will one day crumble and give way to the united *umma* (again, echoing Marx). None of this analysis can be found in the Qur'an or the Hadiths. It arises in a particular historical circumstance: the modern world.

Another dimension of Islamist states that Islamoskeptics miss is that not all—or even most—of their inhabitants are typically Islamists. Islamoskeptics stress uniformity of opinion in Islam, especially in matters manifesting violence and intolerance. It does not follow from Islamism's strong influence in these states, though, that their populations conform to Islamist thinking. As we have seen, Islamist parties have never polled well in democratic elections, often securing only a small percentage of the vote. It is telling of Islamism that it secures its influence largely through nondemocratic channels: authoritarian regimes; constitutional provisions that are difficult to reverse; sectors of the government that are beyond democratic control, for example, the Pakistani intelligence service; and terrorist groups that do not participate in normal politics at all. How Islamists exert influence is little different from how dictators exert influence. So it must be, for Islamism is too narrowly shared to succeed in genuinely open democratic politics.

This mixture of Islamoskeptic and Islamopluralist insights may seem unsatisfactory for those who wish for a straight answer to the question of Islam and religious freedom. Perhaps the best way to synthesize them is to say that Islamism poses a real and direct threat to religious freedom but that Islamism is far from all of Islam. Thus reinforced is this book's central argument that despite the many obstacles and denials of religious freedom in Islam, hope for religious freedom in Islam ought to be tended.

Might Islamist states become more religiously free? Change seems least likely in Iran, Saudi Arabia, and the many other Islamist states where religious repression is ensconced in the ruling structures but is perhaps more likely in Indonesia, where Islamism is not as enshrined legally and where democratic elections and the genuine turnover of power encourage more flux. We must always remember, though, that change, even radical change, is difficult to predict.[92] We do well to recall, too, that few predicted the rise of Islamism in the first place.

The possibility of political change in authoritarian Muslim-majority countries, although not all of them Islamist, is the subject of the next chapter, on the Arab Uprisings.

5

The Arab Uprisings

AT 11:30 IN the morning of December 17, 2010, Mohamed Bouazizi, a produce vendor in the city of Sidi Bouzid, Tunisia, set himself on fire in front of the local government headquarters. Twenty-six years old, Bouazizi had sold fruits and vegetables to support his extended family, including six siblings, in this rural town that suffered from corruption and an unemployment rate of 30%. According to a close friend, Bouazizi was well liked and known for giving produce to the poor without charge.

Earlier that morning, a female city employee, Faida Hamdi, had confiscated Bouazizi's produce cart and his weighing scale, explaining that Bouazizi had lacked a vendor's license. Bouazizi had suffered such treatment many times before but offered to pay a fine. What happened next is disputed, but Hamdi is alleged to have refused his payment, struck him, spat on him, and, when he resisted, called the police, who then beat him. Outraged, Bouazizi went to the provincial headquarters to complain but was refused a hearing. Then, standing in the middle of traffic outside, he doused himself with gasoline and lit himself on fire. Eighteen days later, on January 4, 2011, he died in the hospital.

Had Bouazizi's story ended there it would have remained little more than a tragic commentary on corruption and economic stagnation in Tunisia under the dictatorship of President Zine El Abidine Ben Ali. Instead it provoked a historic wave of demonstrations and uprisings across the entire Arab world. Within hours, protests began in Sidi Bouzid and then spread quickly to all of Tunisia, facilitated by Facebook and other social media. On January 14, 2011, President Ben Ali fled the country with his family and took refuge in Saudi Arabia, where he resigned and ended his 23-year reign. Soon thereafter, Egyptians took to the streets to protest the rule of President Hosni Mubarak, who ended his own 30-year reign when he resigned the next month. Uprisings also broke out in Bahrain, Yemen, Libya, and Syria, and large-scale protests took place in Algeria, Iraq, Jordan, Kuwait, Morocco, and Sudan.

Did the Arab Uprisings succeed? If success means overthrowing a dictator, then uprisings succeeded in four countries—out of six countries in which major uprisings took place (Tunisia, Egypt, Libya, Yemen, Bahrain, and Syria) and out of 14 Arab states that were autocracies and free from foreign occupation and thus ripe for popular challenge.[1] One of the four ousters, that of Muammar Qaddafi in Libya, required air strikes from the world's most powerful military alliance, NATO. In Bahrain, the regime survived through cracking down on the protests with the help of Saudi Arabian troops who crossed the causeway that connects the two countries. Syria's regime has survived overthrow as well but only through a civil war that has killed more than 300,000 people by conservative estimates, displaced some 6.6 million internally, and created 4.8 million refugees outside Syria.[2] All in all, around 90,000 people died across 16 countries where interconnected protests and uprisings took place over the 30 months following Mohamed Bouazizi's self-immolation.[3]

If success means not just the overthrow of a dictator but also the rise of stable liberal democracy, the results are still bleaker. The Western media dubbed the uprisings "the Arab Spring," evoking the democratic revolutions of 1848 in Europe, sometimes called the "Springtime of Peoples," as well as the Prague Spring of 1968, when Czechoslovakian dissidents challenged their Communist government. Perhaps unintentionally, the springtime analogy augured failure, for these other historic vernal developments were occluded by wintry authoritarian reversals not long after their onset. Fitting better the early hopes that liberal democrats around the world harbored for the Arab Uprisings were the far more successful waves of democratization in Latin America in the 1980s and Eastern Europe in 1989, most of whose bumper crop of democracies remain free to this day. Sadly, at the time of this writing, the fate of the Arab Uprisings matches better those earlier episodes dubbed springs, for almost all of the Arab revolts have ended back in authoritarianism. Only one country, Tunisia, now resembles a stable democracy.

What does all of this have to do with the question of this book—is Islam hospitable to religious freedom?—and with the answers to this question that the book has put forth? A great deal, in fact. Admittedly, religion played only a bit part in initially provoking the Uprisings. Most Arabs who took to the streets harbored the same sort of frustrations that led Mohamed Bouazizi to his sad protest: corruption, lack of economic opportunity, unemployment, weariness with dictatorship, and a desire for democracy. Islam, however, entered the stage soon thereafter and critically shaped the course of the drama. Even more so, Muslims' political theologies of religious freedom were crucial to the plot. This chapter investigates this influence by asking these questions: Did the Arab Uprisings advance religious freedom, impede it, or do neither? What role did Islamic political theologies of religious freedom play in shaping the course of the Arab Uprisings? To what extent can the failure of most of the Arab Uprisings be attributed to a dearth of champions of religious freedom and the success of Tunisia be credited to proponents of religious freedom? The importance of religious freedom, I argue, is one of the central lessons of the historic Arab Uprisings.[4]

What Did the Arab Uprisings Do for Religious Freedom?

Taken as a whole, the Arab Uprisings were dismal for religious freedom. Table 5.1 compares the religious freedom scores of 20 countries in the region before, during, and after the uprisings using the Pew Research Center's Government Restrictions Index (GRI). It first lists the 6 countries that saw major uprisings and then presents 14 other countries whose politics were in some way affected by the uprisings, including two non-Arab countries, Turkey, and Iran.[5] This wide inclusion of cases strengthens the judgment that religious freedom did not do well by the Arab Uprisings.

All but two of the countries on the table ended up with worse religious freedom scores in 2013 than they showed in 2007. Thirteen of the countries rose by one point or more on the 10-point GRI scale—a notable increase by the standards of the index—and four or more rose more than two points (recall that the higher the score, the more repressive the regime). Through this entire period, the Middle East–North Africa region remained far above any other region of the world in its restriction of religion.

Social hostilities—the violations of religious freedom that victims suffer at the hand of fellow citizens and nonstate actors—also increased sharply in the Middle East–North Africa region during this period. The region's score in Pew's Social Hostilities Index—also a 10-point scale—increased from a median 3.7 in June 2007 to a peak of 6.4 in 2012, decreasing only somewhat to 5.8 in 2013. Middle East–North Africa remained above Asia–Pacific, the region with the next highest social hostilities, by more than two points.[6] At least four countries—Syria, Libya, Bahrain, and Yemen—broke out into civil war as a direct result of the uprisings.

Were there any bright spots in the region? The only two countries that improved their GRI scores during this period, Saudi Arabia and Libya, did not improve by much. Saudi Arabia remained among the top 10 religiously

Table 5.1. The Fate of Religious Freedom in the Arab Uprisings

Country	Religious freedom pattern in 2009	Pew GRI year ending June 2007	Pew GRI year ending June 2010	Pew GRI year ending December 2011	Pew GRI year ending December 2012	Pew GRI year ending December 2013
Tunisia	Secular repressive	4.8	7.7	5.8	5.1	4.9
Egypt	Secular repressive	7.2	8.7	8.9	8.8	8.2
Yemen	Religiously repressive	4.3	7.0	6.9	6.3	5.8
Libya	Secular repressive	5.1	5.8	6.2	5.5	4.7
Bahrain	Religiously repressive	4.3	4.2	6.2	6.5	8.2
Syria	Secular repressive	4.5	7.3	7.5	8.0	7.4
Algeria	Secular repressive	5.6	6.9	7.5	6.9	6.1
Morocco	Secular repressive	4.9	6.2	5.9	7.0	6.3
Iraq	Religiously repressive	5.1	4.6	5.0	6.8	6.4
Jordan	Secular repressive	4.6	6.5	6.0	5.7	6.2
Kuwait	Religiously repressive	4.8	4.7	5.5	5.1	5.4
Lebanon	Religiously free	1.4	3.7	3.6	3.1	4.0

Oman	Religiously repressive	3.9	5.3	5.5	6.0	5.2
Palestinian Territories	Not coded	3.3	3.5	3.7	3.6	4.5
Qatar	Religiously repressive	3.3	5.6	5.7	6.0	6.0
Saudi Arabia	Religiously repressive	8.0	8.6	8.6	8.6	7.8
Sudan	Religiously repressive	5.7	5.4	6.6	6.9	7.0
United Arab Emirates	Religiously repressive	3.9	4.3	5.5	6.0	4.6
Iran	Religiously repressive	7.9	7.9	8.5	8.6	8.3
Turkey	Secular repressive	6.6	5.8	5.3	6.4	7.4

Sources: Pew Research Center, December 2009, "Global Restrictions on Religion"; Pew Research Center, June 2013, "Arab Spring Adds to Global Restrictions on Religion"; Pew Research Center, February 26, 2015, "Latest Trends in Religious Restrictions and Hostilities."

unfree countries in the world. Perhaps more hope can be found in Libya, whose GRI score rose just prior to and during the period of the Uprisings and then decreased, suggesting that the overthrow of Qaddafi may have improved things. Hope for Libya, though, must be tempered by the violence that beset the country in the immediate aftermath of Qaddafi's fall and then the civil war that convulsed the country—and brought much religiously motivated violence—beginning in 2014. More hope—indeed perhaps the only bright spot—can be found in Tunisia, whose score sharply rose in 2010 and then decreased to a level in 2013 that was only slightly higher than its score in 2007 but where more progress toward religious freedom took place than the numbers alone show.

How Did Muslims Shape the Course of the Arab Uprisings?

When a popular uprising overthrows a secular repressive dictatorship that has held power for decades, what kinds of scenarios are likely to emerge? Worrisome scenarios, observers might be forgiven for suspecting. Recall that the populations living under these dictatorships have remained far more religious than their regimes. Once uncorked, will long-bottled-up religiosity spew forth in radical and vengeful forms? Recall, too, that it was traditional and conservative Muslims—some of them violent *jihadis*—who were jailed and tortured under the old regime. Will they now move to install a religiously repressive dictatorship? If that scenario unfolds, then might we expect resistance from holders of a political theology of secular repression, including members of the overthrown dictatorship who still cling to power? Will not these conflicting political theologies then reinforce each other in polarizing fashion, each claiming that the other will realize what it fears? These worries turned out to be well founded.

Dare we hope for a scenario in which a religious freedom bloc wins the day? It would comprise Muslims whose political theology calls for a democracy that respects the full religious freedom of non-Muslims and different schools of Muslims and perhaps secular allies with a political theology of positive secularism. Most likely the members of this bloc will be pressured from two sides, including religiously repressive Islamists who charge them with apostate secularism and secularists who warn that their religious openness risks empowering Muslim extremists. Will they be able to withstand the pressure of these pincers? This hope, alas, was not borne out, except in Tunisia, which deserves a close look.

Tunisia

Tunisia was the only Arab Uprising country to make a transition to a genuinely competitive constitutional democracy. Certain preconditions, including the best educational system, the largest middle class, and the strongest labor movement in the Arab world, gave Tunisians a strong desire and capacity for democracy, whereas Ben Ali's dictatorship, one of the most repressive in the Arab world, gave Tunisians a strong conviction that democracy was being denied.[7] Choices and strategies mattered a great deal, too. Crucial was the decision of the army to withdraw its support for Ben Ali and stand aside as democracy moved ahead. Essential, too, was the persistence of the popular protest movement, organized by civil society, which did not cease its demonstrations until regnant agents of Ben Ali's dictatorship left power. A council created in March 2011 to chart a course toward elections and a new constitution proved vital for building consensus, bringing together major factions, including Muslim ones as well as secular ones who feared an Islamist takeover.[8] In Tunisia's first national elections since 1956, held on October 23, 2011, a plurality of 37% of Tunisians supported the Ennahda Party, a moderate Islamic party, yet more Tunisians voted against Islamic parties than for them. The secular parties were willing to accept their loss while Ennahda was willing to join in a governing coalition with them. When another national election was held in October 2014, this time Ennahda lost and stepped down from power. Tunisia had passed the "two turnover test" that political scientist Samuel Huntington proposed as a criterion for the consolidation of democracy.[9]

In becoming more democratic, Tunisia also became more religiously free. The very fact that Ennahda, thousands of whose members Ben Ali had imprisoned, could compete in and be allowed to win elections was a breakthrough for the free expression of religion. Once Ennahda was in office, it legalized two far more conservative parties, opening the system further to religious participation.[10]

The Constitution that went into effect in January 2014 stipulated that the country is a civil state and guaranteed freedom of belief, conscience, and the exercise of religious practice. Although the Constitution says that Tunisia's religion is Islam and that the president must be Muslim, it contains no clause saying that *sharia* is a (or, still less, *the*) source of legislation—a triumph for positive secularists and religious freedom advocates and a defeat for religious repression. The new government retained Tunisia's personal status laws, which are among the most progressive in the Muslim world, giving women a strong set of rights in family matters. Tunisia's laws allow no punishment for apostasy either.

The state relaxed its governance of religion. The Ministry of the Interior, Ben Ali's arm of religious repression, ceased to operate, and his police force was disbanded. The government gave mosques more freedom to conduct prayers and education, while requests to build new mosques spiked. Women were permitted to wear headscarves, including in their national identity card photos, and men beards. Religious charities and religious schools enjoyed newfound freedoms, and registration procedures for religious groups were eased. In this 99% Sunni Muslim country, Jews and Christians are permitted to worship freely and conduct education and other activities, though Shias and Baha'is are tolerated far less.[11]

The state has not relinquished its governance of religion, though, and Tunisia remains in the "high" category of Pew's GRI. The Ministry of Religious Affairs still subsidizes mosques, appoints and pays imams, cooperates with civil society groups in training imams to use moderate language in sermons, and appoints the grand mufti of the country. The government justifies ongoing restrictions mainly by the need to control religious groups that are prone to or actually carry out violence. Although it can be debated whether the restrictions are too tight, it cannot be denied that terrorist violence takes place, including two attacks on foreign tourists in 2015 and the assassination of prominent secular opposition leader Chokri Belaid in February 2013.[12]

On the whole, though, the new regime sanded down the rough edges of secular repression and increased the sphere of religious freedom.[13] Nobody played a more important role in securing this development than the Ennahda Party, an Islamic party with a reasonably robust political theology of religious freedom. In the early 2000s, Ennahda's leaders in exile affirmed a commitment to democracy and religious freedom. In June 2003, Ennahda leader Rashid Ghannouchi met in France with three nonregime parties to discuss and sign a "Call From Tunis" that proclaimed the goals of a government based on the sovereignty of the people and a guarantee of religious freedom for all. The Call made friendly references to the 19th-century Tunisian intellectuals and statesmen who had pioneered a politically liberal Islam. In 2005, the four parties thickened their commitments through the "18 October Coalition for Rights and Freedoms in Tunisia," affirming a commitment to the existing personal status laws, a democratic civic state (as opposed to a religious state), and a state where there would be "no compulsion in religion," including the right not to follow a religion.

In a 2011 interview with political scientist Alfred Stepan, Ghannouchi said that he would not seek a *sharia* council to review legislation. Another party leader, Hamadi Jebali, told Stepan in 2011 that he saw the Ennahda Party as closer to the Justice and Development Party (AKP) in Turkey than to a religious party like the Muslim Brotherhood in Egypt.[14] Ennahda has repeatedly stated its willingness to govern in coalition with secular parties and its commitment to respect individual human rights, including the rights of women and minorities. It has pointedly renounced pursuit of an Islamic state or "Iranian option."[15] Once in power, Ennahda did not support a constitutional clause declaring *sharia* as a source of legislation. Importantly, too, Ghannouchi was the one Tunisian political leader who met with the country's tiny Jewish community to affirm Jews' citizenship rights.[16]

As can be expected, the lifting of secular repression released the energies not only of Ennahda but also of far more restrictive Islamists. Prominent among them were Salafists, whose thought is rooted in Wahhabism and who aspire to replace traditional schools of jurisprudence with a direct interpretation of the Qur'an and Sunna, reject all separation of religion from politics and society, and achieve an Islamic state. Tunisian political scientist Hamid Redissi reports an estimate that Salafists range from 10,000 to 50,000 in number.[17]

For some Salafists, making Tunisia properly Islamic is a long-term endeavor that begins with *dawa*, the call to conversion, and shuns revolution or even contesting elections.[18] Others call for political engagement. Since Ben Ali's fall, Salafists have undertaken hundreds of street protests, sit-ins, and other forms of confrontation against what they believe to be the defilement of Islam in universities, the media, and the arts.[19] On March 25, 2012, for instance, thousands of Islamists reportedly demonstrated publicly for an Islamist state.[20] Were politically engaged Salafists to have their way, they would install a religiously repressive regime. A subset of Salafists is composed of violent *jihadis*. As of December 2015, some 5,500 young Tunisians—more than any other nationality—had joined the Islamic State, the world's most powerful Islamist militant group at the time.[21]

Salafists criticize Ennahda for being too soft in its Islam. Illustrative is a dispute over the Zaytuna Mosque, Tunisia's largest and most influential mosque, which Islamists sought to restore as a leader in Islamic education after the fall of Ben Ali, who had crippled Islam's role in education. After the October 2011 election, the Ennahda government and the Ministry of Higher Education and Ministry of Religious Affairs took the position that the mosque is independent in its governance but that the state would supervise its teaching. Salafists, Islamists more broadly, and the leaders of the mosque argued vigorously that the mosque ought to be far more independent, but the government insisted upon the supervision over their objections.[22]

It was also predictable that secularists would organize against the rise of Islamic politics. Some on the left had joined the movement to overthrow Ben

Ali but wanted to retain a French-style *laïcité* that would marginalize Islam from public life. Secularists challenged Islamists as well as the more moderate Ennahda Party over the Constitution and control of the media, higher education, and the religious sphere.[23] They gave public and symbolic prominence to a demand for the deletion of Article 1 from the Constitution, which had declared that Tunisia's "religion is Islam" and had slipped its way into the Constitution of the Bourguiba and Ben Ali governments despite their secularizing ambitions. Ennahda refused to agree to the deletion, arguing that the article was essential to Tunisia's national identity. The secularists rejoined that Ennahda's stance was symptomatic of its religiously repressive aspirations. Article 1, which remained in place, however, was not a repressive one, especially when compared with the laws of other Islamist countries. On Ennahda's right flank, Tunisia's Salafists were demanding a constitutional reference to *sharia* that would make the principle a standard for legislation. Ennahda ruled this out as well, underlying its moderate, pragmatic, and religiously free orientation.[24]

The secular left accused Ennahda of having ties with Islamists of a repressive sort and of practicing authoritarianism. They cited a video in which Ghannouchi reportedly ridiculed skeptics of *sharia* and voiced his goal of making Tunisia an Islamic state, and they alleged that Ghannouchi had called Ennahda's opponents "enemies of Islam."[25] They also accused Ennahda of exercising heavy-handed control over the media, the judiciary, and the police.

It cannot be proven how much Ennahda's Islamist veerings reflect efforts to stave off Salafists through appeasement rather than through some long-term Islamist aspiration of its own. Ennahda is a catchall party composed of many factions, some of them tending Islamist. It was constantly under pressure from its Islamist flank to do more for it and to make gestures in its direction. Its willingness to rule in coalition and its commitment to democratic procedures and policies of moderation once in office speak in favor of the genuineness of its commitments to democracy and freedom.

Ennahda lost power to a secularist party in October 2014, a loss that was due to persistent unemployment, ongoing terrorism, a lack of governing experience, and the sheer difficulty of governing democratically after five decades of dictatorship. Ennahda reacted to defeat by congratulating its opponent, stepping down, and throwing an outdoor party for its workers replete with music and fireworks. That Ennahda lit fireworks rather than took up firearms says much about its politics and about the critical role that it played in making Tunisia more democratic and religiously free than it was when its uprising began.

Egypt

Democracy and religious freedom have fared far worse in Egypt. Although the protesters in Cairo's Tahrir Square were not motivated by religion—their first banners read "Bread, Freedom, Social Justice, and Human Dignity"—the powerful and popular Muslim Brotherhood moved quickly to seize the political opportunity opened up by the fall of its political nemesis of half a century. In February 2011, the Brotherhood was finally allowed to form a political party, the Freedom and Justice Party (FJP), which won a resounding victory in parliamentary elections ending in early 2012, taking 47.2% of the seats. In contrast with Tunisia, though, it entered into a governing coalition not with secular parties but rather with Salafist parties, which had won 24% of the seats.

On June 30, 2012, FJP leader Mohammed Morsi became the first democratically elected head of state in Egypt's history. His presidency, though, was a rocky one on account both of the Islamist course that he charted and of the persistent power of Egypt's military and judiciary, bastions of secularism. In contrast to Tunisia, when Mubarak fell in February 2011, the Supreme Council of the Armed Forces controlled and supervised the transition to an elected government. Just prior to Morsi's election, the military, acting on a ruling of the Supreme Constitutional Court of Egypt, had closed the parliament and assumed many of parliament's powers for itself. In November 2012, after Morsi had been in office for several months, he resisted the military and the courts by seizing emergency executive powers in order to further passage of Egypt's new Constitution. In December, the new Constitution, more Islamist than Egypt's Constitution under Sadat and Mubarak, was approved by a popular referendum.

Both Morsi's seizure of power and his Islamic trajectory touched off major popular protests, which continued on and off for several months, culminating in a military coup d'état that removed him from office on July 3, 2013. The new government, under General Fattah el-Sisi, cracked down on the Muslim Brotherhood, arrested hundreds of its leaders, banned the movement once again, and, on August 14, 2013, attacked popular pro-Morsi protesters, killing hundreds (the numbers are disputed) and injuring some 4,000 of them. On March 24, 2014, an Egyptian court sentenced 529 members of the Brotherhood to death, and then on April 15, 2014, a court banned current and former members of the Brotherhood from running in presidential and parliamentary elections. The democratic experiment was over; secular repressive dictatorship had returned.

Over the course of these events, Egypt remained one of the most religiously unfree countries in the world, as its extremely high GRI scores in

Table 5.1 show. It was religiously unfree in all of the 20 different types of restrictions that make up the GRI ratings. For instance, the government actively used force against religious groups, failed to act against religious discrimination, highly favored one religion over others, instituted effective prohibitions on Muslims converting to other faiths, and strongly restricted religious literature and broadcasting.[26] Egypt also ranked high in social hostilities. Muslim mobs attacked Christian churches, for instance, almost always with impunity.

Up to 2011, Egypt's repression of religious freedom combined both secular and religiously repressive elements, although the regime was broadly secular repressive in its orientation, as I argued in the previous chapter. The fall of Mubarak and then the rise of Morsi changed the mix of repressive measures so as to relax some of the secularist restrictions and to increase the religious ones. The legalization of the Muslim Brotherhood as a political party and the granting of greater independence to Al-Azhar University, for instance, realized great freedom for Muslims.[27] The December 2012 Constitution, though, added restrictions of an Islamist sort.[28]

Why did Egypt fail to follow the comparatively sunny path of Tunisia? One major reason was that the Muslim Brotherhood was more traditionally Islamic than its counterpart, the Ennahda Party. Like Ennahda, the Brotherhood was its country's strongest organized Muslim voice in social and political affairs, more moderate than the Salafist parties, and thus a pivotal player in determining whether a religiously free democracy would be advanced. The Brotherhood, however, did not articulate religious freedom and principled pluralism as clearly as Ennahda did, created worries that it would subvert these values, and failed to assuage the fears of secularists who were chary of the Brotherhood's political participation. It could not serve as a credible carrier, then, of a more open political system.

During the decades prior to the uprising of 2011, the Brotherhood had committed itself to the rules of the democratic game. It had renounced violence and would stand in elections, abide by the will of the majority, cooperate in the political system with secular parties, respect the separation of powers and an independent judiciary, and uphold the rights of women and non-Muslims. It stood for these things even though it suffered being outlawed as a political party, the imprisonment of its leaders, and the blatant rigging of elections in which it fielded candidates for parliament under a banner other than the Brotherhood. It insisted that its democratic commitments were grounded in Islamic principles and made clear that, playing by the democratic rules, it would seek laws that reflected these principles and that would further its long-term goal of a religiously faithful society. For instance, it would promote an

Islamic understanding of family and sexuality and might well restrict the consumption of alcohol.[29]

The Brotherhood continued to voice these commitments when it finally gained the freedom to contest its views in the political arena after Mubarak's fall. Stressing Islamic foundations, the 2012 platform of the FJP defined *sharia* as the "frame of reference" that fosters "faith, worship, and morality."[30] The political theology of the Brotherhood, then, favored democracy as a form of regime that could be grounded in Islamic doctrine and could serve to advance the principles of Islam.

There is no reason to doubt the sincerity of the Brotherhood's commitment to the rules of the democratic game in order to raise questions about its commitment to religious freedom. Remember from previous chapters that a commitment to democracy—elections, the rule of law, separation of powers—does not necessarily mean a commitment to religious freedom. True, in Morsi's 2012 campaign, he said that Coptic Christians "are certainly just as Egyptian as I am, and have as much a right to this homeland as I do," that religious freedom is a right grounded in Allah's commands, and that respect for non-Muslims on the part of Muslims is a command of *sharia*.[31] Even such a broad affirmation of the right of religious freedom and the rights of minorities, though, leaves open the question of how these rights might be qualified. Do they extend to blasphemous speech? The public expression of non-Islamic religious beliefs or Islamic views that depart from Sunni orthodoxy? The opportunity to construct Christian or Baha'i houses of worship? The freedom to convert away from Islam without punishment? These are not idle questions but exactly the sort that Egypt has long faced and that were thrown open again by the demise of Mubarak's secular repressive dictatorship.

Unfortunately the Muslim Brotherhood's answers to these questions, both before and after Mubarak's fall, did not yield confidence in its commitment to religious freedom. In its 2007 draft party platform, the Brotherhood proposed a *sharia* council based at Al-Azhar to review laws—something akin to an Islamist veto power. Although the Brotherhood dropped this plank from later versions of its platform, it retained a separate plank holding that no woman or Christian could be president. The FJP's platform of 2012 favored a *private* right to *worship* to be enjoyed by minority faiths—a classic formula for a curtailed right to religious freedom—alongside a public "right to be governed according to religious values owed to the majority faith"—a troubling bifurcation in light of the demands of religious freedom.[32]

In the 2012 presidential campaign, partly in response to Salafist pressures, Morsi and other FJP candidates waxed Islamist. At one rally, Islamist preachers crowed that Morsi would restore the Caliphate. Morsi declaimed that "the Quran has been and will continue to be our constitution, [and] we believe in the application of *sharia* now rather than in the future."[33] Morsi's campaign touted its endorsements by Salafi leaders. Not long after he was elected, he made Islamist appointments that seemed to confirm the fears of his opponents.[34]

When the FJP published its draft Constitution in late 2012, many viewed it as compromising the religious rights of minorities.[35] Language in Articles 10 and 11 granted the state the role of safeguarding ethics, morality, and the family, promoting "religious and patriotic values," and guarding religion both for its own sake and because it is integral to the "national heritage."[36] This Constitution retained the famous provision from the previous Constitution holding that *sharia* is *the* principle source of legislation. Article 81 makes clear that the rights and freedoms of the people are subject to this provision, that *sharia* is the basis of legislation, and that Islam is the religion of the state. Under Salafi pressure, the FJP inserted a consultative role for Al-Azhar University on matters related to *sharia* and gave the Azhari Council of Senior Scholars enhanced powers of judicial review. This Constitution also contained strong prohibitions on blasphemy against all religious prophets.[37] All of these were classic features of a religiously repressive regime.

Beyond the Islamist tendencies of the Muslim Brotherhood and its political arm, the FJP, the second reason why Egypt's trajectory was less free than Tunisia's was the power of Salafist parties. Their size, their power, and their influence meant that the FJP had to show sympathy for their agenda to prevent voters from fleeing to them, enter into coalition with them after the first parliamentary elections, and continue to appease them during the FJP's tenure in office.

The Salafist movement was founded in Egypt in the 1970s, centered on its main group, the Salafi Call, and grew over subsequent decades. It had espoused a quietist political theology that shunned political involvement, viewing democracy as a Western corruption, interpreting Islam to forbid political participation, and stressing the *dawa*, or "call," which translated to a long-term Islamization of society that would eventually encompass politics. Salafists took the Muslim Brotherhood to task for involving itself in a system rooted in the laws of man, not of God.[38]

After Mubarak's fall, though, Egypt's Salafists changed course, abandoned their quietism, and formed political parties that would stand for elections, the most important of these being Al Nour [the Party of Light]. Although Al Nour stressed the civil character of the state, it called for a rigid application of *sharia*, stressed the strong role of the *ulema* in politics, and demanded measures like a strict segregation of the sexes and a ban on women and Christian presidents. Part of the secret of their success was their outreach: "they [liberals and seculars] didn't come to our streets, didn't live in our villages, didn't walk in our hamlets, didn't wear our clothes, didn't eat our bread, didn't drink our polluted water, didn't live in the sewage we live in and didn't experience the life and misery and hardship of the people," one Salafi leader put it.[39]

In February and March 2013, the Salafists broke with the FJP, their leaders making strong attacks on the FJP and Morsi for failing in leadership, grabbing power, and creating a weak government. The Salafis' exit made Morsi all the more vulnerable to overthrow a few months later.[40]

A third reason for the failure of Egypt's revolution was the forces of repressive secularism, namely the army and the judiciary. Much like Turkey's Atatürk, Nasser had established these two institutions as sentries of the republic's secularism, charged with fending off the zealous encroachments of the Muslim Brotherhood and other Islamist factions. Whereas the army in Tunisia largely refrained from involving itself in the country's political transition, power in Egypt continued to repose in these institutions as the uprising ran its course. They controlled the transition to parliamentary and presidential elections; they greatly weakened Morsi; and they eventually overthrew him. They secured passage of a new Constitution in a 2014 referendum, one that was much like the 1971 Constitution that existed up to Mubarak's ouster. The Sisi regime, like the Mubarak regime, was secular repressive in its orientation, though its law and policies contained an alloy of both Islamist and secular repressive elements.

Being powerful, the army and the judiciary were able to intervene against the Islamist government. Being secular in their political theology, they were inclined to intervene, even though the government was democratically elected. The Islamist course that the FJP steered, pressured by Salafis, quickened their intervention. The forces of secular repression and religious repression are mutually repulsive, each mobilizing the other to aggressive action, undermining democracy and freedom.

Two other sectors help explain the outcome in Egypt as well. One is Coptic Christians, about 10% of the population at the time of the uprising. When the demonstrations began, Coptic Pope Shenouda backed Mubarak and ordered his clergy not to participate. Ever since Shenouda had returned from exile in 1985, he had been loyal to Mubarak, to whom Copts looked for protection against the Islamists who attacked them regularly. Following the uprising, Islamist attacks on Copts greatly increased, and by 2013, an estimated 100,000 Copts had fled the country.[41] Because of the Copts' treatment at the hands of the Islamists, they could not trust the Morsi government; they favored the return of secular repression; and they constituted an important bloc of the population whose support for the democratic experiment was, understandably, lacking. Pope Tawadros, who succeeded Shenouda following his death in 2012, was a part of the small group of top leaders who supported Sisi's coup in July 2013. Sisi reciprocated with protection and support for Copts. The new Constitution of 2014, for instance, established an antidiscrimination commission and required parliament to pass a law that makes easier the construction and renovation of churches. Meanwhile, Sisi tightened his governance of mosques and imams.[42]

The other relevant sector was the Wasat Party, formed in 1996, an Islamic party with a strong commitment to liberal democracy, including a robust favor for religious freedom and a flexible view of *sharia* law. Among the party's top leaders were three women and two Copts. Wasat, though, was weak, having won only 3.7% of the vote in the parliamentary election that ended in January 2012. Wasat and other liberal parties—and the hope for a religiously free democracy that they carried—were vastly outnumbered by the coalition of Islamic parties.[43]

Libya

In February 2011, the month after protests broke out in Egypt and Tunisia, popular demonstrations took place in Libya against another secular repressive ruler, Muammar Qaddafi. Qaddafi's forces fired on the crowds, igniting a civil war that, with the indispensable aid of NATO military intervention in March 2011, succeeded in overthrowing Qaddafi and founding a new regime. An angry crowd killed the dictator after they discovered him hiding in a drain pipe in his hometown of Sirte in October 2011.

In February 2015, four years after Libya's uprising began, Sirte was the site from which the international violent *jihadi* network, the Islamic State, kidnapped 21 people—20 Egyptian Coptic Christian migrant workers and a Ghanaian construction worker[44]—whom they took to a Mediterranean beach and beheaded. The Islamic State released a video of the beheadings on the Internet, which went viral and became one of the most memorable images of religious brutality—and of the savage denial of religious freedom—in recent years. "You've seen us . . . chopping off heads that had been carrying the cross delusion for a long time," declared one of the killers in the video.[45]

The Islamic State had gained a foothold in Libya in a milieu of civil war and anarchy. In an article in *The New Yorker* published in early 2015, journalist Jon Lee Anderson wrote this description:

> There is no overstating the chaos of post-Qaddafi Libya. Two competing governments claim legitimacy. Armed militias roam the streets. The

electricity is frequently out of service, and most business is at a stand-still; revenues from oil, the country's greatest asset, have dwindled by more than ninety per cent. Some three thousand people have been killed by fighting in the past year, and nearly a third of the country's population has fled across the border to Tunisia. What has followed the downfall of a tyrant—a downfall encouraged by NATO air strikes—is the tyranny of a dangerous and pervasive instability.

In the same piece he tells of the 170,000 migrants who had fled across the Mediterranean to Europe and of the more than 3,000 who died at sea trying.[46]

Why did Libya's uprising descend into civil war? The country had been riven for years by tribal and regional loyalties, which Qaddafi had contained through his security forces and their characteristic methods, and was denuded of state institutions and civil society, which Qaddafi had stunted in his quest for purely personal control.[47] Governing institutions were plagued with one of the world's highest levels of corruption.[48] Vast oil wealth was concentrated in a tiny number of hands. Religion—and rival notions of religion's place in governance, or political theology—did much to propel the descent as well, though.

The regime that replaced the deposed Qaddafi nevertheless laid out a blue-print for a constitutional democracy and even achieved some initial success in building it. The blueprint was the interim constitutional declaration that the National Transitional Council published in August 2011, which led to national elections in July 2012, which in turn yielded governance to a new legislature, the General National Congress, and a new prime minister. In contrast to Egypt's first election, Islamic forces, represented by the political arm of the Muslim Brotherhood, the Justice and Construction Party, won only 10.3% of the vote and were defeated by the liberal and centrist National Forces Alliance (NFA), which won 48.1% of the vote.[49]

In some respects, the new regime opened up space for religion, which Qaddafi had closely monitored and controlled. It legalized the Muslim Brotherhood and allowed Muslims to express their views openly and to organize politically. The interim constitution protected religious freedom, accorded non-Muslims the right to practice their faith, and forbade religious discrimination. The government allowed religious scholars to form organizations that could issue *fatwas* and provide advice to followers.[50]

In other respects, though, the regime began to look religiously repressive. It came under strong pressure from Islamists who, despite their paltry electoral showing in 2012, found more thuggish ways to exert influence. In May 2012, for instance, Islamist militants burst into government offices demanding passage of a law that would prohibit virtually anyone who had been involved in Qaddafi's government from holding further office—a draconian effort to cleanse perceived secular oppressors from power.[51] The Muslim Brotherhood, which participated in the political system, called for legislation that would advance a traditional Islamic agenda and was moderate in comparison with the Salafis and violent *jihadis* who strode to its right. Even the NFA, the big winner of the first elections, disavowed describing itself as "secular" or "liberal" in order to demonstrate its religious *bona fides*. In February 2012, the NFA's leader, Mahmoud Jibril, stated that "the rulings [*ahkām*] of *sharia* are a principal source of legislation."[52]

While loosening Qaddafi's secularist restrictions, the new regime retained structures for governing religion and steered them in an Islamist direction. A Ministry for Endowments and Islamic Affairs continued to administer mosques, oversee the work of clerics, furnish texts for Friday sermons, and ascertain that religious practices in Libya met Islamic standards. In 2012, the National Transitional Council established a grand mufti to serve as the most authoritative religious scholar in the country and to issue official *fatwas*, appointing a Salafist cleric, Sheikh Sadeq al-Gharyani, as the first holder of the position. Al-Gharyani would take strongly traditional stances, declaring, for instance, that gender integration in educational institutions is immoral.[53]

Whereas no law was passed that prohibits conversion away from Islam, the government would detain and deport people, especially Christians, whom it perceived to be proselytizing. Christians thought to be spreading religious literature were charged with sowing division and insulting Islam, crimes that carry a maximum sentence of death. The government has done little to stop or punish frequent Islamist attacks on Sufis, Coptic Christians, and their houses of worship and sacred sites.[54] Most important, a December 2013 statement of the General National Congress declared *sharia* the only source of legislation and voided laws that contradict *sharia*. Recalling the evolution of Egypt's Constitution, using the words "the only" rather than "a" to describe "source of legislation" strongly indicated an Islamist trend.[55]

Whatever the level of religious freedom or democracy of the new regime, it was increasingly beset by its lack of control over the country and its legion strongmen, warlords, and *jihadis*. In summer 2014, open civil war broke out. National elections were held in June that were meant to establish a new legislature, the House of Representatives, to replace the General National Congress. When Islamists lost the elections, they complained of irregularities, claimed the General National Council as the legitimate legislature, and established it in Tripoli. Meanwhile, the new House of Representatives met in Tobruk as a rival legislature. Thereafter, the country has been controlled by two governments, each associated with an armed faction. Each faction is in turn supported by outside powers, Qatar being on the side of the Islamists and the United Arab Emirates being on the side of the (relatively) more secular parties, thus rendering the conflict a regional one.[56]

Watching this disintegration take place from his home in Virginia was Khalifa Haftar, a high-ranking defector from Qaddafi's army who had lived in exile in the United States for about 20 years. Returning to Libya in 2011, he assembled a coalition of factions that he called Operation Dignity and launched a military offensive against Islamist factions. Although there is little record of Haftar expressing anything more than a rough account of how Libya ought to be governed religiously and although his loyalties have shifted many times over the course of his career, it is clear that he began his career as a secularist and an admirer of Nasser and that he now declares it his goal to rid Libya of Islamic influence, making no distinction between moderates and extremists. It is safe to say that Haftar's victory would bring with it secular repression.[57]

Arrayed against Haftar's coalition is Operation (Libya) Dawn, an opposing coalition of Islamists and their close allies. In 2014, Grand Mufti al-Gharyani urged Libyans to view their country's conflict in religious terms, declaring that a person who died fighting against Operation Dignity could be considered a martyr, and speaking of Operation Dawn and its cousin, the Benghazi Revolutionaries' Shura Council, as heroes. Late in 2014, al-Gharyani exhorted the General National Council to enact Islamic law immediately. Several of the factions in the coalition are violent *jihadi* extremists, and where they control territory, they institute religious repression of the harshest kind. In the eastern city of Derna, two *jihadi* groups closely affiliated with the Islamic State executed and flogged residents for violating *sharia* law—drinking alcohol, for instance—and ordered segregation of the schools. When *jihadis* invaded Benghazi in summer 2014, they undertook a merciless campaign of assassination. The Islamic State also took root and gained strength in Libya during this period of civil war, beheading its opponents and pursuing its dream of a Caliphate.[58]

Syria

Another civil war sparked by the Arab Uprisings, this one dwarfing Libya's, has convulsed Syria. "This conflict did not begin as a strictly religious conflict," observes Nicole Bibbins Sedaca, "[i]t began much as the uprisings in other Arab countries throughout the Arab Spring: average citizens of all walks of life going to the street to claim the freedoms that had long been denied them by a dictator with a tight grip on power."[59] These citizens were peaceful and belonged to diverse religions and sects.[60] Soon after they began to protest in March 2011, the dictator with a tight grip on power, President Bashar al-Assad, met them with prompt and disproportionate violence.[61] By September 2011, civil war was underway. In summer 2012, the opposition was still led by the Free Syrian Army, an assemblage of relatively moderate forces who sought a civic democracy. Soon thereafter, though, *jihadi* rebel groups came to dominate. By the end of 2012, a United Nations report determined that the conflict had become a sectarian one.[62] Each side deployed acidic religious rhetoric, affixing the other with epithets like infidel and Satan's army.[63] As of September 2015, the Islamic State held 35%–45% of Syria's territory and most of its oil and gas production. Yet, in contrast to the pattern in Tunisia, Egypt, and Libya, the Assad regime was still in power.[64]

"The sectarian divide in Syria," continues Sedaca, "is neither a perception nor a secondary point of analysis. It is a reality that is central to the roots of the conflict as well as to why it is being fought and how it will be resolved."[65] The conflict is not only religious but is centrally one between two political theologies whose positions on religious freedom are what each side fears in the other. Assad's Ba'athist regime has always been secular repressive, protecting Alawites and Christians while outlawing the Muslim Brotherhood and tightly controlling Sunni Islam. From the moment the protests broke out, Assad has portrayed the opposition to his regime as one of Islamic terrorism.[66] With such appeals, and with no small amount of corroborating evidence available to cite, Assad has consolidated his support among Alawites and Christians and marshaled it against Sunni Muslims. Reciprocating Sunni *jihadis'* brutality, local Alawite security forces—known as *shabiha*—are responsible for some of the war's worst massacres.[67]

The conflict's religious cleavages are not only between Assad's secular repression and the dominant opposition forces' religious repression but also between Shia Muslims, who demand freedom to practice their faith, including building shrines, and Sunni Muslims, making up 75% of Syria's population, many of whom would deny Shias that freedom.

It is largely these religious divisions that have rendered the conflict a regional one. Shias from Lebanon, Iraq, and Iran have descended on Syria to protect Shia sacred sites and to defend Assad's regime. The government of Iran has funded Assad, while in May 2013, the Lebanese militant group Hezbollah entered the conflict on Assad's side and provided critical force in pushing back rebel advances.[68]

On the other side of the conflict, Sunni Muslims from outside Syria have supported the *jihadis* of Syria for their opposition to Assad's secularism and his support for Shias. Saudi Arabia and Qatar have supported Sunni opposition groups diplomatically and financially.[69] Yusuf al-Qaradawi, the international celebrity Sunni cleric, signed a *fatwa* in August 2011 calling on Muslims all over the world to "assist the Syrian people with words and actions" against the "heretical Syrian regime." Then, in January 2012, 70 religious scholars, Qaradawi among them, proclaimed that *"jihad* in Syria is an obligation for any Muslim." Qaradawi also called for *jihad* against the Syrian regime on the television program, Aljazeera Arabic, which is viewed by 40–50 million people.[70] He has exhorted Sunnis to fight against Shiites and Hezbollah, calling them the "Party of the Devil." When Mohamed Morsi was president of Egypt, Qaradawi cut off ties with Syria and took up opposition to Hezbollah under the strong urging of Sunni clerics.[71] Another supporter of Syria's Sunni opposition is Al-Qaeda in Iraq, who has carried on its own fight against the Shia government of Iraq. Finally, some 25,000 fighters from tens of countries, including at least 4,500 westerners, have come to join the Islamic State, encouraged by the calls of radical Muslim preachers.[72]

Those rebel armies who have conquered the most territory also have implemented the most religiously repressive governance. All of them Sunni, they have enforced a rigid *sharia* that allows little deviance or dissent among Muslims and little room for non-Muslims to practice their faith. The Islamic State earned a genocide designation from the US government in March 2016 for its treatment of Yazidis, Christians, Mandaeans, Shias, and other religious minorities, involving expulsions, massacres, and the sexual enslavement of women. Aside from the Islamic State, the most powerful army has been al-Nusra, who has practiced frequent suicide bombings, maintained allegiance to Al-Qaeda, and severely mistreated religious minorities. In September 2013, 13 Islamic rebel armies spurned the more moderate Syrian National Coalition and averred that *sharia* law is the "sole source of legislation."[73]

Some Sunni opponents of Assad are more moderate, for instance, the alliance known as the Syrian Coalition. The Muslim Brotherhood in Syria, which holds the most seats in the Syrian Coalition of any group, affirmed in March 2012 its support for "a civil and democratic republican state with a parliamentary system, in which all the people are treated equal regardless of faith or ethnicity."[74] As in Egypt, the Brotherhood has affirmed its willingness to participate in democratic politics, though it is reasonable to ask whether, once it is in office, it will advance legislation that compromises religious freedom. All of these relative moderates, though, have been overpowered by the forces of religious repression, who are in turn marshaled against the forces of secular repression.

Yemen

In contrast to the four uprisings analyzed so far, which were aimed at a sec-ular repressive regime, in two Gulf States, Yemen and Bahrain, uprisings took place against a religiously repressive regime. On January 15, 2011, one day after President Ben Ali was ousted in Tunisia, demonstrators, mostly youth, took to the streets in Sanaa, Yemen's capital, to protest corruption and au-thoritarianism in the regime of President Ali Abdullah Saleh. Over the next couple of months, their numbers grew into the thousands. In March, Saleh's troops fired their guns upon them, causing Saleh to lose the support of his key army leaders and coming under pressure to resign. Saleh finally stepped down in November 2011, in accordance with a proposal brokered by the Gulf Cooperation Council that would allow him to receive immunity from prosecu-tion. Saleh's vice president, Abd Rabbuh Mansur Hadi, was elected president in February 2012 and formed a government that included opposition leaders and set a timetable for a constitution to be developed and multiparty and pres-idential elections to be held.

These strides toward governance, however, were then swept over by vio-lent rivalries between regional and religious factions. Like Syria and Libya, Yemen then descended into civil war, which began in 2015. Opposing the state were the Houthis, an armed group representing Yemen's 35% Shia popula-tion, located in the north of the country. Tensions between Shias and Sunnis, north and south, had been accumulating since 1990 and had taken the form of violence since 2004, displacing some 300,000 people.[75] The Islamic State and Al-Qaeda also expanded in Yemen during this time and took up arms against the state. By March 2016, the Houthis controlled the western portion of the state, including the capital city, Sanaa; the government controlled the middle band of the country, including the port city of Aden; and Al-Qaeda and its allies controlled swaths of land in the middle and eastern portions of the country.

What was the fate of religious freedom through all of these events? Prior to the uprising, Yemen's Constitution did not prescribe religious freedom; the Constitution specified that Islam is the state religion and *sharia* is the source of all laws; blasphemy laws were in place; other laws prohibited conversion away from Islam with the death penalty attached; non-Muslims were barred from running for parliament; Muslim women were not permitted to marry non-Muslim men while Muslim men were prohibited from marrying women who are something other than Muslim, Jewish, or Christian; and other meas-ures characteristic of religiously repressive regimes existed. The country's tiny

Christian community (some 3,000 people in a country of 26 million people in 2014) could worship but was barred strictly from proselytizing.[76] The Jewish community suffered harassment, often violent, from fellow Muslim citizens, not long before the uprisings began; the government did little to stop it; and many of the 1,000 remaining Jews in the country fled. The national government restricted Shias in the north, for instance, prohibiting their holiday celebrations and forbidding their mosques from being open outside of prayers—restrictions that Shias regarded as an unjust curtailment of their freedom but that the government insisted were measures to curb separatist violence.[77]

Yemen's Constitution and basic laws remained in place after its uprising, unlike in Egypt and Tunisia, where they were thrown out. Still, Yemen made efforts to ease its religious restrictions. The National Dialogue Conference, whose several hundred delegates were tasked with developing inclusive laws, established the Rights and Freedoms Working Group, which made numerous recommendations for enhancing religious liberty. It was a mouthpiece for a political theology of religious freedom, proposing measures to safeguard against discrimination; better protections for religious minorities; the abolition of blasphemy laws; and educational materials designed to further respect for other religions.[78]

It is not clear whether any of these measures have been adopted, but some religious restrictions have been loosened. Non-Muslims may now run for elected office except for the presidency. The government has lifted its bans on the public commemoration of Shia holidays, Shia literature, and permits for Shia libraries and book clubs. The participation in government of the relatively moderate Islamist Islah Party, which has connections to the Muslim Brotherhood, has resulted in looser restrictions on Islamic institutions.[79]

Religious freedom has suffered greatly, though, from the rise of *jihadi* extremist groups. Salafi religious figures have accused wide groups of people—political activists, journalists, bloggers, scholars, and human rights activists—of apostasy. Ardent Sunni Islamists engage the practice of *takfir*, or naming as apostate, Shias and others whom they believe have compromised the faith, including members of the government. Shias return the favor. In addition, Al-Qaeda in the Arabian Peninsula has carried out attacks in Yemen beginning in the 2000s and increasing during the time of transition and civil war. The group has assaulted government installations, soldiers, and other individuals whom it accuses of immoral behavior. In the regions where it rules, it institutes and harshly enforces a rigid form of *sharia*.[80] By and large, Yemen remains religiously repressive.

Bahrain

To the north, protests in the tiny island country of Bahrain ended in an outcome unique among the Arab Uprisings: neither the overthrow of a regime
nor civil war but rather the suppression of protest by the state. Bahrain has a
population of about 1.3 million people, about half a million of whom are citizens, the rest being foreign workers. Of the citizens, an estimated 65%–75%
are Shia Muslims, though no official numbers are available; almost all the
rest are Sunni Muslims.[81] The Shias, though, by and large do not govern the
country or hold high positions in business or other sectors of society. The
government is rather a monarchy that rests in the hands of the Khalifa family,
who has run the country since 1783, enjoys the support of Saudi Arabia and
the United States, and ensures Sunni domination in the government and
other sectors of society. It was out of a pervasive and enduring sense of enforced inequality that mostly Shia protesters took to the streets in February
2011, occupied Pearl Roundabout in the capital city of Manama, and called
for human rights, political participation, and an end to discrimination. One
month after a Day of Rage was held on February 14, 2011, troops from Saudi
Arabia and the Gulf Cooperation Council crossed the King Fahd causeway that
connects Saudi Arabia and Bahrain and supported Bahrain's security forces in
clearing the area. Thousands of protesters were arrested, an estimated 64% of
detainees were tortured, and tens of people died in the crackdown.[82]

Prior to the uprising, Bahrain practiced a moderate to high degree of restriction of a religiously repressive kind. Along with the standard features of
regimes of this sort went the state's heavy discrimination against Shias and
tight control of Shia religious practice. Sunnis enjoyed a privileged legal and
social status in government, business, and education as well as superior mu-
nicipal services in the locales where they lived. Against Shia activism and protest, the government would practice arbitrary arrests, use force excessively,
and carry out other forms of mistreatment, including torture. It would also
closely monitor and restrict Shia mosques and holiday celebrations, claiming
that it was promoting security, not discrimination. Of course, the government
deemed security to include quelling public protest. To justify its repression,
the regime argued that, were Shias to accrue power, they would establish a
Shia theocracy like that in Iran.[83]

In the conduct and aftermath of the crackdown, religious freedom in
Bahrain plummeted. As the security forces repressed demonstrators, so,
too, they destroyed Shia mosques, centers, and shrines; proclaimed a "State
of National Safety" law that facilitated the detaining and torture of Shia
protesters; smeared Shias in the government-run media, including comparing

them, in terms evocative of the Rwandan genocide, to termites who should be exterminated; and dismissed thousands of Shias from their jobs in both the public and private sectors. In 2014, the High Court ordered the disbanding of the Islamic Ulema Council, the main organization of Bahrain's Shia clerics, whom the government said was using religion as a mask for political opposition.[84]

In certain ways, the government also sought to soften its suppression. It pledged to rebuild the Shia mosques that it had destroyed and had reconstructed 23 by the end of 2014. It granted Shias greater leeway for worship and holiday processions, though it still placed restrictions on them. It increased recruiting of Shia police and pursued the religious integration of institutions in other ways. Still, Bahrain remained religiously repressive, especially for Shias.[85]

Lessons for Religious Freedom

The Arab Uprisings reinforce this book's argument. From a satellite view, they appear to corroborate skepticism about religious freedom in Islam. Five years after the protests of early 2011, the preponderance of these predominantly Muslim countries was not more religiously free. The dreams of the brave people who first took to the streets, risking being trampled by the forces of a dictatorship, were largely dashed as well. Democracy in the vast majority of cases failed to advance. Muslim countries along with a vast failure of religious freedom and democracy: Does such a correlation bolster the judgment that Islam is inhospitable to religious freedom?

Here again, zooming in on the cases reveals a more complex picture. Islamoskeptics will depict this picture as one of traditional Islamic forces—radical *jihadi* militant groups, Salafists, and their ideological confreres—obstructing freedom's emergence. The power of Salafists in Egypt, Morsi's need to appease their demands, and Morsi's own Islamist signals stoked the fears of proponents of religiously free democracy, and even more so the fears of secularists and of Coptic Christians, that religious repression was in the offing. In Libya, the refusal of radical Islamist militants and Salafists to join the nascent and fragile democratic government doomed its prospects more than any other factor. In Syria, radical Islamist militants took over the opposition to the Assad government and conquered a substantial portion of the country's territory, where they fomented a religious repression of beheadings and expulsion. In Yemen, too, radical Islamic groups, especially Sunni ones, have attacked members of the government, harshly discriminated against

Shias, and ruled the territories they control with religious repression. In Bahrain, the Sunni minority government has continued to discriminate sharply against the minority Shias well after the Shias rose up. Without a doubt, bearers of the religiously repressive pattern of denying freedom have exercised strong sway over the direction of the Arab Uprisings.

To leave matters there, though, leaves a great deal unexplained. The secular repressive dictatorships that ruled Arab countries for decades also bear much of the blame for the failure of religiously free democracies to develop. Decades of secular repression in Egypt, Libya, and Syria choked off opportunities for Islamic parties with inclinations toward democracy or religious freedom to gain experience in organizing politically and participating in democratic governance. Many Islamic groups reacted to repression by becoming militant opponents of the political system. Thus, when secular repressive dictatorships fell, Islamic parties were ill-equipped to govern effectively, especially in the face of economic tumult and institutions rotten with corruption. Even in Tunisia, whose post-uprising trajectory was far more positive, the difficulty of facing these burdens rendered the Ennahda Party an electoral loser when it faced its second round at the polls.

Secular repressive forces persisted after the uprisings in Egypt, Libya, Tunisia, and Syria, where they both weakened Islamic sectors who sought democracy and religious freedom and contributed to a mutually reinforcing polarization between secular and religiously repressive parties. While the powerful and secularist Egyptian army hung like a Sword of Damocles over Egypt's democratic experiment, the religiously repressive tendencies of President Morsi's government provoked protesters to return to the streets and gave the army the pretext to drop the sword and return the country to a secular repressive dictatorship. In Libya, forces who carry the prospect of secular repression vie for dominance with Islamist forces who foment religious repression. The secular repressive government in Syria has not been overthrown but continues to fight a civil war in which both this government and its religiously repressive Muslim opponents have muffled moderate Muslim voices who call for democracy and religious harmony. A mutually fortifying opposition between secular repression and religious repression, then, accounts for freedom's failure better than religious repression alone.

The fate of freedom in the Arab Uprisings is made still more complex by the presence of Muslim proponents of religious freedom—that is, people and parties committed both to an Islamic vision for the society and to an expansion of democracy and religious freedom. Tunisia's Ennahda Party is the best example of such a party, one that articulated principles of religious freedom and mostly resisted religiously repressive demands from Islamists.

Ennahda is far from perfect in its fidelity to freedom, as is true of Tunisia's Constitution, laws, and democracy. But Ennahda represents a genuine force for religious freedom in the Arab world. In each of the other countries where major uprisings took place, there were also people and factions who stood for religious freedom on Islamic grounds.

The Muslim Brotherhood is more mixed in its support for religious freedom. For a generation now, in Egypt and in other countries, it has voiced its commitment to participating democratically in a political system that it coinhabits with secular parties. This does not mean, however, that the Brotherhood will cease supporting laws that confine the religious behavior of both Muslims and Christians. It favors religious freedom more than the parties on its right flank, but this is a low standard. The Brotherhood's performance in Egypt under Morsi leaves it lacking a track record of advancing freedom while actually in power, although it is difficult to know how much its behavior was due to the need to appease the Islamists with whom it shared governance. On the religious freedom spectrum, the Brotherhood lies between parties like Ennahda and the Justice and Development Party in Turkey (of 2002–2011) on the one hand, and Salafists on the other.

The fate of religious freedom in the Arab world, then, cannot be explained simply as an upshot of Islam or of Islamism. Rather, it results from the interplay among factions holding political theologies of religious freedom, secular repression, and religious repression. Where religious freedom champions were strong enough and could position themselves favorably to the advocates of the other two political theologies, as was the case in Tunisia, religious freedom could be advanced. In most cases, though, partisans of religious freedom did not enjoy such advantages.

The interplay between these factions in turn explains much about the fate of democracy, the aspiration of Mohamed Bouazizi and the other protesters who first took to the Arab streets. Political theologies of religious freedom, of course, are not the only determinant of the success of democracy. A country's level of economic development, the repressive capacities of the state, and other factors obviously will be crucial.[86] Where parties or factions holding a political theology of religious freedom are relatively strong, though, democracy stands a much better chance, and where forces of secular repression and religious repression are relatively strong, democracy will be handicapped. Religion matters, and religious freedom matters.

In Egypt, if secularism had not been lodged so strongly in the army and if Salafist forces had not been as popular as they were, the democratic experiment might not have been cut short so brusquely. Were Libya not riven by Islamists who shun the system and secularist forces who would expel all advocates of an Islamic politics, the nascent democratic government would not be so beleaguered. If Syria were not cleft among a secular dictator and Islamist militants who each mortally fear the other's religious agenda—and fear the ways in which the other would curtail religious freedom—a peace settlement and possible national elections would stand a much better chance. If the governments of Yemen and Bahrain were more inclusive of Shias and that of Yemen not forced to fight religiously repressive militants, both governments would be in a better position to stage free elections. In Tunisia, by contrast, the impressive size and influence of an Islamic political party committed to greater religious freedom, the relative weakness of Salafists, and the willingness of secular parties to form a coalition with the Muslim religious freedom party were all crucial to the democratic success that Tunisia has enjoyed so far.

To say that democracy would fare better were religious freedom stronger may smack of utopianism. It might recall to mind the old joke about the physicist, the chemist, and the economist who are stranded on a desert island with a tin can of food and nothing to open it with, whereupon the chemist and physicist invent clever prying mechanisms while the economist declares: Assume a can opener! To say that religious freedom is the solution to the Arab world's political problems may seem to beg for something that is not on the horizon: Assume religious freedom. Yet, if one can identify how the presence or absence of a certain quality has a direct impact on the political fate of a country, then perhaps the consensus upon the importance of developing that quality will grow in numbers and strength. This development may take place only over the long term, but the same could be said about other political principles that were once rare and are now widely accepted around the globe. Recall that the success of democratization movements in Eastern Europe and Latin America in the 1980s were preceded historically by failed springs. We cannot discount that a spring may yet emerge in the Arab world or rule out that religious freedom might help to melt the snows of repression.

6

Seven Seeds of Freedom

THE PAST FOUR chapters have looked at the state of religious freedom in the Muslim-majority world. In the aggregate, the Muslim-majority world is less religiously free than the rest of the world and in religiously repressive countries is severely lacking religious freedom. Yet, religious freedom exists and is supported by Islamic teachings, and where it does not exist, Islam is not always the reason for its absence. This combination of absence and presence leads us to ask whether Islam contains potential for expanding religious freedom. We look to the tradition.

Behind the question of Islam is the horizon of history. Partisans of warring paradigms believe that they stand atop 14 centuries of scriptures and schools of thought, wars and conquests, empires and regimes that serve as evidence for their case. Scholars will demur, appealing for complexity, but conform equally well to the maxim: What one thinks Islam is derives from what one thinks Islam has been.

Assessing the prospects for religious freedom in Islam likewise requires a look at history. Are we dealing with a religion whose past overwhelmingly lacks religious freedom? Or is it one in which religious freedom was once achieved and then lost? Or has it been present in certain schools of thought, periods of history, or geographic locales, and not others? Or has religious freedom long been absent but is now emergent among modern Islamic voices?

The present argument aims to respect historical complexity without being drowned in it. Generalizations can be made; dominant trends can be found. To venture one such generalization, through most of Islam's history, it has lacked religious freedom of the sort that today's human rights conventions set forth: a recognition of every person and religious community's right to practice and express religious faith free from overt coercion, heavy forms of pressure, discrimination, or penalties. This is admittedly a high standard and evokes this question: Compared with what? Much the same generalization could be made about any of the major world religions. It is quite late in history that we find any religious body espousing a stable, enduring, principled commitment to religious freedom. When the historian Bernard Lewis wrote that "[f]or Christians and Muslims alike, tolerance is a new virtue, intolerance a new crime," he might have extended his observation to every world religion.[1]

If Islamic history predominantly lacks religious freedom, however, the same history suffers great distortion if this dearth becomes the leading headline. Islam has also contained "seeds of freedom," that is, concepts or practices that express religious freedom in a significant way but that fall short of a full human right of religious freedom that is articulated in its many dimensions, enshrined in law, protected in contemporary political orders, and broadly accepted by Muslims. If nurtured, these seeds might grow into religious freedom in full bloom. That such a development is possible is illustrated in Chapter 7 through a comparison with the Catholic Church, which adopted a teaching of religious freedom in 1965—a late moment in history but one that was anticipated by the thoughts and actions of early figures like Thomas Aquinas, Augustine, Lactantius, Tertullian, and the Roman Emperor Constantine. This chapter aims to identify parallel seeds in the Islamic tradition—seven in all—and to indicate how they might be nurtured into the full flower of a doctrine of religious freedom that is found widely in the thought of jurists, the constitutions of states, the opinions of Muslims, and, most of all, actual practice.

The First Seed of Freedom: Verses in the Qur'an and Their Interpretation

Numerous verses in the Qur'an stress that the Islamic faith must be lived freely.[2] The Qur'an is the most authoritative source of guidance for Muslims, who understand it to be the direct revelation of God delivered by the Angel Gabriel to the Prophet Muhammad in periodic episodes spanning from 610 CE to the end of his life in 632 CE.

One verse in the Qur'an more than any other conveys the importance of freedom: "There is no compulsion in religion: true guidance has become distinct from error, so whoever rejects false gods and believes in God has grasped the firmest hand-hold, one that will never break."[3] There is no compulsion in religion. The statement is striking for the directness and simplicity with which it forbids the very coercion that religious freedom prohibits. It is rare to find such a direct exhortation of freedom in the central texts of any religious tradition. The verse—Qur'an 2:256—has not been forgotten or stranded in the Qur'an's 114 surahs, or books, but rather has been asserted by proponents of freedom time and again through the Islamic tradition. In the early centuries of Islam, for instance, the Mutazilite school, which stressed rationality, argued on the basis of this verse that faith must be an "action of the heart" and thus unhindered. Freedom undergirds this school's understanding of the world as an "Abode of Trial" in which peoples' choices carry consequences for the hereafter. Tenth-century philosopher Al-Farabi applied this Mutazilite insight to the political realm, which he thought should be one of complete freedom. Today, "the verse is being used constantly in order to substantiate the notion of religious tolerance in Islam," writes scholar Yohanan Friedmann.[4]

Echoing Qur'an 2:256 are verses such as Qur'an 50:45, which counsel against coercion: "We know best what the disbelievers say. You [Prophet] are not there to force them, so remind, with this Qur'an, those who fear My warning." Multiple verses emphasize the importance of a personal decision for faith, for instance, Qur'an 6:104, which reads, "Now clear proof has come to you from your Lord: if anyone sees it, that will be to his advantage; if anyone is blind to it, that will be to his loss—[Say], I am not your guardian." Other verses hold that God has not willed directly that all would believe in Islam, at least in a way that circumvents freedom. Qur'an 10:99, for instance, holds that "[h]ad your Lord willed, all the people on earth would have believed. So can you [Prophet] compel people to believe?" Similarly, Qur'an 5:48 reads, "If God had so willed, He would have made you one community, but He wanted to test you through that which He has given you, so race to do good: you will all return to God and He will make clear to you the matters you differed about," and Qur'an 2:62 states, "The [Muslim] believers, the Jews, the Christians, and the Sabians—all those who believe in God and the Last Day and do good—will have their rewards with their Lord." Still another group of verses foster freedom in stating the proper duty of the Prophet Muhammad to deliver the message of Islam but to leave people free to choose it. Witness Qur'an 3:20: "If they argue with you [Prophet], say, 'I have devoted myself to God alone and so have my followers'. Ask those who were given the Scripture, as well as those without one, 'Do you too devote yourselves to Him alone?' If they do, they will be guided, but if they turn away, your only duty is to convey the message. God is aware of his servants."

The Qur'an's munificent invocations of the free character of faith, however, have not stood in the way of Muslim jurists sanctioning heavy religious coercion and Muslim rulers carrying it out over the course of history. This is a favorite point of today's Islamoskeptics, who tell a much different story about the Qur'an and its interpretation. For two and a half centuries following the life of Muhammad, a period of vigorous debate over *ijtihad*, or interpretation, ensued. Within the majority Sunni Islam, four legal schools emerged along with a philosophical and theological debate centering on the role of human reason in interpreting Islamic teachings. The schools differed on many issues, not least the degree of allowable religious tolerance.

By and large, Islamoskeptics are keen to stress, the skeptics of human reason and the proponents of harsh religious restriction—the school of thought known as the Asharites and the emergent Hanbali legal school—won the debate while the faction favoring reason, the Mutazilites, lost.[5] In the 10th century, in the setting of the Abbasid Empire, the traditionalists "closed the gates of *ijtihad*" and crystallized Muslim orthodoxy for centuries to come, runs this line of reasoning.

What, though, of Qur'an 2:256, that is, there is no compulsion in religion? When verses in the Qur'an conflict, interpreters often argue that one of them trumps, or "abrogates," the other, usually the one that was revealed latest to the Prophet Muhammad. It was verses that called for *jihad*, or warfare against unbelievers, that interpreters of the early centuries thought to have trumping force in matters of religious coercion. They cited Qur'an 9:73, for instance, which says, "Prophet, strive against the disbelievers and the hypocrites, and be tough with them. Hell is their final home—an evil destination." Some interpreters thought that the counsel against compulsion in Qur'an 2:256 applied only to "people of the book"—meaning Christians, Jews, and Zoroastrians, to whom Islam has traditionally given special protection—and thus left the door open to the forcible conversion of others.[6] Still other verses appear to command warfare on religious grounds. Qur'an 9:5, for instance, says, "When the [four] forbidden months are over, wherever you encounter the idolaters, kill them, seize them, besiege them, wait for them at every lookout post." In the same spirit, Qur'an 2:193 prescribes, "[f]ight them until there is no more persecution, and worship is devoted to God." And then there is Qur'an 9:123: "You who believe, fight the disbelievers near you and let them find you standing firm."

The interpretation of the Qur'an that most convinces Islamoskeptics that Islam is hardwired for violent intolerance is that which mandates the death penalty for apostasy, the act of leaving the Islamic faith. Espousers of this interpretation often claim that apostasy is one of seven *hudud* crimes, those for which the Qur'an mandates a specific penalty. The verse in the Qur'an usually cited is 4:89: "They would dearly like you to reject faith, as they themselves have done, to be like them. So do not take them as allies until they migrate [to Medina] for God's cause. If they turn [on you], then seize and kill them wherever you encounter them."

It is not just the Qur'an that proponents of death for apostasy cite, though, but also a separate source to which Muslims accord nearly as much authority, namely the *hadith*, or collections of reports of what the Prophet Muhammad said on numerous matters. The entire corpus of *hadith* comprises several thousand sayings, some of which sanction coercion in religious matters. The most direct says, "whoever changes his religion, kill him."[7]

During the early centuries of Islam—what is known as the classical period—"almost all early jurists took a hard line, believing that apostasy was to be punished by death," observes even Abdullah Saeed, a contemporary Muslim intellectual who dissents from this line and champions religious freedom. Still, today, Saeed acknowledges, "[t]he vast majority of Muslim scholars writing on the issue of apostasy . . . follow the pre-modern jurists on apostasy. They rely on the *ijtihad* of pre-modern jurists on apostasy with all of its details."[8] The upshot, claim Islamoskeptics, has been executions by the Saudi government, vigilante threats upon the life of Egyptian intellectual Abu Zayd, and scores of other incidents of violence that have taken place around the world in the past couple of decades.

Muslim proponents of religious freedom, although they swim against the dominant stream of interpretation, believe this interpretation to be mistaken. They hold that Qur'an 2:256 remains the central reference point on matters of religious freedom and coercion. It is binding on all Muslims and toward members of all other religions and has not been abrogated. Saeed argues that advocates of abrogation misread verses that call for fighting unbelievers as a command to convert them through force. The many verses that stress the free character of faith, he says, come from both the earlier and later parts of the Prophet's life. Decisively, no verse clearly commands forced conversion and many speak against it.[9]

One of the most common arguments among Islamopluralists is that the Qur'an commands violence against unbelievers, polytheists, idolaters, and the like only when the same practitioners of heterodoxy are also engaged in attacks on the Muslim community from within or without—that is, sedition or aggression.[10] The justice of religious coercion, then, turns out to be little more than the ethics of war. Qur'an 9:11–13 illustrates what at first appears to be a command against fighting unbelievers but evolves into one against armed aggression:

> If they repent, keep up the prayer, and pay the prescribed alms, then they are your brothers in faith: We make the messages clear for people who understand. But if they break their oath after having made an agreement with you and revile your religion, then fight these leaders of

disbelief – oaths mean nothing to them – so that they may stop. How could you not fight a people who have broken their oaths, who tried to drive the Messenger out, who attacked you first? Do you fear them? It is God you should fear if you are true believers.

The "disbelief" of those who "break their oath after having made an agreement with you"—that is, who leave Islam—is closely tied to their "attack" and their effort to "drive the Messenger out." So, too, other verses enjoining violence against the religiously wayward can be shown to be revealed amid circumstances in which the heterodox were armed and hostile. Therefore, argue Islamopluralists, the Qur'an offers no enduring doctrine of religious coercion, only one of self-defense.

No verse prescribes judicial execution for apostasy, in contrast to the verses that prescribe specific punishments for other *hudud* crimes like adultery and theft. The Qur'an does warn of punishment for apostasy, but it is to be experienced in the hereafter at the hands of Allah, not in the here and now at the hands of an executioner in Riyadh or a gunman in Lahore. For *hudud* crimes, Islamopluralists offer an important principle of interpretation: The Qur'an prescribes strong punishments only for crimes that sever relations between persons and within communities; wrongs that pertain primarily to a person's standing with God are only sins, not crimes, and will be dealt with by God in the afterlife. It turns out, too, that even in the classical period, when interpretation overwhelmingly favored the death penalty for apostasy, one important group of jurists, including the founder of the Hanafi legal school, held that the death penalty is justifiable only when apostasy poses a threat to the physical safety of the community.[11]

Islamopluralists take the same analysis to the *hadith*, arguing that those sanctioning force in matters of religion can be shown to be bound up with the defense of the community.[12] A strong tradition of interpretation, for instance, holds that the *hadith*, "whoever changes his religion, kill him," is to be understood in the context of rebellion. Sarakhsi, an 11th-century jurist of the Hanafi legal school, held just this view.[13] In other cases, Islamopluralists point out, *hadiths* commending coercion are baldly politically motivated. A caliph wishing to dispatch with his critics might well have accused them of apostasy. Similarly, Islamopluralists argue that the closing of the gates of *ijtihad* was enabled by a new Abbasid caliph in 847 who suppressed Mutazilites and gave official support to traditionalists.[14]

Even should the Islamopluralist interpretation of the Qur'an and *hadith* prevail, these sources do not prescribe the full human right of religious freedom. That is what makes them seeds of freedom. Qur'anic verses and sayings in the *hadith* alone do not establish that every person and religious community enjoys a right to practice the full range of legitimate religious activities and that public law ought to guarantee this right. The point is not to demand that the Qur'an contain the content of modern human rights conventions. None of the world religions' holy books could meet such a standard. It is rather to show what sorts of developments are needed if this seed is to grow into the full human right of religious freedom. The view that the Qur'an and the *hadith* prescribe religious freedom would have to garner more and more adherents, who would have to look upon these sources as the basis for the wide range of obligations that contemporary human rights set forth.

The Second Seed of Freedom: The Life of the Prophet Muhammad

Muslims regard the life of the Prophet Muhammad—what he said, what he did—as recorded in *hadith* to be nearly as important as the Qur'an as a source of faith, law, and morals. In his life, we can find pointers to religious freedom.

The Prophet's life following the first revelations to him in 610 is typically divided into two periods: one in the city of Mecca (610–622) and one in the city of Medina (622–632). During the Meccan period, his followers increased but they remained a minority and were persecuted. It was to this period that scholars attribute a verse in the Qur'an that appears to stress tolerance in matters of religion, Qur'an 109:6, "you have your religion and I have mine," but in all likelihood the verse is an appeal by Muslims for tolerance from fellow Meccans.[15] The real test of whether the Prophet Muhammad's life points to religious freedom lies in his behavior when he wielded the power of a political ruler and conqueror. That test would come in the Medina portion of his life.

One of the most defining episodes in Islamic history came in 622, when Muhammad and his followers made the *hijra*, or migration, to the city of Yathrib, which soon came to be known as Medina. It is from this year that the Muslim calendar is dated. The city leaders invited Muhammad to settle divisions among quarreling factions. He did so while planting Islam, which grew quickly. It was in Medina that the first mosque, the foundations of ritual life, and the first Muslim community all were established. Here, Muhammad became a political and military ruler. In 630, he conquered Mecca and by the time of his death in 632, he had conquered the entire Arabian Peninsula. Once empowered, how did he treat non-Muslims and allegedly wayward Muslims?

Soon after Muhammad's arrival in Medina, he negotiated what is known as the Constitution of Medina between the tribes of Yathrib, an agreement that established them as a single community.[16] The Constitution by and large sets forth religious freedom. It grants something close to equality to the Jewish community in Medina, whom it says "are one community with the believers. The Jews have their religion and the Muslims theirs."

Other words and deeds of the Prophet point toward lenience as well. When the Prophet's companions asked him if hypocrites in Medina ought to be executed, he replied no, insisting that he was prohibited from performing such an act. After the Prophet's conquest of Mecca, he issued a general amnesty. On many occasions, he insisted that he could not discern other people's states of belief.[17]

Islamopluralists commonly claim that Muhammad never put anyone to death for simple apostasy. The tradition, they say, offers evidence that he refused just such a possibility. One *hadith* tells of Muhammad releasing a Bedouin who openly renounced his pledge of allegiance to Muhammad and Islam. Another relates the story of Muhammad refusing to punish a Christian who converted to Islam and then returned to Christianity and even called Muhammad a self-created prophet and a liar. Tradition also has it that Qur'an 2:256 (no compulsion) was revealed in a context in which a father asked Muhammad to pursue his two sons, who had converted to Christianity and left Medina for Syria, and to force them to convert back to Islam—and Muhammad refused. The Treaty of Hudaybiyyah, which Muhammad concluded with Mecca, permits a Muslim to renounce Islam and to remain in Mecca as an apostate. The only case in the *hadith* where the Prophet orders death against apostates was against a group of renegades who were also guilty of robbery, torture, and murder.[18] These episodes from Muhammad's life are seeds of freedom.

Against this account, Islamoskeptics respond with Muhammad the Conqueror. The Constitution of Medina may have been tolerant, they argue, but subsequently Muhammad expelled three Jewish tribes from Medina. The first, Banu Qaynuqa, posed a military threat to Muhammad's forces. The second, Banu Nadir, had conspired to kill Muhammad. He expelled this tribe to Khaybar, where he later conquered them and subjected them to a regime in which they could practice their faith but owed Muhammad a tribute of one-half of their crops. A third tribe, the Banu Qurayza, conspired against Muhammad, who subdued them and executed 400–900 of them. In conquering the Arab Peninsula, Muhammad forced Christians in the northern Hijaz (region surrounding Mecca and Medina) and southern Arabia into a submission by which they could practice their faith but were required to pay tribute. He gave pagans a choice between Islam or death. A tradition was begun that the Hijaz, the region of Islam's most holy sites, is for Muslims only and would be off-limits to people of other faiths.[19]

Islamopluralists respond that Muhammad the Conqueror was just that—a conqueror, not a forcible converter. His battles with people who had not accepted true Islam were driven mostly by a political and military logic, not the desire to force them to convert. Thus, the life of Muhammad did not leave a legacy of religious repression. Islamoskeptics might retort that Muhammad's conquests were themselves driven by the goal of spreading Islam. Whatever the outcome of this debate, the question of religious freedom in Islam must deal with the fact that this religion's founder was also a political ruler, unlike, say, Jesus, who died at the hands of political authority. Islamopluralists will say that this fact makes Muhammad's acts of tolerance and leniency all the more significant. Islamoskeptics will say that this combination of political power and religious authority would bode ill for religious freedom in Islam.

The Third Seed of Freedom: The History of Muslim Toleration of Non-Muslims

From Muhammad's rule emerged one practice that can be regarded as a seed of freedom: the creation of the status of the *dhimmi*, a permanent arrangement for non-Muslims living under Muslim rule that allows them to practice their faith freely while paying tribute to the government. Again, to call this practice a seed of freedom is to say that the glass is both half full and half empty. A measure of freedom exists but falls well short of the full human right of religious freedom. Islamopluralists and Islamoskeptics—categories onto which scholars' views of *dhimmis* map quite well—respectively claim the glass as half full, viewing the *dhimmi* status as a laudable tradition of tolerance, and half empty, regarding it as a demeaning plight of second-class citizenship.[20]

The roots of the *dhimmi* lie in the Qur'an, whose verse 9:29 says "[f]ight those of the People of the Book who do not [truly] believe in God and the Last Day, who do not forbid what God and His Messenger have forbidden, who do not obey the rule of justice, until they pay the tax promptly and agree to submit." Muhammad's treatment of the Jews of Khaybar, allowing them to practice their faith but demanding a tribute, is regarded as a founding precedent for the status of *dhimmis*, and his treatment of Christians in the Hijaz is also a precedent, though of lesser importance. What is known as the Pact of Umar, a *dhimmi* arrangement with Christians and Jews in Syria and Palestine dating to the 630s, was later judged to be a fabrication but nevertheless served as a common reference point for the status of *dhimmis* in classical Islam.[21]

Subsequently, the status of *dhimmis* developed amid Islamic conquest, which began during Muhammad's life and accelerated after his death, so that by 750, Islam governed a geographic expanse extending from present-day Portugal and Morocco in the West to present-day Pakistan in the East.

The *dhimmi* status arose as an answer to the question of how to treat members of other faiths living in *dar al-Islam*, meaning the realm of rule by Muslims. Much depended on the faith in question. The classical form of the practice was for "People of the Book," as the Qur'an phrased it, which included Jews, Christians, and Zoroastrians. Members of these faiths could be seen as *dhimmis*, meaning that they were subject to the *dhimma*, which in turn means something much like covenant. These faiths also had going for them their monotheism, their scriptures, and their shared history with Islam. Pagans and idolaters, by contrast, lacked these qualities and so did not deserve protection. Because Muslims regarded Islam as the final revelation, they expected their religion to expand and others not to grow. They reserved their harshest treatment for religions that emerged subsequently to Islam's founding but were wary, too, of the expansion of Judaism and Christianity.

Dhimmis would live under a Muslim regime and obey its laws. They would receive protection and could practice their faith. In return, they would have to pay the *jizya*, or poll tax, as well as the *kharaj*, a tax on land. They could not build new houses of worship—that is, expand their faith—though they could repair their existing ones. Never, never, could they proselytize among Muslims. All of this is more or less a standard picture of the *dhimmi* status, which existed widely in the heartlands of Islam over the course of its history—the Umuyyad Caliphate of 661–750, based in Damascus; the Abbasid Caliphate of 750–1258, based in Baghdad; and the Ottoman Empire, spanning from 1299 to 1922, where the *dhimmi* arrangement, known as the Millet System, dates back at least as far as the 17th century. The Ottomans abolished the *dhimmi* category in the 19th century, but some Muslim states like Iran have revived something very much like it today. In some times and places, the treatment of *dhimmis* was more harshly restrictive, and in others, it was more relaxed—a variance that provides grist for both Islamopluralists and Islamoskeptics.

Islamopluralists would concur with Bernard Lewis's judgment that "[i]n general," meaning in most times and places over the course of Islamic history, "the *dhimmīs* were allowed to practice their religions, pursue their avocations, and live their own lives, so long as they were willing to abide by the rules."[22] In the same general sense, Islam has rarely practiced forcible conversion of non-Muslims. Although, during the centuries of Islamic expansion, a major purpose of conquest was to open up lands for Islam, Muslims usually did not force the residents to convert.[23] Instead, they offered them *dhimmi* status.

Contemporary scholar Mahmoud Ayoub derives from the *hadith* a highly sympathetic interpretation of the *dhimmi* status as a covenant between God and man by which Muslims were obligated to protect non-Muslims, not subdue or separate them. It was later that the practice was corrupted into a legal, contractual relationship, Ayoub claims.[24] Other scholars stress the capacious character of the practice, pointing out, for instance, that when Muslims ruled India during the Mughal Empire, spanning the 16th through 18th centuries, they extended the *dhimmi* arrangement beyond the People of the Book to Hindus and Buddhists.[25]

In the contemporary public debate over Islam, one of the noisiest controversies, in which Islamopluralists and Islamoskeptics vociferously volley myth and countermyth, is that over medieval Spain and its treatment of minorities. In 2010, a controversy took place over the construction of an Islamic community center a few blocks from the site in lower Manhattan where the twin towers of the World Trade Center stood prior to their destruction in the attacks of September 11, 2001. One of the chief bones of contention was the center's name, the "Cordoba House," named for a medieval Spanish city.

In the view of Islamoskeptics—chief among them, former Speaker of the House of Representatives, Newt Gingrich—the "Ground Zero Mosque," as they termed the building, was a plot by radical Muslims to establish a beachhead for propagating their message at the site of conquest. "It is a sign of [the developers'] contempt for Americans and their confidence in our historic ignorance that they would deliberately insult us this way," declaimed Gingrich on the Internet. Gingrich and friends held that in medieval Cordoba, Muslims conquered Christian Spaniards and even converted a church into the world's third largest mosque complex. Gingrich closed his posting with a battle cry: "No mosque. No self-deception. No surrender. The time to take a stand is now—at this site on this issue."

Such bigotry toward a minority group is the first step toward another "Holocaust," countered Keith Olbermann, host of MS-NBC's "Countdown." His view, that of an Islamopluralist, was shared by comrades in the media and in politics. The Ground Zero Mosque was neither a mosque nor at Ground Zero, they retorted. Rather, it was to be a community center, modeled on a Jewish center on the Upper West Side, that would include a basketball court, a swimming pool, a cooking school, and a prayer space, all of this five blocks away from Ground Zero, from where it was not even visible. The developer, Sharif El-Gamal, had responded to the attacks of September 11 by spending two days handing out water to victims, while the designated religious leader of the center, Feisal Abdul Rauf, had written books criticizing radical Islam and terrorism. Rauf had founded the Cordoba Initiative in 2004 to counter extremism and promote interfaith understanding and named the proposed center Cordoba in recognition of the harmony among Jews, Christians, and Muslims that existed in this medieval Spanish town.

Both sides evoked medieval Spain to make their arguments. For Islamopluralists, medieval Spain was a model of interfaith harmony, often referred to as La Convivencia (or "the coexistence"). The period for which they make their strongest case is the years 711–1031, when Spain was ruled by the Umayyad dynasty. Under a laxly enforced arrangement, minority Jewish and Christian *dhimmi* populations enjoyed broad freedom to practice their faith and to participate in society as roughly equal citizens. Particularly for the Jewish population, it was a time of flourishing in the fields of art, architecture, philosophy, literature, and culture.[26]

Islamoskeptics look upon medieval Spain far more warily.[27] Cordoba, the alleged city of tolerance, was the site of the martyrdom of 50 Christians for blasphemy and apostasy in the middle of the ninth century.[28] The Christians had been provocateurs, historians tell us, but they were nevertheless killed for their beliefs. In Granada in 1066, a persecution of Jews took place that involved the massacre of up to 1,500 families.[29] Following the century 900–1000, often portrayed as the high point of tolerance, two Islamic movements, the Almoravids and the millenarian Almohads, took over and ruled far less tolerantly, even practicing what has been rare in Islamic history, expulsions of Christians and Jews.[30]

More generally, Islamoskeptics look upon the condition of *dhimmis* as one of humiliation and subordination.[31] Islamoskeptics, too, can find support in Lewis, whose balanced interpretation acknowledges the darker dimension of the practice. Over the course of Islamic history, as Lewis renders it, there have taken place episodes of repression—not violent persecution, but rather heavy subordination. Rulers' motivations ranged from desiring to restore religious rigor, to exploiting minorities for money, to stopping minorities from collaborating with outside enemies. Lewis broadly characterizes the history of the treatment of *dhimmis* as increasing in tolerance up through the 12th and 13th centuries and decreasing thereafter.[32]

Other Islamoskeptics find repression in Islam's early days when Caliph Umar, Muhammad's immediate successor, expelled non-Muslims, including Christians and Jews, from the Arabian Peninsula. The subsequent treatment of *dhimmis* was designed to subordinate. "[T]he *jizya* was not only a tax but also a symbolic expression of subordination," Lewis observes. In many instances, payers of the tax had to adopt a bent posture and even submit to beatings.[33] The *kharaj* tax was imposed on minorities when conquerors seized their property and leased it back to them. It was usually the case that Muslims could not inherit from *dhimmis* nor *dhimmis* from Muslims; that *dhimmi* men could not marry Muslim women; that *dhimmis* were required to wear distinctive garb and hold funerals in secret; and that *dhimmis* were prohibited from building tall buildings, ringing bells, drinking wine in public, riding noble animals, and carrying out certain religious processions. And the arrangement was insecure. Writes Islamoskeptic Bat Ye'or, "[i]n reserving the right to revoke the *dhimma* unilaterally at any time, the victors placed the *dhimmis* in a situation of permanent insecurity."[34]

Who is right about *dhimmis*? Lewis's even-handed judgment seems on the mark: *dhimmi* status was second-class citizenship, but it was nonetheless citizenship, not expulsion or death.[35] It was not full religious freedom, but it was tolerance. Jews, Christians, Zoroastrians, and sometimes members of other faiths were subordinated, but they could practice their faith relatively freely. In some times and places, *dhimmi* status was harsher, in some, gentler. Again, a comparison with other religions provides perspective. Whatever mixture of tolerance and repression obtained in Islamic medieval Spain, Christian rule of Spain in subsequent centuries involved expulsions of Jews and Muslims on at least as great a scale as anything that took place under Muslim rule. Indeed, it was the Muslim Ottoman Empire that took in and protected Jews that the Christians expelled.[36] For the seed of *dhimmi* status to flower into full religious freedom, all dimensions of subordination would have to be shed and full equality of citizenship would have to emerge.

Fourth Seed: Liberal Islam

In certain pockets of history, certain Muslim countries have hosted liberalism. Liberalism here means a constitutional regime marked by the rule of law, equal citizenship, an elected legislature, civil liberties, free markets, and, yes, religious freedom. To say that a country has hosted liberalism is to say that a substantial number of intellectuals, politicians, civil servants, and citizens espoused liberal ideas and advocated for liberal institutions and that liberal institutions actually were founded and developed. A liberalism rooted in Islam is a form of political theology. Here, the focus is on the 19th and early 20th centuries, when Islamic liberalism reached its apogee. Then, an international network of liberal thinkers and activists flourished, so much so that by the first couple decades of the 20th century, liberalism was the dominant trend in Islamic political thought.[37]

The locales where liberalism most gained ground were the Ottoman Empire in the 19th century; Iran in the early 20th century; Egypt in the late 19th and first half of the 20th century, especially the period 1923–1952; Tunisia in the mid-19th century; and heavily Muslim regions of the Russian Empire—what are today known as the Central Asian Republics—in the late 19th and early 20th centuries, where a reform movement known as the Jadids existed.

Islamic liberalism was influenced by the West, where the Enlightenment had promoted liberal ideas and institutions, and advanced by Western countries like Britain and France, who began to assert colonial political and military power in the Middle East, beginning with Napoleon's invasion of Egypt in 1798. Muslim reformers, though, were keen to place democracy, equality, and civil liberties on an Islamic footing. To this end, they engaged in *ijtihad*, a reopening of the tradition of interpretation. Common among liberals was their resuscitation of the Mutazilite, or rational, tradition of thought, their appeals to the Hanafi school of jurisprudence, and their evocation of what contemporary scholar Recep Senturk calls the universalist tradition of classical Islamic thought, which stresses the inviolability and indeed the natural rights of every human being.[38]

The West itself could hardly claim a patent on liberalism, given the stops and starts in its political progress. Throughout the West, the right to vote was expanded only gradually over the 19th and early 20th centuries; the United States maintained legalized slavery until 1865; Western European countries developed liberties in some respects but not others; and by the 1920s through the mid-1940s, authoritarianism and totalitarianism were ascendant in Europe. So, too, in those Muslim states where liberalism found a foothold, its achievement was partial and reversible. In most of these states, liberalism was championed by a small elite and a small middle class. Still, liberals' achievements exceeded their numbers, and for this stretch of history, certain Muslim societies rivaled Western states in the development of liberal institutions.

The most important experiment in Islamic liberalism was in the Ottoman Empire. In the 18th century, worried that it was falling behind Europe, the empire undertook reforms that imitated Europe in military organization, administration, law, and even clothing and architecture. In the 19th century, the empire also became increasingly threatened by rising nationalism on the part of its Christian populations in southeastern Europe and Armenia.

In the early 19th century, Ottoman sultans began to embrace equal citizenship, in part to modernize and in part to appease Christian minorities and the European states who pressured the sultans on their behalf. Between 1839 and 1876, what is known as the *Tanzimat* [reorganization] reforms, propelled by civil servants, a rising middle class, and an emerging liberal intelligentsia, introduced a whole host of modernizing and liberalizing measures in government, economics, and culture. Among these were equality among Muslim and non-Muslim citizens. Sultan Abdülmecid I's edict of 1856 abolished the Millet System, proclaiming that "[e]very distinction or designation tending to make any class whatever of the subjects of my Empire inferior to another class, on account of their religion, language, or race, shall be forever effaced from the Administrative Protocol."[39]

Religious freedom was an important facet of Ottoman liberalism, as Turkish writer Mustafa Akyol explains in his book, *Islam Without Extremes*. In 1844, an Ottoman court decreed that "[n]o subject of the Sublime [Ottoman] State shall be forced by anyone to convert to Islam against their (*sic*) wishes." Although apostasy laws mandating death remained on the books, Ottoman citizens became effectively free to convert away from Islam, Akyol explains. The 1856 edict declared that "[a]s all forms of religion are and shall be freely professed in my dominions, no subject of my empire shall be hindered in the exercise of the religion that he professes, nor shall he be in any way annoyed on this account. No one shall be compelled to change their (*sic*) religion." In the following year, a government commission gave its legal approval to a case of conversion from Islam to Christianity, declaring that "[t]he Musselman is now as free to become a Christian as the Christian is free to become a Musselman . . . . The government will know no difference in the two cases." Akyol cites a Turkish historian, Selim Deringil, who surveyed the era's apostasy cases and concluded that "[t]he orders from the center [were] always in the same vein . . . . No force or compulsion is admissible in matters of conversion."[40]

In 1878, Ottoman liberalism suffered a major setback when, shortly after achieving a liberalized constitution, a new parliament, and the first general election in Ottoman history, Sultan Abdülhamid (II) suspended the Constitution and inaugurated 30 years of absolutist rule. In 1908, under pressure from the Young Turks, what became known as the Second Constitutional Period began, featuring the revival of the constitution, the reconvening of parliament, the flourishing of free thought, and the advancement of women's rights. Although the Young Turks were secular in outlook, Muslim intellectuals in the same period continued to offer Islamic justifications for liberal institutions. The end of these liberal institutions came with the end of the Ottoman Empire, which collapsed in World War I and was followed by the abolition of the sultanate and the founding of the secular repressive Republic of Turkey in 1923.[41]

Two nominal provinces of the Ottoman Empire in the 19th century, each enjoying substantial autonomy, were zones of liberal innovation in the mid-19th century. They were Tunisia and Egypt—"arguably the most liberal and rights-friendly polities in the Arab world," according to political scientist Alfred Stepan.⁴² It was in Tunisia in 1861 that the first written Constitution in Arab history established religious equality and built upon a recent legacy of religious freedom. Although these laws were not enforced totally, they stood out as pioneering achievements for their time—even in comparison with Europe. Contemporary intellectuals defended them on Islamic grounds. Parallel to the Ottoman experience, Tunisian Islamic liberalism came to an end in through the victory not of Islamism but of secular repression, which triumphed in 1956 in the government of Habib Bourguiba. Liberal Islam, however, built a legacy that shaped the emergence of the Ennahda Party in the 2000s.⁴³

Liberal Islam is a seed of freedom because it demonstrates the possibility that liberal democratic thought and liberal institutions, entailing religious freedom, can thrive among Muslim people who support them for Islamic reasons. Liberal Islam is evidence that Islam is not hardwired for repression.

Liberal Islam is only a seed of freedom, though, because it has been episodic and scattered. Muslim sympathizers with liberalism amounted to a minority of the global Muslim population; only a handful of liberal regimes existed; and these regimes all came to an end and were superseded by far less liberal regimes. The mottled presence of liberalism on Islam's global map, though, does not warrant dismissal of liberal Islam's testimony to the compatibility of religious freedom and Islam. There were reasons for the defeat of liberal Islam other than Islamic doctrine. Two sorts of regimes succeeded liberal Islam, the very two sorts of regimes that characterize the unfree Muslim-majority world according to the argument of this book—secular repressive ones and Islamist ones. Islamist ones admittedly detract from the case for religious freedom's possibility in Islam. As we have seen, though, secular repressive regimes are imports from the West, emanating from the French Revolution and its model of religious governance. Secular repressive governance was what succeeded the Ottoman Empire in Turkey; what ended the liberal experiment in Iran, when Reza Shah Pahlavi took power in 1925; and what emerged in Egypt through the Free Officers Coup of 1952, which brought Gamal Abdel Nasser to power.

In the case of the Ottoman Empire, another major stressor on liberalism was the threat to stability posed by nationalist movements and by outside powers who intervened aggressively on behalf of these movements and on behalf of the empire's Christian and sometimes Jewish minorities. When Sultan Abdülhamid muzzled liberal institutions in 1878, he argued that Turkey needed order and discipline following a brutal war against Balkan nationalist movements and Russia that had cost the Ottoman Empire two-fifths of its territory. Over the course of the 19th and 20th centuries, nationalist conflict and ethnic cleansing wrought death and displacement for millions of people on all sides. One scholar's judgment is that over five million Ottoman Muslims died in these conflicts between 1821 and 1922.[44] The Ottomans and their successors in the Turkish Republic committed their own share of atrocities, including the killing of about 1.5 million Armenians as well as hundreds of thousands of Assyrian and Greek Christians, between 1913 and 1922.[45] Religious freedom in Islam was pressured by forces far more colossal than this or that Qur'anic verse or *hadith*.

Fifth Seed: Contemporary Muslim Advocates of Religious Freedom

Even if early experiences in liberal Muslim regimes were swept over by one or another form of illiberalism, numerous Muslim intellectuals have continued to advocate principles of liberalism, including religious freedom. The full human right of religious freedom means one that is extended to all Muslims, including those judged to be heretical, as well as to all non-Muslims. Religious freedom forbids the death penalty, and indeed all legal sanctions, for apostasy and blasphemy and forbids the *dhimmi* status in favor of full legal equality for members of all religious faiths (or no religious faith).

Today, there exist Muslim scholars, jurists, clerics, and activists who advocate religious freedom as an Islamic principle. They are a seed of freedom. Their arguments admit of variation. Some focus on abolishing the death penalty for apostasy and blasphemy, issues that have pervaded the global headlines in recent years. Some call for abolishing the death penalty for these infractions but retaining other legal sanctions. Others call for religious freedom in full: no criminalizing apostasy and blasphemy, no *dhimmi* status, no discrimination. Consonant with the concept of a seed of freedom, religious freedom is partially and variously realized.

It is difficult to say how many Muslims support religious freedom. A couple of organized global initiatives have garnered impressive numbers of followers. Following Pope Benedict XVI's Regensburg Address of September 2006, whose short remark about Islam and violence stirred Muslim protests around the world, a coalition of 138 prominent Muslims signed "A Common Word," a statement of peace that affirmed religious freedom.[46] Another organized effort is that of Mohammad Omar Farooq, an American scholar of Islam who compiled a list of more than 100 "notable Islamic voices affirming freedom of faith" and renouncing the death penalty for apostasy. The voices hail from all over the world.[47] In like spirit, in 2016, 250 prominent Muslim scholars, religious leaders, and heads of state signed the Marrakesh Declaration affirming the rights of religious minorities.[48]

The voices also vary in the kinds of arguments they make for religious freedom. To characterize these arguments, I adapt religious freedom sociologist Charles Kurzman's threefold classification of justifications for liberal Islam.[49]

One type of argument, corresponding to what Kurzman calls "liberal *sharia*," says that religious freedom is the true interpretation of the Qur'an and *hadith*. This view stresses the free character of religious faith and cites Qur'an 2:256—there is no compulsion in religion—as its central text. It is this line of argument that reinforces the pivotal contention of this book, which is that religious freedom is a universal principle rooted in the nature of the human person as a being who searches for and often embraces religious truth. The grounds that these proponents cite for the free character of religious belief—and the verse, Qur'an 2:256, itself—are ones that pertain to all of humanity and are not confined to Islamic belief.[50]

The same movement aims to refute interpretations of the Qur'an and *hadith* that favor coercion. One line of reasoning is the method of counter-abrogation, deployed by Sudanese intellectual, Ustadh Mahmoud Mohammed Taha, whom the Sudanese state executed in 1985, and his pupil, Emory University scholar, Abdullahi Ahmed An-Na`im, who is one of the boldest proponents of Islamic liberalism today. For Taha and An-Na`im, it is the verses from the more tolerant Meccan period of Muhammad's life that contain the true, enduring message of Islam, whereas the coercion-friendly verses from the Medinan period were a contingent adaptation to historical circumstances. The Meccan verses, argues An-Na`im in his first book of 1990, *Toward an Islamic Reformation*, ought to be retrieved for the contemporary cause of human rights, equality, and religious freedom in Islam today.[51]

Refutations of religious coercion rooted in the Qur'an and *hadith* also lie in other arguments that we have encountered. Some point to textual evidence that the Qur'an does not prescribe penalties for apostasy, blasphemy, or "religious sins" in general and that the *hadith* do not show Muhammad favoring death for these sins. Some argue that *hadith* that appear to favor harsh penalties either do not in fact mean what they seem to say or else are inauthentic, originating, say, in the baldly political motives of a potentate. Perhaps the quintessential mistake of proponents of coercion, text-based arguments for freedom run, is confusing apostasy for treason. The texts mainly advocate the killing of apostates or blasphemers when these miscreants are engaged in sedition, rebellion, aggression, or subversion of the Islamic community.

When apostasy or blasphemy is only a sin against Allah or the sinner's own soul, it does not merit such punishment.

The second type of argument corresponds to what Kurzman calls "silent *sharia*" and holds that the texts of the Qur'an and *hadith* do not speak to or at least do not definitively settle the issue of religious freedom. Therefore, Muslim scholars are free to make arguments for religious freedom drawn from history and political experience. Arguments in this vein might point to the way in which political rulers across history have abused apostasy and blasphemy laws or to various developments in modernity that make restrictions on religious freedom no longer suitable: the modern state, the international system of sovereign states, globalization, population movements, and the religiously mixed character of populations.[52]

The final type of argument parallels what Kurzman calls "interpreted *sharia*" and holds that views of religious freedom ought to appeal to the Qur'an but that the Qur'an is subject to diverse interpretations and that interpretations evolve over the course of history. Interpreted *sharia* is not relativism. Allah's word is constant, this view holds, but interpretation is human and adaptable to the insights of every age. A practitioner of interpreted *sharia*, for instance, might hold that the emergence of modern human rights covenants helps Muslims to see the deeper meaning of "there is no compulsion in religion," namely that it implies a legally enshrined human right.[53]

Contemporary proponents of religious freedom deploy all three of these strategies and contribute to the Islamopluralist view that Islam contains grounds for religious freedom. How do Islamoskeptics respond? Whatever Muslim voices for religious freedom may have right, they say, these voices are vastly outnumbered by those who believe that Islam mandates the death penalty for apostasy or for blasphemy or that it requires something short of full equal rights for religious minorities. We saw earlier the admission of scholar Abdullah Saeed, whose own case for religious freedom combines all three types of arguments, that the vast majority of Muslims writing on apostasy today follow the premodern view that the death penalty is warranted. "They rely on the *ijtihad* of pre-modern jurists on apostasy with all of its details, as if that *ijtihad* was immutable," comments Saeed.[54] Islamoskeptics also point out that most of the vocal defenders of religious freedom live in liberal democracies that are not Muslim-majority countries. Some of them cannot return to their Muslim home countries without risking their lives.

For the majority of jurists who defend premodern thinking, there is no viable distinction between apostasy and treason; apostasy simply is treason. The religious and political dimensions of the social order are closely intertwined, they insist. For a person to leave the faith is not only to defy Allah and to harm one's soul but is also to harm others in the community—a wrong that needs to be dealt with here, not just in the hereafter. Classical jurists were nearly unanimous on this point, and we should follow their lead, holders of this view argue.

The Islamoskeptic argument that scholars and jurists favoring religious freedom are a global minority is hard to dispute. This does not, of course, call into question the quality of proponents' arguments, but it indicates the amount of work to be done if these arguments are to be accepted widely among intellectuals. Islamopluralists find more evidence that Muslims support religious freedom and liberal institutions in general if they expand the field to Muslim public opinion. Arab Barometer polls conducted among 12 Arab Muslim-majority countries for the year 2013 show strong support for civil liberties; the rights of non-Muslims; democracy with religious participation but not religious domination; and a separation of religious authority from political authority. The Arab world is significant, for it is often argued to be the part of the Muslim world that is most hostile to religious freedom. Illustrative are the following polling results aggregated across the 12 countries (see Table 6.1). For each statement, majorities are in favor of the responses that favor liberalism, democracy, and religious freedom.

Not every result supports the position of liberalism and freedom entirely. Majorities favor statements like, "the government and parliament should enact laws in accordance with Islamic law"; and "[t]he government and parliament should enact penal laws in accordance with Islamic law"; and in support of "[a]pplying shari'a more strictly." We should be wary of drawing too pessimistic a conclusion from these results, though. Islamic law is a broad concept, and support for it does not specify what measures respondents favor or do not favor.

A separate survey, this one conducted by the Pew Forum on Religion and Public Life on 39 Muslim-majority countries selected from around the entire world, published in 2013, also shows Muslim support for liberalism, democracy, and religious freedom.[55] The following two results in Tables 6.2 and 6.3 show Muslim support.

Table 6.4, drawn from the same study, however, shows that in 7 out of 37 countries, more than 50% of Muslims favor the death penalty for those who leave the Muslim religion.

Finally, solid majorities in four out of six regions favor enshrining *sharia* in law, as Table 6.5 shows. Again, though, the meaning of *sharia* can vary widely and does not necessarily negate freedom.

Put together, all of the preceding evidence and the arguments of both Islamoskeptics and Islamopluralists bear out the metaphor of seed of freedom

Table 6.1. Arab Barometer Polling Results (figures are percentages)[66]

Statement	I strongly agree	I somewhat agree	I somewhat disagree	I strongly disagree	Don't know	Refuse
In a Muslim country, non-Muslims should enjoy less political rights than Muslims	8.2	21.9	38	25.3	6	0.7
Democracy is a system that contradicts the teachings of Islam	7.8	18.6	40.9	23.1	8.9	0.6
The government and parliament should enact laws in accordance with citizens' wishes with regard to certain subjects and in accordance with Islamic law with regard to other subjects	26.4	38	18.6	10.6	5.4	0.9
Religious practices are private and should be separated from social and political life	26.7	32.7	23.9	10.4	5.3	1.1
Religious associations and institutions (excluding political parties) should not influence voters' decisions in elections	31.8	42.8	13.9	4.8	5.4	1.3
Your country is better off if religious people hold public positions in the state	10.4	29.1	32.9	20.1	6.4	1.1
Religious leaders (imams, preachers, priests) should have influence over government decisions	8.9	24	38	22.1	6	1.1

(continued)

Table 6.1. Continued

Question	Very appropriate	Appropriate	Somewhat appropriate	Absolutely appropriate	Don't know	Refuse
Appropriate for your country: A system governed by Islamic law without elections or political parties	9.5	13.1	16.1	52.1	7.9	1.4
Appropriate for your country: A parliamentary system in which nationalist, left wing, right wing, and Islamist parties compete in parliamentary elections	33.1	30.1	13.7	14.8	7.5	0.8
Appropriate for your country: A parliamentary system based on Islamic Law (Shari'a) in which only Islamist parties compete in parliamentary systems	3.5	8	9.3	25.1	3.6	0.5
Appropriate for your country: A parliamentary system in which only Islamists parties compete in parliamentary elections	3.1	7.1	8.7	26.8	3.6	0.6
Appropriate for your country: A parliamentary system in which only non-religious parties compete in parliamentary elections	7.1	8.9	13.4	61.4	8.2	1

Statement	I strongly support	I somewhat support	I do not support	I strongly do not support	Don't know	Refuse
Support: Individual freedoms such as freedom of the press, freedom of expression, and freedom to establish associations	50.8	37.3	5.4	1.5	4.6	0.4

**Table 6.2. Median Percentage of Muslims Who Say
Religious Freedom Is a Good Thing**

South Asia	97
Southeast Asia	93
Middle East–North Africa	85
Sub-Saharan Africa	94
Southern–Eastern Europe	95
Central Asia	92

**Table 6.3. Support for Religious Freedom:
Percentage of Muslims who say it is good that others
are very free to practice their faith**

Russia	95
Kosovo	95
Albania	98
Bosnia-Herzegovina	94
Azerbaijan	95
Tajikistan	93
Uzbekistan	92
Kyrgyzstan	91
Kazakhstan	91
Turkey	89
Malaysia	83
Thailand	97
Indonesia	93
Pakistan	96
Bangladesh	97
Palestinian Territory	85
Egypt	77
Jordan	91
Iraq	91
Lebanon	83
Tunisia	86
Morocco	79
Ghana	98
Tanzania	98
Nigeria	97
Mozambique	96

Table 6.3. Continued

Senegal	96
Guinea-Bissau	95
Chad	94
Ethiopia	94
Liberia	94
Uganda	94
DR Congo	92
Kenya	90
Mali	90
Cameroon	89
Djibouti	84
Niger	76

to describe contemporary Muslim opinion on the question of religious freedom. There is significant and substantial support for religious freedom, but religious freedom is far from a consensus position in the Muslim world. For this seed of religious freedom to grow, there must be an expansion in the number and proportion of those who believe that religious freedom is a valid and universal principle, that apostasy is not treason, that by its nature a religious commitment must be free, that the Qur'an and *hadith* support religious freedom, and that modern constitutional states with human rights are the superior form of political order.

Sixth Seed: Freedom in Law and Institutions in Muslim-Majority States

Whereas the fifth seed of religious freedom involves the realm of thought, a sixth seed involves the realm of law and practice—constitutions, legislation, and international law. Today, the legal entity in which Muslims, like the vast majority of the world's population, reside is the sovereign state—a territorially bounded polity in which a single locus of authority is supreme. When the Ottoman Empire died in the early 1920s, so did one of the last alternatives to the sovereign state in the Muslim world—the last empire, the last caliph. The vast majority of the Muslim world came under the domination of a colony or a mandate controlled by a European country. Countries like Turkey that remained independent had already taken the form of a sovereign state and belonged to the community of sovereign states. Over the following decades,

Table 6.4. Death Penalty for Leaving Islam:
Do you favor or oppose the following: the death penalty for people who leave the Muslim religion?

Country	Favor	Oppose	Don't know/refuse
Russia	12	80	8
Kosovo	3	80	17
Albania	2	91	7
Bosnia-Herzegovina	4	93	3
Azerbaijan	1	93	6
Tajikistan	8	82	9
Kyrgyzstan	9	86	5
Kazakhstan	1	96	3
Turkey	8	89	3
Malaysia	58	23	19
Thailand	23	66	11
Indonesia	16	77	7
Pakistan	75	16	9
Bangladesh	43	49	8
Afghanistan	79	18	3
Palestinian Territory	62	29	9
Egypt	88	10	1
Jordan	83	14	3
Iraq	41	48	12
Lebanon	17	81	2
Tunisia	18	79	3
Ghana	28	70	3
Tanzania	23	74	3
Nigeria	29	65	6
Mozambique	27	70	3
Senegal	35	61	4
Guinea-Bissau	33	63	4
Chad	32	67	1
Ethiopia	25	74	2
Liberia	30	65	5
Uganda	26	70	3
DR Congo	44	48	9
Kenya	32	67	1
Mali	36	55	9
Cameroon	19	79	2
Djibouti	62	32	6
Niger	32	60	7

Table 6.5. Median Percentage of Muslims Who Favor
Enshrining *Sharia*

South Asia	84
Southeast Asia	77
Middle East–North Africa	74
Sub-Saharan Africa	64
Southern–Eastern Europe	18
Central Asia	12

every colony and mandate would achieve independence from its European ruler and its borders would become the boundary of a new sovereign state. Thus Muslims came to live within a form of political organization that originated in Christian Europe.[56]

Were religious freedom to be enshrined in law in Muslim-majority states, it would be established first of all as a civil liberty within a constitution, which, in all but about two Muslim-majority states, is the locus of supreme authority. It would be reinforced by legislation. And it would be strengthened through the state's accession to international law conventions. To what degree is religious freedom realized in law within the Muslim world?

Religious freedom has a significant presence in the law within many Muslim-majority states. All Muslim-majority states except for Saudi Arabia and Oman have a constitution and many of these constitutions articulate religious freedom as a civil right.[57] A report published in March 2005 by the US Commission on International Religious Freedom (USCIRF), analyzing the role of religious freedom in the constitutions of Muslim countries, shows that 21 of these countries have constitutional provisions that "compare favorably" with international standards of religious freedom. Ten of these countries have established safeguards against religious coercion.[58] Eleven constitutions proclaim the state to be secular while another eleven constitutions proclaim neither an Islamic nor a secular state.

The laws of other Muslim states protect religious freedom far less. According to the USCIRF report, 22 Muslim states make "no [provision]" for religious freedom or "provision only for the right to worship," a standard formula for a constricted reading of religious freedom. The laws of 12 Muslim states contain "provisions that do not define rights on an individual basis or limit rights to one or more enumerated groups." The Constitution of Iran, for instance, establishes a modern form of the *dhimmi* status that affords some recognition to Christians, Jews, and Zoroastrians—though hardly full religious freedom—while denying recognition to Baha'is and in fact heavily persecuting them. The laws of 15 Muslim states contain "provisions that permit limitations not enumerated under international standards."[59]

Legal scholar Ann Elizabeth Mayer warns of "human rights schemes" in which certain Muslim states commit themselves to human rights in their laws or pronouncements while at the same time positing other principles that sharply curtail these same commitments.[60] They may, for instance, declare that they are an Islamic state; establish Islam as the state religion; proclaim Islam to be the "basis for," "a principle source of," or "a source of" legislation; or enunciate a clause holding that no law shall be passed that is repugnant to Islam. The USCIRF report relates that 10 Muslim states declare themselves to be an Islamic state and Islam to be the state religion whereas another 12 declare Islam to be the state religion but do not declare themselves to be an Islamic state.

Pakistan illustrates how such principles offset religious freedom. Its Constitution declares that "every citizen shall have the right to profess, practice, and propagate his religion," while also proclaiming that Islam is the state religion and mandating the federal court to judge whether any law is repugnant to Islam. Whatever religious freedom means in Pakistan, it does not stand in the way of outlawing the Ahmadi sect of Islam, viewed by Sunnis as heretical, or passing draconian blasphemy laws, like those that resulted in the prosecution of Asia Bibi as recounted in Chapter 4.

Muslim states have also supported religious freedom, along with other human rights, in their international legal commitments. Of the small number of independent Muslim-majority states in the world in 1948, eight voted in favor of that year's Universal Declaration of Human Rights; Saudi Arabia was the only one to abstain, which it did on account of its objections to Article 18, on religious freedom, and Article 16, on equal marriage rights. As of today, 39 Muslim-majority states have signed and ratified the United Nations Covenant on Civil and Political Rights, whose Article 18 also articulates religious freedom. Only seven Muslim-majority states have neither signed nor ratified this covenant; one other (Comoros) has signed but not ratified.[61]

Countering this support are the extensive efforts of Muslim states since 1980 to promote human rights instruments that sharply compromise the human right of religious freedom—international versions of Mayer's human rights schemes. Disputes between Muslim countries and the United States over what became the 1981 UN Declaration on the Elimination of All Forms of Intolerance and of Discrimination Based on Religion or Belief help to account for the two decades that it took to negotiate the convention and for the fact that it never became a legally binding instrument, remaining a declaration. Particularly contentious was the clause, "this right includes the freedom to change his religion or belief," which, for Muslims, amounts to apostasy and never made it into the final document. Then, in 1981, what is known as the Universal Islamic Declaration of Human Rights (UIDHR) was proclaimed by several Muslim-majority countries, including Egypt, Pakistan, and Saudi Arabia under the coordination of the Islamic Council, a London organization affiliated with the Muslim League, whose headquarters are in Saudi Arabia.[62] It is testimony to the power of the idea of human rights that these states saw fit to create a human rights declaration modeled on the UDHR of 1948; it is testimony to the resurgent power of Islam that the declaration differs so much from the UDHR. Article 12 declares religious freedom—that every person "has the right to express his thoughts and beliefs"—but then adds, "so long as he remains within the limits prescribed by the Law." The Arabic version of the declaration makes clear what the law means:

> Everyone may think, believe, and express his ideas and beliefs without interference or opposition from anyone as long as he obeys the limits [hudud] set by the Shari'a. It is not permitted to spread falsehood [al-batil] or disseminate that which involves encouraging abomination [al-fahisha] or forsaking the Islamic community [takhdhil li'l-umma].[63]

Then, in 1990, the Cairo Declaration on human rights in Islam was adopted by the Nineteenth Islamic Conference of Foreign Ministers of the Member States of the Organization of the Islamic Conference (OIC)—and contained no article dedicated to religious freedom at all. Finally, in recent years, in response to insults against Islam such as the Danish cartoons that lampooned Muhammad in 2005, the OIC has been promoting international anti-blasphemy norms that would likely pose strong constraints on free speech and the freedom of religion.

Once again, we have a seed of freedom. Religious freedom, even a robust form of the principle, has a deposit in the law of Muslim states. It is opposed, however, by other legal arrangements that would sharply truncate the principle and that are quite common in Islam. For this seed to grow, religious freedom would have to become far more robustly ensconced in the laws of Muslim states and these states' commitments to religious freedom in international law would have to become far less qualified.

Seventh Seed: Separation of Religion and State

Islamoskeptics often say that Islam's problem is that it knows no separation between religion and state. They often contrast this feature of Islam with

Christianity, in which Jesus established two spheres when he taught, as recorded in the Gospel of Matthew, "[r]ender unto Caesar what is Caesar's and unto God what is God's," and in which these two spheres have remained separate in subsequent centuries, at least in Latin Christendom. In Islam, by contrast, religious authority and temporal authority are said to be fused, resulting in the violent imposition of religion on the part of states and in claims of religious authorities to control politics.

Historian Ira Lapidus argues differently. A close examination of the history of Islam reveals that except for a few periods, religious and temporal authorities have been differentiated.[64] There are many varieties of this differentiation, and at times, religious and temporal authorities have interpenetrated each other thoroughly. Differentiation has not always meant what Thomas Jefferson had in mind when he wrote of a wall of separation between church and state in a letter to the Danbury Baptist Association. The same can be said about medieval Christianity, though. What differentiation means is that two separate authorities exist and are not fused into one. "Two there are," as Pope Gelasius put it in 494 CE. In most of Islam's history, as in most of Christianity's history, there have been two.

True, religious and temporal authorities were fused in the person of the Prophet Muhammad and in the first century of caliphs but not thereafter. In the Middle East, the caliphs evolved into monarchs while religious authority migrated into the hands of scholars and holy men; a state apparatus developed and so did religious communities; the caliph and the *ulema* struggled for authority. In ensuing empires over subsequent centuries—the Saljuqs, the Ottomans, and the Safavids—dual authorities persisted, however various their roles and relationships. True, not all Muslim jurists have accepted this duality. A rejection of it fuels the resistance of certain contemporary Islamist militants. Even in most Islamist states today, though, a duality exists in fact and is widely accepted in theory.[65]

The differentiation that Lapidus describes falls short of religious freedom. Even if authorities are dual, nothing stands in the way of them suppressing the heretical, the heterodox, and the non-Muslim. Yet, differentiation is a step toward religious freedom, for it means that the political authority has accorded the religious authority and community some measure of autonomy. Differentiation is a seed of freedom.

So it goes for all of the seeds of freedom discussed in this chapter. They point both to the presence of religious freedom in Islam but also to its incomplete realization. Is there a basis for hope that religious freedom will grow and expand, rather than retreat and contract, within the Muslim world? The next chapter points to one religious community's pathway to freedom.

7

A Pathway to Freedom

WHAT ISLAM NEEDS is a Reformation. This is a claim that one often hears in the Western media.[1] In another version, it is an Enlightenment that Islam really needs. In either rendering, Western history is invoked to reveal a pathway for Islam. The West, too, once knew a time when intolerance reigned, the logic runs, but then a revolution took place that ushered in freedom. Should Islam experience a similar revolution, it, too, would realize freedom.

These historical parallels are defective. Consider the Protestant Reformation. True, it challenged the hierarchical authority of the Catholic Church, which had repressed dissent for centuries, and it preached the primacy of each believer's decision for faith. Protestants, however, proved just as capable of religious repression as Catholics. Martin Luther, who launched the Reformation in 1517, came to urge execution for Protestant "Anabaptist" heretics who dissented from his teaching on key matters of doctrine. John Calvin, another major father of the Reformation, had renegade theologian Michael Servetus burned at the stake for heresy.

The reigning conviction among both Protestants and Catholics during this period was that a political order ought to be uniform in its religious faith. As the Reformation spread through Central and Northern Europe, taking root in some territories but not others, Protestants would seek an alliance with a prince or king, and, where they succeeded, the prince or the king would establish a particular Protestant church as the religion of the realm, protect its members against external enemies, and outlaw dissenters, including other kinds of Protestants. So, when Henry VIII seized control of the Catholic Church in England, he executed powerful dissenters, most famously Sir Thomas More and Bishop John Fisher. When Henry's daughter Mary reigned from 1553 to 1558, she reestablished the Catholic Church and had 283 Protestants burned at the stake, earning the sobriquet, "Bloody." When her younger sister,

Elizabeth, succeeded her, she reestablished the Anglican Church and proved no less bloody toward Catholics. Throughout the 17th century, Anglican kings persecuted Catholics and Puritans, except during the brief midcentury reign of Puritan Oliver Cromwell, who persecuted Catholics. Across the continent, competition to establish each territory as *"une foi, une loi, un roi"* ["one faith, one law, one king"], as a contemporary French formulation put it, ignited over a century of war, culminating in the Thirty Years' War of 1618–1648.

By the 17th century, certain Protestants began to teach that the state must not coerce religious faith, and they deserve to be lauded as pioneers of modern religious freedom. These were a minority among Protestants, though, and most of them belonged to sects that were not established as national churches.[2] Most established Protestant churches continued to enforce their faith at the expense of other Christian believers well into the future. Consider, for instance, Britain's American colonies. Although many of them were havens for Europe's religious refugees, 8 out of the 13 maintained established churches and practiced persecution or heavy discrimination against nonmembers up to the time of the American Revolution.[3] England discriminated harshly against non-Anglican Protestants and Catholics until it gradually established equality through a series of laws spanning from 1778 to 1926. As late as the 1870s and 1880s, Germany's Lutheran chancellor, Otto von Bismarck, carried out a *Kulturkampf* [cultural struggle] against Catholics in which he dissolved the Jesuit order, placed Catholic Churches and schools under state control, and jailed 1,800 priests along with every bishop in Prussia.[4] The Reformation, then, turns out to be a dubious pathway for Islam, at least if the goal is religious freedom and peace.

What about the Enlightenment? This philosophical movement of the late 17th and 18th centuries, whose most famous figures include John Locke, Jean-Jacques Rousseau, Immanuel Kant, David Hume, Voltaire, Montesquieu, and Thomas Jefferson, advanced individual rights, stressed the autonomy of reason from religious authority, professed skepticism that religious revelation could be understood reliably and consensually, interpreted recent history as a period of bloodshed and hatred wrought by irresolvable religious conflict, and sought to minimize religion's role in politics.

Like the Reformation, however, the Enlightenment has a mixed track record in promoting religious freedom. Some Enlightenment thinkers advocated religious freedom, at least for individuals. Their doctrines of religious freedom, though, were highly selective, especially toward Catholics. Enlightenment thinkers almost uniformly regarded the Catholic Church as the great enemy of religious freedom, the purveyor of inquisitions. But were they prepared to allow Catholics and their Church their own religious freedom?

Diderot's biliousness toward priests and Locke's cold shoulder toward atheists, Catholics, and Muslims were mentioned earlier. Add to them Rousseau, who thought that the Catholic Church's hierarchy and dogmas created intolerance and diverted citizens' loyalties from the state. He called for the invention of a civic religion that would direct allegiances to the sovereign state and even advocated that apostates from this religion "should be punished with death"—a proposal for the Enlightenment's own inquisition.[5]

The French Revolution of 1789 followed Rousseau's script. Although it proclaimed the rights of man, it lopped off the heads of Catholic men and women. Although it can be credited for extending toleration to Protestants and Jews, it attacked the authority of Catholic bishops, dissevered them from the authority of the pope, forced priests and nuns to sign an oath of loyalty to the revolutionary regime, executed about 3,000 priests, exiled many of them, expropriated Church lands, and carried out genocidal violence against Catholics in the Vendée region.[6] It invented alternative religions, the Cult of Reason and the Cult of the Supreme Being, that would replace Christianity and serve the state and fitted them out with rites and teachings.

In the 19th and 20th centuries, regimes and parties based on Enlightenment ideas sought to establish an ideology of secularism that sharply curtailed the freedom of the Catholic Church in Western Europe and Latin America. They did so in the expectation that Catholicism, and indeed religion altogether, would fade from history.

Muslims have experienced the European Enlightenment directly on their own turf. Enlightenment ideas have inspired what this book has termed the secular repressive model of regime.[7] As we have seen, this model found its prototype in the Republic of Turkey and was imitated in regimes across the Arab world after World War II, which restricted and managed Islam in the name of modernization, expecting all the while that Islam, like all religion, would become marginalized.

Islam did not become marginalized. In the 1970s a worldwide resurgence of Islam took place that saw both a revival of religious faith and demands for political influence. It was Enlightenment-inspired regimes—most of them highly authoritarian—that devout Muslims found objectionable. And still find objectionable. The problem with the Enlightenment is that its commitment to freedom stands in contradiction to its typical truncation of religious liberty, underwritten by its religious skepticism. Muslims are well familiar with this pathway through history, and a good many of them find it wanting.

Should westerners, then, abstain altogether from commending their own history as a pathway for Muslims? Before we abandon the search for analogies, I want to propose that Western history does in fact contain a pathway to freedom that is promising for Islam. Ironically, it can be found in the religious body that the Reformation and the Enlightenment both considered freedom's greatest enemy: the Catholic Church. It can hardly escape notice that the Catholic Church came around to religious freedom quite late in history upon the Second Vatican Council's promulgation of *Dignitatis Humanae*, its Declaration on Religious Liberty, in 1965—three centuries after certain Protestant and Enlightenment voices began to articulate religious liberty. The Church's long historical pathway to *Dignitatis Humanae*, however, can prove instructive for Islam.

Clearly there are respects in which the Catholic Church's experience will not apply to Islam. Islam does not contain a single locus of authority that speaks for all Muslims in the way that the Catholic Church does through its pope, its bishops, and its theology of the Church as one body. Although caliphs have aspired to speak with such authority, no claimant to the caliphate enjoys such authority today. No doctrine of religious freedom, then, will be proclaimed authoritatively on behalf of all Muslims.

Nor does Islam face a related issue that surrounded *Dignitatis Humanae*—that of doctrinal development. The authors of *Dignitatis Humanae* at the Second Vatican Council were keen to teach religious freedom in a way that was consistent with the authoritative teachings of previous popes. Islam does not demand continuity in the same manner.

These differences, though, leave intact the sense in which I will argue that *Dignitatis Humanae* is directly relevant for Islam—namely, that it shows how a religious body that for many centuries did not teach religious freedom eventually found a way to embrace religious freedom that was compatible with its traditional teachings about religious faith and that avoided the compromise of its teachings that it saw in the Reformation and the hostile secularism that it found in the Enlightenment. *Dignitatis Humanae* illustrates how seeds of freedom planted within a tradition can later sprout into an authoritative and widely embraced doctrine of religious freedom.

How the Catholic Church Forgot Religious Freedom

The way in which we understand the Catholic Church's long historical pathway to *Dignitatis Humanae* matters a great deal for this pathway's relevance for Muslims. A commonly heard story says that the Christian church favored repression of other faiths from the moment that it had the opportunity to be allied with temporal power. That moment was the conversion of the Roman Emperor Constantine to Christianity in 312 CE. Prior to this time, the story runs, the Roman Empire had persecuted Christians, intensifying and widening this repression in the third century, bringing it to a climax in the Diocletian persecution of 303–313. Now, with a Christian emperor, the persecuted would become the persecutors. It was not until religious repression reached an apex in the religious wars of the 16th and 17th centuries that European thinkers began to conceive of a more tolerant politics, the story runs.

This story is alive and well both among latter-day Enlightenment secularists and among Protestant Anabaptists—Mennonites like theologian John Howard Yoder, for instance—who hold that with Constantine, the Christian church fell from purity by turning to worldly power to fight its battles.[8] However, just as the Enlightenment and Protestant versions of the West's pathway to freedom have problems, as we have seen, so, too, does the story of Constantine's conversion as a moment of reversed repression.

Tradition has it that Constantine became a Christian after the sign of the cross appeared in the sky and delivered him and his troops a victory at the Battle of Milvian Bridge in 312. He, along with his co-emperor at the time, Licinius, legalized Christianity in the empire in the Edict of Milan the next year, 313. Legalizing Christianity was also good politics. The Diocletian persecution had failed to stem the growth of Christianity in the empire. Rather than continuing to treat Christians as disloyal citizens for practicing a faith at odds with paganism, why not make Christians allies of the empire and thus mobilize their civic energies?

Did the onset of a Christian emperor, then, usher in the repression of non-Christians, replacing one form of intolerance with another? No. The Edict of Milan grants "both to Christians *and to all others* free facility to follow the religion which each may desire" and mandates that "no one who has given his mental assent to the Christian persuasion nor to any other which he feels to be suitable to him should be compelled to deny his conviction."[9] The Edict of Milan was no ephemeral tactic. Its intellectual godfather was Lucius Lactantius, a Christian scholar and adviser to Constantine who had penned his important work on religion, *Divine Institutes*, during the Diocletian persecution. There, he made a case for religious freedom for all human beings that was rooted not in practical political arguments for toleration but rather in the very character of religious belief. Because religion involves an inward assent of love, it cannot be coerced, he argued. On this basis, he enunciated the equivalent of the modern human right of religious freedom—the immunity of every person from coercion.[10]

Without question, Constantine favored Christianity in his subsequent rule. To speak in the language of the First Amendment to the US Constitution, he instituted both religious freedom and establishment. He established the Catholic faith by according it the strong favor of the state. He built basilicas;

promoted Christians to high office; restituted property that Christians lost during the persecution; gave the Church land and other forms of wealth; commissioned the publishing of Bibles; instituted legal reforms based on Christian teachings; built a new imperial capital at Byzantium that featured churches and Christian architecture and was bereft of pagan temples; and convened the first ecumenical (or universal) council of the Christian church at Nicea in 325. To a great extent, though, he allowed pagans freedom and influence. Up until the end of his life, for instance, two-thirds of his government officials were non-Christian.

That Constantine favored religious freedom is a critical point for understanding Christian history and Western history. Contrary to much contemporary thinking, religious freedom is not solely the product of the early modern religious wars or of modern secular thought. Religious repression is not endemic to Christianity. It is not the case, then, that *Dignitatis Humanae* was a historical straggler, a ratification of something that the Western world outside the Catholic Church had discovered long earlier. It is more accurate to say that *Dignitatis Humanae* resurrected a principle that the Catholic Church had long placed on reserve.

To make the point that religious freedom found strong expression at this early time is not meant to obscure the subsequent onset of a long era in which establishment would expand while religious freedom would be occluded. "By the end of the fourth century," writes classicist Robert Wilken, "Christianity was declared the official religion of the Roman Empire, and as the state granted more privileges to Christianity the Church's bishops put greater pressure on imperial officials to restrict the practice of other forms of religious belief."[11] Fitting this description most famously was St. Ambrose, bishop of Milan, who pressured Emperor Theodosius to outlaw paganism and repress pagans in the final decade of the fourth century. Over subsequent centuries, well after the fall of the Roman Empire in the 5th century, this trajectory would continue. At the Twelfth Council of Toledo in 681, an assembly of Spanish bishops ruled that Jews who had been converted to Christianity through force could be compelled to keep the faith.

By the high Middle Ages—11th through 13th centuries—the papacy was greatly strengthened, and the pope and other bishops could urge and assist the state in enforcing the practice and expression of Christian beliefs. The most carefully organized of these efforts—taking on the status of a historical legend—was the Inquisition. Put better, there were inquisitions, several episodes of them, each occurring in a particular locale, timespan, and set of circumstances. They took place in France, Italy, the Papal States, Rome, Spain, the Netherlands, Portugal, and Spanish and Portuguese colonies from the

13th to the 19th centuries, most intensely between the 13th and 16th centuries and with increasing rarity afterward. An inquisition was a court conducted by the Church for the purpose of investigating and trying heretics, meaning baptized Christians who espoused views contrary to the teachings of the Church. Typical inquisitions were carried out according to careful procedures and, when they found a defendant guilty of a serious offense, handed him or her over to the state to mete out punishment. One study of the Spanish Inquisition found that 1.5% of trials resulted in executions, which numbered 1,303, during the period 1540–1700—not the scale of legend.[12] Whatever the subsequent legend, though, there is no denying that inquisitions took place and that they tortured and executed defendants.

Inquisitions were hardly the only sharp curtailments of religious freedom, many of them far less systematic and law governed. Kings and princes violently repressed heresy and apostasy. Jews suffered heavy discrimination, including being confined to ghettos, barred from offices and professions, forced to wear badges and distinctive clothing, and subjected to coercive attempts at conversion. Jews were expelled from numerous European countries, as were Muslims from Spain. Jews and Muslims were attacked in the Crusades. All such measures sharply infringed upon religious freedom and the dignity of the person.

What was the thinking behind these practices? Or did they spring from an inchoate desire for domination? They cannot be understood apart from how both the Church and the temporal authorities—emperors, kings, princes—came to understand their proper relationship with one another and with the larger society during the period of Christendom, which began in the late 4th century and lasted into modern times.[13]

Christendom's defining idea is that both the Church and the temporal governing authorities are stewards of a thoroughly Christian society, one that manifests the Christian gospel in its laws, customs, architecture, calendar, and daily life so as to lead its members to Christian virtue in this life and eternal salvation in the next. Thomas Aquinas wrote in his treatise, *On Kingship*, that "[t]he final end of organized society then is not [merely] to live the life of virtue but through a life of virtue to attain the enjoyment of God" and that "it is the duty of the king to promote the good life of the community so that it leads to happiness in heaven."[14]

Unlike certain other civilizations, including the Roman Empire prior to Constantine, Christendom did not fuse spiritual and temporal governing authority into the hands of a single ruler. The Church governed sacramental and spiritual life while temporal authorities commanded armies, collected taxes, and built roads. If distinct, though, these spheres overlapped far more than in modern society. Kings and princes upheld the prerogatives of the Church, while the Church would crown kings, counsel them on how to rule, and excommunicate them if they sinned egregiously in their political behavior. Although in theory the spheres of Church and king were complementary and their mutual assistance fraternal, they also could clash over their prerogatives, sometimes to the death. Thomas à Becket, the English archbishop of Canterbury portrayed in modern drama and film, for instance, was assassinated by the henchmen of King Henry II in 1170 when he refused to concede the Church's rights.

In a society in which Church and state worked together to promote a Christian culture that would lead its members to salvation and in which the unity, stability, and welfare of the public order were thought to depend on shared Christian beliefs, heresy and apostasy on the part of once-baptized Christians were considered not only spiritual and moral faults but also public crimes. As historian Brad S. Gregory writes, "The spreading of heresy was religious reckless endangerment by spiritual serial killers. Indeed, heretics were worse than multiple murderers, because their victims lived on to harm others in turn."[15] This was the theory behind the coercion of people with respect to their religious beliefs and practices. Aquinas compared heretics to counterfeiters of money, meaning that they corrupt not only their own souls but even more so the spiritual ecology that sustains the faith of others. The Church, he wrote, "*provides for the salvation of others* by separating [heretics] from the church by the sentence of excommunication and then leaves [them] to the secular judge to be exterminated from the world by death."[16] In describing the English statute *De Haeretico Comburendo* of 1401, contemporary philosopher John Finnis writes,

> Parliament makes clear that it is acting to assist the 'Church of England' because the [Oxford-based] heretics now troubling the Church by their anti-Catholic teaching and preaching 'may excite and stir [people] to sedition and insurrection, and make great strife and division among the people' and subvert the Church which has brought great honour and other benefits to the realm for centuries; and since the Church's own penalties ('censures') for this are ignored, evaded, and derided by heretics, it is right for the sake of the 'honour and prosperity' of the realm to accede to the request of the Church's authorities for state assistance, which will be given in the form of public burning of those whom the Church has found guilty of persistence in heresy – all of this with a view to extirpating the heresy from the realm, a realm conceived implicitly as a (part of) *christianitas*, Christendom.[17]

In the same vein, Sir Thomas More, who oversaw the burning of Lutheran heretics as lord chancellor under King Henry VIII, perceived crime in their active proselytization, not in their mere holding of a false belief, and viewed heresy as a source of social disintegration. As nation-states began to develop, kings grafted national identity onto religion as indispensable sources of national unity: one faith, one law, one king, and one nation.[18] Thus, when Spanish kings expelled Moriscos—former Muslims who converted to Christianity, sometimes under coercion—from Spain in the 16th and 17th centuries, they were seeking not only religious uniformity but also ethnic and national purity.

Does this mean that the Church was concerned only with the heretic's threat to others and not with the heretic's soul? Nothing so simple can be said. The historical record is replete with the Church's hope that the threat of death would lead heretics to repent. "The church," writes Aquinas, "is merciful and desires the conversion of those who are in error. Therefore she does not condemn them immediately 'but after a first and second admonition', as the Apostle [Paul] teaches."[19] In fact, the heretic's own faith and a spiritual ecology that would lead everyone to faith were not easily disentangled as goals of coercion. What the Church never taught authoritatively was forced conversion— that the salvation of the heretic's soul alone merited coercing him—though its members surely sanctioned it in practice in certain historical episodes. Still less did it teach that those who never had held the Christian faith could be forced into it, though again, exceptions dwell in the historical record.

The Catholic Church continued to advocate the basic tenets of Christendom, including the legitimacy of coercion in religious matters, right up to the eve of *Dignitatis Humanae* in 1965. Positively, the Church adhered to Christendom as an authentically Christian model of society: Church and state ought to work closely together in furthering God's creative and redemptive purposes. After the French Revolution of 1789, however, the Church's advocacy of Christendom also took on a more defensive tone in an increasingly hostile political milieu. While, during the three centuries leading up to the revolution, monarchs had asserted more and more power over the Catholic and other Christian churches, they still called themselves "the most Christian king" and professed Christian ideas. Now, however, a form of politics emerged that was altogether hostile to Christianity, seeking to marginalize and, in later forms, to eliminate the Christian church. The French Revolution's attacks on Catholics were the first installment of this new politics, the Church perceived.[20]

Faced with this hostility, 19th century popes denounced, often vehemently, "liberty of conscience," "liberty of worship," and other civil rights that later became staples of modern liberal democracy. Such denunciations arose in reaction to the form in which these rights were advocated, namely in close association with hostility to the Church's powers and privileges and with philosophies and theologies sharply at odds with the Church's teaching: an "indifferentism" toward religious truth; a "latitudinarianism" by which all religions and churches are equally valid; a desire to marginalize and privatize the Church in society; an elevation of autonomous human reason lacking in reference to God as the arbiter of truth; a confinement of reason to the methods of natural science; and other opinions that the Church judged false.[21] Popes also criticized civil liberties for being unlimited and unrestrained.

Certain pontifical utterances attracted great attention in contemporary debates. Pope Gregory XVI, for instance, called "liberty of conscience" an "absurd" and "erroneous" proposition in his 1832 encyclical, *Mirari Vos*. He echoed the 19th century papacy's negative judgment of liberties as being rooted in the "shameful font of indifferentism" as well as its positive view of Christendom in warning against breaking the "mutual concord between temporal authority and the priesthood" and the "concord which always was favorable and beneficial for the sacred and the civil order."[22]

The most famous papal pronouncement in the eyes of 19th-century European publics was Pope Pius IX's *Syllabus of Errors*, a catalogue of modernity's mistakes that appeared as the appendix to his 1864 encyclical, *Quanta Cura*. In the body of the encyclical, Pius IX begins by noting widespread doctrinal errors abroad in the land, proceeds to quote Gregory XVI's condemnation of liberty of conscience, and then adds his own condemnation of arguments against the Church's right to restrain "offenders against the Catholic religion." He rejects both liberty of conscience and religious liberty for being based on misguided doctrines.[23] In the *Syllabus of Errors*, he condemns the proposition that "[e]very man is free to embrace and profess that religion which, guided by the light of reason, he shall consider true" a formulation that clearly links religious freedom with a wayward autonomous reason. So, too, in the body of *Quanta Cura*, he approves that "mutual fellowship and concord of counsels between Church and State which has ever proved itself propitious and salutary, both for religious and civil interests."[24]

Pius IX's successor, Pope Leo XIII, cracked open the door to democracy and liberty in his encyclical, *Immortale Dei* of 1885, where he asserts the traditional teaching that the Church prescribes no one form of regime and that democracy contains laudable virtues like popular participation in governance. In the same letter he develops a distinction between a liberty that promotes virtue and a liberty that amounts to license, thus allowing that a sound version of liberty might exist.[25] However, he also repeats Gregory

XVI's and Pius IX's criticisms of freedom of conscience, freedom of the press, and the separation of church and state, and links them to the liberty of license and the rejection of God as the basis of government. He adheres to Christendom in arguing that the best regime is one where state and church play different but cooperative and complementary roles in upholding a Christian social order.

Leo XIII voiced his increased openness to democracy and political liberty again in his encyclical of 1895 written to the bishops of the United States, *Longinqua Oceani*. There, Leo profusely praises the laws and Constitution of the American Republic for allowing the Church its freedom to flourish. He then goes on to clarify that "though all this is true, it would be very erroneous to draw the conclusion that in America is to be sought the type of the most desirable status of the Church, or that it would be universally lawful or expedient for State and Church to be, as in America, dissevered and divorced." His view became known as the thesis/hypothesis doctrine, holding that an ideal state would establish the Catholic Church and uphold its teachings, even through laws that restrict dissent and apostasy, but that where such a state is not possible, for instance where Catholics are in a minority, something less is acceptable. For all that God has blessed the American church, Leo continued in his letter to America, this church could "bring forth more abundant fruits if, in addition to liberty, she enjoyed the favor of the laws and the patronage of the public authority."[26] Complementing this fealty to Christendom was Leo's warning against "Americanism," a version of liberty that fails to accept the full authority of the pope, in his encyclical of 1899, *Testem Benevolentiae Nostrae.*[27]

As late as the early 1950s, this view prevailed as the authoritative teaching of the Catholic Church. When, in the late 1940s and early 1950s, American Jesuit theologian John Courtney Murray began to advocate for full religious freedom in the political realm, the Vatican responded by forbidding him from writing on the topic. Representative of Vatican opinion was a short comment composed in 1951 by Father Francis Connell, dean of the School of Sacred Theology at the Catholic University of America, on a memorandum that Murray wrote in 1950 for Monsignor Giovanni Battista Montini, the future Pope Paul VI, who was then a substitute secretary of state in the Vatican. "Certainly, Pope Leo XIII clearly taught," write Connell, "that per se [in principle] a government is bound to show special favor to the Catholic Church . . . and he enunciated this principle for all forms of government, including democracy. It is by virtue of this principle that a Catholic government, in order to protect the faith of the Catholic citizens, is per se justified in restricting heretical propaganda."[28] Here endorsed is Christendom.

The Road to *Dignitatis Humanae*

A few short years later, the Church lifted its ban on Murray's writings on religious liberty and declared the very principle an enduringly valid doctrine in its proclamation, *Dignitatis Humanae*, of December 7, 1965:

> [T]he human person has a right to religious freedom. This freedom means that all men are to be immune from coercion on the part of individuals or of social groups and of any human power, in such wise that no one is to be forced to act in a manner contrary to his own beliefs, whether privately or publicly, whether alone or in association with others, within due limits.

What the Church proclaimed was essentially the human right to religious freedom that the Universal Declaration of Human Rights had set forth in 1948, that the International Covenant on Political and Civil Rights would enunciate almost exactly a year later in December 1966, and that this book defends as universal.

Our puzzle, then, is how the Church came to this juncture. Seven factors, I propose, propelled the Church along its pathway to *Dignitatis Humanae* and point to a potential pathway for Islam.

First, much as we saw in Chapter 6 in the Islamic tradition, "seeds" of religious freedom were planted all along over the course of the Christian tradition. Again, a seed is a concept or practice that expresses religious freedom in a significant way but that falls short of the wide and deep articulation, acceptance, and legal enshrinement of the modern human right. One robust form of the seed of religious freedom is the remarkable articulations of the human right of religious freedom in the first three centuries of the Church's history. These articulations did not spell out the many dimensions of religious freedom in the way that *Dignitatis Humanae* or the modern human rights conventions do, or receive the authoritative endorsement of the Church in the way that *Dignitatis Humanae* did, but they did assert the human right of religious freedom.

Dignitatis Humanae footnotes Lactantius as an early exponent of the right. As political philosopher Timothy Samuel Shah shows, and as I noted earlier, the second- and third-century theologian, Tertullian, also appealed to officials of the Roman Empire to acknowledge that "it is a fundamental human right [*humani iuris*], a privilege (or inherent capacity) of nature [*naturalis potestatis*], that every man should worship according to his own convictions: one man's religion neither harms nor helps another man."[29] Shah argues that "the very phrase *libertatem religionis* is one that Tertullian seems to have invented" and quotes Tertullian urging the Romans, "[s]ee that you do not give a reason for impious religious practice by taking away religious liberty (*libertatem religionis*) and prohibiting choice (*optione*) in divine matters."[30] Shah also makes a case that early defenses of religious freedom can be found in the writings of Justin Martyr and Athenagoras of Athens, though they did not articulate religious freedom as a human right as strongly and clearly as did Tertullian and Lactantius.

An important feature of all of these thinkers' concepts of religious freedom, Shah points out, is that they grant immunity from coercive interference not only to individuals but also to the Church as an ecclesiastical, corporate body. Most remarkable of all, Shah contends, these thinkers virtually invented religious freedom, for they had no precedent to work from, including in the Greek world, the Roman world, the Old Testament, or the New Testament. Certainly they drew from Christian teachings to make their case, but they articulated the principle for the first time.[31]

Fitting the description of seed are also numerous statements by Christian theologians, philosophers, and church officials that religious faith itself cannot be compelled. *Dignitatis Humanae* footnotes a phalanx of thinkers who stressed this point in the early centuries of Christianity. These are seeds insofar as they contain important strands of the principle of freedom even if they do not spell out the full human right of religious freedom.

Sometimes, the same scholars or officials who affirmed the free nature of faith also justified the coercion and even execution of heretics. The Council of Toledo of 681, previously mentioned for its endorsement of the compulsion of Jews, also stated in some six different ways, as Finnis explains, that religious faith cannot be coerced.[32] This combination of commitments—a strenuous defense of the freedom of faith alongside an advocacy of strong coercion—can be found in the thought of Augustine of Hippo and Thomas Aquinas, arguably the two greatest thinkers in the Christian tradition and both widely known for their sanctioning of coercion. Augustine's reluctant acceptance of the forcible suppression of the heretical Donatist sect by the Roman authorities in the late fourth and early fifth centuries is still widely considered a turning point in the Church's history of sanctioning coercion. Yet, in numerous writings, Augustine insisted that religious faith is of necessity adopted out of a free will, that the will is guided by the intellect, and that people should therefore be brought to faith by reasoning and persuasion.[33] On many occasions, he counseled against coercing heretics, including the Donatists, before he later changed his mind.

Aquinas, as we have seen, held that heretics could be punished, even with execution. Like Augustine, though, he, too, held strongly that faith could only be adopted authentically through free choice. He forbade conversion of non-Christians by force, holding that Jews and Muslims, for instance, "should in no way be forced to believe, for faith is a matter of the will."[34] He also stressed the importance of the individual's conscience to a degree exceeding that of any previous philosopher, teaching that a person is bound to follow his conscience even if it tells him to do wrong.

How did these great minds reconcile these seemingly contradictory commitments—the freedom of faith and the legitimacy of coercion? The broad answer, again, has to do with the spiritual ecology. Although Augustine continued to hold that the decision for faith could not be coerced, he thought that the Donatists were a danger to social peace and to the faith of the community. They were indeed. Bands of Donatists known as Circumcellions were cultish terrorists. They would commit suicide in dramatic fashion, even bizarrely forcing highway travelers to take their lives. Thomas thought that heretics endangered the souls of others and could be punished also for breaching their baptismal promise.

In certain respects, both thinkers allowed that coercion might encourage faith and thus approached the precipice of contradicting their commitment to free will in matters religious. When Augustine finally came around to accepting coercing the Donatists, he argued that coercion could limit the harm that they did to themselves by their heresy and even compel them to examine their beliefs. He was impressed by the success that coercion seemed to have achieved in leading Donatists to renounce their heresy. Still, he held even here that the actual choice to believe orthodox Christianity must in the end be a free one. Coercion would lead heretics to a decision for faith, it seems, but only they could make the decision. Similarly, Aquinas thought that the threat of death might have the side effect of leading heretics to believe even though the threat was primarily aimed to halt the heretic's damage to the social order. Here, too, though, the decision for faith could be made, in the end, only by the believer.[35]

The achievement of *Dignitatis Humanae*, of course, was that it rejected coercion in matters of religion, just as do most citizens of contemporary Western liberal democracies. This dimension of Augustine and Aquinas they no longer find acceptable. What is important, though, is that despite these thinkers' justifications of coercion, their insistence that a person's basic decision to adopt faith could not be coerced, along with the same insistence on the part of many other Christian thinkers throughout the tradition, amounts to seeds that later germinated.

The second factor that propelled the Catholic Church along its historical pathway to *Dignitatis Humanae* was the efforts of modern Catholic intellectuals to develop a defense of religious freedom as a human right in full—something more than mere tolerance, something fuller than the free nature of faith, but rather a civil right to practice any or no faith that merits enshrinement in public law. Critically, they defended religious freedom on grounds that were fully consonant with Catholic doctrine and tradition. That is, they provided an alternative justification to the "indifferentism" and "latitudinarianism" that characterized Enlightenment arguments for religious liberty and other civil liberties and that led 19th-century popes to reject these arguments.

In the 19th century, German Bishop Wilhelm von Ketteler argued that human dignity was manifested in each person's liberty to choose God and was denied when the state enforced religious orthodoxy. English intellectual Lord John Acton was another prominent defender of religious liberty during the second half of the 19th century. In the 20th century, French Catholic philosopher Jacques Maritain—who emigrated to the United States in the 1930s—tapped Aquinas's thought to develop arguments for democracy and human rights, including religious liberty.[36]

Another Catholic émigré from fascist Europe, German intellectual Heinrich Rommen, is less well known than Maritain or Murray for his defense of religious freedom, yet formulated his arguments on grounds that were arguably closer to those of *Dignitatis Humanae* than either of those of his more famous contemporaries. In a 1950 article in the *Review of Politics*, he defends religious freedom on grounds of conscience, the dignity of the person, and the nature of religious faith.[37]

It was Murray, though, whose influence on *Dignitatis Humanae* was most direct. Once the Church lifted its interdict, it invited him to the Second Vatican Council, where he wrote early drafts of the document. At the core of his thinking was the American experience, which, he thought, had much to teach the whole world about the relative roles of Church and state authority, namely that they ought to be far more separate than Christendom had conceived them. The state's function was to uphold justice and peace, which would include upholding the freedom of the Church to conduct its work but would not include promoting individual salvation directly. Suppressing dissenting opinion was outside the state's competence. The First Amendment's Free Exercise clause, he thought, carried global significance for the Church. Although Murray's arguments were only partially reflected in the text of *Dignitatis Humanae*, which evolved through vigorous discussion and debate, Murray's role in giving prominence to religious freedom and in seeing it through at the Council makes him, more than anyone else, the father of *Dignitatis Humanae.*[38]

The intellectual groundwork that he and these many other scholars laid gave the bishops at the Second Vatican Council a basis from which to formulate and give their approval to *Dignitatis Humanae.*

A third factor in the pathway to *Dignitatis Humanae* was the abatement of anticlericalism in European states. After World War II, France, the Federal Republic of Germany, and Italy firmly rejected Fascism, managed to stave off Communism, and established constitutional democracies that robustly guaranteed religious freedom and other civil and political liberties. The value and fragility of political freedoms in the context of democracy was one of the leading lessons of the war, as Pope Pius XII stressed in his Christmas Address of 1944. After the war, Catholic Christian Democratic parties rose to prominence and succeeded in electing Catholic politicians into top leadership positions: Konrad Adenauer as chancellor of Germany, Alcide de Gasperi as prime minister of Italy, Robert Schuman as foreign minister of France, and Paul Lévy, a Belgian convert to the Catholic faith, as the first chief of the Department of Culture in the newly created Council of Europe. In addition to promoting religiously informed democracy at home, these statesmen served as the key founders of the institutions that would eventually become the European Union. Through federal institutions, they were convinced, European states could recover the unity of medieval Christendom, though now it would be infused with democracy and religious freedom, and they could pursue reconciliation and forgiveness after World War II.[39] That European states who were once hostile to the Catholic Church would respect the Church's freedom and even prove hospitable to Catholic politics did much to convince the Church's bishops that religious freedom was an acceptable principle.

A fourth factor, the American experiment, was an amplification of the third factor. If the Western democracies were still embryonic and experimental in the years between World War II and the Second Vatican Council, across the ocean was a constitutional democracy that had guaranteed religious freedom almost from its beginning—and that provided an environment where, astonishingly in the eyes of the Church in Rome, the Catholic Church had flourished. The American experiment was astonishing to the Vatican because close outside its walls, all across the European continent, liberalism had brought assaults on the Church's internal authority, property, schools, universities, monasteries, and the papal lands in central Italy. European liberalism deigned to replace Christendom with a secular government that would regulate religion heavily though a bureaucracy.

The United States developed a very different model of relationship between Church and state than continental Europe did. The First Amendment to the US Constitution guaranteed the free exercise of religion and forbade the establishment of a national church. Yet, in this environment of full religious freedom, the Church grew by leaps and bounds as Catholic immigrants from Italy, Ireland, Germany, and Eastern Europe flooded the shores of the United States. Monsignor Denis O'Connell, who would become the Catholic bishop of the diocese of Richmond, Virginia, remarked in 1887:

> Americans never suppressed a religious order, never confiscated a sou of church property, never suppressed the salary of a bishop, never sent a seminarian into the army, never refused permission to open a Catholic university, never forbade anyone to become a religious, never forbade a meeting of bishops nor claimed a voice in naming them. In the United States the government of the Church is not carried on by the state over the heads of the bishops.[40]

Here was a state that gave the Catholic Church its freedom, but rather than work in partnership with it, by and large left it alone.

Voices for religious freedom at the time of the US founding had in mind very much what Monsignor O'Connell extolled. James Madison, the leading force behind the Bill of Rights, as the first ten amendments to the US Constitution were known, was the author of a historically enduring defense of religious freedom titled *Memorial and Remonstrance Against Religious Assessments* that bore strong resemblances to the thought of Lactantius and to the argument of *Dignitatis Humanae*. There, he defended religious freedom on the basis of the value of religion. "It is the duty of every man," he continued,

> to render the Creator such homage and such only as he believes to be acceptable to him. This duty is precedent, both in order of time and degree of obligation, to the claims of Civil Society. Before any man can be considered as a member of Civil Society, he must be considered as a subject of the Governor of the Universe.

Madison's close friend and fellow Virginian, Thomas Jefferson, was also a champion of religious freedom, having been an author of the Virginia Statute for Religious Freedom.

To be sure, American culture has hosted a strong streak of anti-Catholicism. Jefferson loved religious freedom but not the Catholic Church, having written to Alexander von Humboldt in 1813 that "[h]istory, I believe, furnishes no example of a priest-ridden people maintaining a free civil government. This marks the lowest grade of ignorance of which their civil as well as religious leaders will always avail themselves for their own purposes."[41] Twentieth-century historian Arthur Schlesinger wrote that anti-Catholicism is "the deepest-held bias in the history of the American people."[42] Anti-Catholicism has meant violence, mockery, unjust discrimination, charges of disloyalty, and state constitutional clauses aimed at denying public funding for Catholic schools known as the Blaine Amendments.

Despite this obstacle, however, the Catholic Church flourished in the United States, just as Pope Leo XIII recognized in *Longinqua Oceana*, even while he argued that legal religious freedom was a second-best adaptation to circumstances rather than a universal principle. It should come as no surprise that seven decades later, at the Second Vatican Council, it was the contingent of bishops from the United States who urged that the Church complete its job and make a right of religious freedom its authoritative teaching. In the company of Father Murray, they were the strongest bloc in favor of *Dignitatis Humanae*, which they looked upon as an export.

If Western Europe and the United States showed the Catholic Church that it could grow in peace and safety under a regime based on religious freedom, other countries motivated the Church to adopt religious freedom from the other direction—by posing new levels of threat. The Communist regimes in the Soviet Union, Eastern Europe, and China that took power in the early and mid-20th century exceeded European liberal regimes' earlier aspirations to manage and marginalize the Church and actively sought to eradicate it. These threats were the fifth factor that led to *Dignitatis Humanae*. Against such regimes, the human right of religious freedom became a source of safety, much like a plumb line dangled to a prisoner in the darkness of the bottom of a well. At the Council, one of the most forceful advocates of *Dignitatis Humanae* was Polish Archbishop Karol Wojtyla, later to become John Paul II. Working to secure the survival of his Church under a Communist regime, he understood religious freedom through the harshness of its denial.

The sixth and seventh factors that led to *Dignitatis Humanae* take us into the deliberations of the Council itself. That there would be a declaration of religious liberty and exactly what it would say were subjects of heated contention. The Council fathers had to come to terms with previous papal teachings and with 16 centuries of Christendom. *Dignitatis Humanae* was not promulgated until December 7, 1965, the penultimate day of the Council, which had lasted over three years. It saw numerous drafts and only gradually came to garner the overwhelming majority of bishops who favored it in the end by a vote of 2,308 to 70. Conservatives worried that the declaration would open the door to religious relativism and compromise the Church's claims to enduring truth—essentially, the worries that the popes of the 19th century expressed. The dialectic between supporters and skeptics resulted in a defense of religious freedom that also affirmed the Church's teachings and its desire for a Christian society and polity.

The sixth factor that paved the pathway to *Dignitatis Humanae*, then, was the Council's success in finding a religious basis for religious freedom. The core of the declaration's argument is what its name conveys—the dignity of the human person. It is a certain dimension of this dignity, though, that grounds each person's immunity from coercion in religious matters—namely, his duty to search for, find, and live out religious truth. Religious liberty is not grounded in skepticism about religious matters. Rather, it is grounded in the claim that the search for religious truth must be free.[43]

The declaration does not back away from the Church's enduring claims about truth. One of the chief skeptics was Alfredo Cardinal Ottaviani, head of the Holy Office and the overseer of Murray's suppression in the 1950s. Ottaviani's worry was that a declaration of religious liberty would sanction the proposition that "error has rights" and thus legitimate doctrines contrary to the Church's truth. *Dignitatis Humanae*, though, did not declare the rights of error but rather the rights of the person in matters of religion. The civil right of religious liberty, the declaration notes, "leaves whole and entire the traditional Catholic teaching concerning the moral duty, owed by men and by societies, towards the true religion and the sole Church of Christ."[44]

Nor does *Dignitatis Humanae* call for governments to abandon their role in promoting the religious lives of their citizenry. True, it closes out Christendom's sanction of force against public dissent from Catholic teachings and widens the separation of Church and state functions, but it also calls for governments to help create conditions "which foster a religious way of life."[45] This includes safeguarding the freedom of religious communities as well as supporting these communities through measures such as tax exemptions or public funding of religious education. The declaration allows for the possibility that a constitution might give "special civil recognition" to one religious community—as several Western European states still do—and is consistent with religiously based laws such as ones that prohibit certain businesses or government offices to be closed on Sunday or that establish religious feast days as national holidays.

The seventh propellant of *Dignitatis Humanae* was an achievement that was critical for winning over skeptical bishops and delivering an overwhelming majority in favor of passage: the formulation of religious freedom in a way that was compatible with previous dogmatic teachings of the Catholic Church.

Dogmatic teachings are those that the Church professes to be a part of its "deposit of faith." They embody divine revelation and so cannot be contradicted.

Whether and how *Dignitatis Humanae* is consistent with previous teachings is a matter of some dispute among Catholics. Those who hold that *Dignitatis Humanae* contradicts previous dogmatic teachings include liberals and Lefebvrists. Liberals celebrate the contradiction because they believe it opens the door for further changes in church teaching on issues like contraception and the male priesthood. Lefebvrists are the followers of Archbishop Marcel Lefebvre and include most of the 70 bishops who dissented from *Dignitatis Humanae* at the Council. Because *Dignitatis Humanae's* right of religious liberty contradicted previous dogmatic teaching, they charged, neither it nor the Council as a whole was legitimate. Eventually, Lefebvre and his followers became separated from the Catholic Church through a schism.

In my view, both liberals and Lefebvrists are wrong. As the text of *Dignitatis Humanae* explains, "the council intends to develop the doctrine of recent popes on the inviolable rights of the human person and the constitutional order of society." A "development of doctrine" is a concept proposed by the 19th-century English churchman John Henry Cardinal Newman to explain that a new, authoritative teaching could emerge that was not previously clear and consensual but that nevertheless embodies universal truth about God's revelation. The declaration holds that the human dignity that undergirds religious freedom is "known through the revealed word of God and by reason itself"—and therefore enduringly valid. Yet this has only become clear over time. "A sense of the dignity of the human person," the declaration reads, "has been impressing itself more and more deeply on the consciousness of contemporary man" and "has come to be fully known to human reason through centuries of experience."

These "new things" are "in harmony with the old," the declaration claims. The "old" to which it refers are the "principles of Catholic doctrine . . . that man, in the act of believing, must respond to God of his own accord." The declaration states that this doctrine is "contained in the word of God, and constantly preached by the Fathers" and refers to Lactantius and other leading theologians of the Church's first few centuries. The teaching of *Dignitatis Humanae*, however, could emerge only if another doctrine was abandoned, namely that a Christian society required the enforcement of religious uniformity to maintain unity and ensure the salvation of its members. This doctrine was a political one and, although it persisted for centuries, had never been proclaimed as a dogmatic teaching. Thus, it could be left behind. And was left behind.[46]

What, then, of Gregory XVI, Pius IX, and Leo XIII and their condemnations of religious liberty? Does not *Dignitatis Humanae* contradict them? We must look carefully at what these popes were condemning. To be sure, they were rejecting the right of religious liberty, but they rejected it because it was rooted in philosophical and theological skepticism—latitudinarianism and indifferentism, as they put it. That is, they were condemning a religious freedom that was tethered to relativism. Because they did not conceive of a religious freedom that was not thus tethered, they could only turn down the whole package. What they were not condemning was religious liberty as *Dignitatis Humanae* formulated it—a human right rooted in human dignity. Whereas *Dignitatis Humanae* drew upon the old truth that religion could not be coerced, it developed it, justified it, and applied it to society in a new manner, a manner that was still foreign to the 19th-century popes.[47]

Dignitatis Humanae and Islam

The factors that paved the way for the Catholic Church's historical pathway to *Dignitatis Humanae* contain important lessons for Muslims. Most important, the declaration put forth a basis for religious freedom that was rooted in the teachings and traditions of the Catholic faith rather than secularism. Muslims who look askance upon religious freedom as an import from the West packaged in secularist containers should find such a basis attractive.

Like Catholicism, Islam is a religion that long predates the Reformation and the Enlightenment and has a history of suppressing or curtailing religious freedom in the public realm. Historically as well as today, Muslims widely have considered the promotion of religious faith to be critical for public order and for the true good of Muslims. In this respect, Islam is similar not only to the Catholic Church, but also to many Protestant churches for several centuries, Hindu nationalist parties in contemporary India, Buddhist states in Sri Lanka and Burma, the Roman Empire, and, for that matter, the vast majority of countries prior to and outside of the (recent) modern West. If Muslims are to embrace religious freedom, then, they must be convinced that it is an authentically Islamic development.

Like the Catholic Church, Islam has been challenged by the Enlightenment, the French Revolution, and their historical legatees—Atatürk and the modernist dictatorships that came to power in the Arab world after World War II. These regimes have promoted secular public philosophies aggressively and marginalized traditional Muslims through force. If they are the carriers of religious freedom, then it is no surprise that Muslims, much like the popes of the 19th century, will want little to do with the principle.

Muslims are likely to find far more promise in a basis for religious freedom that is rooted in religion—the religious nature of the person, the nature of religious faith, and the communal dimensions of religious faith. They will accept religious freedom if it can be shown to develop seeds of the principle that have been present in the tradition for centuries and that were identified in the last chapter.

Muslims will also find religious freedom to be appealing insofar as actual liberal democracies incorporate it into their laws, uphold it robustly, and safeguard the conditions for Muslim communities to flourish. Actual experience with liberal democracies where devout Muslims prosper in their religious life will go a long way toward making the case for religious freedom, as the American experience did for the Catholic Church. Liberal democracies in which the government broadly supports religious communities and in which public policy is informed and shaped by religion will likewise serve to convince. The form and extent of the mutual influence of government and religion within a context of religious freedom will continue to be debated. Ought states to construct bureaucracies for managing religion? Or ought they to pass laws that encourage and enable religion but keep a distance from its activities?

Religious freedom, of course, also requires something important of Muslims—that they allow members of other religions the same freedom to proclaim and to practice that they ask for themselves. The Catholic Church had to come to terms with this requirement as it came to espouse religious freedom over mere tolerance or hypothesis. Muslims will be far more likely to follow this path if they, paralleling Catholics, become convinced that it is a genuinely Islamic one.

8

Realizing Religious Freedom in Islam

LET US NOW reconsider the public debate over Islam that is ever roiling in the West. On the criterion of religious freedom, I have argued that both and neither side is right.

Complicating our categories and cooling tempers on cable news shows, though, is not my ultimate aim. Religious freedom is a call for action, not just a criterion. It demands that the dignity of all Muslims as people who submit to Allah, both in the vertical sense of worship and prayer and in the horizontal sense of their relationships and communities, be honored. It demands that the dignity of non-Muslims surrounded by Muslims be honored as well. It promises derivative benefits of peace, democracy, and economic development. It calls Western states to treat Muslim people and communities, both within and outside the West, more justly and promises that in doing so, these states, too, will reap stability and the reduction of violence and terrorism. Religious freedom is good for Islam, good for Muslims, good for non-Muslims living in Muslim societies, good for Muslims in non-Muslim societies, good for relationships between men and women in Muslim societies, and good for relations between the West and Islam.

The fog of cultural war occludes this potential. Islamoskeptic and Islamopluralist paradigms each obscure how religious freedom can animate change. Religious freedom places demands on secular repressive as well as on religiously repressive societies, as well as on the foreign policies of Western states. Religious freedom is not a lone pursuit, an isolated cause, or a single solution to violence, intolerance, and injustice, but a principle that both holds intrinsic value and promises attendant benefits.

How can religious freedom be realized? Six recommendations show the way. Derived from the analysis heretofore, they are addressed to Westerners but also invite a dialogue with Muslims outside the West. The first four call for changes in thought that break out of ruts in current debates. The last two call for action on the part of Western states and on the part of transnational constituencies for religious freedom.

Recommendation One: Affirm Religious Freedom as a Universal Human Right, Not a Western Value

One recommendation emerges especially insistently: a gestalt shift by which religious freedom comes to be regarded not as a Western value but rather as a human value. Religious freedom's enshrinement in international human rights conventions should be looked upon neither as a historical hiccup nor as a product of American hegemony but rather as a manifestation of "the conscience of mankind" that the Universal Declaration of Human Rights declares human rights to be in its preamble.

This gestalt shift would take place among all those who are fixed on perceiving religious freedom as bounded by Western history and sensibility. In the perception of the new critics of religious freedom engaged in the first part of the book, religious freedom is parochial and presumptuous. Religious freedom, they say, emerged from historical events in the West, reflects Western power, and should not be exported, as Western states have done. A milder version of the new critics' view, one that does not see the social world so thoroughly as a product of power, is nevertheless beset by guilt from Western colonialism and Cold War abuses and now recoils from anything smacking of moral export.

To Islamoskeptics, who can be found on both the right and the left, religious freedom is not so much a product as it is a unique achievement of the West and is unlikely to be adopted by a religion lacking in the West's values or history. The West, then, should forget about realizing religious freedom outside the West and steel up for a long twilight struggle of civilizations.

All of these parties perceive religious freedom as tightly tethered to the West. There is truth to the perception. New voices for religious freedom did emerge in the wake of the Reformation and the religious wars. By the end of World War II, religious freedom was ensconced in the constitutions, law, and practice of most constitutional liberal democracies—and was far less common outside this zone. The West played a major role in articulating religious freedom in the major human rights conventions. It is Western states who are promoting religious freedom today in their foreign policies.

If religious freedom is concentrated in the West, though, it does not follow that it is bound to the West. An expanded historical field of vision renders this view myopic. To summarize the arguments briefly, voices articulated religious freedom over a millennium prior to the Reformation and the Enlightenment, the events that allegedly brought the principle to the West. Voices in many traditions outside of Protestantism and of Christianity altogether have articulated religious freedom. The human right of religious freedom is not intelligible only in terms of a Protestant religion that centers upon inward individual belief while shedding external rituals. Even Protestantism—a term that includes diverse forms of Christianity—does not easily fit the description, whereas the human rights conventions accord religious freedom not just to belief but also to practices, not just to individuals but also to communities. The perception that the modern West is a realm of religious freedom must be radically revised, for it has seen the brutal, even eradicationist, denial of religious freedom as much as it has the protection of religious freedom. Contrary to religious freedom being a tool of the powerful, it has been advocated most consistently by and on behalf of the powerless. Finally, there is a case for religious freedom that is grounded in human reason and human experience, stressing the universality of religion and the central importance of inward commitment in religions of virtually all times and places.

It is not parochial to believe that religious freedom is universal; rather it is parochial to believe that it is modern and Western. It follows that it is parochial to think that Islam is inherently incapable of religious freedom.

Recommendation Two: Recognize Islam's Capacity for Religious Freedom

Not only is religious freedom Western, Islamoskeptics say, but Islam is hardwired against it. The problem lies in Islam's texts and its founding. Islamoskeptics tirelessly upbraid fellow citizens, and especially policymakers, for their naïveté toward Islam's violence and intolerance.

The new critics described in Chapter 1 decline to recognize and encourage Islam's capacity for religious freedom from their different standpoint of relativism. Islam is the way it is, and Westerners ought to leave it alone, they say.

Both are wrong. Islam is capable of religious freedom. Seeds of freedom can be found in verses in the Qur'an and their interpretation, the life of the Prophet Muhammad, the *dhimmi* tradition, historical instances of liberal Islam, contemporary Muslim advocates of religious freedom, and strands of freedom in law and institutions around the Muslim world. A string of West African countries show that religious freedom not only exists in Islam but can be rooted in Islam. Muslim parties and movements, also acting on the basis of Islamic beliefs, have acted as forces for freedom in many other countries, including Turkey, Tunisia, and Indonesia. The Catholic tradition provides testimony that a religious community that predates modernity and once was locked in conflict with modernity can embrace religious freedom and do so on the basis of its own religious commitments and not by contracting the issue out to secular thought.

We must beware certain fallacies. The fact that one religious tradition is less religiously free than the rest of the world at a given time does not mean that it is consigned to religious unfreedom. And that fact that a religious tradition has not taken the West's historical pathway to freedom does not mean that no other pathway is available.[1]

The form of Islam that is behind violence, terrorism, and religious repression today has historically contingent roots. Much can be attributed to the ideology of Islamism, or Radical Islamic Revivalism, which arose in the early and middle 20th century among intellectuals who were convinced that Islamic civilization had reached a nadir because of both internal corruption and external domination. Islamism became increasingly radicalized and violent, weaponized by transnational terrorist groups, and empowered by its marriage to the modern sovereign state, yielding the pattern of religious repression. Advocates of religious freedom in these settings remain silent, are muzzled, or are exiled. Islamism, though, is not permanent, baked into Islam's founding, or the natural upshot of Islam's texts and traditions. Absent the formidably coercive apparatus of repressive states, this would be far more apparent.

Recommendation Three: Recognize That Negative Secularism is Not the Answer

Secularism says that religion can become tolerant only when it ceases being religious. Repression and terrorism in Islam will cease only when Islam becomes secularized. What is meant here is the negative, or hostile, form of secularism, as opposed to positive, or healthy secularism. Negative secularism took shape in the European Enlightenment of the 17th and 18th centuries and gained a new spurt of momentum in the 2000s in the writings of the New Atheists.

Secularism holds that religion is irrational, claiming to know things that cannot be known reliably like the Trinity and Allah's revelation to the Prophet Muhammad. Because religious doctrines deal with matters of ultimate importance yet are prone to irresolvable disputes, they beget division and violence. Religion may contain some salvageable core virtues like love and courage, but these can be fully embraced by secular people and do not require religion's doctrinal baggage. Because religion is irrational, though, it cannot last. Eventually it will flame out, quenched by the forces of rationality, science, and open inquiry.

Much like religious predictions that the world will come to an end soon, secularism has not been borne out. As the renowned sociologist Peter Berger quipped in 1998 when he humbly retracted his prediction of religion's demise 30 years earlier, "[t]he world today . . . is as furiously religious as it ever was."[2] A Pew Research Center study showed that in 2010, 84% of the world's population was affiliated with a religion.[3] In the past half century, a resurgence in religion's influence on global politics has taken place in every religious tradition and every region of the world, as Monica Duffy Toft, Timothy Samuel Shah, and I argued in our 2011 book, God's Century. Religion sometimes manifests a violent face but has also motored a global wave of democratization, forged peace settlements, and promoted reconciliation, economic development, humanitarian aid, and the rights of women.

More troubling for the secularization thesis than religion's exaggerated death is secularism's own history of death and destruction. Secularization is not merely an impersonal historical force that intellectuals have hypothesized but also a program that powerful people have propelled. Secularism is an ideology—an ism—meaning a vision to be realized in politics. Much like Islamism, secularism contains parallels to Leninism, which called for a vanguard party to do what history was doing too slowly. Secularism seeks what I have called negative secular political orders in which religion is sidelined if not hastened along in its envisioned exit from history.

Unsurprisingly, when secularism gains power, the resulting regimes are repressive. Most of the purveyors of the past century's most colossal mass atrocities have been secular: Adolf Hitler, Joseph Stalin, Mao Zedong, Saddam Hussein, and Imperial Japan. Within Islam, we have seen the secular repressive pattern and its aggressive and intentional efforts to promote its program: Turkey's Atatürk, Egypt's Nasser, Iraq's Hussein, Indonesia's Suharto, Iran's Shah Pahlavi, and Syria's Assad. All of these regimes have been authoritarian and associated with severe repression. All of them have radicalized Islamists and elicited violent backlash. Some of them have committed mass atrocities or spurred civil war. All of them have been unstable and eventually overthrown or frontally challenged by their religious opponents. Secularism is not the answer to Islam's problems.[4]

Recommendation Four: Expand Religious Freedom in the Muslim World

If Islam is capable of religious freedom and if secular repression—and of course religious repression—are not the answers, it also remains the case that Islam contains a dearth of religious freedom. Here, Islamoskeptics are on their strongest ground. As pointed out in the introduction, on average, Muslim-majority states are considerably less religiously free than both Christian-majority states and the rest of the world. The Islamoskeptics' view is also confirmed by the fact that the largest category of unfree Muslim-majority states is religiously repressive, governed by a political theology of Islam.

Islam's simultaneous capacity for and dearth of religious freedom combine to elicit a call for an expansion of religious freedom in the Muslim world. Religious freedom is good for Muslims. It is not Western decadence. It does not require a mimicking of the relationship between religion and state in the United States or any other Western state in all of its particulars—only a floor of freedom from coercion and heavy discrimination. It embodies the positive secularism that enables religious faith, not the negative secularism that constrains it. In a religiously free state, Muslim clerics and their communities have wide latitude to preach, to educate their children, and to finance, organize, and govern their communities. Muslims may persuade non-Muslims to convert to Islam. Their religion is no bar from holding office. They may participate in politics and undertake great efforts to make their societies more faithful to the tenets of Islam.

Religiously free states do not allow Muslims—or anyone else—absolute freedom, and Muslims will have to accept certain restrictions and make certain allowances that they would not be faced with in religiously repressive states. Muslims would be allowed to convert away from Islam without sanction and non-Muslims permitted to persuade them to do so. Members of other religions and Muslims considered heterodox would have full rights of citizenship, including freedom to practice their faith. Women would be allowed to doff their headscarves in Iran and don theirs in Turkey. For many heads of state and religious leaders in contemporary Muslim-majority countries, these limitations will be liabilities and perhaps too high a price to pay for freedom. Hopefully, though, the benefits of freedom for Muslims will become apparent as well to more devout Muslims in positions of influence.

Religious freedom will beget further benefits for Muslim-majority societies as well as for Muslims where they are minorities. It will reduce terrorism and civil war, strengthen democracy, encourage economic development, and create the space for religious leaders to negotiate peace, promote reconciliation, provide aid during disasters and emergencies, and carry out social services of a wide variety. Obviously, these goods, like religious freedom itself, depend on many other factors: economic, political, cultural. But insofar as religious freedom makes a difference—and much evidence shows that it does make a difference—these benefits will be realized.[5]

Recommendation Five: Western States and the European Union Ought to Make Religious Freedom Far More Central and Integral to Their Foreign Policies Toward Muslim-Majority States

The first and historically the most enthusiastic country to promote religious freedom beyond its borders has been the United States. Although the American colonies were a mixture of religiously free and religiously repressive regimes, the First Amendment to the US Constitution prevented national law from impeding the free exercise of religion and became a landmark in global history. Although the United States has exported religious freedom steadily through its history—though not always unanimously or successfully—a moment of special intensity was World War II, when President Franklin Roosevelt appealed to religious freedom to justify the US participation in the war, and after which the United States pressed hard to include religious freedom in the Universal Declaration of Human Rights.[6]

The other major historical moment for the policy was the International Religious Freedom Act (IRFA), which the US Congress passed in 1998. More recently, the European Union, Canada, the United Kingdom, Austria, Germany, Italy, the Netherlands, and Norway have adopted religious freedom into their foreign policies in one way or another. Canada reversed course, though, closing its Office of Religious Freedom in March 2016.

In the United States, IRFA has institutionalized religious freedom into human rights policy. The ambassador-at-large roves the world meeting with repressive governments and seeking the release of political prisoners. The annual reports of the State Department's Office of International Religious Freedom (OIRF) provide information on and analyses of religious freedom in every country and among virtually every religion in a professional, measured, and thorough fashion. The independent US Commission on International Religious Freedom (USCIRF) also publishes high-quality annual reports on religious freedom in both the global landscape and in particular contexts. Every year, the secretary of state designates certain states "Countries of

Particular Concern," giving public attention to their severe violations of religious freedom.

The policy can count successes to its name. The annual reports ensure that religious freedom violations are widely known. This is critical, in turn, for the work of human rights activists, journalists, scholars, and other governments. The reports are drawn upon by the authors of the leading indices of religious freedom, including the Pew Research Center measures cited in this book as well as the Religion and State Dataset of political scientist Jonathan Fox. Exposure can also encourage the persecuted. After the fall of the Berlin Wall, human rights dissidents in Eastern Europe reported having been strengthened and heartened by Western human rights groups who would speak on their behalf, as political scientist Daniel Thomas has shown.[7] The same kind of encouragement could be realized by victims of religious freedom violations.

But is a human rights policy enough? The argument of this book is that religious freedom—in the Muslim world and everywhere—depends in good part on regimes and their political theologies. Violations of religious freedom are more than a collection of individual acts committed against individual victims. I have also shown ways in which the abridgement of religious freedom is connected to war, terrorism, violence, and instability, the reduction of which is a core interest of the United States. That religious freedom is a human right, but also much more than a human right, points to the need for new thinking in which religious freedom is integrated into the high politics of national security and alliances.

The need for such new thinking is the thesis of Thomas F. Farr in his book of 2008, *A World of Faith and Freedom: Why International Religious Liberty is Vital to American National Security.*[8] Farr had served as the first director of the Office of International Religious Freedom, established by IRFA, from 1999 to 2003, after which he retired from government service and devoted himself to advocating religious freedom in the private sector.[9] He had become convinced that religious freedom policy ought to be more than a "reaction to the outrages of persecuting governments," as he put it in an article of 2006, adding that "while [the State Department's] actions sometimes help move an individual or family out of harm's way, [it] does not attack the structures of persecution— let alone promote religious freedom as a centerpiece of democracy and human flourishing."[10] Religious freedom should not be "quarantined" to an obscure corner of the State Department at Foggy Bottom, Farr reasoned, but should be kneaded into thinking and strategy on the Seventh Floor, where the secretary of state and his or her closest advisers work, as well as in the Pentagon and the White House.[11]

Farr's call for new thinking has everything to do with the Muslim-majority world, where the United States and other Western states have encountered some of their most difficult foreign policy crises in the past generation.[12] Just as Chapter 5 showed for the Arab Uprisings, religious freedom (or, more precisely, its absence) is integral to both the causes of and the solutions to these crises.

Scholar of Iran James A. Bill tells a story of a CIA analyst named Earnest Oney who, before the Iranian Revolution of 1979, proposed to his superiors a study of Iranian religious leaders. Scholar of Iran James A. Bill describes the response:

> His bureaucratic superiors vetoed the idea, dismissing it as "sociology." The work climate was such that he was sometimes condescendingly referred to be others in the government as "Mullah Ernie." It was not until the revolution and after his retirement that he was able to do his study on the force of religion in Iran. He did it for the agency on con-tract – *after* the force of religion had been felt not only in Iran but by America as well.[13]

The Iranian Revolution created a crisis that brought down a US president, enduringly reconfigured Middle Eastern politics, and led directly to a war be-tween Iran and its neighbor, Iraq, that went on for eight years and took an estimated one million lives. Iran's revolutionary government is a Shia theoc-racy in which religious repression is endemic to the ruling ideology and that rose to power directly in reaction to the secular repression of the previous regime. A major source of enmity between Iraq and Iran was the secular re-pressive policies of Iraq President Saddam Hussein, who violently dominated the country's Shia majority and not unsurprisingly feared an alliance between this majority and Iran over and against his own rule.

The attacks of September 11, 2001, gave rise to dilemmas that have preoccupied US foreign policy ever since. Countering terrorism has stood at the center of the United States' global goals. The attacks led directly to a war in Afghanistan fought by the United States and its allies against Islamist militants that continues through this day. The attacks contributed to, or at least legitimated, the US war against Iraq in 2003, one that kept the United States in Iraq until 2011 and whose effects remain at the center of US problems in the Middle East.

The terrorists who carried out the attacks of September 11 as well as many other attacks against the United States, other Western states, and still other countries like Indonesia hold a political theology of Radical Islamic Revivalism, which repressive regimes helped to cultivate and radicalize. The willingness of a religiously repressive regime in Afghanistan to harbor such terrorists in the 1990s enabled the terrorists to organize against the United States. After the United States toppled Saddam Hussein in 2003, the United States faced a civil war in Iraq that U.S. officials had not anticipated, one that was caused in important part by the bottled-up hostilities of Shias under Saddam Hussein and by the rise of radical Sunni militants. When the United States exited from Iraq in 2011, it left in power a Shia majority government that failed substantially to include the Sunni minority, which in turn created fertile ground for the rise of the Islamic State, which drew upon the sympathy (or at least neutrality) of many Sunnis in its capture of wide territory in Iraq and Syria. The Islamic State, of course, installed a severely repressive Islamist regime that has committed atrocities against Christians, Yazidis, Mandaeans, and Muslims who did not conform to its rule. It and other Islamist militant forces came to dominate the opposition to President Bashar Assad in Syria's civil war. That war, as we have seen, was caused in important part by Assad's secular repressive rule.

To be clear, religious freedom is not a single cause of any of the diplomatic or security dilemmas that have faced the United States and other Western states. As these examples show, though—and there are many others—it makes good sense, both morally and strategically, to incorporate religious freedom into the analysis and formulation of high foreign policy. Nor is religious freedom the only relevant dimension of religion for foreign policy. Officials and analysts in many Western states and the European Union now speak also of "religious engagement," involving partnership and dialogue with religious leaders and communities in a wide variety of pursuits: building democracy and civil society, economic development, the delivery of humanitarian aid, promoting human rights, and others. Religious freedom is central to, but not exhaustive of, religious engagement.

What would a foreign policy consist of that incorporates religious freedom, embedded in religious engagement, into high diplomacy? At the time of this book's writing, the Iraqi army, supported militarily and diplomatically by the United States and its many allies, has achieved virtual success in defeating the Islamic State while war persists in Syria. Should the Islamic State be defeated, what will ensure the stability of the victory? Stability in Iraq will depend critically on a government that is both democratic and inclusive of minorities like Sunnis and Kurds. Although the granting of federal autonomy to Iraqi Kurdistan has helped to assuage the Kurd problem (though exacerbated tensions with Turkey), the dilemma of the Sunnis remains and can be resolved only if they are included in the sharing of power and are free from discrimination and persecution—that is, the letter and spirit of religious freedom. Progress toward such inclusion would profit greatly from reconciliation efforts among religious leaders who carry authority in their community. In 2007 and 2008, reconciliation among these leaders was a central theme in the "surge" operation led by US General David Petraeus, which succeeded in calming Iraq's civil war.[14] When the US government exited in 2011, so did its religious engagement. A few brave civil society leaders were left to continue these efforts.[15] If Iraq is to attain stability and future US military involvement to be avoided, such efforts ought to be resumed and religious freedom for all ought to be at their center. Peace in Syria will likewise require a frontal approach to the "religion problem," involving reconciliation, religious inclusion, and the end of religious discrimination.

This is only a brief sketch of one example of how religious freedom might be incorporated into foreign policy. Reforms in the structure and process of making foreign policy are needed. Some have already taken place. In 2013, the Obama Administration established an Office of Religion and Global Affairs in the State Department and charged it with pursuing religious engagement and coordinating numerous officials and initiatives in the government. One religious freedom expert, Judd Birdsall, noted in 2016 that the State Department had hired more than 50 employees to work on religion and foreign policy.[16] President Obama incorporated religious freedom into his public diplomacy, making it a prominent theme of his speech redefining the United States' relationship to the Muslim world in Cairo in June 2009, and exhorting India's Hindu nationalist government to address religious repression on a state trip in January 2015. The US State Department's designation of the Islamic State's atrocities against religious minorities in March 2016 as genocide— only the second time that the United States has made such a designation— was an important recognition of religious freedom's importance. The Obama Administration's last ambassador-at-large for religious freedom, Rabbi David Saperstein, brought dynamic leadership and a high profile to religious freedom policy, as has the current ambassador at this writing, Sam Brownback.

Much else can be done. Farr, along with religious freedom expert Dennis R. Hoover, outlined comprehensively how religious freedom can be elevated in US foreign policy in their recommendations for the incoming president in 2009 and 2017.[17] For instance, they call for placing the ambassador-at-large for religious freedom directly under the secretary of state rather than lodging him or her in the Bureau of Democracy, Human Rights, and Labor. They recommend requiring every US mission overseas and every regional bureau at the State Department to develop a religious freedom strategy. They advocate that such measures pervade counterterrorism policy, democratization policy, the promotion of civil society, engagement with multilateral organizations, and public diplomacy. I would add that with respect to the Muslim-majority world, the US government's religious freedom policy gains great credibility by giving special attention to the religious freedom of persecuted Muslims: Uighurs in China, Rohingyas in Burma, and Muslims in many parts of India. All of this is what is needed if religious freedom policy is to make its way from Foggy Bottom to the White House.

Recommendation Six: Religious Freedom Should Be Advocated as Universally as Possible, Including Through Transnational Networks of Religious Freedom Constituencies

This book began with a defense of the premise that religious freedom is a universal human right. The credibility and effectiveness of policies to realize religious freedom—in the Muslim world, everywhere—depend on these policies being shared in a way that reflects this universality. The best way to ensconce religious freedom in the common conscience of mankind rather than allow it to become one side of a clash of civilizations is to expand the network of people and organizations who share a stake in it.[18] Religious freedom cannot only be the cause of the US and other Western governments.

Consider the wide range of actors who promote religious freedom, at least in some way. Again, there are now numerous officials in the US government who promote religious freedom. At times, the president and top foreign policy officials promote it. US embassies around the world are charged with reporting on and encouraging religious freedom in the countries where they operate. A recent initiative has sought to build and network together religious freedom constituencies in Western parliaments.[19] A United Nations Special Rapporteur on Freedom of Religion or Belief advocates for religious freedom around the world. Human rights organizations as well as other nongovernmental organizations (NGOS) dedicated entirely to religious freedom take up the cause. Scholars, both inside and outside the West, advocate religious freedom. Within certain Muslim countries, political parties and movements support religious freedom. Muslim clerics and jurists from many countries advocate for it, although nobody knows how many they are in total. In certain Muslim countries, especially the democracies where open contestation coexists with societal and governmental repression (Pakistan, Malaysia, Indonesia, Bangladesh), a constituency for religious freedom is found among politicians and civil society leaders and activists. A strong, though often-ignored, global constituency for religious freedom is business leaders, who benefit from environments free from religious repression.[20]

The challenge is to link these constituencies together into a transnational network for religious freedom. Scholars of human rights Margaret E. Keck and Kathryn Sikkink have pioneered something very much along these lines through their concept of "transnational issue networks."[21] Political scientist Maryann Cusimano Love has shown how Christian transnational networks have worked to protect the religious freedom of Christians in countries like Iraq and Syria.[22] Similarly, scholar and peacebuilding activist John Paul Lederach has developed a paradigm of "conflict transformation," another version of which is "strategic peacebuilding," which calls for a holistic approach that builds relationships among all stakeholders in a conflict.[23] An example of success for such an approach that is well known among students and practitioners of peacebuilding is the role of the Community of Sant'Egidio, a Catholic lay community, in bringing peace to a 16-year-long civil war in Mozambique in 1992. By linking together the combatant parties, the Catholic bishop in Mozambique, the Vatican hierarchy, the United Nations, US diplomats, the Italian Communist Party, and a British businessman, the Community was able to conduct nine rounds of negotiations that brought a lasting settlement to a conflict that had taken over a million lives.[24]

Might such an approach be brought to bear on religious freedom? Coordinating a global network among so many parties would be a daunting task. Perhaps, though, efforts to knit together a wide network of constituencies, internal and external, could be brought to bear upon individual countries where religious repression is high. A government that practices repression would be surrounded by a large number of variously situated parties exerting pressure, public and private, as well as offering positive incentives and forms of empowerment to pursue religious freedom. Likewise, practitioners of religious repression would be blocked. Leadership in coordinating the network would be needed and is best provided by an international official—say the United Nations rapporteur—or by a respected Muslim leader, preferably from the country in question. Again, such a strategy would work best in the religiously repressive Muslim democracies.

The best way to realize religious freedom is to expand the sphere of people who are persuaded by the principle. The more people around the world who undergo the gestalt shift toward perceiving religious freedom as a universal human right, the stronger and wider the political demand for change will be. New possibilities for global cooperation will emerge as well. Religious freedom is a norm of peace. It is a principled commitment, not just a pragmatic accommodation, and is a commitment not simply to coexist but also to respect the full and equal citizenship rights of the people who hold and live out divergent answers to the most important questions about human existence. Religious freedom is a norm of reconciliation. With respect to the public debate that rages in the West, it is a criterion that reveals both Islamoskeptics and Islamopluralists to be both right and wrong and that, were both sides willing to acknowledge what is right in the other side's position, could do much to calm the dispute. With respect to the West and the Muslim world, religious freedom summons a new set of relationships that are different from those of many centuries past when both sides failed to treat the members of the other side as equals in their most ultimate commitments—and far worse. The ability to choose this new history and to prove false the inevitability prescribed by the past is another dimension of freedom, not to be overlooked.

Notes

INTRODUCTION

1. One of the recurrent issues pertaining to matters in this book is usage of the terms Islam, Muslim, and the Muslim world. Generally, I take Islam to mean an entire religious tradition—equivalent to Christianity, Buddhism, etc.—whereas Muslim serves to describe a person, a place, a country, or another noun. In using the term Islam in this opening chapter, I am adopting the terms of the contemporary public debate, in which the two sides argue about Islam as a religious tradition. The very argument of the book, though, which I soon introduce, is that we ought to adopt the specificity and nuance that arises from speaking about "Muslim-majority states" for instance. In Chapter 6 I return to the tradition of Islam but seek to deploy carefully the terms Islam and Muslim where appropriate. Generally, I use the term "Muslim world" to mean the collective set of the world's Muslims, wherever they live.

2. Victor Davis Hanson, "Same Old, Same Old Horror: The Orlando Massacre Brings Up Familiar Lessons That We Never Quite Learn," *City Journal*, June 13, 2016, accessed January 12, 2017; find at http://www.city-journal.org/html/same-old-same-old-horror-14574.html.

3. Alexis Simendinger, "Clinton: Trump's Anti-Muslim Talk Increases U.S. Risks," *RealClearPolitics*, June 13, 2016, accessed January 12, 2017; find at http://www.realclearpolitics.com/articles/2016/06/13/clinton_trumps_anti-muslim_talk_increases_us_risks.html.

4. Ian Schwartz, "Obama: What Exactly Would Using 'Radical Islam' Change? A Political Distraction," *RealClearPolitics*, June 14, 2016, accessed January 12, 2017; find at http://www.realclearpolitics.com/video/2016/06/14/obama_what_exactly_would_saying_radical_islam_change_a_political_distraction.html, quote edited slightly for clarity.

5. For a thoughtful exploration of the public debate over Islam in the West— referred to as "the Muslim Question," see Anne Norton, *On the Muslim Question* (Princeton, NJ: Princeton University Press, 2013).

6. For the hawkish position, I choose the term "Islamoskeptic" over "Islamophobe," which unfairly centers upon fear. Islamoskeptics may well fear Muslims, but my point is that they are pessimistic toward Islam's capacities for tolerance, democracy, human rights, peace, and religious freedom. The term "Islamopluralist," on the other hand, is also imperfect because it does not fully convey the optimism about Islam's capacity for religious freedom that I mean for this position to entail. Language is imperfect.

7. Peter Beinart, "Religious Experience," *New Republic*, February 20, 2006, 6.

8. Andrew McCarthy, "The Great War on Militant Islam," *American Spectator*, July/ August 2004, 32.

9. Reuel Marc Gerecht, "The Pope's Divisions," *Wall Street Journal*, sec. A, September 21, 2006, A16.

10. Ayaan Hirsi Ali, "Islam Is a Religion of Violence," *Foreign Policy*, accessed January 13, 2017; find at http://foreignpolicy.com/2015/11/09/islam-is-a-religion-of-violence-ayaan-hirsi-ali-debate-islamic-state/.

11. David Pryce-Jones, "Islamists and Men in Khaki," *National Review*, April 16, 2012, 20.

12. Martin Peretz, "Counting," *New Republic*, September 24, 2001, 18.

13. Ali, "Islam Is a Religion of Violence."

14. John L. Esposito, "Want to Understand Islam? Start Here." *Washington Post*, sec. B, July 22, 2007.

15. Karen Armstrong, "Think Again: God," *Foreign Policy* (November 2009), 175: 55–60.

16. Fareed Zakaria, "The Politics of Rage: Why Do They Hate Us?" *Newsweek*, October 14, 2001.

17. Armstrong, "God."

18. John L. Esposito and John O. Voll, *Islam and Democracy* (New York: Oxford University Press, 1996), 27.

19. Edward W. Said, *Orientalism* (New York: Random House, 1978).

20. For examples of Islamoskeptics on the left, see Ayaan Hirsi Ali's many writings, including *Heretic: Why Islam Needs a Reformation Now* (New York: HarperCollins, 2015); Paul Berman, *Terror and Liberalism* (New York: Norton, 2004); Bill Maher, the talk show host; and the "New Atheists," who are subsequently discussed. Whereas it may sound strange to say that there are Islamopluralists on the right, what I have in mind are conservatives who find in Islam a partner for common social causes like marriage and the family, thus believing that Islam both has a positive message on these issues and that it is capable of dialogue and partnership. See Peter Kreeft, *Ecumenical Jihad: Ecumenism and the Culture War*

(San Francisco, CA: Ignatius Press, 1996); and Dinesh D'Souza, *The Enemy at Home: The Cultural Left and Its Responsibility for 9/11* (New York: Broadway Books, 2007). For a criticism of Kreeft and D'Souza from a conservative Islamoskeptic, see Robert Spencer, *Not Peace But a Sword: The Great Chasm Between Christianity and Islam* (San Diego, CA: Catholic Answers, 2013). For an interest variant of a conservative Islamopluralist position, see Michael Novak, *Universal Hunger for Liberty: Why the Clash of Civilizations Is Not Inevitable* (New York, NY: Basic Books, 2004), an argument for the possibility of development of liberty in the Muslim world.

21. See, for instance, two very prominent books that are either on Islam or give prominence to Islam: Samuel P. Huntington, *The Clash of Civilizations and the Remaking of World Order* (New York: Simon & Schuster, 1996); and Bernard Lewis, *What Went Wrong: Western Impact and Middle Eastern Response* (Oxford: Oxford University Press, 2002). Both books were widely portrayed as ones of Islamoskepticism within the context of public debates. Both, however, are more nuanced. Neither Huntington nor Lewis holds an "essentialist" view that says that Islam is inherently violent on account of its doctrines, contrary to how their views were widely portrayed, especially in western universities. Each tells a story of historical stages, the most recent of which sees the rise of Islamism. As we will see in Chapter 6, Lewis has argued that Islam has been at least as tolerant as Christianity toward religious minorities over the course of history. Huntington counsels the West against fighting a struggle with Islam and calls for cultural accommodation and dialogue. For him, a clash of civilizations is descriptive, not prescriptive. These are not the typical arguments of Islamoskeptics.

22. Eric Lichtblau, "U.S. Hate Crimes Surged 6%, Fueled by Attacks on Muslims," *New York Times*, November 14, 2016; find at https://www.nytimes.com/2016/11/15/us/politics/fbi-hate-crimes-muslims.html, accessed December 21, 2017.

23. The term democracy is complex and contested both among scholars and in the larger public discourse. Although the origins of the word imply rule by the people, and thus mechanisms of election, representation, and participation, some would argue that today, democracy means not only this but also the entire set of features embodied in full-fledged constitutional liberal democracy, replete with the rule of law, separation of powers, and a wide portfolio of civil and political rights, including those that protect minorities. In my view, the usage of the term democracy should not be confined to this more ambitious view, although it certainly embodies a worthy moral aspiration. Many scholars, including myself and many mentioned in this book, wish to discuss an important combination of features that obtains in numerous Muslim-majority countries, namely the existence of the electoral mechanisms and popular rule that are characteristic of democracy side by side with the maltreatment of and denial of freedom

to religious minorities, religious dissenters, and even religious majorities. To make this point, they and I use the classic, more restricted notion of democracy as rule by the people. It is also important to be able to speak of "illiberal democracy," "unsecular democracy," and so on. Respecting the term democracy's multivocality, I seek to use it in this book in a way that makes clear its meaning in each instance. Where the context does not convey this clarity, I couple the word with an adjective, as in the term "electoral democracy."

24. Fareed Zakaria, *The Future of Freedom: Illiberal Democracy at Home and Abroad* (New York: Norton, 2004).

25. Daniel Philpott, "Explaining the Political Ambivalence of Religion," *American Political Science Review* 101, no. 3 (2007): 520. See also Assaf Moghadam, "Motives for Martyrdom: Al-Qaida, Salafi Jihad, and the Spread of Suicide Attacks," *International Security* 33, no. 3 (2008): 46–78.

26. Monica Duffy Toft, "Getting Religion Right Redux: Hypotheses on Religion and Civil War," unpublished ms., 11–12. In this piece, Toft updates the findings from her previous piece, "Getting Religion? The Puzzling Case of Islam and Civil War," *International Security* 31, no. 4 (2007): 97–131.

27. Ahmet T. Kuru, "Authoritarianism and Democracy in Muslim Countries: Rentier States and Regional Diffusion," *Political Science Quarterly* 129, no. 3 (2014): 399. Kuru adopts the figure of 49 Muslim-majority countries.

28. Political scientists dispute whether Islam is the cause of the dearth of democracy in the Muslim world. Alfred Stepan and Graeme Robertson, for instance, argue that once Arab geography and economic development are controlled for, the effect of a Muslim-majority population disappears in "Arab, Not Muslim Exceptionalism," *Journal of Democracy* 15, no. 4 (2004), 140–146.

29. My coauthors and I referred to religion as a "force multiplier" in Monica Duffy Toft, Daniel Philpott, and Timothy Samuel Shah, *God's Century: Resurgent Religion and Global Politics* (New York: Norton, 2011), 216.

30. Brian J. Grim and Roger Finke, *The Price of Freedom Denied: Religious Persecution and Conflict in the Twenty-First Century* (Cambridge: Cambridge University Press, 2011), 206.

31. Pope Benedict XVI, "Religious Freedom, the Path to Peace," January 1, 2011, accessed January 17, 2017; find at http://www. vatican.va/holy_father/benedict_xvi/messages/peace/documents/hf_ben-xvi_mes_20101208_xliv-world-day-peace_en.html.

32. Nilay Saiya, *Weapon of Peace: How Religious Liberty Combats Terrorism* (Cambridge: Cambridge University Press, 2018).

33. Nilay Saiya, "The Religious Freedom Peace," *International Journal of Human Rights* 19, no. 3 (2015): 369–382. Other work arguing that religious repression causes violence can be found in Matthias Basedau, Birte Pfeiffer, and Johannes Vüllers, "Bad Religion? Religion, Collective Action, and the Onset

of Armed Conflict in Developing Countries," *Journal of Conflict Resolution* 60, no. 2 (2016): 226–255; Matthias Basedau, George Strüver, Johannes Vüllers, and Tim Wegenast, "Do Religious Factors Impact Armed Conflict? Empirical Evidence From Sub-Saharan Africa," *Terrorism and Political Violence* 23, no. 5 (2011): 752–779; Yasemin Akbaba and Zeynep Taydas, "Does Religious Discrimination Promote Dissent? A Quantitative Analysis," *Ethnopolitics* 10, no. 304 (2011): 271–295; Jonathan Fox, Patrick James, and Yitan Li, "Religious Affinities and International Intervention in Ethnic Conflicts in the Middle East and Beyond," *Canadian Journal of Political Science* 42, no. 1 (2009): 161–186; Nilay Saiya and Anthony Scime, "Explaining Religious Terrorism: A Data-mined Analysis," *Conflict Management and Peace Science* 32, no. 5 (2015): 487–512.

34. Brian J. Grim, Greg Clark, and Robert Edward Snyder, "Is Religious Freedom Good for Business?: A Conceptual and Empirical Analysis," *Interdisciplinary Journal of Research on Religion* 10 (2014): 1–19; Ilan Alon and Gregory Chase, "Religious Freedom and Economic Prosperity," *Cato Journal* 25, no. 2 (2005): 399–406.

35. Christopher Hitchens, *God is Not Great: How Religion Poisons Everything* (New York: McClelland, 2007); Richard Dawkins, *The God Delusion* (New York: Houghton Mifflin, 2006); Daniel C. Dennett, *Breaking the Spell: Religion as a Natural Phenomenon* (New York: Penguin, 2006); and Sam Harris, *The End of Faith: Religion, Terror and the Future of Reason* (New York: Norton, 2004).

36. There are even scholars who argue that religion most flourishes when it exists in an environment of freedom. These are scholars who take a "rational choice" approach to religion and governance that draws on the tools of economics. In a "free market," they claim, religions will have to compete for followers and are thus incentivized to perform effectively. Although several scholars belong to this field, perhaps the best known is Rodney Stark. See, for instance, his book with Roger Finke, also a prominent scholar in this school, *The Churching of America, 1776–1990: Winners and Losers in Our Religious Economy* (New Brunswick, NJ: Rutgers University Press, 1992).

37. I will discuss Pew's rankings in chapters ahead. The numbers here are drawn from Pew Research Center, "Global Restrictions on Religion," December 2009.

38. Grim and Finke, *The Price of Freedom Denied*, 169–171.

39. The Religion and State Dataset can be found at http://www.thearda.com/ras/. The analysis here is my own, conducted on 47 Muslim-majority countries. The Dataset list differs slightly from the list that appears in this book. It includes Guinea-Bissau and omits Kazakhstan, whereas this book includes Kazakhstan, which is a Muslim-majority country and leaves out Guinea-Bissau, which is not.

40. Jonathan Fox, *The Unfree Exercise of Religion: A World Survey of Discrimination Against Religious Minorities* (Cambridge: Cambridge University Press, 2016), 122–124. Fox elaborates on his finding by pointing out the strong level of

regional diversity within the Muslim-majority world, noting sub-Saharan Africa as a region where discrimination is low and compares favorably with Christian majority states in some regions, including those in which the Orthodox Church predominates as well as the former Soviet bloc. Fox's broad finding about the Muslim-majority world—high in discrimination in the aggregate yet diverse in the particular—closely parallels the argument of this book.

CHAPTER 1

1. Robert J. Joustra writes, "Just when we thought we'd survived the Culture Wars, the front lines in the Religious Freedom Wars are forming up," in his book, *The Religious Problem with Religious Freedom: Why Foreign Policy Needs Political Theology* (Oxon, UK: Routledge, 2018), 1.

2. See, for instance, Brian Leiter, *Why Tolerate Religion?* (Princeton, NJ: Princeton University Press, 2012); and Winnifred Fallers Sullivan, *The Impossibility of Religious Freedom* (Princeton, NJ: Princeton University Press, 2005), 155–159. I discuss Sullivan at greater length in the subsequent text.

3. See the subsequent discussion of the "new critics of religious freedom."

4. Alastair Sharp and Mara Awad, "Liberal Koran Expert Dies in Egypt, After Exile," *Reuters*, July 5, 2010, accessed April 7, 2017; find at http://www.reuters.com/article/ozatp-jon-egypt-islam-expert-idAFJOE66401E20100705.

5. Eric Schelzig, "Tenn gov hopeful questions if Islam is a 'cult,'" *AP Online*, July 27, 2010, accessed April 7, 2017; find at https://www.highbeam.com/doc/1A1-D9H7L7H00.html.

6. Travis Loller, "Planned US Mosque Draws Opponents, Supporters," AP, accessed July 2, 2013; find at http://www.highbeam.com/doc/1A1-D9GV6I8G0.html.

7. Bob Smietana, "Religious Conflict Isn't New to Murfreesboro," *The Tennessean*, October 24, 2010.

8. Bob Smietana, "Murfreesboro Mosque Opens After Years of Controversy," *The Tennessean*, August 11, 2012.

9. Martin Riesebrodt, *The Promise of Salvation: A Theory of Religion* (Chicago: University of Chicago Press, 2010), xi.

10. Christopher Hitchens, *God Is Not Great: How Religion Poisons Everything* (New York: Twelve, 2007); Richard Dawkins, *The God Delusion* (New York: Houghton Mifflin, 2006);; Daniel C. Dennett, *Breaking the Spell: Religion as a Natural Phenomenon* (New York: Penguin, 2006); Sam Harris, *The End of Faith: Religion, Terror, and the Future of Reason* (New York: Norton, 2004).

11. For a small sampling of these scholars, see Jose Casanova, *Public Religions in the Modern World* (Chicago: University of Chicago Press, 1994); Rodney Stark, "Secularization, R.I.P.," *Sociology of Religion* 60, no. 3 (1999): 249–273; and

Jonathan Fox, *Political Secularism, Religion, and the State* (Cambridge: Cambridge University Press, 2015).

12. That people know the world and its features in this way was explained in ancient Greece by Aristotle, who thought that we attain knowledge first and foremost by observing the world around us. This does not mean that people are not sometimes mistaken about things, but rather that they can know reality reliably through their faculties. In the Western tradition of philosophy, a major departure from this view took place through the French philosopher, René Descartes (1596–1650), who held that we know anything only by first doubting all that we think we know, confronting a blank screen and then asking what cannot be denied. In the commonsense view, by contrast, it is through our ordinary experience with and participation in life that we apprehend basic phenomena—like religion.

   Broadly speaking, two scholars besides Riesebrodt whose views about the definability of religion I share include Kevin Schilbrack, who outlines his views on religion in an interview, "Realism and 'Religion': An interview with Kevin Schilbrack Pt. 1," January 16, 2013; and "Realism and 'Religion': An interview with Kevin Schilbrack Pt. 2," January 17, 2013, accessed June 6, 2017; find at http://bulletin.equinoxpub.com/2013/01/6253/; and Ivan Strenski, *Why Politics Can't Be Freed From Religion* (West Sussex, UK: Wiley-Blackwell, 2010).

13. These questions are similar to what Michael J. Perry has called "limit questions." See his *The Idea of Human Rights: Four Inquiries* (Oxford: Oxford University Press, 1998), 15.

14. Martin Riesebrodt, *The Promise of Salvation: A Theory of Religion*, trans. Steven Rendall (Chicago: University of Chicago Press, 2010), xii, 75, 84–89.

15. My view that religions share family resemblances around certain defined traits is influenced by the view of philosopher William P. Alston, articulated in "Religion," *Encyclopedia of Philosophy* (New York: Macmillan, 1972), vol. 7, 140–145. My coauthors and I make use of it in Toft, Philpott, and Shah, *God's Century*, 21.

16. See, for instance, David Miller, *On Nationality* (Oxford: Oxford University Press, 1997); and Anthony D. Smith, *Theories of Nationalism* (London: Duckworth, 1971), 171, 175.

17. Riesebrodt, *The Promise of Salvation*, xiiv.

18. Riesebrodt, *The Promise of Salvation*, 19.

19. I was alerted to this story by the Witherspoon Institute Task Force on International Religious Freedom, *Religious Freedom: Why Now? Defending an Embattled Human Right* (Princeton, NJ: Witherspoon Institute, 2012), 13. Timothy Samuel Shah is the report's principal author.

20. Tertullian and Lactantius frequently use the word religion as something that could denote several different religions. See Tertullian, *Apology and De*

Spectaculis. Minucius Felix: Octavius, trans. T. R. Glover and Gerald H. Rendall, Loeb Classical Library edition (Cambridge, MA: Harvard University Press, 1931); Lactantius, *Divine Institutes*, trans. Anthony Bowen and Peter Garnsey (Liverpool, UK: Liverpool University Press, 2004).

21. Thomas Aquinas, "Question 81: Of Religion," in *Summa Theologica*, vol. III, trans. Fathers of the English Dominican Province (Notre Dame, IN; Ave Maria Press), 1522–1528.

22. Riesebrodt, *The Promise of Salvation*, 26–27.

23. See, for instance, the world of anthropologist Talal Asad, which is subsequently explored.

24. Justin L. Barrett, "On the Naturalness of Religion and Religious Freedom," in *Homo Religiosus? Exploring the Roots of Religion and Religious Freedom in Human Experience*, ed. Timothy Samuel Shah and Jack Friedman (Cambridge: Cambridge University Press, 2018), 67.

25. See Justin L. Barrett, *Why Would Anyone Believe in God?* (Lanham, MD: AltaMira Press, 2004); Jesse Bering, *The Belief Instinct: The Psychology of Souls, Destiny, and the Meaning of Life* (New York: Norton, 2011).

26. Brian J. Grim and Roger Finke, *The Price of Freedom Denied: Religious Persecution and Conflict in the Twenty-First Century* (Cambridge; Cambridge University Press, 2011), 203–204.

27. "'Nones' On the Rise: One-In-Five Adults Have No Religious Affiliation," Pew Forum on Religion and Public Life, accessed June 20, 2013; find at http://www.pewforum.org/Unaffiliated/nones-on-the-rise.aspx.

28. See, for instance, Joseph Boyle, "The Place of Religion in the Practical Reasoning of Individuals and Groups," *American Journal of Jurisprudence* 43 (1998), 1–24; and Christopher Tollefsen, "Conscience, Religion and State," *American Journal of Jurisprudence* 54 (2009), 111–136. Their work builds on the work of Germain Grisez, *The Way of the Lord Jesus* (Chicago, IL: Franciscan Herald Press, 1983), vol. 1, 124; and John Finnis, *Natural Law and Natural Rights* (Oxford: Oxford University Press, 2011), 89.

29. Witherspoon Institute, *Religious Freedom: Why Now?*, 29.

30. My argument, then, is fully compatible with the central claim of Stephen Prothero in his book, *God Is Not One* (New York: HarperCollins, 2010). I make no claim that all religions are all essentially the same or different versions of the same path to salvation.

31. Indeed, I contend that my argument ought in principle to be convincing to an agnostic. Only one who categorically denies even the possibility of superhuman reality is compelled to hold that religion cannot be real and that therefore religious freedom cannot be justified. Such a skeptic is probably, though not necessarily, a materialist. For a refutation of materialism, see David Bentley Hart, *The Experience of God: Being, Consciousness, Bliss* (New Haven, CT: Yale University Press, 2015).

32. Lactantius, *Divine Institutes*, trans. and intro. by Anthony Bowen and Peter Garnsey (Liverpool, UK: Liverpool University Press, 2003), 321–322, quoted in Timothy Samuel Shah, "Introduction," in *Christianity and Freedom: Historical Perspectives,* ed. Timothy Samuel Shah and Allen D. Hertzke (Cambridge: Cambridge University Press, 2016), vol. 1, 9–10.

33. Kyai Haji Abdurrahman Wahid, "Foreword: God Needs No Defense," in *Silenced: How Apostasy and Blasphemy Codes Are Choking Freedom Worldwide,* ed. Paul Marshall and Nina Shea (Oxford: Oxford University Press, 2011), xx.

34. Note that the *Report of the Special Rapporteur on Freedom of Religion and Belief* of January 17, 2017, strongly stresses the right to change one's religion or belief. See para. 27. Accessed June 13, 2017; find at https://documents-dds-ny.un.org/doc/UNDOC/GEN/G17/008/79/PDF/G1700879.pdf?OpenElement.

35. A thorough discussion of the many "on the ground"—that is, legal, practical, and institutional—dimensions of religious freedom can be found in Fox, *The Unfree Exercise of Religion,* 11–32.

36. The symposium was later revised and republished as Winnifred Fallers Sullivan, Elizabeth Shakman Hurd, Saba Mahmood, and Peter G. Danchin, eds., *Politics of Religious Freedom* (Chicago: University of Chicago Press, 2015). Two of the main contributors to the symposium later published monographs elaborating on their critique of religious freedom. See Elizabeth Shakman Hurd, *Beyond Religious Freedom: The New Global Politics of Religion* (Princeton, NJ: Princeton University Press, 2015); and Saba Mahmood, *Religious Difference in a Secular Age: A Minority Report* (Princeton, NJ: Princeton University Press, 2015). For a critique of these works, see Daniel Philpott and Timothy Samuel Shah, "In Defense of Religious Freedom: New Critics of a Beleaguered Human Right," *Journal of Law and Religion* 31, no. 3 (2017): 380–395.

37. Winnifred Fallers Sullivan, *The Impossibility of Religious Freedom* (Princeton, NJ: Princeton Press, 2005).

38. Winnifred Fallers Sullivan, "The World That *Smith* Made," *Immanent Frame,* accessed February 19, 2013; find at http://blogs.ssrc.org/tif/2012/03/07/the-world-that-smith-made/.

39. Saba Mahmood, "Religious Freedom, Minority Rights, and Geopolitics," *Immanent Frame,* accessed February 26, 2013; find at http://blogs.ssrc.org/tif/2012/03/05/religious-freedom-minority-rights-and-geopolitics/.

40. Elizabeth Shakman Hurd, "The Global Securitization of Religion," *Immanent Frame,* accessed March 5, 2013; find at http://blogs.ssrc.org/tif/2010/03/23/global-securitization/; Elizabeth Shakman Hurd, "Believing in Religious Freedom," *Immanent Frame,* accessed February 10, 2017; find at http://blogs.ssrc.org/tif/2012/03/01/believing-in-religious-freedom/. In the same vein, Lori G. Beaman, a scholar of religion at the University of Ottawa, writes that "[r]eligious freedom and religious establishment have come to mean many

things to many people . . . . The shifting nature of these two concepts makes normative assessment—religious freedom is good, religious freedom is bad—extremely difficult to carry out in any meaningful way." See Lori Beaman, "Beyond Establishment," *Immanent Frame*, accessed March 4, 2013; find at http://blogs.ssrc.org/tif/2012/04/27/beyond-establishment/. Bolstering this view is Evan Haefeli, then a historian at Columbia University, who concludes from his historical investigation of religious tolerance that "toleration, however described, whether as an ideal state of being, or religious freedom, religious liberty, secularism, or pluralism, is not an objective status or transcendent condition." See Evan Haefili, "The Problem With the History of Toleration," *Immanent Frame*, accessed February 26, 2013; find at http://blogs.ssrc.org/tif/2012/04/09/the-problem-with-the-history-of-toleration/.

41. I am thankful to one of the two reviewers of this book for this example.

42. See Amy Zegart, "Controversy Dims as Public Opinion Shifts," *New York Times*, January 7, 2013, accessed June 28, 2013; find at http://www.nytimes.com/roomfordebate/2013/01/07/the-right-or-wrong-experience-for-the-job/controversy-dims-as-public-opinion-shifts-5.

43. Talal Asad, "Modern Power and the Reconfiguration of Religious Traditions: Interview With Saba Mahmood," *Stanford Electronic Humanities Review* 5, no. 1, February 27, 1996, accessed February 10, 2017; find at https://web.stanford.edu/group/SHR/5-1/text/asad.html.

44. Talal Asad, "Anthropological Conceptions of Religion: Reflections on Geertz," *Man* 18, no. 2 (1983): 251. Emphasis in original. In the words "products" and "disciplines," one can detect the imprint of French philosopher Michel Foucault, who influenced Asad and, in turn, several of the other new critics, including Saba Mahmood and Elizabeth Shakman Hurd.

45. Talal Asad, "Thinking about Religious Beliefs and Politics," in *The Cambridge Companion to Religious Studies*, ed. Robert Orsi (Cambridge: Cambridge University Press, 2012), 56.

46. Elizabeth Shakman Hurd, "Believing in Religious Freedom," *Immanent Frame*, accessed February 19, 2013; find at http://blogs.ssrc.org/tif/2012/03/01/believing-in-religious-freedom/.

47. Winnifred Fallers Sullivan, "The Extra-Territorial Establishment of Religion," *Immanent Frame*, accessed March 5, 2013; find at http://blogs.ssrc.org/tif/2010/03/22/extra-territorial/; Webb Keane, "What is Religious Freedom Supposed to Free?" *Immanent Frame*, accessed February 26, 2013; find at http://blogs.ssrc.org/tif/2012/04/03/what-is-religious-freedom-supposed-to-free/; Robert Yelle, "Christian Genealogies of Religious Freedom," *Immanent Frame*, accessed February 26, 2013; find at http://blogs.ssrc.org/tif/2012/04/06/christian-genealogies-of-religious-freedom/; Peter Danchin, "'Sorry Comforters' and the

New Natural Law," *Immanent Frame*, accessed March 5, 2013; find at http://blogs.ssrc.org/tif/2010/04/12/sorry-comforters/; Peter Danchin, "*Hosanna-Tabor* in the Religious Freedom Panopticon," *Immanent Frame*, accessed February 26, 2013; find at http://blogs.ssrc.org/tif/2012/03/06/hosanna-tabor-in-the-religious-freedom-panopticon/.

48. See Perez Zagorin, *How The Idea of Religious Toleration Came to the West* (Princeton, NJ: Princeton University Press, 2003).

49. Portions of this section, responding to the third claim of the new critics, are adapted from Daniel Philpott and Timothy Samuel Shah, "In Defense of Religious Freedom.".

50. The story of Protestantism's mixed and frequently negative record on religious freedom is well told in Joseph Lecler's magisterial two-volume study, *Toleration and the Reformation* (London: Longmans, 1960); see also Richard A. Helmstadter, ed., *Freedom and Religion in the Nineteenth Century* (Stanford, CA: Stanford University Press, 1997).

51. John Locke, *A Letter Concerning Toleration*, ed. James H. Tully (Indianapolis, IN: Hackett,1983), 50.

52. See Yvonne Sherwood, "On The Freedom of the Concepts of Religion and Belief," *Immanent Frame*, accessed April 12, 2017; find at http://blogs.ssrc.org/tif/2012/11/13/on-the-freedom-of-the-concepts-of-religion-and-belief/.

53. Jonathan Fox makes the case that even today, religious discrimination is common in Western democracies. See *The Unfree Exercise of Religion*, 65–75.

54. Elizabeth DePalma Digeser, *The Making of a Christian Empire: Lactantius & Rome* (Ithaca, NY: Cornell University Press, 2000); Robert Louis Wilken, "The Christian Roots of Religious Freedom," in *Christianity and Freedom: Volume 1, Historical Perspectives*, ed. Shah and Hertzke, 62–89; Timothy Samuel Shah, "The Roots of Religious Freedom in Early Christian Thought," in *Christianity and Freedom: Volume 1, Historical Perspectives*, ed. Shah and Hertzke, 33–61.

55. Elizabeth DePalma Digeser, "Lactantius on Religious Liberty and His Influence on Constantine," in *Christianity and Freedom: Volume 1, Historical Perspectives*, ed. Shah and Hertzke, 96–97.

56. Unless otherwise noted, all quotes from the Qur'an are taken from *The Qur'an*, trans. M. A. S. Abdel Haleem (Oxford: Oxford University Press, 2004). This quotation is from Surah 2:256 and is found on p. 29. For the examples in this paragraph, I am indebted to Timothy Samuel Shah, who brought them into the writing of our co-authored piece, Daniel Philpott and Timothy Samuel Shah, "In Defense of Religious Freedom.".

57. The phrase "stripping the altars" was adapted from Christian tradition by historian Eamon Duffy, who used it as the title for his book on the English

reformation. See Eamon Duffy, *The Stripping of the Altars: Traditional Religion in England, 1400–1580* (New Haven, CT; Yale University Press, 2005).

58. Of course, there may be ways in which these practices are carried out that can infringe upon religious freedom. If, for instance, the government funds religious education in a way that creates strong inequalities in education for members of one religion, then a kind of religious discrimination takes place that may amount to an interference with religious freedom. Unjust discrimination, though, is not inherent in the government funding of religious education.

59. Benjamin Schonthal, "Reading Religious Freedom in Sri Lanka," *Immanent Frame*, accessed March 4, 2013; find at http://blogs.ssrc.org/tif/2012/05/08/reading-religious-freedom-in-sri-lanka/.

60. Saba Mahmood, *Politics of Piety: The Islamic Revival and the Feminist Subject* (Princeton, NJ: Princeton University Press, 2005).

61. Saba Mahmood, "Religious Freedom, Minority Rights, and Geopolitics," *Immanent Frame*, accessed February 26, 2013; find at http://blogs.ssrc.org/tif/2012/03/05/religious-freedom-minority-rights-and-geopolitics/.

62. Greg Johnson, "Social Eugenics, Unintended Consequences, and Dropped Balls," *Immanent Frame*, accessed March 5, 2013; find at http://blogs.ssrc.org/tif/2012/06/21/social-eugenics-unintended-consequences-and-dropped-balls/.

63. Anna Su, *Exporting Liberty: Religious Liberty and American Power* (Cambridge, MA: Harvard University Press, 2016).

64. One of the leading new critics, Elizabeth Shakman Hurd, presented the US policy toward Iran during the Cold War as one that was blinded by secularism in her previous book, *The Politics of Secularism in International Relations*. I agree with her analysis by and large. But if the United States supports repressive secularism outside its borders, then how can it be a country that promotes religious freedom as a tool of its power at the very same time?

65. Su, *Exporting Freedom*, 148–158.

66. Su, *Exporting Freedom*, 145. See also the careful account of IRFA's passage in Allen D. Hertzke, *Freeing God's Children: The Unlikely Alliance for Global Human Rights* (Oxford: Rowman & Littlefield, 2004).

CHAPTER 2

1. "Latest Trends in Religious Restrictions and Hostilities," Pew Research Center. Last modified February 26, 2015. Find at http://www.pewforum.org/2015/02/26/religious-hostilities/. The researchers assessed these dimensions through 17 authoritative sources of information:
   1. Country constitutions
   2. US State Department annual reports on International Religious Freedom
   3. US Commission on International Religious Freedom annual reports

4. UN Special Rapporteur on Freedom of Religion or Belief reports
5. Human Rights First reports in first and second years of coding; Freedom House reports in subsequent years of coding
6. Human Rights Watch topical reports
7. International Crisis Group country reports
8. United Kingdom Foreign & Commonwealth Office annual report on human rights
9. Council of the European Union annual report on human rights
10. Global Terrorism Database
11. European Network Against Racism Shadow Reports
12. United Nations High Commissioner for Refugees reports
13. US State Department Annual Country Reports on Terrorism
14. Anti-Defamation League reports
15. US State Department Country Reports on Human Rights Practices
16. The Uppsala Conflict Data Program, Armed Conflict Database
17. Human Rights Without Frontiers "Freedom of Religion or Belief" newsletters

2. The six reports are Pew Research Center, "Global Restrictions on Religion," December 17, 2009, accessed February 6, 2017; find at http://www.pewforum.org/2009/12/17/global-restrictions-on-religion/ ; Pew Research Center, "Rising Tide of Restrictions on Religion," September 20, 2012, accessed February 6, 2017; find at http://www.pewforum.org/2012/09/20/rising-tide-of-restrictions-on-religion-findings/; Pew Research Center, "Arab Spring Adds to Global Restrictions on Religion," June 20, 2013; find at http://www.pewforum.org/2013/06/20/arab-spring-restrictions-on-religion-findings/; Pew Research Center, "Latest Trends in Religious Restrictions and Hostilities," February 26, 2015, accessed February 6, 2017; find at http://www.pewforum.org/2015/02/26/regions-and-countries/ ; Pew Research Center, "Trends in Global Restrictions on Religion," June 23, 2016, accessed February 6, 2017; find at http://www.pewforum.org/2016/06/23/trends-in-global-restrictions-on-religion/ ; and Pew Research Center, "Global Restrictions on Religion Rise Modestly in 2015, Reversing Downward Trend," April 11, 2017, accessed June 13, 2017; find at http://www.pewforum.org/2017/04/11/global-restrictions-on-religion-rise-modestly-in-2015-reversing-downward-trend/.

3. See "Global Restrictions on Religion," 53–63.

4. Pew Research Center, "Global Restrictions on Religion Rise Modestly in 2015, Reversing Downward Trend" April 11, 2017, p. 14.

5. For a more extensive discussion, see Toft, Philpott, and Shah, *God's Century*, 16–19.

6. John L. Allen, Jr., "Benedict Makes A Case For 'Healthy Secularism,'" *National Catholic Reporter*, accessed January 20, 2017; find at https://www.ncronline.org/

news/benedict-makes-case-healthy-secularism. The pope's distinction is similar to political scientist Ahmet Kuru's distinction between passive secularism and assertive secularism in Kuru, *Secularism and State Policies Toward Religion: The United States, France, and Turkey* (New York: Cambridge University Press, 2009), as well as Elizabeth Shakman Hurd's distinction between the laicist tradition of secularism and the Judeo-Christian tradition of secularism in *The Politics of Secularism in International Relations* (Princeton, NJ: Princeton University Press, 2008), 23.

7. Alfred Stepan, "The World's Religious Systems and Democracy: Crafting the Twin Tolerations," in Alfred Stepan, *Arguing Comparative Politics:* (Oxford: Oxford University Press, 2001), 213–253. For an argument for positive secularism that is rooted in Islamic thought and history and applied to the Muslim world, see Nader Hashemi, *Islam, Secularism, and Liberal Democracy* (Oxford: Oxford University Press, 2009).

8. Guinea-Bissau does not have a majority of Muslims according to US State Department estimates. Still, with a 40% Muslim population, close proximity to the Muslim-majority West African states, and a similar level and kind of religious freedom, Guinea-Bissau can broadly be included as evidence for religiously free Islam. To be clear, though, it is not included in the 47 Muslim-majority countries that are the primary source of data in this book.

9. The estimates are taken from each country's 2014 International Religious Freedom Report.

10. Quoted in Alfred Stepan, "Stateness, Democracy, and Respect: Senegal in Comparative Perspective," in *Tolerance, Democracy, and Sufis in Senegal*, ed. Mamadou Diouf (New York: Columbia University Press, 2013), 221.

11. Jonathan Fox documents the frequent disparity between constitutional provisions and the reality of religious freedom in *Political Secularism*, 201–230.

12. See Fox, *Political Secularism*, 169–179.

13. Report of the special rapporteur on freedom of religion or belief, Heiner Bielefeldt, Addendum: Mission to the Republic of Sierra Leone, UN Doc. A/HRC/25/58/Add. 1, accessed July 12, 2016; find at http://www.ohchr.org/Documents/Issues/Religion/A.HRC.25.58.Add1.pdf.

14. Fox, *The Unfree Exercise*, 153–157. To be sure, Fox identifies the region as sub-Saharan Africa rather than West Africa, and looks at 13 Muslim-majority states. He finds that 9 out of 13 fit the pattern of low discrimination. Eight of these nine are in West Africa, and the other is Djibouti. Three of the four that are higher are all outside of West Africa: Comoros, Mauritania, Somalia, and Nigeria, the latter of which is on the eastern edge of the region. His findings, then, corroborate my argument that West Africa is remarkably religiously free.

15. "Guinea 2014 International Religious Freedom Report," US Department of State, accessed May 30, 2016; find at http://www.state.gov/documents/organization/238434.pdf.

16. "Senegal 2014 International Religious Freedom Report," US Department of State, accessed May 30, 2015; find at http://www.state.gov/documents/organization/238466.pdf.

17. "Gambia—Researched and Compiled by the Refugee Documentation Centre of Ireland on 26 March 2009, How Enforceable/Prevalent is Sharia Law in Gambia?," Refugee Documentation Centre of Ireland, accessed May 30, 2016; find at http://www.justice.gov/sites/default/files/eoir/legacy/2013/06/11/sharia%20law_0.pdf.

18. "Guinea 2014 International Religious Freedom Report," US Department of State, accessed May 30, 2016; find at http://www.state.gov/documents/organization/238434.pdf; "Senegal 2014 International Religious Freedom Report," US Department of State, accessed July 11, 2016; find at http://www.state.gov/documents/organization/238466.pdf.

19. "Burkina Faso 2013 International Religious Freedom Report," US Department of State, accessed May 30, 2016; find at http://www.state.gov/documents/organization/222235.pdf.

20. Monica Cantilero, "Christians in Niger Struggle to Rebuild 70 Churches Destroyed by Islamic Militants," *Christianity Today*, last modified July 25, 2015, accessed February 12, 2016; find at http://www.christiantoday.com/article/christians.in.niger.struggle.to.rebuild.70.churches.destroyed.by.islamic.militants/60160.htm.

21. "Senegal 2014 International Religious Freedom Report," US Department of State, accessed July 11, 2016; find at http://www.state.gov/documents/organization/238466.pdf.

22. Sheldon Gellar, *Senegal: An African Nation Between Islam and the West*, 2nd ed. (Boulder, CO: Westview, 1995), 117–118.

23. Stepan, "Stateness, Democracy, and Respect," 217;

24. Donal Cruise O'Brien, *Symbolic Confrontations: Muslims Imagining the State in Africa* (New York: Palgrave Macmillan, 2003), 58–59; Paul Marshall, gen. ed., *Religious Freedom in the World* (Lanham, MD: Rowman & Littlefield, 2003), 352.

25. Marshall, *Religious Freedom in the World*, 282.

26. Thomas M. Turay, "Civil Society and Peacebuilding: The Role of the Inter-Religious Council of Sierra Leone," *Conciliation Resources Accord Series*, no. 9 (2000), accessed May 30, 2016; find at http://www.c-r.org/downloads/Accord%2009_10Civil%20society%20and%20peacebuilding_2000_ENG.pdf.

27. Sebastian Elischer, "Autocratic Legacies and State Management of Islamic Activism in Niger," *African Affairs* 114, no. 457 (2015): 577–597.

28. "Gambia 2014 International Religious Freedom Report," US Department of State, accessed May 30, 2016; find at http://www.state.gov/documents/organization/238430.pdf.

29. "Burkina Faso 2013 International Religious Freedom Report," US Department of State, accessed May 30, 2016 find at http://www.state.gov/documents/organization/222235.pdf.

30. Gellar, *Senegal*, 117–118.

31. Benjamin F. Soares, "The Attempt to Reform Family Law in Mali," *Die Welt des Islams*, 49, (2009): 427–428; and Carine Debrabandère, "Women's Rights Languish in Mali," *Deutsche Welle*, March 8, 2010, accessed May 30, 2016; find at http://www.dw-world.de/dw/article/0,,5323121,00.html.

32. Momodou Darboe, "ASR Focus: Islamism in West Africa: Gambia" *African Studies Review* 47, no. 2 (2004): 73–82; "Gambia 2013 International Religious Freedom Report," US Department of State, accessed May 30, 2016; find at http://www.state.gov/documents/organization/222265.pdf; "Gambia 2014 International Religious Freedom Report," US Department of State, accessed May 30, 2016; find at http://www.state.gov/documents/organization/238430.pdf.

33. "Guinea 2013 International Religious Freedom Report," US Department of State, accessed May 30, 2016; find at http://www.state.gov/documents/organization/222269.pdf.

34. Sebastian Elischer, "Autocratic Legacies and State Management of Islamic Activism in Niger," *African Affairs* 114, no. 457(2015):577–597.

35. "Gambia 2014 International Religious Freedom Report," US Department of State, accessed May 30, 2016; find at http://www.state.gov/documents/organization/238430.pdf.

36. See, for instance, Robert A. Dowd's explanation for religious freedom in Nigeria in *Christianity, Islam, and Liberal Democracy: Lessons from Sub-Saharan Africa* (Oxford: Oxford University Press, 2015).

37. For a good account of the view of religion promoted by Western secularism, see William T. Cavanaugh, *The Myth of Religious Violence: Secular Ideology and the Roots of Modern Conflict* (Oxford; Oxford University Press, 2009), 3–56.

38. Pew Research Center, *Tolerance and Tension: Islam and Christianity in Sub-Saharan Africa*, 2010, 25, 27; find at http://www.pewforum.org/files/2010/04/sub-saharan-africa-full-report.pdf.

39. Pew Research Center, *The World's Muslims: Unity and Diversity*, 2012, 40; find at http://www.pewforum.org/2012/08/09/the-worlds-muslims-unity-and-diversity-executive-summary/.

40. Stepan, "Stateness, Democracy, and Respect," 220. Stepan cites an article in a Dakar newspaper entitled, "Une famille, deux religions," *Le Soleil*, October 23, 2001.

41. Pew Research Center, *Tolerance and Tension*, 39. Pew does not report scores for the other Muslim-majority countries considered in this chapter.

42. Philip Jenkins, "Mystical Power," *Boston Globe*, January 25, 2009, accessed June 3, 2016; find at http://archive.boston.com/bostonglobe/ideas/articles/2009/01/25/mystical_power/.

43. Jenkins, "Mystical Power."

44. Stepan, "Stateness, Democracy, and Respect," 219.

45. Sheldon Gellar, *Democracy in Senegal: Tocquevillian Analytics in Africa* (New York: Palgrave Macmillan, 2005), 112.

46. For the civil society influence, see Leonardo A. Villalón, *Islamic Society and State Power in Senegal: Disciples and Citizens in Fatick* (New York: Cambridge University Press, 1995), 2.

47. Report of the special rapporteur on freedom of religion or belief, Heiner Bielefeldt, Addendum: Mission to the Republic of Sierra Leone, UN Doc. A/HRC/25/58/Add. 1, accessed July 12, 2016; find at http://www.ohchr.org/Documents/Issues/Religion/A.HRC.25.58.Add1.pdf.

48. Lamin Sanneh, *Beyond Jihad: The Pacifist Tradition in West African Islam* (Oxford: Oxford University Press, 2016), 13.

49. John Azumah, "Patterns of Christian-Muslim Encounters in Africa," in *The African Christian and Islam*, ed. John Azumah and Lamin Sanneh (Carlisle, UK: Langham Monographs, 2013), 44; Lamin Sanneh, *West African Christianity: The Religious Impact* (Maryknoll, NY: Orbis Books, 1983), 212–213; Victor T. LeVine, "Mali: Accommodation or Coexistence?" in *Political Islam in West Africa: State-Society Relations Transformed*, ed. William F. S. Miles (Boulder, CO: Lynne Rienner Publishers), 79.

50. John Hunwick, "Secular Power and Religious Authority in Muslim Society: The Case of Songhay," *Journal of African History* 37, no. 2 (1996): 175–194.

51. Azumah, "Patterns of Christian-Muslim Encounters," 44–45; Martha T. Frederiks, "Methodists and Muslims in the Gambia," *Islam and Christian–Muslim Relations* 20, no. 1 (2009): 61–72; Ousman Murzik Kobo, *Unveiling Modernity in 20th Century West African Islamic Reforms* (Leiden, Netherlands: Brill, 2012), 55.

52. See Sanneh, *Beyond Jihad*.

53. Azumah, "Patterns of Christian-Muslim Encounters," 45–48, quote on p. 47.

54. See Thomas Pakenham, *The Scramble for Africa: White Man's Conquest of the Dark Continent From 1876 to 1912* (New York: Avon Books, 1991).

55. I say virtually because Guinea-Bissau under Portugal was a partial exception. There, Portugal promoted Christian supremacy over Islam. For the support of Islam by colonial governments in the region, see Lamin Sanneh's chapter, "Christianity, Islam, and African Traditional Religions," in his *West African Christianity: The Religious Impact*, 210–241, especially 216; David E. Skinner, "Islam and Education in the Colony and Hinterland of Sierra Leone

(1750–1914)," *Canadian Journal of African Studies* 10, no. 3 (1976): 499–520; Andrew Francis Clark, "Imperialism, Independence, and Islam in Senegal and Mali," *Africa Today* 46, no. 3 (1999): 149–167; Kobo, *Islam in Africa*, 62; Benjamin Soares and Rüdiger Seesemann, "'Being as Good Muslims as Frenchmen': On Islam and Colonial Modernity in West Africa," *Journal of Religion in Africa* 39, no. 1 (2009): 91–120.

56. Stepan, "Stateness, Democracy, and Respect: Senegal in Comparative Perspective," 211.

57. Stepan, "Stateness, Democracy, and Respect: Senegal in Comparative Perspective," 227. Stepan cites David Robinson, *Paths of Accommodation Muslim Societies and French Colonial Authorities in Senegal and Mauritania, 1880–1920* (Athens: Ohio University Press, 2000), 75–96; and Donal Cruise O'Brien, "Toward an 'Islamic Policy' in French West Africa, 1854–1914," *Journal of African History* 8, no. 2 (1967): 303–316.

58. Stepan, "Stateness, Democracy, and Respect: Senegal in Comparative Perspective," 212; Stepan cites Robinson, *Paths of Accommodation*, 221–222.

59. Sanneh, *West African Christianity: The Religious Impact*, 216–222, 242–251; Azumah, "Patterns of Christian-Muslim Encounters"; Elom Dovlo, "The African Christian and Islam: Insights From the Colonial Period," in *The African Christian and Islam*, ed. John Azumah and Lamin Sanneh (Carlisle, UK: Langham Monographs, 2013), 85–102.

60. Report of the special rapporteur on freedom of religion or belief on his mission to Lebanon, para. 3 A/HRC/31/18/Add.1, accessed 13 July, 2016; find at http://www.ohchr.org/Documents/Issues/Religion/A.HRC.31.18.Add1.pdf.

61. The figures in this paragraph are from the "International Religious Freedom Report: Lebanon 2014," US Department of State, accessed June 7, 2016; find at http://www.state.gov/documents/organization/238678.pdf.

62. Habib Badr, "The Religious Landscape of Lebanon," *Near East School of Theology Theological Review* 35, no. 1/2, (2014): 7–12.

63. "Casualties of Middle East Wars," *Los Angeles Times*, March 8, 1991, accessed February 9, 2017; find at http://articles.latimes.com/1991-03-08/news/mn-2592_1_civil-war.

64. Report of the special rapporteur on his mission to Lebanon, paras. 56–58.

65. Report of the special rapporteur on his mission to Lebanon, paras. 42–44 and 65–66.

66. "International Religious Freedom Report 2014: Lebanon," US Department of State, accessed June 7, 2016; find at http://www.state.gov/documents/organiza-tion/238678.pdf.

67. Yvonne Yazbeck Haddad and Rahel Fischbach, "Interfaith Dialogue in Lebanon: Between a Power Balancing Act and Theological Encounters" *Islam and Christian-Muslim Relations* 26, no. 4 (2015): 423–442.

68. Quoted in International Religious Freedom Report: Lebanon, 2014.

69. "Muslims Defend Christians' Freedom in Beirut Declaration," *Asia News.it*. Last modified August 25, 2015, accessed June 7, 2016; find at http://www.asianews. it/news-en/Muslims-defend-Christians%E2%80%99-freedom-in-Beirut-Declaration-35135.html.

70. In the country's 2011 census, 20% of respondents declined to answer an optional question about religion. The US State Department cites that census as reporting that Muslims are about 59% of the population with Roman Catholics at 10% and Orthodox Christians at 7%. Tiny communities of Baha'is, Jehovah's Witnesses, and Mormons inhabit Albania, where there are also 230 religious organizations of various kinds. See "International Religious Freedom Report: Albania 2014," US Department of State, accessed June 6, 2016; find at http://www.state.gov/ documents/organization/238560.pdf.

71. Registration is not mandatory for all religious groups. The committee maintains records and statistics only on foreign religious groups that solicit its assistance. Otherwise, the government does not require registration or licensing for religious groups. See International Religious Freedom Report, Albania, 2014.

72. "Religion in Europe," *WOW*, accessed February 9, 2017; find at http://www. wow.com/wiki/Religion_in_Europe.

73. "The World's Muslims: Religion, Politics, and Society," Pew Research Center, last modified April 30, 2013, accessed June 6, 2016; find at http://www.pewforum. org/Muslim/the-worlds-muslims-religion-politics-society.aspx.

74. Marcus Tanner, "'A Hardliner's Nightmare': Religious Tolerance in Europe's Only Majority-Muslim Country," *Newsweek*, March 31, 2015, accessed June 6, 2016; find at http://www.newsweek.com/2015/04/03/hardliners-nightmare-religious-tolerance-europes-only-majority-muslim-country-318212.html.

75. Tim Judah, *Kosovo: What Everyone Needs to Know* (Oxford: Oxford University Press, 2008), 9.

76. On this history, see Romeo Gurakuqi, "Pope Francis and Martyrs to Communism," *Wall Street Journal*, May 19, 2016, accessed February 9, 2017; find at https:// www.wsj.com/articles/pope-francis-and-martyrs-to-communism-1463700394.

77. "Kosovo 2014 International Religious Freedom Report," US Department of State, accessed June 6, 2016; find at http://www.state.gov/documents/organiza-tion/238608.pdf.

78. See "Multiethnicity, Territory, and the Future of Kosovo's Serbs," *European Stability Initiative*, Berlin/Pristina, accessed June 7, 2004; find at http://www. esiweb.org/pdf/esi_document_id_53.pdf. The report favors the lower number of 65,000.

79. "Trends in Global Restrictions on Religion," 50. This is the 2016 report, and the figure 5.3 is for the year ending December 2013. It reports a figure of 5.1 for the year ending December 2014.

80. "Kosovo 2014 International Religious Freedom Report," US Department of State, accessed June 6, 2016; find at http://www.state.gov/documents/organization/238608.pdf.

81. "Djibouti 2008 International Religious Freedom Report," US Department of State, accessed July 14, 2016; find at http://www.state.gov/j/drl/rls/irf/2008/108365.htm.

82. "Djibouti 2014 International Religious Freedom Report," US Department of State, accessed June 7, 2016; find at http://www.state.gov/documents/organization/238420.pdf.

83. Sanneh, *Beyond Jihad*, 1–17.

CHAPTER 3

1. See Kuru, *Secularism*, 136–160; and Stathis N. Kalyvas, *The Rise of Christian Democracy in Europe* (Ithaca, NY: Cornell University Press, 1996).

2. Kuru, *Secularism and State Policies Toward Religion*, 145–149.

3. In The Pew Research Center's report, "Global Restrictions on Religion" of 2009, France scores a 3.4 on the Government Restrictions Index, placing it in the "moderate" bracket, which is higher than the "low" bracket, in which most democracies are located.

4. On the relationship between secularism and Islam in France and elsewhere, see Olivier Roy, *Secularism Confronts Islam*, trans. George Holoch (New York: Columbia University Press, 2005), 13–64.

5. On the ways in which states can control religion by supporting it, see Fox, *Political Secularism*, 64–104.

6. M. Şükrü Hanioğlu, "The Historical Roots of Kemalism," in *Democracy, Islam, and Secularism in Turkey*, ed. Ahmet T. Kuru and Alfred Stepan (New York: Columbia University Press, 2012), 42.

7. Akyol, *Islam Without Extremes*, 156.

8. Erik-Jan Zürcher, "Ottoman Sources of Kemalist Thought" in *Late Ottoman Society: The Intellectual Legacy*, ed. Elisabeth Özdalga (New York: Routledge Curzon, 2005), 26, quoted in Kuru, *Secularism*, 215.

9. The Turkish Parliament awarded him the honorific, or "Father of the Turks," in 1934. Herein, for simplicity's sake, I refer to him as Kemal Atatürk, the name by which he continues to be known, even when discussing his life prior to 1934.

10. On Atatürk's effort to remake society, see Hanioğlu, "The Historical Roots of Kemalism," 48.

11. Turkey's Constitution of 1982 With Amendments Through 2002; find at https://www.constituteproject.org/constitution/Turkey_2002.pdf.

12. Kuru, *Secularism and State Policies Towards Religion*, 219–221.

13. Kuru, *Secularism and State Policies Towards Religion*, 218.

14. At the time, the school was known as Darülfünun and was on its way to becoming the University of Istanbul. Akyol, *Islam Without Extremes*, 206; Kuru, *Secularism and State Policies Towards Religion*, 224.

15. Kuru, *Secularism and State Policies Towards Religion*, 234.

16. Kuru, *Secularism and State Policies Towards Religion*, 222.

17. Eric Lawlor, "His Name Meant 'Father Turk," and That He Was," *Smithsonian* 26, no. 12 (1996): 116–117.

18. The figures on the decline of the non-Muslim population in the Ottoman Empire and in the Republic of Turkey are cited in Ergun Özbudun, "Turkey-Plural Society and Monolithic State," in Kuru and Stepan, eds., *Democracy, Islam, and Secularism in Turkey*, 65–67. The figure of five million Muslims comes from Justin McCarthy, *Death and Exile: The Ethnic Cleansing of Ottoman Muslims, 1821–1922* (Princeton, NJ: Darwin Press, 1996), 1, quoted in Akyol, *Islam Without Extremes*, 167.

19. David Shankland, *The Alevis in Turkey: The Emergence of a Secular Islamic Tradition* (London: Routledge, 2003); Elisabeth Özdalga, "The Alevis—A New Religious Minority?," in Dietrich Jung and Catharina Raudvere (New York: Palgrave Macmillan, 2008), 189.

20. "Sufism in Turkey," Harvard Divinity School Religious Literacy Project, find at http://rlp.hds.harvard.edu/faq/sufism-turkey.

21. *In Response to Persecution: Findings of the* Under Caesar's Sword *Project on Global Christian Communities*, report published April 20, 2017, p. 21; see also the excellent analysis of Nukhet Sandal, "Public Theologies of Human Rights and Citizenship: The Case of Turkey's Christians," *Human Rights Quarterly* 35, no. 3 (2013): 631–650.

22. Jean-Philippe Plateau, *Islam Instrumentalized: Religion and Politics in Historical Perspective* (Cambridge: Cambridge University Press, 2017), 359. Plateau's interpretation of Turkey follows closely the analysis of Kuru and Zürcher (see subsequent discussion).

23. Kuru, *Secularism*, 173.

24. Erik Jan Zürcher, *Turkey: A Modern History* (New York: Tauris, 2004), 173; cited in Ahmet T. Kuru and Alfred Stepan, "*Laïcité* as an 'Ideal Type' and a Continuum: Comparing Turkey, France, and Senegal," in Kuru and Stepan, eds., *Democracy, Islam, and Secularism*, 108.

25. Kuru, *Secularism*, 182, 234.

26. Niyazi Berkes, *The Development of Secularism in Turkey* (New York: Routledge, 1998), 481, 482, 507. On the Constitutional Court's endorsement of his writing, see Kuru, *Secularism*, 174.

27. Timur Kuran, *The Long Divergence: How Islamic Law Held Back the Middle East* (Princeton, NJ: Princeton University Press, 2011), 298–301. For a book with a broadly similar argument, see Jared Rubin, *Rulers, Religion, & Riches: Why The*

West Got Rich and the Middle East Did Not (Cambridge: Cambridge University Press, 2017). Kuran and Rubin together made a fascinating argument that Muslims in 17th- and 18th-century Istanbul actually suffered economically from their privileged access to courts, which in turn led creditors to charge them higher rates on loans in Timur Kuran and Jared Rubin, "The Financial Power of the Powerless: Socio-Economic Status and Interest Rates Under Partial Rule of Law," *Economic Journal* 128, no. 609 (2018): 758–796.

28. Kuran, *The Long Divergence*, 253.
29. Zürcher, *Turkey: A Modern History*, 208–220.
30. M. Hakan Yavuz, *Islamic Political Identity in Turkey* (New York: Oxford University Press, 2003), 133–205.
31. M. Hakan Yavuz, *Secularism and Muslim Democracy in Turkey* (New York: Cambridge University Press, 2009), 4; Angel Rabasa and F. Stephen Larabee, *The Rise of Political Islam in Turkey* (Arlington, VA: Rand Corporation, 2008), 54–55.
32. Hakan Yavuz, *Secularism and Muslim Democracy in Turkey*, 14–78; Vali Nasr, *Forces of Fortune: The Rise of the New Muslim Middle Class and What It Will Mean for Our World* (New York: Free Press, 2009).
33. Ali Çarkoğlu and Binnaz Toprak, *Türkiye'de Din, Toplum ve Siyaset* (Istanbul: TESEV, 2006), 75, quoted in Kuru, *Secularism*, 172.
34. Yavuz, *Secularism and Muslim Democracy in Turkey*, 3.
35. Quoted in Yavuz, *Secularism and Muslim Democracy in Turkey*, 159.
36. "The Survey of *Milliyet* and Konda," *Milliyet*, December 3–4, 2007, quoted in Kuru, *Secularism*, 191–192.
37. Akyol, *Islam Without Extremes*, 204.
38. The Turkish Constitutional Court, March 7, 1989, no 1989/12, quoted in Kuru, "Reinterpretation of Secularism in Turkey: The Case of the Justice and Development Party," in *The Emergence of a New Turkey: Democracy and the AK Party*, ed. M. Hakan Yavuz (Salt Lake City: University of Utah Press, 2006), 148.
39. In part, these figures are from Ahmet Kuru, "Islam and Democracy in Turkey: Analyzing the Failure," *Montréal Review*, accessed February 14, 2018; find at http://www.themontrealreview.com/2009/Islam-And-Democracy-In-Turkey.php.
40. "Al-Malarkey," *The Economist*, August 27, 2016, 17, find at https://www.economist.com/news/europe/21705842-president-erdogans-threat-realign-towards-russia-more-bark-bite-al-malarkey.
41. "The Decline of Turkish Schools," *The Economist*, September 30, 2017, accessed February 23, 2018; find at https://www.economist.com/news/europe/21729784-out-goes-evolution-comes-islamic-piety-and-loyalty-regime-decline-turkish.
42. Scott W. Hibbard, *Religious Politics and Secular States: Egypt, India, and the United States* (Baltimore: Johns Hopkins University Press, 2010), 63.

43. Richard P. Mitchell, *The Society of Muslim Brothers* (New York: Oxford University Press, 1993), 127; Hibbard, *Religious Politics and Secular States*, 56–66.

44. Hazem Fahmy, "The Root Causes of the Egyptian Revolution," 367.

45. "Egypt: Systematic Abuses in the Name of Security," Amnesty International, accessed February 1, 2016; find at https://www.amnesty.org/en/documents/mde12/001/2007/en/.

46. Pew Research Center, "Global Restrictions on Religion."

47. On the persistence of presidential power over religion, see Nathan J. Brown, "Contention in Religion and State in Postrevolutionary Egypt," *Social Research*, 79, no. 2 (2012): 534.

48. Carrie Rosefsky Wickham, *Mobilizing Islam; Religion, Activism, and Political Change in Egypt* (New York: Columbia University Press, 2002). See entire book, but especially pp. 1–20, 119–175.

49. Barbara H. E. Zollner, *Muslim Brotherhood: Hasan al-Hudaybi and Ideology* (Abingdon, UK: Routledge, 2009), 23; Mitchell, *The Society of Muslim Brothers*, 64–71.

50. Scott Atran, "Egypt's Bumbling Brotherhood," *New York Times*, February 2, 2011, accessed January 23, 2017; find at http://www.nytimes.com/2011/02/03/opinion/03atran.html?_r=0.

51. Italics added for emphasis.

52. Derek Hopwood, *Egypt: Politics and Society, 1945–1990* (New York: Routledge, 1991), 3rd edition, 117, quoted in Hibbard, *Religious Politics & Secular States*, 77; Hibbard, *Religious Politics & Secular States*, 66–78.

53. Sumita Pahwa, "Secularizing Islamism and Islamizing Democracy: The Political and Ideational Evolution of the Egyptian Muslim Brothers 1984–2012," *Mediterranean Politics*, 18, no. 2 (2013): 197–200.

54. Fahmy, "The Winter of Discontent," 370–371.

55. Mohammed H. Hafez, *Why Muslims Rebel: Repression and Resistance in the Islamic World* (Boulder, CO: Lynne Rienner Publishers), 82–90.

56. Bruce K. Rutherford, *Egypt After Mubarak: Liberalism, Islam and Democracy in the Muslim World* (Princeton, NJ: Princeton University Press, 2008), 70.

57. Samuel Tadros, *Motherland Lost: The Egyptian and Coptic Quest for Modernity* (Stanford, CA: Hoover Institute Press, 2013), 185.

58. Samuel Tadros, *Religious Freedom in Egypt*, No. 2487 (Washington, DC: Heritage Foundation, 2010).

59. Samuel Tadros, *Motherland Lost*, 188–189; Magdi Guirguis, "The Copts and the Egyptian Revolution: Various Attitudes and Dreams," *Social Research*, 79, no. 2 (2012): 515–522.

60. Salli Nabil, "Egypt's Jewish Community's Lost Future," *BBC News*, September 18, 2014, accessed February 2, 2016; find at http://www.bbc.com/news/world-asia-29249033.

61. Sandra Mackey, *The Reckoning: Iraq and the Legacy of Saddam Hussein* (New York: Norton, 2003), 187.

62. P.J. Tobia, "Why Did Assad, Saddam, and Mubarak Protect Christians?," *PBS Newshour*, October 14, 2011, accessed February 3, 2016; find at http://www.pbs.org/newshour/rundown/mid-easts-christians-intro/. On the sharp decline of Iraq's Christian population after 2003, see the previous chapter.

63. "Annual Report on International Religious Freedom 2001," US Department of State, December 2001, 438–440.

64. Khalil F. Osman, *Sectarianism in Iraq: The Making of State and Nation Since 1920* (Oxon, UK: Routledge, 2014), 85.

65. Michael Driessen, *Religion and Democratization: Framing Religious and Political Identities in Muslim and Catholic Societies* (Oxford: Oxford University Press, 2014), 135–144.

66. Hafez, *Why Muslims Rebel*, 36–48.

67. Jennifer Noyon, *Islam, Politics, and Pluralism: Theory and Practice in Turkey, Jordan, Tunisia, and Algeria* (London: Royal Institute of International Affairs, 2003), 96.

68. Alfred Stepan, "Tunisia's Transition and the Twin Tolerations," *Journal of Democracy*, 23, no. 2 (2012): 99–100; and Hamadi Redissi, "The Decline of Political Islam's Legitimacy: The Tunisian Case," *Philosophy and Social Criticism*, 40, no. 4-5 (2014):383.

69. Pew Research Center, *Global Restrictions on Religion*, 2009.

70. US Department of State, *International Religious Freedom Report 2012*; Emanuela Dalmasso and Francesco Cavatorta, "Political Islam in Morocco: Negotiating the Kingdom's Liberal Space," *Contemporary Arab Affairs* 4, no. 4 (2011): 484–500; Ezzoubeir Jabrane, "Morocco's High Religious Committee Says Apostates Should Not Be Killed," *Morocco World News*, accessed June 8, 2017; find at https://www.moroccoworldnews.com/2017/02/207505/moroccos-high-religious-committee-says-apostates-should-not-be-killed/.

71. See Jason Brownlee, Tarek Masoud, and Andrew Reynolds, *The Arab Spring: Pathways of Repression and Reform* (Oxford: Oxford University Press, 2015), 158.

72. US Department of State, *Report on International Religious Freedom*, 2010, accessed February 6, 2017; find at https://www.state.gov/j/drl/rls/irf/2010/148832.htm.

73. Michael Robbins and Lawrence Rubin, "The Rise of Official Islam in Jordan," *Politics, Religion, and Ideology* 14, no. 1 (2013): 59–74.

74. Glenn E. Robinson, "Can Islamists Be Democrats? The Case of Jordan," *Middle East Journal* 51, no. 3 (Summer 1997): 373–388; Nathan J. Brown, "Jordan and Its Islamic Movement: The Limits of Inclusion?," *Carnegie Papers Middle East Series* 74 (2006); and Michael Robbins and Lawrence Rubin, "The Rise of

Official Islam in Jordan," *Politics, Religion, and Ideology* 14, no. 1 (2013): 59–74; Jillian Schwedler, *Faith in Moderation: Islamist Parties in Jordan and Yemen* (Cambridge: Cambridge University Press, 2006), 65–69, 86–96, 130–134, 155–169.

75. John Anderson, *Religion, State and Politics in the Soviet Union and Successor States* (Cambridge: Cambridge University Press, 1994), 183; Shireen T. Hunter, "Religion, Politics, and Security in Central Asia," *SAIS Review* 21, no. 2, (Summer-Fall 2001): 73.

76. An exception is Azerbaijan, which is predominantly Shia.

77. Edward W. Walker, "Islam, Islamism, and Political Order in Central Asia," *Journal of International Affairs* 56, no. 2 (2003): 24; see also Tadeusz Swietochowski, "Azerbaijan: The Hidden Faces of Islam," *World Policy Journal* 19, no. 3 (Fall 2002): 69–76.

78. Hunter, "Religion, Politics and Security in Central Asia," 68.

79. Hunter, "Religion, Politics and Security in Central Asia," 70, 71.

80. Sarah Wilson, "The Rise of Islamic Militancy in Central Asia: Causes and Consequences," *Briefing Notes on Islam, Society and Politics* 4, no. 1 (September 2001): 13.

81. US State Department, *International Religious Freedom Report for 2011*, accessed January 30, 2017; find at https://www.state.gov/j/drl/rls/irf/2011religiousfreedom/#wrapper; US State Department, *International Religious Freedom Report for 2012*, accessed January 30, 2017; find at https://www.state.gov/j/drl/rls/irf/2011religiousfreedom/#wrapper.

82. Ahmed Rashid, *The Resurgence of Central Asia* (Karachi, Pakistan: Oxford University Press, 1994), 132–133.

83. Ahmed Rashid, *Jihad: The Rise of Militant Islam in Central Asia* (New Haven, CT: Yale University Press, 2002), 42.

84. Hunter, "Religion, Politics and Security in Central Asia," 74.

85. Kathleen Collins, "Ideas, Networks, and Islamist Movements: Evidence from Central Asia and the Caucuses," *World Politics* 60, no. 1 (2007): 84–85.

86. Collins, "Ideas, Networks, and Islamist Movements," 89–92.

87. Collins, "Ideas, Networks, and Islamist Movements," 76.

88. Hunter, "Religion, Politics and Security in Central Asia," 77.

89. Hafez, *Why Muslims Rebel*, 202.

90. Collins, "Ideas, Networks, and Islamist Movements," 87–88.

91. On the tension between Enlightenment-based regimes and Islam, see John M. Owen IV and J. Judd Owen, "Enlightened Despots, Then and Now," *Foreign Affairs*, August 10, 2015, accessed March 5, 2018; find at https://www.foreignaffairs.com/articles/2015-08-10/enlightened-despots-then-and-now.

92. On different versions of rationality, see Alasdair MacIntyre, *Whose Justice? Which Rationality?* (Notre Dame, IN: University of Notre Dame Press, 1999).

CHAPTER 4

1. "Asia Bibi Faces another lonely Christmas in her 'Death Row' Cell in Pakistan," *Crossmap*, December 20, 2016, accessed September 17, 2018; find at https://www.crossmap.com/news/asia-bibi-faces-another-lonely-christmas-in-her-death-row-cell-in-pakistan.html.

2. Seyyid Qutb, *Milestones* (Damascus, Syria: Dar Al-Ilm, n.d), 8. This edition spells Qutb's forename as Seyyid, whereas I use the more common Sayyid.

3. Qutb, *Milestones*, 12.

4. Qutb, *Milestones*, 50, 81–82.

5. Qutb, *Milestones*, 11.

6. Qutb, *Milestones*, 35.

7. Qutb, *Milestones*, 27.

8. Qutb, *Milestones*, 56, 57, 70.

9. Sayyid Qutb, *Fe Zilal al-Qur'an* [*In the Shade of the Qur'an*] (Cairo, Egypt: Dar al-Shuruq, 1996), vol. 1, 291–292, quoted in Abdullah Saeed and Hassan Saeed, *Freedom of Religion, Apostasy and Islam* (Aldershot, UK: Ashgate, 2004), 75.

10. Qutb, *Milestones*, 58, 59.

11. Olivier Roy, *The Failure of Political Islam*, trans. Carol Volk (Cambridge, MA: Harvard University Press, 1994), 40, 41.

12. Sohail Hashmi, "Islamic Ethics in International Society," in *International Society: Diverse Ethical Perspectives*, ed. David R. Mapel and Terry Nardin (Princeton, NJ: Princeton University Press, 1998), 223–224.

13. Bassam Tibi, *The Challenge of Fundamentalism: Political Islam and the New World Order* (Berkeley: University of California Press, 1998), 144–146.

14. On the comparison with Marx, see Roy, *The Failure of Political Islam*, 4. On Islamism, see also Bassam Tibi, *Islamism and Islam* (New Haven, CT: Yale University Press, 2012).

15. Roy, *The Failure of Political Islam*, 3, 37.

16. Quoted in Kyai Haji Abdurrahman Wahid, "God Needs No Defense," foreword to Paul Marshall and Nina Shea, *Silenced: How Apostasy and Blasphemy Codes Are Choking Freedom Worldwide* (Oxford: Oxford University Press, 2011), xvii.

17. Seyyed Vali Reza Nasr, *Islamic Leviathan: Islam and the Making of State Power* (Oxford: Oxford University Press, 2001), 82–101.

18. Paul Marshall and Nina Shea, *Silenced: How Apostasy and Blasphemy Codes Are Choking Freedom Worldwide* (Oxford: Oxford University Press, 2011), 38, 39, 59.

19. "International Religious Freedom Report for 2012," US Department of State, accessed March 23, 2017; find at https://www.state.gov/j/drl/rls/irf/2012religiousfreedom/index.htm?year=2012&dlid=208388; Marshall and Shea, *Silenced*, 41.

20. Vali Nasr, *The Shia Revival: How Conflicts Within Islam Will Shape the Future* (New York: Norton, 2007), 75, 121–125.

21. *In Response to Persecution*, 23; "Annual Report of the U.S. Commission on International Religious Freedom," US Commission on International Religious Freedom, accessed June 26, 2016; find at http://www.uscirf.gov/sites/default/files/USCIRF%202014%20Annual%20Report%20PDF.pdf.

22. Thomas Hegghammer, *Jihad in Saudi Arabia: Violence and Pan-Islamism Since 1979* (Cambridge: Cambridge University Press, 2010), 3.

23. *Kingdom of Saudi Arabia: Criminal Laws, Regulations, and Procedures Handbook* (Washington, DC: International Business Publications, 2016), 108.

24. "International Religious Freedom Report for 2012," US Department of State, accessed March 23, 2017; find at https://www.state.gov/j/drl/rls/irf/2012religiousfreedom/index.htm?year=2012&dlid=208388, Marshall and Shea, *Silenced*, 22–23.

25. Gilles Kepel, *Jihad; The Trail of Political Islam* (Harvard, MA: Harvard University Press, 2002), 176–184.

26. "Policy Focus: Nigeria," US Commission on International Religious Freedom, August 2004, 2–3, accessed July 26, 2016; find at http://www.uscirf.gov/sites/default/files/resources/stories/PDFs/PolicyFocus_Nigeria_Summer2004.pdf, "International Religious Freedom Report for 2012," US Department of State, accessed July 26, 2016; find at http://www.state.gov/documents/organization/208394.pdf.

27. "Tolerance and Tension: Islam and Christianity in Sub-Saharan Africa," Pew Research Center on Religion and Public Life, April 15, 2010, 11, 64, accessed July 26, 2016; find at http://www.pewforum.org/2010/04/15/executive-summary-islam-and-christianity-in-sub-saharan-africa/.

28. Toyin Falola, *Violence in Nigeria: The Crisis of Religious Politics and Secular Ideologies* (Rochester, NY: University of Rochester Press, 1998), 24–78; Toyin Falola, *The History of Nigeria* (Westport, CT: Greenwood Press, 1999), 37–120; Jonathan Reynolds, "Good and Bad Muslims: Islam and Indirect Rule in Northern Nigeria," *International Journal of African Historical Studies* 34, no. 3 (2001): 601–618; and Chima J. Korieh, "Islam and Politics in Nigeria: Historical Perspectives," in *Religion, History, and Politics in Nigeria: Essays in Honor of Ogbu U. Kalu*, ed. Chima J. Korieh and Ugo G. Nwokeji (Lanham, MD: University Press of America, 2005), 114–120.

29. "Policy Focus: Nigeria," US Commission on International Religious Freedom, August 2004, 1, accessed July 26, 2016; find at http://www.uscirf.gov/sites/default/files/resources/stories/PDFs/PolicyFocus_Nigeria_Summer2004.pdf.

30. "'I Lit the Match,'" *The Guardian*, February 17, 2003, accessed March 23, 2017; find at http://www.guardian.co.uk/world/2003/feb/17/gender.pressand publishing; "Nigerian Government Rejects 'Fatwa,'" *BBC*, November 26, 2002, accessed March 23, 2017; find at http://news.bbc.co.uk/2/hi/africa/2514821.stm.

31. Vali Nasr, "Rise of 'Muslim Democracy,'" *Journal of Democracy*, 16, no. 2 (2005). Open elections, Nasr reports, have taken place in Bangladesh in 1991, 1996, and 2001; in Indonesia in 1999 and 2004; in Malaysia in 1995, 1999, and 2004; in Pakistan in 1990, 1993, and 1997; and in Turkey in 1995, 1999, and 2002.

32. See Alfred Stepan and Graeme B. Robertson, "Arab, Not Muslim, Exceptionalism," *Journal of Democracy* 15, no. 4 (October 2004), 140–146..

33. Charles Kurzman and Ijlal Naqvi, "Islamic Political Parties and Parliamentary Elections," US Institute of Peace Working Paper (Grant SG-055-06S), January 15, 2009, revised March 17, 2009, accessed September 12, 2014; find at http://www.unc.edu/~kurzman/elections/Kurzman_Naqvi_USIP_Working_Paper.pdf.

34. On this possibility of a Muslim-majority country that has electoral democracy but a lack of certain individual freedoms, including religious freedom, see the work of Jocelyne Cesari, who calls these regimes "unsecular democracy," in Jocelyn Cesari, *The Awakening of Muslim Democracy: Religion, Modernity, and the State* (Cambridge: Cambridge University Press, 2014), 237–263. See also Shadi Hamid, *Temptations of Power: Islamists and Illiberal Democracy in a New Middle East* (Oxford: Oxford University Press, 2014), for an argument that democracy does not necessarily moderate Islam but often also empowers Islamists.

35. Ayesha Jalal, *The State of Martial Rule: The Origins of Pakistan's Political Economy of Defence* (Cambridge: Cambridge University Press, 2008), 17–22; Akbar Ahmed, *Jinnah, Pakistan and Islamic Identity: The Search for Saladin*, 1st ed. (London; Routledge, 1997), 10.

36. Mohammed Ali Jinnah, *Quaid-e-Azam Mohammed Ali Jinnah Speeches: As Governor-General of Pakistan, 1947–1948* (Lahore, Pakistan: Sang-e-Meel Publications, 2004), 3.

37. Shahid Javed Burki et al., *Pakistan Under the Military: Eleven Years of Zia ul-Haq* (Boulder, CO: Westview Press, 1991); Ian Talbot, *Pakistan: A Modern History* (New York: St. Martin's Press, 1998), 273–275.

38. Pew Research Center, "Arab Spring Adds to Global Restrictions on Religion," June 2013, 11, 80.

39. Ali Riaz, "The Politics of Islamization in Bangladesh," in *Religion and Politics in South Asia*, ed. Ali Riaz (New York: Routledge, 2010), pp. 63–65.

40. Freedom House 2011 Report: Bangladesh, accessed at https://freedomhouse.org/report/freedom-world/2011/bangladesh.

41. Ali Riaz and C. Christine Fair, "Introduction," in *Political Islam and Governance in Bangladesh*, ed. Ali Riaz and C. Christine Fair (New York: Routledge, 2011), 3.

42. Pew Research Center on Religion and Public Life, *Global Restrictions on Religion* (2009), 12, 22, 49.

43. Jalal Alamgir, "Bangladesh's Fresh Start," *Journal of Democracy* 20, no. 3 (2009): 42.

44. Figures are found at US State Department, *International Religious Freedom Report for 2015*, accessed June 8, 2017; find at https://www.state.gov/documents/organization/256331.pdf.

45. Albert Sundararaj Walters, "Issues in Christian-Muslim Relations: A Malaysian Christian Perspective," *Islam and Christian-Muslim Relations* 18, no. 1 (January 2007), 72.

46. Pew Research Center, April 11, 2017, "Global Restrictions on Religion Rise Modestly in 2015, Reversing Downward Trend," pp. 50, 53, 57.

47. Abdullah Saeed and Hassan Saeed, *Freedom of Religion, Apostasy and Islam* (Surrey, UK: Ashgate, 2004), 124–125, 128–130; Liz Gooch, "In a Muslim State, Fear Sends Some Worship Underground," *New York Times,* January 27, 2011, accessed March 23, 2017; find at http://www.nytimes.com/2011/01/28/world/asia/28iht-malay28.html?_r=0.

48. Joseph Chinyong Liow, *Piety and Politics: Islamism in Contemporary Malaysia* (Oxford: Oxford University Press, 2009), 144–147; "Malaysian Court Tells Convert She Must Stay Muslim," *Christian Century* 124, no. 13 (2007), accessed March 23, 2017; find at http://www.christiancentury.org/article/2007-06/malaysian-court-tells-convert-she-must-stay-muslim-0.

49. Liow, *Piety and Politics*, 70.

50. "Federal Court: Unilateral Conversion of Indira Gandhi's 3 Children is Null and Void," *The Star,* January 29, 2018, accessed February 23, 2018; find at https://www.thestar.com.my/news/nation/2018/01/29/federal-court-unilateral-conversion-of-indira-gandhis-3-children-is-null-and-void/.

51. Saeed and Saeed, *Freedom of Religion*, 127; Walters, "Issues in Christian-Muslim Relations," 74–75; "International Religious Freedom Report for 2010," US Department of State, accessed July 24, 2014; find at http://www.state.gov/j/drl/rls/irf/2010/148881.htm.

52. "Malaysia's Highest Court Backs a Ban on Allah in Christian Bibles," June 23, 2014, accessed March 23, 2017; find at https://www.theguardian.com/world/2014/jun/23/malaysia-highest-court-allah-bible-ban.

53. Nasr, *Islamic Leviathan*, 54.

54. Michael G. Peletz, "Islam and the Cultural Politics of Legitimacy: Malaysia in the Aftermath of September 11," in *Remaking Muslim Politics: Pluralism, Contestation, Democratization*, ed. Robert W. Hefner (Princeton, NJ: Princeton University Press, 2009), 265–267.

55. Abdul Rahman Embong, "Islam and Democracy in Malaysia," in *Democracies in Muslim Societies: The Asian Experience*, ed. Zoya Hasan (Los Angeles: Sage, 2007), 144–158.

56. "Freedom in the World: 2011: Malaysia," Freedom House; find at http://www.freedomhouse.org/report/freedom-world/2011/malaysia#.U9Jsf2RVAhw.

57. For instance, there are the Allied Coordinating Committee of Islamic NGOs; the Malaysian Consultative Council of Buddhism, Christianity, Hinduism, Sikhism, and Taoism; the Majlis Dakwah Negara, the Gabungan Bertindak Malaysia; and the Friendship Group of Inter-Religious Services.

58. Robert W. Hefner, "Muslim Democrats and Islamist Violence in Post-Soeharto Indonesia," in Hefner, ed., *Remaking Muslim Politics*, 279. On the contribution of these mass organizations to religious tolerance in Indonesia, see the important, complex, and subtle book, Jeremy Menchik, *Islam and Democracy in Indonesia, Tolerance Without Liberalism* (Cambridge: Cambridge University Press, 2016).

59. "International Religious Freedom Report 2013: Indonesia," US Department of State, accessed July 29, 2014; find at http://www.state.gov/j/drl/rls/irf/religiousfreedom/index.htm#wrapper.

60. Robert Hefner, *Civil Islam: Muslims and Democratization in Indonesia* (Princeton, NJ: Princeton University Press, 2000).

61. The Pew Research Center, *Trends in Global Restrictions on Religion*, June 23, 2016, 45.

62. See Michael Buehler, "Subnational Islamization Through Secular Parties: Comparing Shari'a Politics in Two Indonesian Provinces," *Comparative Politics* 46, no. 10 (2013), quoted in Christian Solidarity Worldwide, *Indonesia: Pluralism in Peril: The Rise of Religious Intolerance Across the Archipelago*, 2014, 27–28. The Christian Solidarity Worldwide document is a report researched and written by Benedict Rogers. Although it was presented by a Christian organization, it covers the compromise of religious freedom with respect to every religion.

63. Hefner, "Muslim Democrats Islamist Violence," 276–278.

64. *Indonesia: Pluralism in Peril*, 8.

65. Melissa Crouch, "Regulating Places of Worship in Indonesia: Upholding Freedom of Religion for Religious Minorities," *Singapore Journal of Legal Studies* 1 (2007): 100. http://www.heinonline.org.proxy.library.nd.edu/HOL/Print?collection=journals&handle=hein.journals/sjls2007&id=105.

66. International Crisis Group, "Indonesia: Implications of the Ahmadiyah Decree," *Asia Briefing*, no. 78 (July 7, 2008): 8–10. http://www.genocidewatch.org/images/Indonesia_08_07_07_Implications_of_the_Ahmadiya_Decree.pdf

67. *Indonesia: Pluralism in Peril*, 30.

68. Robert Pringle, *Understanding Islam in Indonesia: Politics and Diversity* (Honolulu: University of Hawaii, 2010), 172–173.

69. Crouch, "Regulating Places of Worship," 98–116; Frans Wijsen and Gerrit Singgih, "Regulation on Houses of Worship: A Threat to Social Cohesion?," in *Religion, Civil Society and Conflict in Indonesia*, ed. Carl Sterkens, Mumammad Machasin, and Frans Wijsen (Zweigniederlassung Zurish: Lit-Verlag, 2009), 91–94.

70. *Indonesia: Pluralism in Peril*, 32–33.

71. Alwi Shihab, "The Muhammadiyah Movement and Its Controversy With Christian Mission in Indonesia," PhD dissertation, Temple University, 1995 (Ann Arbor: University of Michigan Press), 205–206, 251–252, 277–281, 306–307, 313–314.

72. *Indonesia: Pluralism in Peril*, 35–36.

73. International Crisis Group, "Indonesia: Implications of the Ahmadiyah Decree," 5–7.

74. *Indonesia: Pluralism in Peril*, 33–34, 71–86.

75. *Indonesia: Pluralism in Peril*, 32. On the number of discrimination laws, the report quotes Musdah Mulia, "The Problem of Implementation of the Rights of Religious Freedom in Indonesia," *EU-Indonesia Conference: Human Rights and Faith in Focus*, 24–25 October 2011.

76. *Indonesia: Pluralism in Peril*, 37–39; Buehler, "Subnational Islamization."

77. The Pew Research Center, *Trends in Global Restrictions on Religion, 2015*, 49.

78. Setara Institute, 2012, http://www.setara-institute.org/en/content/report-freedom-religion-and-belief-2012-0. Similar findings are reported by another Indonesian NGO, the Wahid Institute, as recounted by Greg Fealy, "The Politics of Religious Intolerance in Indonesia: Mainstream-ism Trumps Extremism?" in *Religion, Law, and Intolerance in Indonesia*, ed. Tim Lindsey and Helen Pausacker (London: Routledge, 2016), 116.

79. Hefner, "Muslim Democrats Islamist Violence," 274.

80. *Indonesia: Pluralism in Peril*, 9, 12, 20, 49.

81. Hefner, "Muslim Democrats and Islamist Violence," 283.

82. John T. Sidel, *Riots, Pogroms, Jihad: Religious Violence in Indonesia* (Ithaca, NY: Cornell University Press, 2006), 140. See also the analysis of Hefner, "Muslim Democrats and Islamist Violence."

83. *Indonesia: Pluralism in Peril*, 32.

84. Fealy, "The Politics of Religious Intolerance in Indonesia," 117–119.

85. I have relied here on Marshall and Shea, *Silenced*, 101–116.

86. Pew Research Center, "Latest Trends in Religious Restrictions and Hostilities," 2015, 51. Somalia and Comoros are "moderate" in their levels of restrictions; those falling into the "high" category are Kuwait, Yemen, Bahrain, Qatar, United Arab Emirates, Oman, Maldives, and Mauritania; and Brunei is "very high."

87. Figures here are taken from US Department of State, *International Religious Freedom Report for 2013*.

88. "Qatar 2013 International Religious Freedom Report," US Department of State, accessed June 26, 2016; find at http://www.state.gov/documents/organization/222521.pdf.

89. See the analysis of Hafez, *Why Muslims Rebel*, 9–19. Hafez looks at the evidence from multiple studies of the economic basis of Islamist movements and militancy and summarizes it here.

90. Nikki R. Keddie, "The Revolt of Islam, 1700 to 1993: Comparative Considerations and Relations to Imperialism," *Comparative Studies in Society and History* 36, no. 3 (1994): 463–487. See also Hashemi, *Islam, Secularism, and Liberal Democracy*, 23–66.

91. On the convergence of Islam and the modern state, see Cesari, *The Awakening of Muslim Democracy*.

92. At this writing, some degree of liberalization appears to be afoot in Saudi Arabia, though nobody knows its direction.

CHAPTER 5

1. Here, I follow the analysis of Jason Brownlee, Tarek Masoud, and Andrew Reynolds, *The Arab Spring: Pathways of Repression* (Oxford: Oxford University Press, 2015), 13.

2. As this book was being produced, this war continued and its death toll was rising. The Syrian Human Rights Observatory, whose figures are widely respected, offered a death toll figure of 312,000 in 2016. See "Death Toll in Syria War Rises to 312,000: Syrian Observatory for Human Rights," *Economic Times*, December 13, 2016, accessed February 1, 2017; find at: http://economictimes. indiatimes.com/news/defence/death-toll-in-syria-war-rises-to-312000-syrian-observatory-for-human-rights/articleshow/55961579.cms. Some estimates have run considerably higher, placing the figure at well over 400,000 deaths. On internally displaced people and refugees, see the estimates of the Internal Displacement Monitoring Center, drawn in part from the office of Coordination of Humanitarian Affairs. The figures are accurate as of December 31, 2015. See http://www.internal-displacement.org/middle-east-and-north-africa/syria/figures-analysis (accessed February 1, 2017).

3. This figure is drawn from Brownlee, Masoud, and Reynolds, *The Arab Spring*, 10. This paragraph is situated in their overall description of the Arab uprisings on pp. 5–12.

4. For a perspective also stressing political theology, see Ebrahim Moosa, "Political Theology in the Aftermath of the Arab Spring: Returning to the Ethical," in *The African Renaissance and the Afro-Arab Spring*, ed. Charles Villa-Vicencio, Erik Doxtader, and Ebrahim Moosa (Washington, DC: Georgetown University Press, 2015), 101–119. On Islam and the Arab Spring, see also Bassam Tibi, *The Sharia State: Arab Spring and Democratization* (Oxon, UK: Routledge, 2013).

5. Broadly speaking, the 18 countries apart from Iran and Turkey are Arab ones. Even this assessment must be complexified, though. As discussed in Chapter 4, the Gulf States contain guest worker populations, mostly non-Arab, who in many cases far outnumber native citizens. In addition, a careful definition of "uprising" can be found in Brownlee, Masoud, and Reynolds, *The Arab Spring*, in which the

authors award the term uprising to the events that took place in the first six countries arrayed in Table 5.1. Three features of an uprising, they argue, are "1. the eruption of non-violent mass protests over multiple days. 2. the spread of protest to multiple geographic sites, and 3. the seizure and control by protesters of public spaces—for example, Bourguiba Avenue in Tunis, Tahrir Square in Cairo, the Pearl Roundabout (Dawwār al-Lu'lu'ah) of Manama, and Bahrain." See pp. 20–25.

6. Pew Research Center, "Latest Trends in Religious Restrictions and Hostilities," 2015, 24.

7. Lisa Anderson, "Demystifying the Arab Spring: Parsing the Differences Between Tunisia, Egypt, and Libya," *Foreign Affairs* 90, no. 3, (May/June 2011): 3; Brownlee, Masoud, and Reynolds, *The Arab Spring*, 183.

8. Alfred Stepan, "Tunisia's Transition and the Twin Tolerations," *Journal of Democracy* 23, no. 2, (April 2012): 92–94.

9. Brownlee, Masoud, and Reynolds, *The Arab Spring*, 100–101, 137; Samuel P. Huntington, *The Third Wave: Democratization in the Late Twentieth Century* (Norman: University of Oklahoma Press, 1991), 267.

10. Teije Hidde Donker, "Re-Emerging Islamism in Tunisia: Repositioning Religion in Politics and Society," *Mediterranean Politics* 18, no. 2 (2013): 211.

11. Teije Hidde Donker, "Re-Emerging Islamism in Tunisia," 213; Pew Research Center, "Arab Spring Adds to Global Restrictions on Religion," June 2013, 34.

12. US State Department, *International Religious Freedom Report for 2014*, accessed February 1, 2017; find at https://www.state.gov/documents/organization/238692.pdf.

13. Here is where a fine-grained qualitative analysis argues for a trend that is not fully reflected in the Pew Research Center numbers. The relaxation of restrictions by the Ennahda Party, an Islamic party, itself can be seen as a gain for religious freedom, for instance, though it is not necessary reflected in the Pew numbers.

14. Stepan, "Tunisia's Transition," 95–97.

15. Jeffrey Haynes, "The 'Arab Uprising', Islamists and Democratization," *Mediterranean Politics* 18, no. 2 (2013): 177.

16. Emanuela Dalmasso and Francesco Cavatorta, "Democracy, Civil Liberties and the Role of Religion After the Arab Awakening: Constitutional Reforms in Tunisia and Morocco," *Mediterranean Politics* 18, no. 2 (2013): 232–234.

17. Hamadi Redissi, "The Decline of Political Islam's Legitimacy: The Tunisian Case," *Philosophy and Social Criticism* 40, no. 4-5 (2014): 387.

18. Donker, "Re-Emerging Islamism in Tunisia," 214.

19. Redissi, "The Decline of Political Islam's Legitimacy," 387.

20. Brownlee, Masoud, and Reynolds, *The Arab Spring*, 141.

21. Rafika Bendermel, "Why Are So Many Tunisians Joining IS?," *Middle East Eye*, accessed March 25, 2013; find at http://www.middleeasteye.net/news/why-are-so-many-tunisians-joining-748811153.

22. Donker, "Re-Emerging Islamism in Tunisia," 221.

23. Donker, "Re-Emerging Islamism in Tunisia," 221.

24. Dalmasso and Cavatorta, "Democracy, Civil Liberties and the Role of Religion After the Arab Awakening," 231–233.

25. Brownlee, Masoud, and Reynolds, *The Arab Spring*, 141.

26. Pew Research Center, "Arab Spring Adds to Global Restrictions on Religion," 26.

27. On Al Azhar, see Nathan J. Brown, "Contention in Religion and State in Postrevolutionary Egypt," *Social Research* 79, no. 2 (Summer 2012): 540–542.

28. US State Department, *International Religious Freedom Report for 2013*, accessed February 1, 2017; find at https://www.state.gov/documents/organization/222499.pdf.

29. Haynes, "The 'Arab Uprising', Islamists and Democratization," 175; Pahwa, "Secularizing Islamism and Islamizing Democracy," 200.

30. Pahwa, "Secularizing Islamism and Islamizing Democracy," 202.

31. "Full English Translation of Dr. Mohamed Morsi's Interview on Dream TV with Wael Ibrashi," Ikhwanweb, accessed March 25, 2016; find at http://www.ikhwanweb.com/article.php?id=29405.

32. Pahwa, "Secularizing Islamism and Islamizing Democracy," 202. Italics added.

33. Pahwa, "Secularizing Islamism and Islamizing Democracy," 201–202.

34. Brownlee, Masoud, and Reynolds, *The Arab Spring*, 120.

35. Haynes, "The 'Arab Uprising', Islamists and Democratization," 179.

36. Pahwa, "Secularizing Islamism and Islamizing Democracy," 202.

37. Pahwa, "Secularizing Islamism and Islamizing Democracy," 203.

38. Khalil al-Anani and Maszlee Malik, "Pious Way to Politics: The Rise of Political Salafism in Post-Mubarak Egypt," *Digest of Middle East Studies* 22, no. 1 (2013): 59–64.

39. Anani and Malik, "Pious Way to Politics," 62–65.

40. Anani and Malik, "Pious Way to Politics," 180.

41. "Does Coptic Christian Persecution Under Morsi Signal Egypt's Collapse?," *Jewish News Service*, accessed March 25, 2016; find at http://www.jns.org/latest-articles/2013/4/15/does-egyptian-religious-violence-under-morsi-point-to-an-impending-collapse#.VvSUFmTF9vo.

42. Magdi Guirguis, "The Copts and the Egyptian Revolution: Various Attitudes and Dreams," *Social Research* 79, no. 2 (Summer 2012): 502–519.

43. Haynes, "The 'Arab Uprising', Islamists and Democratization," 181.

44. The identity of the Ghanaian construction worker has been disputed somewhat, but one story seems to establish his identity reasonably well. See "Ghanaian Beheaded in Libya?" *GhanaWeb*, February 17, 2015, accessed June 14, 2017; find at http://www.ghanaweb.com/GhanaHomePage/NewsArchive/artikel.php?ID=346906. Other reports reveal that he pledged his Christian faith moments before his death. See Stefan J. Bos, "African

Man Turns to Christ Moments Before Beheading," *BosNewsLife*, April 23, 2015, accessed June 14, 2017; find at http://www.bosnewslife.com/35141-african-man-turns-to-christ-moments-before-beheading#comments.

45. "Islamic State Video Shows Beheading of 21 Egyptian Christians," *Rediff News*, February 16, 2015, accessed March 29, 2016; find at http://www.rediff.com/news/report/islamic-state-video-shows-beheading-of-21-egyptian-christians/20150216.htm.

46. Jon Lee Anderson, "The Unravelling," *The New Yorker*, February 23 and March 2, 2015, accessed March 29, 2016; find at http://www.newyorker.com/magazine/2015/02/23/unravelling.

47. Lisa Anderson, "Demystifying the Arab Spring: Parsing the Differences Between Tunisia, Egypt, and Libya," *Foreign Affairs* 90, no. 3 (May/June 2011): 2–7.

48. Libya ranked 166 out of 175 countries on Transparency International's 2014 Corruption Perceptions Index, reported in https://freedomhouse.org/report/freedom-world/2015/libya(accessed March 29, 2016).

49. Brownlee, Masoud, and Reynolds, *The Arab Spring*, 160.

50. US State Department, *International Religious Freedom Report for 2013*, accessed February 1, 2017; find at https://www.state.gov/documents/organization/222515.pdf.

51. Anderson, "The Unravelling."

52. Brownlee, Masoud, and Reynolds, *The Arab Spring*, 160.

53. US State Department, *International Religious Freedom Report for 2013*, accessed February 1, 2017; find at https://www.state.gov/documents/organization/222515.pdf.

54. US State Department, *International Religious Freedom Report for 2013*, accessed February 1, 2017; find at https://www.state.gov/documents/organization/222515.pdf.

55. US State Department, *International Religious Freedom Report for 2014*, accessed February 1, 2017; find at https://www.state.gov/documents/organization/238680.pdf.

56. Scott Shane and Jo Becker, "A New Libya 'With Very Little Time Left,'" *New York Times*, February 27, 2016, accessed March 29, 2016; find at http://www.nytimes.com/2016/02/28/us/politics/libya-isis-hillary-clinton.html?_r=0.

57. "Khalifah Haftar—A New Al-Sisi in Libya." *Middle East Monitor*, May 20, 2014, accessed February 1, 2017; find at https://www.middleeastmonitor.com/articles/africa/11606-khalifah-haftar-a-new-al-sisi-in-libya.

58. US State Department, *International Religious Freedom Report for 2014*, accessed February 1, 2017; find at https://www.state.gov/documents/organization/238680.pdf; Anderson, "The Unravelling."

59. Nicole Bibbins Sedaca, "The Religious Component of the Syrian Conflict: More Than Perception," *Georgetown Journal of International Affairs* (2013), accessed

March 31, 2016; find at http://journal.georgetown.edu/the-religious-component-of-the-syrian-conflict-more-than-perception-by-nicole-bibbins-sedaca/.

60. Steven Heydemann, "Syria and the Future of Authoritarianism," *Journal of Democracy* 24, no. 4 (October 2013): 62.

61. Heydemann, "Syria and the Future of Authoritarianism," 70.

62. "Syria in Civil War, Says UN Official Herve Ladsous," *BBC News*, June 12, 2012, accessed March 31, 2016; find at http://www.bbc.com/news/world-middle-east-18417952.

63. Daniel Burke, "Syria Explained: How It Became a Religious War," *CNN Belief Blog*, accessed March 31, 2016; find at http://religion.blogs.cnn.com/2013/09/04/syrian-wars-got-religion-and-that-aint-good/.

64. Patrick Cockburn, "ISIS Consolidates," *London Review of Books* 36, no. 16 (2014), accessed March 31, 2016; find at http://www.lrb.co.uk/v36/n16/patrick-cockburn/isis-consolidates; Marc Champion, "To Imagine Syria at Peace, Think Bosnia," *BloombergView*, September 14, 2015, accessed March 31, 2016; find at http://www.bloombergview.com/articles/2015-09-14/syria-at-peace-to-imagine-it-think-of-bosnia-.

65. Sedaca, "The Religious Component of the Syria Conflict."

66. Asad cited sentiments like the one expressed by Sunni cleric Adnan Anour, who announced, "[a]s for those Alawites who violate what is sacred, when the Muslims rule and are the majority of 85%, we will chop you up and feed you to the dogs." In Burke, "Syria Explained."

67. Heydemann, "Syria and the Future of Authoritarianism," 66.

68. Burke, "Syria Explained."

69. Burke, "Syria Explained."

70. Armenak Tokmajyan, "Religion, Religious Leaders, and Violence in the Conflict in Syria," Fragile States, September 28, 2014, accessed March 31, 2016; find at http://www.fragilestates.org/2014/09/28/religion-religious-leaders-violence-conflict-syria-armenak-tokmajyan/.

71. Sedaca, "The Religious Component of the Syria Conflict."

72. Edwin Mora, "Report: Dozens of Americans Have Reentered the U.S. After Joining ISIS," *Breitbart*, September 30, 2015, accessed April 3, 2016; find at http://www.breitbart.com/big-government/2015/09/30/report-dozens-americans-reentered-u-s-joining-isis/.

73. "Syrian Rebels Reject Interim Government, Embrace Sharia," *CNN*, September 25, 2013, accessed March 31, 2016; find at http://www.cnn.com/2013/09/25/world/meast/syria-rebels/.

74. Heydemann, "Syria and the Future of Authoritarianism," 69.

75. Brownlee, Masoud, and Reynolds, *The Arab Spring*, 148.

76. US State Department, *International Religious Freedom Report for 2005*, accessed February 1, 2017; find at https://www.state.gov/j/drl/rls/irf/2005/51614.htm.

77. US State Department, *International Religious Freedom Report for 2009*.
78. US State Department, *International Religious Freedom Report for 2013*.
79. US State Department, *International Religious Freedom Report for 2013*.
80. US State Department, *International Religious Freedom Report for 2013*; US State Department *International Religious Freedom Report for 2014*.
81. Pew Research Center, "Mapping the Global Muslim Population," accessed April 3, 2016; find at http://www.pewforum.org/2009/10/07/mapping-the-global-muslim-population/.
82. Brownlee, Masoud, and Reynolds, *The Arab Spring*, 85–87; Bahrain Center for Human Rights, the Bahrain Youth Society for Human Rights, and the Bahrain Human Rights Society, *Bahrain: The Human Right for Freedom and Social Justice: A Joint Report on Human Rights Violations in Bahrain*, November 22, 2011, 5.
83. See Toby Jones, "Bahrain: Human Rights and Political Wrongs," *Sada: Middle East Analysis*, Carnegie Endowment for International Peace, September 25, 2012, find at http://carnegieendowment.org/sada/?fa=49468; US State Department, *International Religious Freedom Report for 2010*; US State Department, *International Religious Freedom Report for 2014*.
84. Pew Research Center, "Arab Spring Adds to Global Restrictions on Religion," June 2013, 34; US State Department, *International Religious Freedom Report for 2014*.
85. US State Department, *International Religious Freedom Report for 2014*.
86. See the excellent explanation of the trajectory of the Arab uprisings in Brownlee, Masoud, and Reynolds, *The Arab Spring*.

CHAPTER 6

1. Bernard Lewis, *The Jews of Islam* (Princeton, NJ: Princeton University Press, 1984), 3.
2. For an excellent listing and discussion of pro-freedom verses, see Abdullah Saeed and Hassan Saeed, *Freedom of Religion, Apostasy and Islam* (Surrey, UK: Ashgate, 2004), 69–72.
3. *The Qur'an*, 29.
4. Yohanan Friedmann, *Tolerance and Coercion in Islam: Interfaith Relations in the Muslim Tradition* (Cambridge: Cambridge University Press, 2003), 94, 100; Mustafa Akyol, *Islam Without Extremes: A Muslim Case for Liberty* (New York: Norton, 2011), 93–95.
5. The distinction between Mutazilites as being the tradition of reason and Asharites as the tradition of revelation is not a rigid one. George F. Hourani, in his *Reason and Tradition in Islamic Ethics* (Cambridge: Cambridge University Press, 1985), distinguishes five positions on the relationship between reason

and revelation in the Islamic tradition. He refers to the Mutazilite position as independent reason supplemented by revelation and the Asharite position as revelation supplemented by dependent reason. See pp. 270–272.

6. On these interpretations see Friedmann, *Tolerance and Coercion in Islam*, 102–105.

7. Sahih Bukhari (52:260).

8. Saeed and Saeed, *Freedom of Religion, Apostasy, and Islam*, 51, 88. On classical jurists, see also Friedmann, *Tolerance and Coercion in Islam*, 127.

9. Saeed and Saeed, *Freedom of Religion, Apostasy, and Islam*, 74.

10. Saeed and Saeed, *Freedom of Religion, Apostasy, and Islam*, 65, 76–78; Declan O'Sullivan, "The Interpretation of Qur'anic Text to Promote or Negate the Death Penalty for Apostates and Blasphemers," *Journal of Qur'anic Studies* 3, no. 2, (2001), 63–93..

11. Akyol, *Islam Without Extremes*, 277–278. The debate runs similarly with blasphemy. Jurists have interpreted some *hadiths* to propose death for blasphemers. Islamopluralist interpreters respond that the Qur'an threatens punishment in the hereafter but no earthly punishment for blasphemy and call for a nonviolent response. See Akyol, *Islam Without Extremes*, 281–282.

12. See Declan O'Sullivan, "The Interpretation of Qur'anic Text," 87.

13. Saeed and Saeed, *Freedom of Religion, Apostasy, and Islam*, 68.

14. Akyol, *Islam Without Extremes*, 110–111.

15. Friedmann, *Tolerance and Coercion in Islam*, 88.

16. R. Stephen Humphreys comments that "both Western and Muslim scholars agree unanimously that the piece is authentic." See R. Stephen Humphreys, *Islamic History: A Framework for Inquiry* (Princeton, NJ: Princeton University Press, 1991), 92. Some scholars argue that the text that we have now is a composite of several different texts dating back to perhaps prior to the arrival of Muslims in Medina. See R. B. Sarjeant, "The Sunnah Jami'ah, Pacts With the Yathrib Jews, and the Tahrim of Yathrib: Analysis and Translation of the Documents Comprised in the So-Called 'Constitution of Medina,'" *Bulletin of the School of Oriental and African Studies* 41, no. 1 (1978): 1–42; and W. M. Watt, *Muhammad: Prophet and Statesman* (Oxford: Oxford University Press, 1961).

17. Saeed and Saeed, *Freedom of Religion, Apostasy, and Islam*, 82–83.

18. O'Sullivan, "The Interpretation of Qur'anic Text," 83–84; Friedmann, *Tolerance and Coercion in Islam*, 101; Mohammed Kamali, *Freedom of Expression in Islam* (Cambridge: Islamic Texts Society, 1997), 96.

19. Lewis, *The Jews of Islam*, 10–11; W. M. Watt, *Muhammad at Medina* (Oxford: Oxford University Press, 1956), 209–212.

20. Several scholars describe a strikingly similar binary opposition among views of the *dhimmi* status. See Lewis, *The Jews of Islam*, 3–4; Mark R. Cohen, *Under*

Crescent and Cross: The Jews in the Middle Ages (Princeton, NJ: Princeton University Press, 1994), 3–14; Friedmann, *Tolerance and Coercion In Islam*, 1–12.

21. Lewis, *The Jews of Islam*, 24–25.
22. Lewis, *The Jews of Islam*, 45–46.
23. Akyol, *Islam Without Extremes*, 65–66.
24. Mahmoud Ayoub, "Dhimmah in Qur'an and Hadith," in *Muslims and Others In Early Islamic Society*, ed. Robert Hoyland (London: Ashgate, 2004), 26–32.
25. Akyol, *Islam Without Extremes*, 66; Saeed and Saeed, *Freedom of Religion, Apostasy, and Islam*, 13.
26. The strongest case for medieval Spain as a realm of tolerance is Maria Rosa Menocal, *The Ornament of the World: How Muslims, Jews, and Christians Created a Culture of Tolerance in Medieval Spain* (Boston: Little, Brown, 2002). See also Roger Collins, *Early Medieval Spain: Unity in Diversity 400–1000* (New York: St. Martin's Press, 1995).
27. See, for instance, Darío Fernández-Morera, "The Myth of the Andalusian Paradise," *Intercollegiate Review* 41, no. 2 (Fall 2006): 23–31.
28. Ann Christys, *Christians in Al-Andalus, 711–1000* (Surrey, UK: Curzon Press, 2002).
29. Norman Roth, *Jews, Visigoths, and Muslims in Medieval Spain: Cooperation and Conflict* (Leiden: E.J. Brill, 1994), 103–110.
30. Lewis, *The Jews of Islam*, 51–52.
31. Arguably the most prominent Islamoskeptic on *dhimmis* is Bat Ye'or. See her *Islam and Dhimmitude: Where Civilizations Collide*, trans. Miriam Kochan and David Littman (Madison, NJ: Fairleigh Dickinson University Press, 2002).
32. Lewis, *The Jews of Islam*, 46–56.
33. Lewis, *The Jews of Islam*, 14–15.
34. Bat Ye'or, *The Dhimmi* (Madison, NJ: Fairleigh Dickinson University Press, 1985), 52.
35. In addition to Lewis, *The Jews of Islam*, see the balanced perspective of Hugh Goddard, *A History of Christian-Muslim Relations* (Chicago: New Amsterdam Books, 2000), which documents both tolerant and intolerant dynamics on both Christian and Muslim sides over the course of the history of relations between members of the two religions.
36. Akyol, *Islam Without Extremes*, 143.
37. Albert Hourani, *Arabic Thought in the Liberal Age, 1798–1939* (Cambridge: Cambridge University Press, 1983); Mohammad Fadel, "Modernist Islamic Political Thought and the Egyptian and Tunisian Revolutions of 2011," *Middle East Law and Governance* 3 (2011): 94–104. Fadel cites Rifa Rifa'a al-Tahtawi, Khayr al-Din al'Tunisi, and Rashid Rida as important "modernist" intellectuals. Akyol, *Islam Without Extremes*, 172. Among late 19th- and early 20th-century thinkers can be included Ahmad Khan, Muhammad Abduh, Rashid Rida, and

Muhammad Iqbal. See Abdullah Saeed, *Islam and Belief: At Home With Religious Freedom* (Palo Alto, CA: Zephyr Institute, 2014), 20.

An important historical social scientific work on the development of modern Islam, mentioned in Chapter 3, is Timur Kuran, *The Long Divergence: How Islamic Law Held Back the Middle East*, which focuses centrally on economic development but briefly discusses implications for civil society and democracy in its final chapter (pp. 295–296). In the same way that Kuran argues that Islamic law acted as a brake on the economic development of Muslim countries, one might venture to argue that it acted as a brake on the development of modern democracy and political freedom in Muslim countries. This application of Kuran's thought, however, should be treated with caution. Kuran does not strongly assert such an argument himself and, what is more, he acknowledges the possibility of institutional change in Muslim countries, explicitly abjuring the view that Islam is hardwired in political and social affairs (see pp. 6–11).

38. Charles Kurzman, "Liberal Islam and Its Islamic Content," in *Liberal Islam: A Sourcebook*, ed. Charles Kurzman (Oxford: Oxford University Press, 1998), 6, 11–12; Akyol, *Islam Without Extremes*, 172; Saeed, *Islam and Belief: At Home With Religious Freedom*, 20; Recep Şentürk, "Minority Rights in Islam: From *Dhimmi* to Citizen," in *Islam and Human Rights: Advancing a U.S.-Muslim Dialogue*, ed. Shireen T. Hunter and Huma Malik (Washington, DC: Center for International and Strategic Studies (CSIS), Significant Issues Series, 2005), 67–99.

39. For the 1856 "Rescript of Reform—Islahat Fermani," see http://www.anayasa.gen.tr/reform.htm, accessed March 30, 2017.

40. Akyol, *Islam Without Extremes*, 151–152.

41. Akyol, *Islam Without Extremes*, 166–176.

42. Stepan, "Tunisia's Transition," 98.

43. Stepan, "Tunisia's Transition," 96–99.

44. Akyol, *Islam Without Extremes*, 156–167. For the estimate of five million deaths, Akyol cites Justin McCarthy, *Death and Exile: The Ethnic Cleansing of Ottoman Muslims, 1821–1922* (Princeton, NJ: Darwin Press, 1996), 1, in Akyol, *Islam Without Extremes*, 167.

45. On the numbers, see Adam Jones, *Genocide: A Comprehensive Introduction*, 3rd ed. (Oxon, UK: Routledge, 2017), 201–202. This genocide took place even while liberal institutions were revived in the Ottoman Empire, illustrating the complexity of an era characterized by liberalism and nationalism, as well as the breakdown of an empire.

46. Initially, one month after the Regensburg Address, an international coalition of 38 Muslims issued an *Open Letter to His Holiness* that became the nucleus of the Common Word statement. For a volume that contains the Common Word statement and accompanying commentaries, see Miroslav Volf, Ghazi

bin Muhammad, and Melissa Yarrington, eds., *A Common Word: Muslims and Christians on Loving God and Neighbor* (Grand Rapids, MI: Eerdmans, 2010).

47. He includes 120 voices, to be exact. See his "On Apostasy and Islam: 100+ Notable Islamic Voices affirming the Freedom of Faith," http://apostasyandislam. blogspot.com/ (accessed April 2, 2016).

48. See http://www.marrakeshdeclaration.org/ (accessed June 7, 2017).

49. Charles Kurzman, "Liberal Islam: Prospects and Challenges," *Middle East Review of International Affairs* 3, no. 3 (September 1999): 1–19.

50. Examples of this line of argument are Saeed and Saeed, *Freedom of Religion, Apostasy, and Islam*; Abdullah Saeed, *Islam and Belief: At Home With Religious Freedom* (Palo Alto, CA: Zephyr Institute, 2014); Abdulaziz Sachedina, *The Islamic Roots of Democratic Pluralism* (Oxford: Oxford University Press, 2001), 25, 83–93; Abdolkarim Soroush and Mahmoud Sadri, *Reason, Freedom, & Democracy in Islam: Essential Writings of Abdolkarim Soroush* (Oxford: Oxford University Press, 2000); Akyol, *Islam Without Extremes*, 80–95, 262–287; Abdullahi Ahmed An-Na`im, *Islam and the Secular State: Negotiating the Future of Shari`a* (Cambridge, MA: Harvard University Press, 2008), 1–4; Areej Hassan, "Religious Freedom: Arguments From Islam," May 5, 2015, accessed April 3, 2017; find at http://staging.tonyblairfaithfoundation.org/religion-geopolitics/ commentaries/opinion/religious-freedom-arguments-islam; Usama Hasan, *No Compulsion in Religion: Islam & The Freedom of Belief, Religious Reform Series 2* (Quilliam, July 2013), accessed April 3, 2017; find at http://www.islamandrf.org/ no-compulsion-in-religion; "The Beirut Declaration on Religious Freedom," *Makassed Association*, July 20, 2015, accessed April 3, 2017; find at http://www. lebanonrenaissance.org/assets/Uploads/The-Beirut-Declaration-on-Religious- Freedom.pdf; Yoginder Sikand, "A Dissenting Voice on Pakistan's Blasphemy Law, Maulana Wahiduddin Khan," accessed April 3, 2017; find at http:// blasphemylaws.blogspot.com/2011/01/pakistans-blasphemy-law-maulana. html; and Recep Şentürk, "Human Rights in Islamic Jurisprudence: Why Should All Human Beings Be Inviolable?" in *The Future of Religious Freedom: Global Challenges*, ed. Allen Hertzke (Oxford: Oxford University Press, 2013), 270–289. Some writers' arguments span these categories and are thus listed in more than one.

51. Abdullah Ahmed An-na`im, *Toward an Islamic Reformation: Civil Liberties, Human Rights, and International Law* (Syracuse, NY; Syracuse University Press, 1990).

52. Farooq, "Apostasy and Islam"; Saeed and Saeed, *Freedom of Religion, Apostasy, and Islam*. Another example that skirts the second and third categories is Ebrahim Moosa, "Muslim Political Theology: Defamation, Apostasy, and Anathema," published by Heinrich Böll Stiftung, Middle East Office, 2012.

53. For examples of these arguments, see Asma Afsaruddin, "Making the Case for Religious Freedom Within the Islamic Tradition," *Review of Faith and International Affairs* 6, no. 2 (summer 2008), 57–60; Sachedina, *The Islamic Roots of Democratic Pluralism*, 14–15; Naser Ghobadzadeh, *Religious Secularity: A Theological Challenge to the Islamic State* (Oxford: Oxford University Press, 2015); Hashemi, *Islam, Seculariism, and Democracy*, and An-Na`im, *Islam and the Secular State*. For my own interpretation and critique of An-Na`im, see Daniel Philpott, "Arguing with An-Na`Im," *Immanent Frame*, July 14, 2008, accessed April 3, 2017; find at http://blogs.ssrc.org/tif/2008/07/14/arguing-with-an-naim/.

54. Saeed and Saeed, *Freedom of Religion, Apostasy, and Islam*, 88.

55. Pew Research Center, "The World's Muslims: Religion, Politics and Society," April 30, 2013, accessed April 3, 2017; find at http://www.pewforum.org/2013/04/30/the-worlds-muslims-religion-politics-society-overview/.

56. On the Protestant foundations of the sovereign state system and the subsequent expansion of the sovereign state system to the entire globe, see Daniel Philpott, *Revolutions in Sovereignty: How Ideas Shaped Modern International Relations* (Princeton, NJ: Princeton University Press, 2001).

57. Even Oman has a Basic Statute that functions similarly to a constitution.

58. US Commission on International Religious Freedom, *The Religion-State Relationship and the Right to Freedom of Religion or Belief: A Comparative Textual Analysis of the Constitutions of Predominantly Muslim Countries*, prepared by Tad Stahnke and Robert C. Blitt, March 2005, 15. By the report's count, there are 44 "predominantly" Muslim countries, whereas this book identifies 47 Muslim-majority countries. Of course, there will be some differences between 2005 and today. For instance, Iraq was governed by "Transitional Authority Law," whereas today Iraq has its own constitution.

59. USCIRF, *The Religion-State Relationship*, 13.

60. Ann Elizabeth Mayer, *Islam and Human Rights: Tradition and Politics*, 5th ed. (Boulder, CO: Westview Press, 2013), 2.

61. The Muslim-majority states who have neither signed nor ratified are Brunei, Kosovo, Malaysia, Oman, Qatar, Saudi Arabia, and the United Arab Emirates. Comoros has signed but not ratified. Kosovo, who is counted among those who have not signed or ratified and is included in this book's pool of Muslim-majority states, is only partially recognized by other states and is not a member of the United Nations.

62. Kristine Kalanges, *Religious Liberty in Western and Islamic Law: Toward a World Legal Tradition* (Oxford: Oxford University Press, 2012), 147–148.

63. See Mayer, *Islam and Human Rights*, 177–179.

64. Ira M. Lapidus, "State and Religion in Islamic Societies," *Past and Present*, 151, May 1996, 3–27.

65. Lapidus, "State and Religion," 19.
66. "Arabbarometer III Spss-Data File," Arab Barometer, find at http://www. arabbarometer.org/instruments-and-data-files, accessed October 23, 2015.

CHAPTER 7

1. See, for instance, Robin Wright, "Two Visions of Reformation," *Journal of Democracy* 7, no. 2 (1996): 64–75; Ayaan Hirsi Ali, *Heretic: Why Islam Needs a Reformation* (New York: HarperCollins, 2015); Ryan Mauro, "Obama Says Islam Needs Modernist Reformation," *The Clarion Project: Challenging Extremism, Promoting Dialogue,* March 15, 2016, accessed February 2, 2017; find at http://www.clarionproject.org/analysis/obama-says-islam-needs-modernist-reformation; and Reuel Marc Gerecht, "What Hath Ju-Ju Wrought!" *Weekly Standard,* March 14, 2005, accessed June 7, 2017; find at http://www. weeklystandard.com/article/6534, where Gerecht wrote, "you don't get to arrive at Thomas Jefferson unless you first pass through Martin Luther."
2. See Perez Zagorin, *How The Idea of Religious Toleration Came to the West* (Princeton, NJ: Princeton University Press, 2005).
3. A landmark moment for religious freedom was the passage of the First Amendment to the United States Constitution in 1791, which forbade Congress from prohibiting the free exercise of religion and from making a law respecting the establishment of religion. Established churches continued to exist at the state level, though, right up to 1833, when Massachusetts became the last state to disestablish a state church. On the development of religious freedom in the American colonies, culminating in the American Revolution, see Anthony Gill, *The Political Origins of Religious Liberty* (Cambridge: Cambridge University Press, 2008), 60–113.
4. Ronald J. Ross, "The Kulturkampf: Restrictions and Controls on the Practice of Religion in Bismarck's Germany," in *Freedom and Religion in the Nineteenth Century,* ed. Richard Helmstadter (Stanford, CA: Stanford University Press, 1977), 172–195.
5. Jean Jacques Rousseau, *The Social Contract,* in vol. 4, *The Collected Writings of Rousseau,* ed. Roger D. Masters and Christopher Kelly, trans. Judith R. Bush, Roger D. Masters, and Christopher Kelly (Hanover, NH: Dartmouth College and the University Press of New England), 222–223.
6. See Ahmet Kuru, *Secularism and State Policies Toward Religion* (Cambridge: Cambridge University Press, 2009), 139.
7. See Owen and Owen, "Enlightened Despots Then and Now."
8. John Howard Yoder, *The Politics of Jesus,* 2nd ed. (Grand Rapids, MI: Eerdmans, 1994), 135, 167.

9. Emphasis added. Sidney Z. Ehler ed., Sidney Zdeneck and John B. Morrall, trans., *Church and State Through the Centuries: A Collection of Historic Documents With Commentaries* (Westminster, MD: Newman Press, 1954), 5.

10. See the essays in Timothy Samuel Shah and Allen D. Hertzke, *Christianity and Freedom: Volume 1, Historical Perspectives* (Cambridge: Cambridge University Press, 2016), especially Timothy Samuel Shah, "The Roots of Religious Freedom in Early Christian Thought," 33–61; Robert Louis Wilken, "The Christian Roots of Religious Freedom," 62–89; and Elizabeth DePalma Digeser, "Lactantius on Religious Liberty and His Influence on Constantine," 90–102.

11. Robert Wilken, "In Defense of Constantine," *First Things* 112 (April 2001): 38.

12. Gustav Henningsen, *The Database of the Spanish Inquisition. The relaciones de causas Project Revisited*, in *Vorträge zur Justizforschung*, ed. Heinz Mohnhaupt and Dieter Simon (Frankfurt: Vittorio Klostermann, 1992), 84.

13. The end date of Christendom is not easily defined and depends much on one's criteria for what counts as Christendom. As argued shortly in the following text, top officials in the Catholic Church were espousing Christendom as an ideal right up to the eve of *Dignitatis Humanae* in 1965.

14. Thomas Aquinas, "On Kingship," in *St. Thomas Aquinas on Politics and Ethics*, trans. and ed. Paul E. Sigmund (New York: Norton, 1988), 27–28.

15. Brad S. Gregory, *Salvation at Stake: Christian Martyrdom in Early Modern Europe* (Cambridge, MA: Harvard University Press, 2009), 85–86.

16. Thomas Aquinas, "The Summa of Theology," in *Aquinas on Politics and Ethics*, 64. Emphasis added.

17. John Finnis, "Reflections and Responses," in *Reason, Morality, and Law*, ed. John Keown and Robert P. George (Oxford: Oxford University Press, 2013), 573. Finnis quotes from the text of *De Haeretico Comburendo*. Brackets and parentheses are as they appear in Finnis's text.

18. See Anthony W. Marx, *Faith in Nation: Exclusionary Origins of Nationalism* (Oxford: Oxford University Press, 2003).

19. Aquinas, "The Summa of Theology," 63.

20. For an argument that the French Revolution was a key turning point in which an anti-Christian ideology was put forth, see Monica Duffy Toft, Daniel Philpott, and Timothy Samuel Shah, *God's Century: Resurgent Religion and Global Politics* (New York: Norton, 2011), 65–70.

21. See Pope Pius IX, *The Syllabus of Errors Condemned by Pope Pius IX*, December 8, 1864, find at http://www.papalencyclicals.net/Pius09/p9syll.htm.

22. Gregory XVI, *Mirari Vos*, August 15, 1832, para. 14, 20; find at http://www.papalencyclicals.net/Greg16/g16mirar.htm.

23. Pius IX, *Quanta Cura*, December 8, 1964, para. 1–3; find at http://www.papalencyclicals.net/Pius09/p9quanta.htm.

24. Pius IX, *Syllabus of Errors*, 15; Pius IX, *Quanta Cura*, 3.

25. Similar judgments on liberty and on unconditional freedoms of thought, speech, writing, and worship can be found in Leo XIII, *Libertas*, June 20, 1888, http://w2.vatican.va/content/leo-xiii/en/encyclicals/documents/hf_l-xiii_enc_ 20061888_libertas.html.

26. Pope Leo XIII, *Longinqua*, January 6, 1895, para 6; find at http://w2.vatican.va/ content/leo-xiii/en/encyclicals/documents/hf_l-xiii_enc_06011895_longinqua. html.

27. Pope Leo XIII, *Testem Benevolentiae Nostrae*, January 22, 1899, http://www. papalencyclicals.net/Leo13/l13teste.htm.

28. Joseph A. Komonchak, "'The Crisis in Church-State Relationships in the U.S.A': A Recently Discovered Text by John Courtney Murray," *Review of Politics* 61, no. 4 (1999): 675–714.

29. Shah quotes from Tertullian's *Ad Scapulam*. See Timothy Samuel Shah, "Introduction," in Shah and Hertzke, eds., *Christianity and Freedom*, 8.

30. Shah, "The Roots of Religious Freedom," 52, 54.

31. Shah, "The Roots of Religious Freedom," 38–39.

32. Finnis, "Reflections and Responses," 572.

33. In this section, I have been guided by Gabrielle M. Girgis, "The Roots of Religious Liberty in the Thought of Augustine and Aquinas" (MA thesis, Princeton University, 2015).

34. Aquinas, "The Summa of Theology," 61.

35. See Girgis, "The Roots of Religious Liberty."

36. Jacques Maritain, *Man and the State* (Chicago: University of Chicago Press, 1951), 151–181.

37. Heinrich Rommen, "Church and State," *Review of Politics* 12, no. 3 (1950): 329–331.

38. For accounts for the Council's evolution toward *Dignitatis Humanae*, see John W. O'Malley, *What Happened at Vatican II* (Cambridge, MA: Harvard University Press, 2008); and David L. Schindler and Nicholas J Healy, Jr., *Freedom, Truth, and Human Dignity: The Second Vatican Council's Declaration on Religious Freedom* (Grand Rapids, MI: Eerdmans, 2015).

39. Brent F. Nelsen and James L. Guth, *Religion and the Struggle for European Union* (Washington, DC: Georgetown University Press, 2015), 149–207.

40. Arline Boucher and John Tehan, *Prince of Democracy, James Cardinal Gibbons* (Garden City, NJ: Image, 1962), 158.

41. Quoted in Mark A. Beliles and Jerry Newcombe, *Doubting Thomas: The Religious Life and Legacy of Thomas Jefferson* (New York: Morgan James, 2015), 124.

42. David Gibson, *The Coming Catholic Church: How the Faithful Are Shaping a New American Catholicism* (New York: HarperCollins, 2003), 10.

43. *Dignitatis Humanae*, sec. 1–3.

44. *Dignitatis Humanae*, sec. 1.

45. *Dignitatis Humanae*, sec. 6.
46. *Dignitatis Humanae*, secs. 1 and 10.
47. Here I have followed the interpretation of Martin Rhonheimer, "Benedict XVI's 'Hermeneutic of Reform' and Religious Freedom," *Nova et Vetera* 9, no. 4 (2011): 1029–1054.

CHAPTER 8

1. Here, I borrow from Alfred Stepan, who discusses the "fallacy of 'unique founding conditions'" in his article, "The World's Religious Systems and Democracy: Crafting the Twin Tolerations," in Alfred Stepan, *Arguing Comparative Politics:* (Oxford: Oxford University Press, 2001), 226–227.
2. Peter L. Berger, "The Desecularization of the World: A Global Overview," in *The Desecularization of the World: Resurgent Religion and World Politics*, ed. Peter L. Berger (Washington, DC: Eerdmans/Ethics and Public Policy Center, 1999), 2.
3. Pew Research Center, "The Global Religious Landscape."
4. See Timothy Samuel Shah, "Secular Militancy as an Obstacle to Peacebuilding," in *The Oxford Handbook of Religion, Conflict, and Peacebuilding*, ed. R. Scott Appleby, Atalia Omer, and David Little (Oxford: Oxford University Press, 2016), 380–406.
5. I point to some of this evidence in the Introduction.
6. Andrew Preston, "The First Human Right: Religious Liberty and the American Diplomatic Tradition," *Review of Faith and International Affairs* 11, no. 1 (Spring 2013): 11–12.
7. Daniel C. Thomas, *The Helsinki Effect: International Norms, Human Rights, and the Demise of Communism* (Princeton, NJ: Princeton University Press, 2001).
8. Thomas F. Farr, *World of Faith and Freedom: Why International Religious Liberty is Vital to American National Security* (Oxford: Oxford University Press, 2008).
9. Farr became Director of the Religious Freedom Project at the Berkley Center for Religion, Peace, and World Affairs at Georgetown University in 2011 and is currently Director of the Religious Freedom Institute.
10. Thomas F. Farr, "The Diplomacy of Religious Freedom," *First Things* 163 (2006): 18.
11. Farr used the phrase "quarantined" in Thomas F. Farr, "Diplomacy in an Age of Faith: Religious Freedom and National Security," *Foreign Affairs* 87, no. 2 (March/April 2008): 118.
12. Farr laid out his thinking on Islam in "Islam's Way to Freedom," *First Things* 187 (November 2008): 24–28.
13. James A. Bill, *The Eagle and the Lion: The Tragedy of American-Iranian Relations* (New Haven, CT: Yale University Press, 1988), 417, cited in Toft, Philpott, and Shah, *God's Century*, 12.

14. See Peter R. Mansoor, *Surge: My Journey with General David Petraeus and the Remaking of the Iraq War* (New Haven, CT: Yale University Press, 2013).

15. See, for instance, the work of Canon Andrew White, *The Vicar of Baghdad: Fighting For Peace in the Middle East* (Oxford: Monarch Books, 2009).

16. Judd Birdsall, "Keep the Faith: How American Diplomacy Got Religion, and How to Keep It," *Review of Faith and International Affairs* 14, no. 2 (2016): 113.

17. Thomas F. Farr and Dennis R. Hoover, *The Future of International Religious Freedom Policy: Recommendations for the Obama Administration*, 2009; Thomas F. Farr and Dennis R. Hoover, *U.S. Foreign Policy and International Religious Freedom: Recommendations for the Trump Administration and the U.S. Congress*, 2017, find at https://globalengage.org/content/Policy_Brief_FINAL.pdf.

18. See Daniel Philpott, "Culture War or Common Heritage: Recent Critics of Religious Freedom," accessed July 4, 2016; find at https://www.lawfareblog.com/culture-war-or-common-heritage-recent-critics-global-religious-freedom.

19. See the work of the *All-Party Parliamentary Group for International Freedom of Religion of Belief*, accessed July 4, 2016; find at https://freedomdeclared.org/about/.

20. See the work of the Religious Freedom and Business Foundation, of which Brian J. Grim, one of the pioneers of the Pew indices, is the president, accessed July 4, 2016; find at http://religiousfreedomandbusiness.org/brian-j-grim.

21. See their *Activists Beyond Borders: Advocacy Networks in International Politics* (Ithaca, NY: Cornell University Press, 1998).

22. Maryann Cusimano Love, "Christian Transnational Networks Respond to Persecution," in *Under Caesar's Sword: How Christians Respond to Persecution*, ed. Daniel Philpott and Timothy Shah (Cambridge: Cambridge University Press, 2018), 456–491.

23. John Paul Lederach, *Building Peace: Sustainable Reconciliation in Divided Societies* (Washington, DC: United States Institute of Peace, 1997); and John Paul Lederach and R. Scott Appleby, "Strategic Peacebuilding: An Overview," in *Strategies of Peace: Transforming Conflict in a Violent World*, ed. Daniel Philpott and Gerard F. Powers (Oxford: Oxford University Press, 2010), 19–44.

24. See the description in Toft, Philpott, and Shah, *God's Century*, 174–177.

Index

Note: Tables and figures are indicated by a *T* and *F* following the paragraph number.